CASE STUDIES ON PANDEMIC AND EPIDEMIC COMMUNICATION CAMPAIGNS

Spanning over a century of global health crises, *Case Studies on Pandemic and Epidemic Communication Campaigns* examines 25 case studies across 12 major pandemics and epidemics that shaped public health communication and all types of organizations in both the public and private sectors.

Each chapter begins with the historical context when the health crisis occurred to help readers understand the overall magnitude of the health crisis, treatments, media, and available communication tools. Each case study contains a complete overview and details (situation analysis, objectives, strategies, tactics, implementation, results, and measurement), about a specific communication campaign to address the health crisis, as well as theoretical principles and insightful questions to hone critical thinking skills. The book also addresses ethics, social inequities, xenophobia, discrimination, fearmongering, misinformation, and vaccine hesitancy. The case study method is a crucial pedagogical tool for educators and practitioners to make sense of past and present health crises and learn about the similarities and parallels between communication methods and theoretical principles applied across epidemics and pandemics.

The book will appeal to students and academics in public health and crisis communication programs as well as academic associations in communication and crisis management, public relations practitioners, and members of the leading communication industry groups.

Arhlene A. Flowers, formerly a public relations executive based in New York City and Toronto, is a professor in the Advertising, Public

Relations, & Marketing Communications degree program at Ithaca College, United States.

Cory L. Young is a professor in Ithaca College's Department of Strategic Communication, where she has taught 23 different courses on crisis communication, stakeholder relations, and other communication topics.

"This case study book is unlike any other [...] Professors Flowers and Young bring their professional and academic experiences to produce a book that combines history, theory, and ethics of cases and compels users to think outside the box."

Amiso M. George, *Fellow PRSA, Professor of Strategic Communication, Texas Christian University*

"Buckle up and indulge. This book equips PR practitioners and students with strategies for navigating culturally informed solutions and diverse approaches, such as community-led initiatives and innovative communication strategies to ensure business resiliency."

Saud Alsulaiman, *Assistant Professor, Mass Communication Department, King Saud University, Riyadh, The Kingdom of Saudi Arabia*

"It is timely, interdisciplinary, and appropriate for both undergraduate and graduate audiences in health and corporate communication. The case study approach makes it a must-read for any communication practitioner seeking crisis and risk communication analysis and best practices."

David P. Burns, *Professor, Communication Department, Salisbury University*

"This book, which compares communication campaigns on public health crises and risks across time, countries, and disciplines, is long overdue. The authors effectively integrate theory and practice in health-related risk and crisis communication, offering a unique comparative and global perspective that is highly relevant to scholars, students, and practitioners alike."

Andreas Schwarz, *P.D. Dr. habil.; Chair, International Research Group Crisis Communication; Ilmenau University of Technology, Institute of Media and Communication Science; Germany*

"The use of case studies in a course allows students to engage in active learning, specifically in the areas of research, problem solving, critical thinking, creativity and reflection. This book connects theory to practice and lends itself to creative groups and individual activities."

Terry L. Rentner, *Professor, School of Media and Communication, Bowling Green State University*

"It is such an important volume for both practitioners and scholars. Indeed, "those who cannot remember the past are condemned to repeat it", and this book is written specifically to learn from the history to be better prepared for public health crises in the future."

Pavel Rodin, *Ph.D.; Vice Chair, ECREA Risk and Crisis Communication, World Health Organization advisor, University of Gothenburg, Sweden.*

CASE STUDIES ON PANDEMIC AND EPIDEMIC COMMUNICATION CAMPAIGNS

From the 1918 Influenza to COVID-19

Arhlene A. Flowers and Cory L. Young

Routledge
Taylor & Francis Group
NEW YORK AND LONDON

Designed cover image: Getty Images

First published 2026
by Routledge
605 Third Avenue, New York, NY 10158

and by Routledge
4 Park Square, Milton Park, Abingdon, Oxon, OX14 4RN

Routledge is an imprint of the Taylor & Francis Group, an informa business

ISBN: 978-1-032-56199-8 (hbk)
ISBN: 978-1-032-56198-1 (pbk)
ISBN: 978-1-003-43438-2 (ebk)

DOI: 10.4324/9781003434382

Typeset in Sabon
by KnowledgeWorks Global Ltd.

Access the Instructor Resources: www.routledge.com/9781032561981

We dedicate this book to our spouses, Steven Lovass-Nagy and David Beardsley, and our friends and families. We would also like to thank Deanna Sellnow, Ph.D., chair of the Clemson University Department of Communication, and Professor Timothy Sellnow, College of Behavioral, Social and Health Sciences at Clemson University. They are prolific scholars and mavens in the international crisis and risk communication world, as they bridge the gap between academics and practitioners in the International Crisis and Risk Communication Association (ICRCA) annual conference. Because this manuscript represents a collaboration between a practitioner/academic and an academic, this book is a tribute to the conference's mission and to all the scholars and practitioners from this conference. Lastly, we would like to thank our students, some of whom contributed to the case studies, and others who have supported us along the way

CONTENTS

PREFACE

It is quite serendipitous that COVID-19 occurred a little over 100 years after the 1918–1919 H1N1 Influenza (commonly referred to as the "Spanish Flu"). History appears to be repeating itself. The similarities and parallels between these two pandemics are remarkable and provide insight into potential features that exist across epidemics and pandemics. For instance, what is the origin of the flu or the coronavirus? Where did these viruses spread to and how? How did organizations, governments, and others respond, and with what medium? How many people were infected, and what was the death toll? How was the public educated about prevention and treatment?

When we examine the origins of these health crises, both the causes of influenza in 1918–1919 and of COVID-19 were difficult to pinpoint. Scientists and government officials debated in political and medical arenas about how the virus was introduced. Both pandemics are spread airborne via respiratory droplets and through contact with infected individuals, either in social circles or through transportation. Both pandemics occurred in waves, spiking and ebbing as the disease spread (Liang et al., 2021), disrupting people's daily lives. Cities and towns then and now implemented mask mandates that divided people politically around compliance and safety concerns (Lovelace, 2020). Additionally, then President Woodrow Wilson contracted the virus while downplaying it, just as President Trump during his first term was diagnosed with COVID-19 a year after responding that "We have it under control … It's going to be fine" (Doggett, 2022, para. 4). Both presidents also were perceived to be slow in responding. In reference to mortality rates, according to Liang et al. (2021), both pandemics were roughly equal between the H1N1 Influenza and

COVID-19—2.5% to 2.4%—respectively. While this is not an exhaustive list of similarities between the Spanish Flu and COVID-19, it does identify parallels that may mimic across other pandemics.

Similarities aside, this book explores how these and other pandemics and epidemics over a century have diverged, in both positive and negative directions, based on what has been learned over time. Historically, pandemics and epidemics are nothing new. They have been wreaking havoc on the health of humans for thousands of years. We do know that our understanding of medicine and epidemiology from 100 years ago has been enhanced as the medical industry has advanced. Effective vaccines for influenza were not available in 1918 but are available now to treat and potentially eradicate some diseases. Individuals also have greater access to life-saving information and treatments as new techniques have been established. Organizations like the Centers for Disease Control and Prevention (CDC) and World Health Organization (WHO) did not exist in the early 1900s but emerged out of the need to systematically document and log valuable data that helped coordinate preventive efforts to stop the spread of viruses. Without these organizations, we would not have various guidebooks (Reynolds et al., 2007; WHO Global Influenza Programme, 2009) and updated best practices (Assaad & El-adaway, 2021; Omnilert, n.d.) for handling pandemics and epidemics as different countries and territories learned from each other (Sellwood & Van-Tam, 2013).

Methods for communicating health information to the public have evolved as well. For example, in 1918, "libraries were central to disseminating public health information" about the flu (Skinner, 2021, para. 7), as well as posters and newspapers, telephones and newsreels. From the 1950s to the beginning of the new millennium, television, cable and the internet were prominent media for message delivery to the masses (Zhao, 2020) whereas social media is the predominant medium for disseminating, gathering, and generating information about modern epidemics and pandemics. With new technologies comes increased literacy and the ability to discern what is factual and what is manufactured or misleading. As information flows and is mediated, the potential for false origin myths emerges and competes with legitimate scientific information, which can lead to fear, misinformation, distrust, and uncertainty. The spread of diseases has increased alongside the transportation industry as domestic and international borders were crossed geographically. As such, scapegoating of different ethnic, cultural, and animal groups shifted depending on the disease and political, economic, and social factors, for example, gay men and AIDS, Asians and various influenzas, pigs and (A)H1N1 Influenza (commonly called the "Swine Flu"), among others.

In addition to epidemics and pandemics, health crises share many similar features, yet have divergent health implications for human, animal, plant, food, and environmental systems (Law Insider, n.d.). As high-impact events, health crises disrupt normalcy and require urgent actions and responses by organizations and governments on multiple levels from local to regional and national to international. A typical response to a health crisis is a health communication campaign, which is an organized communication-based activity, guided by theory, to promote health behaviors (e.g., risk, medication usage, use of health services, testing and screen for diseases, and methods of prevention) through a similar process of public relations planning: research, targeted audience, goals and objectives, messages, and strategies (Snyder, 2007; Zhao, 2020).

All types of organizations in both the public and private sectors face unique communication challenges during health crises, pandemics and epidemics. *Case Studies on Pandemic and Epidemic Communication Campaigns: From the 1918 Influenza to COVID-19* analyzes communication campaigns involving public relations, advertising, social media, marketing communications, special events, or face-to-face engagement undertaken by governments, corporations, nonprofits, and nongovernmental and intergovernmental organizations.

This book also addresses ethics, social inequities, fearmongering due to the spread of misinformation, the impact of the antivaccination movement, and bias and discrimination against infected people and social locations. Each chapter covers a historical perspective to understand the overall magnitude of the health crisis and its economic, political, or societal impact. Each case study contains a complete overview and details about the campaign (situation analysis, communication programming and execution, results and measurement), theoretical principles, and insightful questions to hone critical thinking skills.

As authors, we are practitioners, instructors, and scholars within the field of strategic communication. We are not doctors, physicians, epidemiologists, nor health researchers; rather, we integrate our experiences and offer a blend of practical and theoretical perspectives in communications. We hope this book takes readers on a fascinating journey from the 1918–1919 H1N1 pandemic to the COVID-19 pandemic while investigating 12 major health crises in the U.S. and worldwide that occurred over a 100-year span.

References

Assaad, R., & El-adaway, I. H.. (2021). Guidelines for responding to COVID-19 pandemic: Best Practices, impacts, and future research directions. *Journal of Management in Engineering*, *37*(3), 1–17. DOI: 10.1061/(ASCE)ME.1943-5479.0000906

Doggett, L. (2022, March 2). *Timeline of Trump's Coronavirus responses.* [Blog]. https://doggett.house.gov/media/blog-post/timeline-trumps-coronavirus-responses

Law Insider. (n.d.). *Health crisis definition*. https://www.lawinsider.com/dictionary/health-crisis
Liang, S. T., Liang, L. T., & Rosen, J. M. (2021, May). COVID-19: A comparison to the 1918 influenza and how we can defeat it. *Postgraduate Medical Journal*, *97*(1147), 273–274. DOI: 10.1136/postgradmedj-2020-139070. PMID: 33563705.
Lovelace, B. Jr. (2020, September 29). *Medical historian compares the coronavirus to the 1918 flu pandemic: Both were highly political*. CNBC. https://www.cnbc.com/2020/09/28/comparing-1918-flu-vs-coronavirus.html
Omnilert. (n.d.). *Definitive guide to pandemic communications*. https://www.omnilert.com/solution-brochures/guide-to-pandemic-communications
Reynolds, B., Deitch, S., & Schieber, R. A. (2007). *Crisis and emergency risk communication: Pandemic influenza*. https://emergency.cdc.gov/cerc/resources/pdf/cerc-pandemicflu-oct07.pdf
Sellwood, C., & Van-Tam, J.. (2013). *Pandemic influenza*. CABI. https://www.cabidigitallibrary.org/doi/book/10.1079/9781845938567.0000
Skinner, J. (2021, April 14). Libraries and pandemics: Past and present. *Daily*. https://daily.jstor.org/libraries-and-pandemics-past-and-present/
Snyder, L. B. (2007). Health communication campaigns and their impact on behavior. *Journal of Nutritional Educational Behavior*, *39*, S32–S40. doi: 10.1016/j.jneb.2006.09.004
WHO Global Influenza Programme. (2009). *Pandemic influenza preparedness and response: A WHO guidance document*. https://www.who.int/publications/i/item/9789241547680
Zhao, X. (2020). Health communication campaigns: A brief introduction and call for dialogue. *International Journal of Nursing Sciences*, 7, S11–S15. https://doi.org/10.1016/j.ijnss.2020.04.009

ACKNOWLEDGMENTS

We received much support financially and otherwise from several constituencies within Ithaca College in New York. From the Department of Strategic Communication, we received sabbatical leave and funds for traveling to the International Crisis and Risk Communication conference. Dean Amy Falkner, Brandy Hawley (administrative coordinator) and Erin Schiefelbein (administrative and financial operations coordinator) supported us with funding made possible in part by two James B. Pendleton Grants from the Roy H. Park School of Communications at Ithaca College. Provost Melanie Stein and Associate Provost Brendan Murday supported us with a faculty development mini-grant. We also would like to thank Felisa Salvago-Keyes, Zoya Gayle, Daniela Santacruz, Riya Bhattacharya, and other staff at Routledge for all their help.

We wish to acknowledge these organizations that granted us permission to use the images contained in the book:

- Beef. It's What's For Dinner, Beef Checkoff
- Centers for Disease Control and Prevention
- David J. Sencer CDC Museum
- Division of Medicine and Science, National Museum of American History, Smithsonian Institution
- Te Ranga Tupua Iwi Collective
- University of Pittsburgh and University of Pittsburgh Library System
- World Health Organization
- Zavalita Brand Building, Art Director Pablo Collantes

Other images were in the public domain or from stock houses.

ACRONYMS

A(H1NI)	Influenza strain also known as the "swine flu"
H1N1	1918–1919 Influenza, "Spanish flu"
ACHD	Allegheny County Health Department
AIDS	Acquired Immunodeficiency Syndrome
AMA	American Medical Association
APhA	American Pharmacists Association
ARC	American Red Cross
ARTA	America Responds to AIDS
ASTHO	Association of State and Territorial Health Officials
BSE	Bovine Spongiform Encephalopathy
BZgA	Bundeszentrale für gesundheitliche Aufklärung/Federal Center for Health Education (Germany)
CAD	Canadian Dollar
CDC	Centers for Disease Control and Prevention
CPI	Committee on Public Information
COVID	Coronavirus Disease
ECDC	European Centre for Disease Prevention and Control
EJAF	Elton John AIDS Foundation
EPI	Expanded Programme on Immunization
EUR	Euro
FAO	Food and Agriculture Organization of the United Nations
FCC	Federal Communications Commission
FDR	Franklin Delano Roosevelt
FDA	Food and Drug Administration
FTC	Federal Trade Commission

Gavi	Global Alliance for Vaccines and Immunizations
GISRS	Global Influenza Surveillance Response System
GPEI	Global Polio Eradication Initiative
GPRB	Government of the People's Republic of Bangladesh
H2N2	"Asian flu"
H3N2	"Hong Kong flu"
HBM	Health Belief Model
HKTB	Hong Kong Tourism Board
HIV	Human Immunodeficiency Virus
IPV	Inactivated Polio Vaccine
KSA	Kingdom of Saudi Arabia
KDCA	Korea Disease Control and Prevention Agency
KPOA	Kick Polio Out of Africa
LGBTQ	Lesbian, Gay, Bisexual, Transgender, and Queer
MERS	Middle East Respiratory Syndrome
MERS-CoV	Middle East Respiratory Syndrome Coronavirus
MMR	Measles, Mumps and Rubella
MOH	Ministry of Health (Kingdom of Saudi Arabia)
MoHFW	Ministry of Health and Family Welfare (Bangladesh)
NAACP	National Association for the Advancement of Colored People
NASPA	National Alliance of State Pharmacy Associations
NCBA	National Cattlemen's Beef Association (U.S.)
NFIP	National Foundation for Infantile Paralysis; now known as the March of Dimes
NPB	National Pork Board
NPIs	Non-Pharmaceutical Interventions
NPPC	National Pork Producers Council
NZD	New Zealand Dollar
OPV	Oral Polio Vaccine
ORI	Outbreak Response Immunization
OSDH	Oklahoma State Department of Health
PADM	Protective Action Decision Model
PAHO	Pan American Health Organization
PATA	Pacific Asia Travel Association
PBS	Public Broadcasting Service
PPE	Personal Protective Equipment
PPS	Pittsburgh Public Schools
PRSA	Public Relations Society of America
PSA	Public Service Announcement
RRT	Rapid Response Team
SARS	Severe Acute Respiratory Syndrome

SARS-CoV	Severe Acute Respiratory Syndrome Coronavirus
SCCT	Situational Crisis Communication Theory
SEAR	South-East Asia Region
SDH	Social Determinants of Health
SIP	SARS Induced Panic
TRT	Te Ranga Tupua Collective in New Zealand
UNESCO	United Nations Educational, Scientific and Cultural Organization
UNICEF	United Nations Children's Fund, since 1953; originally known as the United Nations International Children's Emergency Fund
USD	United States Dollar
USDA	United States Department of Agriculture
USPHSCC	United States Public Health Service Commissioned Corps
USDHHS	United States Department of Health and Human Services
USPHS	United States Public Health Service
vCJD	Variant Creutzfeldt-Jakob Disease
VNNIOSH	Vietnam National Institute of Occupational Safety and Health
VNR	Video News Release
WHO	World Health Association
WHO-AR	World Health Organization-African Region
WHOEMR	World Health Organization Eastern Mediterranean Region

1

INTRODUCTION

Primer on the case study method

Have you ever wondered why case studies have withstood the test of time—over a century—within institutions of higher education? Case studies have been valuable learning platforms for students since 1921 when Harvard Business School (HBS) broke new ground in introducing case studies in management courses. Serendipitously, in 2021 during COVID-19, HBS launched a timeline celebrating the evolution of 100 years of case method teaching and learning. This technique of using real-world situations and strategies continues to be popular in other disciplines such as public relations, crisis communication, health communication and public affairs.

Now more than ever, the case study method is a crucial pedagogical tool for educators and practitioners to employ in helping students make sense of past and present pandemics and epidemics and learn from mistakes.

In this chapter, we provide a primer on the case study method by delineating the salient features, fundamentals, and skills. We then identify unique psychological and communication features of pandemics and epidemics and explain how to use this book effectively. We conclude with an overview of how this book is organized.

Case studies: Salient features, fundamentals, and skills

We begin with the origin of the case method. HBS Professor Jan Rivkin narrates on video the creation of the first case—The General Shoe Company written by Clinton P. Biddle (Kunhardt, 2019). Out of this original case,

DOI: 10.4324/9781003434382-1

salient features, fundamentals, and skills emerged that Dr. Rivkin believes are still relevant today when using case studies. Such features include:

a A shift in teaching about business from a traditional lecture format to discussing an actual organization experiencing a problem.
b An uncertain or ambiguous situation where the outcome is difficult to ascertain but requires a course of action.
c "Detective" questions or a path of inquiry that arise out of the ambiguity and necessitate empathy—being put in the shoes of the decision maker or stakeholder (i.e., What would you do if you were in this situation? What do you need to decide for this community?).

An additional feature of case studies that emerged over time is the application of theory which helps individuals organize thoughts and observations about phenomenon. Case studies allow readers to see public relations theories and principles in action in campaigns (Turk et al., 2017) that can assist students in evaluating organizational actions during a crisis and in forming recommendations (Ray, 1992). Within the field of health communication, theories can be applied to real-life health scenarios to help students understand critical contexts surrounding how individuals and families make decisions or how health campaigns disseminate information about diagnoses, treatments, and associated changes in behavior (Ray, 1992).

Salient features are just as important as fundamentals. Case studies are designed to be interactive, experiential, immersive, and engaging. As an example, the Centers for Disease Control and Prevention (CDC, 2023) developed case studies "based on real-life epidemiologic investigations and used them for training Epidemic Intelligence Service (EIS) officers—CDC's 'disease detectives'" (para. 2).

As students discuss the case with others in class, they will find the emergence of different perspectives that shed light on various complexities, competing voices, and choices. By participating in case studies and taking on different perspectives, students develop these important transferable skills in a safe learning environment: critical thinking, problem solving, independence, foresight, analytical abilities, listening, and the ability to express themselves. Additionally, students gain meta-skills as a "group of long-lasting abilities that allow someone to learn new things more quickly" (Nohria, 2021, para. 5), including preparation, discernment, bias recognition, judgment, collaboration, curiosity, and self-confidence.

We believe understanding the salient features, fundamentals, and skills of case studies provides a valuable scaffolding or structure to approach each case and to use this book effectively.

Definitions of terms

At this point you, as the reader, might be wondering, what is the difference between crisis, epidemic, and pandemic? These terms often become conflated because of similarities but differ in subtle and important ways that necessitate explanation.

From an etymological perspective, crisis evolved from the Greek word *krisis* or "turning point in a disease, a change which indicates recovery or death" (Online Etymology Dictionary, 2019, para. 1). Merriam-Webster (n.d.) adds an additional defining element of "an unstable or crucial time or state of affairs in which a decisive change is impending" (para. 3). The operating assumption is that organizations and individuals are agents who can exert control over how a crisis unfolds by making decisions within a crisis plan and containing the damage. Additionally, when it comes to health, the same operating assumption applies as individuals have agency to exert control of what threatens their health and can make decisions.

The origins of the terms epidemic and pandemic primarily denote people or the public. Pan=all. Epi=among. Demos=people. And emic=cultural phenomenon. More specifically, an epidemic "refers to an increase, often sudden, in the number of cases of a disease above what is normally expected in that population in that area" (CDC, 2012, para. 3), for example, yellow fever, smallpox, measles, and polio. As an epidemic evolves, it has the potential to become a pandemic by jumping boundaries, spreading geographically, and impacting a large number of people (CDC, 2012), thus overwhelming various systems. The operating assumption is that diseases are hard to control as viruses morph while being difficult to contain with permeable boundaries and thereby require multiple plans across multiple levels.

What is fascinating about crises, epidemics, and pandemics is that they exist within the confluence of public relations, health communication, and crisis/risk communication industries.

As Maureen Taylor (2023), professor of strategic communication at the University of Technology Sydney, Australia, observes "Public health campaigns encompass public relations strategies and tactics" (p. 86). PRSA (2021), in its study guide for professional accreditation in public relations, defines strategies as the use of "social media, media relations, public engagement, employee engagement, third-party endorsement, and interactions with opinion leaders" (p. 28). These strategies are used to ethically communicate an organization's stance and showcase its products, clarify or correct an organization's stance on the issue or crisis and to deliver important information to decision makers. Tactics include "scheduling a news conference, sending a newsletter, hosting a meeting, writing a news release, or planning a special event" (PRSA, 2001, p. 28) and are tools to achieve a strategy. Throughout each case, readers explore how organizations, individuals, or governments used these strategies and tactics throughout the various phases of the pandemic or epidemic—before, during, and after a health crisis. The goals and objectives of a health communication campaign are to raise awareness and inform publics of a health crisis (health information) and to prevent and control the spread of diseases by promoting health and safety behaviors (health promotion) through tailoring messages to target audiences.

Crisis communication efforts to combat epidemics tend to focus on building awareness, reducing risk, and increasing positive health behaviors. A mega-crisis like a pandemic requires "a rethinking of preparation, response, and management" and necessitates systemic coordination of communication efforts on multiple levels (Sellnow & Seeger, 2021, p. 6). Additionally, crises present unique communication challenges, nuances, and contradictions or dialectical tensions evident in each case presented in this book.

Pandemics and epidemics: Unique communication features and psychological factors

Recently, numerous books related to pandemic communication have been published. This is not surprising as the recency of COVID-19 has incited interdisciplinary scholarship to explore and make sense of the interconnected nature of the pandemic, its impacts, and changes to our daily lives. Within the field of communication, researchers have sought to capture pandemic communication and reexamine and update existing theories, models, and constructs (Croucher & Diers-Lawson, 2023).

Scope

One of the unique challenges faced by scholars and practitioners is related to scope. The scope of research and practices has widened, challenging scholars and practitioners to think outside their disciplinary or industry boxes and integrate multiple disciplinary aspects to investigate the impacts and changes to health communication, crisis communication, or public relations.

It is increasingly difficult to examine an aspect of a pandemic in isolation or from a single perspective. Inherently, pandemics mimic viruses. They are messy and "tend to transcend geographical boundaries and thus require more coordination across countries and regions to manage ... they implicate diverse cultures, political systems, public health systems, and traditions and practices in response to disease management" (Seeger & Seeger, 2023, pp. 60–61).

For example, Berube (2021) examined the design and delivery of health messages related to outbreaks, epidemics, and pandemics. The scope of his research encompassed digital messaging and social media, literacy, domestic and international audiences, and political communication.

Taylor (2023) investigated how the public relations industry has evolved by identifying changes in topics and themes pre- and post-pandemic. The topics included several areas of specialization indicated above and others: health communication, corporate social responsibility, employee communication, communication engagement on social media, organizational public relationships, social capital, networks, and socially mediated communication. Seeger and Seeger (2023) integrated crisis, and risk and emergency response communication to identify a "unique set of constraints and communication interventions" that pandemics impose (p. 61).

Pandemics affect a large and diverse group of audiences with unique needs, experiences, resources, values, beliefs, levels of trust, and languages. These factors impact access and abilities to process scientific and technical information, which then impact how interventions are created, coordinated, and heard. The overall point is that communication within a global pandemic is a nested and networked phenomenon, representing an exchange of information designed to reduce harm and uncertainty while enabling rapid responses (Seeger & Seeger, 2023).

Adaptability

Another unique feature of pandemic communication is a nuanced understanding of how to adapt and adjust as an outbreak ebbs and flows. No one can predict with certainty how a pandemic is going to spread, how far, and for how long. Unpredictability and uncertainty can derail strategies and plans and raise important questions. Who, what organization, or governmental entity, decides when a health crisis or outbreak becomes an epidemic? When does the epidemic become a pandemic? When is a pandemic officially declared, or declared done?

The World Health Organization (WHO) (2023) declared an end to COVID-19's public health emergency based on increasing immunity due to vaccines and decreasing deaths on May 5, 2023, while "stressing it does not mean the disease is no longer a global threat" (para. 1). Yet, ideas about what the post-pandemic world will look like began emerging six to eight months after it was officially declared a pandemic in March 2020 (Kirsch, 2020; Powell, 2020) while Bokat-Lindell (2021) pleads "Stop saying 'post-pandemic'" in 2021.

As the latest information arises about how a disease is spreading, parallel information arises about which behaviors mitigate the spread. This information convergence requires a complex adaptive system in which "Ongoing research into the disease, its treatment, and prevention potentially provides 'external input' into the systems, which may modify doctors' disease management and alter patient's health outcomes" (Strumberg & Martin, 2020).

CDC and other health officials can put more thought into the intention of messages: "rather than implying that most people are not contagious after day 5 of infection ... officials [should] explain that for a patient with improving symptoms, the chance of spreading infection to others is lower" (Wachter, 2022, para. 7).

Tensions

An additional communication nuance is the ability to recognize "how tensions between organizations and publics influence communication decisions" (Littlefield, 2020, p. 211). Littlefield and Sellnow (2015) illuminate seven tensions organizations might experience during a crisis: timeliness of when to release information, how much information should be revealed, whose voice is heard revealing information, how confident organizations are about the information, whose interests are prioritized, the level of responsibility an organization accepts, and how much emotional connection should an organization maintain with publics. Croucher and Diers-Lawson (2023) identify a challenge these tensions might create: "while people may want certainty, certainty cannot be produced quickly" (p. 3).

Others have researched a) dominant and non-dominant identities that reveal tensions surrounding access and exclusion, b) privilege versus discrimination, c) scientific facts competing with conspiracy theories and misinformation, d) traditional vs. digital and emerging platforms with respect to consistent messaging, and e) trust versus distrust between publics and organizations, between organizations and governments, and between practitioners and academics, among others. Navigating these tensions within a pandemic requires careful planning, a flexible structure, clear intent, the ability to socially listen, and an understanding of psychology.

Psychological factors

These communication nuances and tensions, if managed effectively, can reduce psychological impacts on health promotion efforts. Stephen Taylor (2022), professor and clinical psychologist at the University of British Columbia, Canada, acknowledges the role that psychology plays in the "spreading versus containment of pandemic-related disease" and in determining adherence to mitigation procedures like social distancing (p. 233). If tensions and nuances are managed ineffectively, these psychologically distressing and "socially disruptive, divisive, and potentially harmful phenomena" can emerge:

> racism … anticipatory anxiety … the rise of xenophobia, rumors, and conspiracy theories; panic buying; new-onset or newly worsened emotional disorders (e.g., anxiety and mood disorders); protests over social distancing restrictions and related mandates such as mask wearing; the rise of quack cures and profiteering [and] the occasional rioting and violent protests.
>
> *(pp. 233–234)*

Taylor reminds us that "pandemics are not 'once in a lifetime' events; plan for more to come" (p. 233).

How to use this book effectively

The main theme of our book is explicit in its title: *Case Studies on Pandemic and Epidemic Communication Campaigns: From the 1918 Influenza to COVID-19*. This book covers communication campaigns from businesses, nonprofits, advocacy groups, and nongovernmental and governmental organizations during major health outbreaks that affected the U.S. and countries around the world. The case study structure is adapted from the Public Relations Society of America's (2025) Silver Anvil Awards/Strategic Communication category, the Arthur W. Page Society's (2023) case study competition, author guidelines from University of Southern California Annenberg's (n.d.) former *Case Studies in Strategic Communication* journal, and case study lessons used in the authors' courses. The authors acknowledge that not all information may be available, particularly for the earlier historical campaigns; however, they follow the core structure for each section as closely as possible.

As a way of modeling the case study process, within each section, we reference the National Association for the Advancement of Colored People (NAACP) and highlights of its COVID-19 "We Are Done Dying" campaign.

Historical context

This section sets the scene for the readers to fully understand the circumstances, uncertainties, and challenges of each case, by going back in time or reflecting on the present. It covers when the health crisis began and ended—or if it is continuing; where the epidemic or pandemic began and where it spread to; the death toll and number of people who became ill; the disruptions the affected populations experienced in their daily lives; the medical environment and availability of vaccines; the economic, political, or societal impacts; the variety of communication tools available to reach the public; the spread of misleading information stoking fear and panic; and scapegoating and discrimination against specific audiences.

> *Black and brown communities have endured injustices, police violence, discrimination, marginalization, and violations of civil rights. Black Lives Matter (BLM) emerged in 2013 to vocalize and expose inequities in the justice system, following the acquittal of George Zimmerman who shot Trayvon Martin. As the country faced the COVID-19 pandemic and data was being tracked and collected by CDC and American University's Antiracist Research & Policy Center and the COVID Tracking Project (Williams, 2020), the "virus laid bare the fact that African Americans continue[d] to experience the highest overall morbidity and the most widespread occurrence of disproportionate deaths"*
>
> *(Cox & Cobb, 2020, p. 13)*

> *The mortality rate of African Americans due to COVID-19—over 95 out of every 100,000—is a third higher than Latinos, double that of Whites and Asians (Reyes, 2020). Although the rate of morbidity has significantly decreased overall, CDC's COVID Data Tracker revealed in January 2024, the monthly death rate per 100,000 for Blacks was higher (2.25) than American Indian or Alaskan Natives (2.16), Asians (1.54), and Hispanics (1.12), with Native Hawaiian or Other Pacific Islanders and Whites at 2.4 and 4.41, respectively.*
>
> *(CDC, 2024)*

> *The disruptions to people's personal lives during the pandemic were impacted by various social determinants of health; for example, poor living conditions, social policies and programs, low-wage jobs, homelessness, incarcerations, and lack of access to health insurance, testing, vaccinations, and health care, among other aspects affecting Black communities (Reyes, 2020). Additionally, many Black Americans worked in public service setting like hospitals that exposed themselves and their families to the virus and subjected them to being blamed if they got sick (Williams, 2020). To mobilize people to take action against discrimination and address social and healthcare inequities, the NAACP launched its "We Are Done Dying" campaign in May 2020.*

Situation analysis of the campaign

This section provides information about a specific communication campaign and the major reasons for conducting the campaign; specific challenges facing the government, business, or nonprofit organizations; research conducted and findings, if available; relevant internal organizational factors of the organization, such as its mission, vision, and values; brief background of the organization(s); and the involvement of the organization's in-house marketing, advertising, and public relations staff, and any retained advertising and public relations agencies.

> *NAACP's (2024) mission, displayed on its website, is to "achieve equity, political rights, and social inclusion by advancing policies and practices that expand human and civil rights, eliminate discrimination, and accelerate the well-being, education, and economic security of Black people and all persons of color" (para. 2). The organization envisions itself to be "an inclusive community rooted in liberation where all persons can exercise their civil and human rights without discrimination"*
>
> *(NAACP, 2024, para. 1)*

> *As public acts of police violence and racism involving Breonna Taylor, Ahmaud Arbery, and George Floyd erupted concurrently with the launch of the "We Are Done Dying" campaign in May 2020, the campaign's focus shifted to include broader criminal/economic justice, education, and voting rights (Hunt, 2020). In a press statement, NAACP's President and CEO Derrick Johnson stated, "our community members face tough choices as access to food, good jobs, and a quality education slips further away"(NAACP, 2020a, para. 3). He pled that idleness was no longer an option; the campaign addresses equities and serves as a Call-to-Action with steps on reaching out to elected officials.*
>
> *(NAACP, 2020a)*

Communication programming and execution

This part covers the campaign's objectives, strategies, and target audiences and stakeholders; campaign theme, if any; tactics used to communicate and reach specific audiences, including media relations, website content, social media, video, printed materials, advertisements, events, promotions, and other activities; visual examples to illustrate specific tactics; involvement of celebrities and public opinion leaders, if relevant; timetable of the campaign; and budget, if available.

> *The Crisis Magazine is "the official publication of the NAACP and the nation's oldest African American publication." (NAACP, n.d., para. 1).*

> *The July 2020 issue was dedicated to all efforts associated with the coronavirus, Black America, and declaration "We Are Done Dying." Features included articles about underlying conditions that contributed to erupting protests; the multiple crises facing Black people; an interview with newly elected Mayor Ella Jones of Ferguson, Missouri; an exploration of what change looks like; poems, tweets, and a literary quilt of words in honor of George Floyd; issues and viewpoints; impacts and effects of COVID-19; elder residents at risk; learning gaps; the virus in prison; families coping with challenges; mental health; a forum; and lastly, the NAACP #WeAreDoneDying campaign.*
>
> *The campaign also used in-person and mediated communication tools such as social media, petitions, email, websites, newspapers, television, and radio (NAACP, 2020–2021) to bring to light the inequities.*
>
> *The campaign's target audience is the federal government. The objectives and strategies were to demand police, economic, healthcare, voting, and prison reforms (Hunt, 2020), along with civil rights advocacy recommendations articulated in NAACP's report on Coronavirus equity considerations*
>
> *(NAACP, 2020b)*

Outcomes

This component details the outcomes of the campaign, available results, and any evaluation efforts; for example, how the campaign increased awareness, sold products or services, changed perceptions or behavior, or enhanced fundraising efforts. It also summarizes media coverage and where (newspapers, magazines, TV, radio, or online); measurement and evaluation, such as achieved objectives, facts on media interactivity and engagement, and any significant changes, such as new legislation and public opinion shifts.

> *NAACP's campaign efforts yielded the following outcomes: over 200,000 petition signatures and increased followers of NAACP to 1.5 million within a month (Hunt, 2020) and broader recognition of police violence and race, increased participation in activism as 90,000 people emailed Congress with demands for changes, 6 million visits to NAACP's website—2 million of which were new visitors—and almost 350,000 advocacy actions.*
>
> *(NAACP, 2020–2021)*

Theoretical perspectives

Each case study includes academic theories from various disciplinary perspectives such as health communication, crisis communication, public relations, media, psychology, and sociology to name a few. The relevant theory or theories can help students understand the assumptions and accepted facts that were used to explain what was happening.

> *Critical race theory is an appropriate perspective from which to analyze NAACP and other cases throughout this book. Briefly, this intellectual and social movement led by activists and scholars is rooted in the general idea that race is not a biological but rather a social construct used by dominant groups to rationalize oppression and exploitation of non-dominant groups (Duignan, 2025). Further, the assumption underlying the theory is that racism is inherent in various institutions which function to create inequities.*
>
> *When applied to pandemics and other health crises, critical race theory can be used to understand "structural issues including those related to public health … [and] the experiences and perspectives of discrimination among racially minoritized peoples including how this impacts health outcomes."*
> *(Yashadhana et al., 2021, p. 5)*
>
> *It can also be used to understand how dual pandemics can co-exist—one based in health, the other based in systemic racism—that interact "to exacerbate negative outcomes for communities of color."*
> *(Jones, 2021, p. 427)*

Key words

In this section of each chapter, the authors provide a list of key words.

Arthur W. Page Society Case Study
Centers for Disease Control and Prevention (CDC)
Crisis
Critical Race Theory
Detective Questions
Dialectical Tensions
Epidemic
National Association for the Advancement of Colored People (NAACP)
Pandemic
Risk Communication
World Health Organization (WHO)

Questions for discussion

Readers are prompted with a list of detective questions for analysis and critical thinking about the case study, such as the relevance of the campaign for students studying integrated marketing communications, public relations, health communication, and other communication fields; what components were considered most successful and why, and whether these components could be successful today or be adapted to future events; helpful lessons for communicators nationwide or around the world; how different time periods impact communication planning and execution; recommendations for what could have been done differently or worked more effectively; identification of commonalities or differences across case studies; and other questions about the specific case study.

1 *What would you do if you were the public relations director of the NAACP trying to address health inequities?*
2 *How would you obtain feedback or conduct research on what would be helpful to the African American community related to COVID-19?*
3 *What communication strategies could the NAACP develop to address future epidemics and pandemics?*

How this book is organized

Readers will be able to grasp the historical context of each health outbreak to understand the circumstances and challenges revolving around major health crises in the U.S. and worldwide for a century. The book will help communication and public health students learn the best practices and acquire insight on audiences, objectives, strategies, execution, and evaluation for a wide variety of communication campaigns. Each case study contains theoretical principles and reflective questions for students to examine real-world campaigns in greater depth.

The chapters are organized in chronological order of the health crisis:

- **Chapter 2** focuses on the **H1N1 "Spanish Flu" Influenza** pandemic from 1918–1919 with case studies on communication efforts undertaken by the U.S. Public Health Service and the American Red Cross to educate public safety; how telephone companies attempted to curb personal usage of telephones for emergency services during the pandemic; and how panic profiteers in the U.S. and the U.K. used questionable tactics to promote their "cure-all" products.
- **Chapter 3** looks at the **polio** epidemic from 1927 to the present with case studies on how the 32nd U.S. President Franklin Roosevelt helped form the March of Dimes to raise funds for polio research and to build public awareness of the disease; how the largest U.S. medical field test persuaded parents to volunteer their children as "Polio Pioneers" to test a new vaccine and the subsequent approved vaccine's rollout in

public schools nationwide; and how the pan-African "Kick Polio Out of Africa" campaign helped eradicate polio in many countries with the support of soccer athletes.

- **Chapter 4** spans the **H2N2 "Asian Flu" Influenza** pandemic from 1957–1958 and the **H3N2 "Hong Kong Flu" Influenza** pandemic from 1968–1969 with case studies on how the U.S. Public Health System and American Medical Association educated the public and encouraged vaccinations with the growing influence of television; and how a health communication campaign combatted the spread of the Asian Flu in Singapore.
- **Chapter 5** examines outbreaks of the **measles** since the MMR (Measles, Mumps, Rubella) vaccine in 1971 with case studies on how a British medical journal sparked antivaccination protests with research claiming that the MMR vaccine causes autism in children; how two U.S. cities developed vaccination campaigns for their residents; and how advocacy communication strategies led to the world's largest vaccination rollout in Bangladesh.
- **Chapter 6** studies the **HIV/AIDS (Human Immunodeficiency Virus/Acquired Immunodeficiency Syndrome)** pandemic from 1981 to the present with case studies on how U.S. health groups united to prevent HIV/AIDS; how celebrities in sports and music formed foundations to create educational campaigns on HIV/AIDS; and how Germany's "Don't Give AIDS a Chance" campaign educated the public about condom use and risky behavior.
- **Chapter 7** covers the **Mad Cow Disease (Bovine Spongiform Encephalopathy)** from 1986 with case studies on how the National Cattlemen's Beef Association created campaigns to promote safety measures by the U.S. beef industry; and how McDonald's, the largest buyer of beef worldwide, beefed up its public image and dealt with the health crisis at its restaurants.
- **Chapter 8** investigates **SARS (Severe Acute Respiratory Syndrome)** from 2002–2003 and **MERS (Middle East Respiratory Syndrome)** beginning in 2012 with case studies on how Toronto increased public awareness of SARS when Canada dealt with the highest number of fatalities and cases outside of Asia; how the Hong Kong Tourism Board faced bad timing with its "Take Your Breath Away" tourism campaign and quickly rebranded to deal with SARS; and how Saudi Arabia's public health campaign, "We Can Stop It," warned the public to avoid contact with camels as natural hosts of MERS, leading to camel farmers undertaking their "Kiss Your Camel" social media outreach.
- **Chapter 9** looks at the **(A)H1N1 "Swine Flu"** pandemic starting in 2009 with case studies on how the U.S. pork industry's "Pork is Safe"

campaign overcame misinformation about pork consumption; and how the leading American pharmacy trade group set up industry initiatives to promote certification and communication tools as U.S. pharmacies nationwide were allowed to inoculate customers.

- **Chapter 10** focuses on the **COVID-19** pandemic beginning in 2019 with case studies on how South Korea's COVID-19 public health campaign, "TRUST," instilled solidarity among citizens; how the "Getty Museum Challenge" from the Los Angeles museum sparked creativity with people stuck indoors during the pandemic lockdown; how Mexico, Peru, and Vietnam communicated preventive measures with impactful video storytelling; and how culturally appropriate campaigns reached Aboriginal people in Australia and Māori communities in New Zealand.

References

Arthur W. Page Society. (2023). *Case study competition*. https://page.org/study_competitions

Berube, D. M. (2021). *Pandemic communication and resilience*. Spring International Publishing.

Bokat-Lindell, S. (2021, June 5). Debatable: Stop saying 'post-pandemic.' *New York Times (Online)*. https://www.nytimes.com/2021/06/15/opinion/vaccination-pandemic-world.html

CDC. (2012). *Lesson 1: Introduction to epidemiology*. https://archive.cdc.gov/www_cdc_gov/csels/dsepd/ss1978/lesson1/index.html

CDC. (2023, February 21). *EIS case studies*. https://archive.cdc.gov/#/details?q=epidemiologic%20case%20studies%20+%202019&start=0&rows=10&url=https://www.cdc.gov/eis/request-services/casestudies.html

CDC. (2024). COVID-19 monthly death rates per 100,000 population by age group, race and ethnicity, and sex. https://covid.cdc.gov/covid-data-tracker/#demographicsovertime

Coombs, W. T. (2014). *Applied crisis communication and crisis management: Cases and exercises* (1st ed.). SAGE Publications.

Cox, C., & Cobb, C. C. (2020, July). Protest, race and the American future. *The Crisis- the official publication of the NAACP*. https://naacp.org/articles/protest-race-and-american-future

Croucher, S. M., & Diers-Lawson, A. (Eds.). (2023). *Pandemic communication*. Routledge.

Duignan, B. (2025, September 22). Critical race theory. *Encyclopedia Britannica*. https://www.britannica.com/topic/critical-race-theory

Hunt, J. (2020). NAACP declares: "We Are Done Dying [Article]. *The crisis: We Are Done Dying*, *127*, 69–71. https://naacp.org/resources/crisis-we-are-done-dying-vol-127

Jones, J. M. (2021). The dual pandemics of COVID-19 and systemic racism: Navigating our path forward. *School Psychology*, *36*(5), 427–431. https://doi.org/10.1037/spq0000472

Kirsch, M. (2020, December 4). Considering a post-pandemic future: At home newsletter. *New York Times*. https://www.nytimes.com/2020/12/04/at-home/newsletter.html

Kunhardt, A. (2019). *1921—The first case: General Shoe Company*. President and Fellows of Harvard College. https://www.hbs.edu/case-method-100
Littlefield, R. S. (2020). The tensions of strategic decision-making: An exploratory examination of theory and practice. *Journal of International Crisis and Risk Communication Research*, *3*(2), 211–242. https://doi.org/10.30658/jicrcr.3.2.4
Littlefield, R. S., & Sellnow, T. L. (Eds.). (2015). *Risk and crisis communication: Navigating the tensions between organizations and the public*. Lexington Books.
Merriam-Webster. (n.d.). Crisis. In *Merriam-Webster.com dictionary*. https://www.merriam-webster.com/dictionary/crisis
NAACP. (n.d.). *History of the crisis*. https://naacp.org/find-resources/history-explained/history-crisis
NAACP. (May 2020–June 2021). Impact report: Imagining a more just world. *Issuu*. https://issuu.com/naacphq/docs/naacp_impact_report_final
NAACP. (2020a, May 7). *NAACP Launches #WeAreDoneDying Campaign, Empowering Black and Brown communities to take action against senseless killings of African Americans*. [Press Statement]. https://naacp.org/articles/naacp-launches-wearedonedying-campaign-empowering-black-and-brown-communities-take-action#:~:text=%22With%20crumbling%20economic%20infrastructure%2C%20our,leadership%20from%20the%20White%20House.
NAACP. (2020b, April 3). *Coronavirus equity considerations: The imperative for civil rights advocacy, monitoring, and enforcement*. https://naacp.org/sites/default/files/documents/Coronavirus-Equity-Considerations.pdf
NAACP. (2024). *We're on a mission. Civil rights and social justice for all*. https://naacp.org/about/mission-vision
Nohria, N. (2021, December 21). What the case study method really teaches. *Harvard Business Review*. https://hbr.org/2021/12/what-the-case-study-method-really-teaches
Online Etymology Dictionary. (2019). *Crisis (n.)*. https://www.etymonline.com/search?q=crisis
Powell, A. (2020, November 24). What will the new post-pandemic normal look like? *Harvard Gazette*. https://news.harvard.edu/gazette/story/2020/11/our-post-pandemic-world-and-whats-likely-to-hang-round/
Public Relations Society of America. (2021). *Study guide for the Examination for Accreditation in Public Relations*. https://accreditation.prsa.org/MyAPR/Content/Resources/Resources_for_Candidates.aspx
Public Relations Society of America. (2025). *Silver Anvil Strategic Campaign Awards*. https://www.prsa.org/conferences-and-awards/awards/anvil-awards
Ray, E. B. (Ed.) (1992). *Case studies in health communication* (1st ed.). Routledge.
Reyes, M. V. (2020, December). Student essay—The disproportional impact of COVID-19 on African Americans. *Health and Human Rights Journal*, *22*(2), 299–307.
Seeger, M. W., & Seeger, H. S. (2023). Pandemic communication: CDC and WHO approaches to emergency risk communication and emerging infectious disease crises. In S. Croucher & A. Diers-Lawson (Eds.). *Pandemic communication* (pp. 59–78). Routledge, New York. https://doi.org/10.4324/9781003214496
Sellnow, T. L., & Seeger, M. W. (2021). *Theorizing crisis communication* (2nd ed.). Wiley Blackwell.
Sellwood, C., & Van-Tam, J. (2013). *Pandemic influenza*. CABI. https://www.cabidigitallibrary.org/doi/book/10.1079/9781845938567.0000
Strumberg, J. P., & Martin, C. M. (2020, October). COVID-19 – how a pandemic reveals that *everything is connected to everything else* [emphasis in

title]. *Journal of Evaluation in Clinical Practice*, *26*(5), 1361–1367. https://doi.org/10.1111/jep.13419

Taylor, M. (2023). Public relations and pandemics. In S. Croucher & A. Diers-Lawson (Eds.), *Pandemic communication* (pp. 79–95). Routledge. https://doi.org/10.4324/9781003214496

Taylor, S. (2022). The psychology of pandemics: Lessons learned for the future. *Canadian Psychology*, *63*(2), 233–246. https://doi.org/10.1037/cap0000303

Turk, J. V., Valin, J., & Paluszek, J. (Eds.). (2017). *Public relations case studies from around the world*. Peter Lang.

University of Southern California Annenberg. (n.d.). *Case Studies in Strategic Communication*. [On-line Journal]. https://cssc.uscannenberg.org/index.html

Wachter, R. M. (2022, July 14). Nailing the nuance on COVID-19. *Science*, *377*(6603), 243. DOI: 10.1126/science.add8599. PMID: 35857614

WHO. (2023, May 5). WHO chief declares end to COVID-19 as a global health emergency. [UN News]. https://news.un.org/en/story/2023/05/1136367

Williams, S. (2020, July). Black America and the coronavirus pandemic. [Article]. *The crisis: We Are Done Dying (Vol 127)*, 28–33. https://naacp.org/resources/crisis-we-are-done-dying-vol-127

Yashadhana, A., Derbas, A., Biles, J., & Grant, J. (2021, October 1). Pandemic-related racial discrimination and its health impact among non-Indigenous racially minoritized peoples in high-income contexts: a systematic review. *Health Promotion International*, 37(2), 1–16. https://doi.org/10.1093/heapro/daab144

2

CASE STUDIES ON THE H1N1 "SPANISH FLU" INFLUENZA PANDEMIC, 1918–1919

2.1 INTRODUCTION

The H1N1 Influenza in context

"I had a little bird, and its name was Enza. I opened the window, and in-flew-Enza" was a common rhyme chanted by children as they jumped rope during the devastating pandemic from 1918 to 1919 that spread around the world. The lyrics turned out to be accurate about the influenza originating from a bird—an avian flu of an unknown type and origination. Considered the "greatest tidal wave of death since the Black Death" (Spinney, 2017, p. 4) or potentially throughout the entire history of pandemics, the H1N1 influenza reportedly resulted in more fatalities than the death toll of an estimated 20 million (Mougel, 2011) in WWI and possibly other wars. Approximately one-third of the global population became infected with the H1N1 influenza (Taubenberger & Morens, 2006). The death toll varies based on the source from under 50 million to 100 million (Spinney, 2017), with an estimated 675,000 deaths in the U.S. (CDC, 2018a) and 228,000 in Britain (Honigsbaum, 2013). India experienced the highest death toll in the world, with estimates ranging from 12 to 20 million (Chandra & Kassens-Noor, 2014).

The first widely reported cases of the H1N1 influenza were in Europe near the end of WWI, which were attributed to soldiers living in overcrowded barracks and cramped spaces in the trenches. Approximately 20 million military personnel and civilians lost their lives, and 21 million were wounded in WWI (Mougel, 2011). These figures do not include deaths by influenza for

DOI: 10.4324/9781003434382-2

civilians. Four million Americans were mobilized in the U.S. Armed Forces, resulting in 116,708 military deaths and 205,690 wounded (Mougel, 2011).

A major cause of the spread of H1N1 influenza was the return of military troops to their home countries by rail or ships after WWI. The first reported outbreak of the influenza in the U.S. occurred in the spring of 1918, which was part of the first wave until the summer of 1918. The second wave, considered the most severe phase, occurred in fall 1918 and the third wave in spring 1919 (Taubenberger & Morens, 2006). In temperate and tropical climates, incidences of flu occur as a season: "the disease is thought to exist at a low level throughout the year but exhibits a marked seasonal increase, typically during the winter months" (Lofgren et al., 2007, p. 5429).

Although the H1N1 influenza has been referred to as the "Spanish Flu," the origin, whether from the U.S., Europe, or Asia, remains widely debated to this day. Since Spain was a neutral country free of wartime censorship, it was the first country where journalists reported on the H1N1 influenza. As the media coverage spanned beyond Spain's borders, the "Spanish Flu" misnomer stuck. Rupert Blue, U.S. surgeon general in 1918, stated:

> there is no reason to believe it originated in Spain. Some writers who have studied the question believe that the epidemic came from the Orient [sic] and they call attention to the fact that the Germans mention the disease as occurring along the eastern front in the summer and fall of 1917.
>
> *(USPHS, 1918, p. 2)*

Alternatively, Barry (2004) and Humphries (2014) attributed the origin to two other possibilities: the wave hypothesis of purulent bronchitis outbreaks in military trenches in England and France, espoused by British scientist and virologist J.S. Oxford, and the first case of influenza in U.S. military camp in Haskell County, Kansas, a fact accepted by the USDHHS (Fargey, 2019).

Several well-known people perished during the pandemic, including Austrian artists Gustav Klimt and Egon Schiele, German sociologist Max Weber, and Frederick Trump, who became better known a century later as the grandfather of the 45th and 47th U.S. President Donald Trump. The list of survivors spans many famous people such as artists Edvard Munch and Georgia O'Keeffe; actors Greta Garbo and Mary Pickford; writer Franz Kafka; animator and entrepreneur Walt Disney: political figures such as King Alfonso XIII of Spain, U.S presidents Woodrow Wilson and Franklin Delano Roosevelt, Indian anti-colonial nationalist Mahatma Gandhi, U.K. Prime Minister David Lloyd George, and Kaiser Wilhelm II of Germany (Barro et al., 2020; Lovett, 2017).

Changes in public transportation also exacerbated infection transmission. The days of horse transportation were becoming outdated, particularly in urban areas. Buses, trains, trams, and subways eclipsed the horse with speedier, yet more crowded conditions, for people to travel. Purveyors of horse-related products (e.g., wagons, horse feed, and saddles) turned into owners of gas stations and auto repair shops. Stables later became parking lots. People with more financial resources could travel by car. In 1918, 59,690 Americans owned vehicles and 72,500 people owned cars the following year (Davis, Diegel, & Boundy, 2014).

Transmission and symptoms

Infected people could easily spread the influenza by expelling droplets from their coughs and sneezes, or even by conversing with healthy people. In addition, the virus could have been contagious when healthy people touched surfaces contaminated by ill people. The initial symptoms of the H1N1 influenza resembled ordinary flu, with fever, chills, sore throat, dry coughs, achiness, fatigue, and loss of appetite. Seriously infected people later developed pneumonia and heliotrope cyanosis, resulting in their noses, ears, mouths, and fingers turning a bluish-purple shade as their lungs filled up with fluids while they struggled to breathe and eventually suffocated (Fujimura, 2003). The infection spread rapidly with some people dying within 24 hours of experiencing symptoms. For example, a healthy person could be feeling well in the morning, then quickly succumb to influenza, and perish in the evening. "Influenza is particularly dangerous when it leads to pneumonia, which can be fatal in vulnerable populations, such as the very young, the malnourished, and those under considerable stress" (Merrill, 2009, p. 68).

Unlike other pandemics, the mortality rate was unusually high for healthy people between 20 and 40 years old. Other affected age groups were primarily people under 5 years old and over 65 years old (CDC, 2019). The cause fatality rate, which indicates the percentage of people who become infected or die, of the influenza was 2.5% (Taubenberger & Morens, 2006).

The concept of syndemic may explain why the influenza virus defied expectations in terms of typical flu symptoms and why mortality rates were higher in the younger age group, and in those of lower economic status, because: 1) there were two or more epidemics, in this case influenza and pneumonia, 2) the epidemics co-occurred in military and civilian contexts, 3) the interaction of the two epidemics occurred biologically and through social or psychological processes; for example, through coughing and sneezing in mass gathering or places overcrowded with people, or through resistance to compliance efforts to stop the spread of disease, and lastly, 4) the co-occurrence included structural, social, cultural, environmental, or economic factors (Mendenhall et al., 2022).

Treatments and preventive measures

In 1918, no reliable influenza test, vaccine for the influenza, or antibiotic for secondary infections were available. No major disease control organization in the U.S. and a global health organization existed; the Centers for Disease Control and Prevention was launched in 1946 and the World Health Organization in 1948. Healthcare workers, particularly nurses, played a significant role tending to ill people at their homes or hospitals, many of which were running out of beds. Without tests to diagnose the influenza and medication to treat it, medical staff had to examine the patients' symptoms and provide as much care as they could before the patients recovered or died. With a nursing shortage increased by nurses serving abroad during WWI and others succumbing to the influenza on the front or back home, nurses worked longer days, some up to 18 hours or longer (Paton, 2020). Meanwhile, the public desperate for immediate help sought out readily available remedies widely advertised with dubious claims.

Non-pharmaceutical preventive measures became widely used worldwide, such as wearing masks covering the nose and mouth, washing hands often, quarantining and isolating infected people, curbing public events, and closing non-essential services. Local health authorities launched different restrictions for the public to follow based on the spread of the influenza. Many schools were also closed temporarily, except for public schools in New York City, Chicago, and New Haven (Stern et al., 2010). Health officials in New York City, for example, believed that school environments with sanitary conditions and strict health monitoring were safer than the homes of many students.

Not all public events were curtailed. After the influenza spread to Philadelphia where 600 sailors contracted H1N1 from the Philadelphia Navy Yard, the city still held a Liberty Loan Parade about a week later in September 1918 to encourage civilians to buy government bonds to cover expenses for WWI (Davis, 2018). The city of 1.7 million residents experienced serious rates of infection and deaths, with 12,000 fatalities and 47,000 cases six weeks later due to the parade, unsanitary employment, and residential circumstances, which was followed by 16,000 deaths and 500,000 cases within six months (Davis, 2018). The Liberty Loan Parade would be called a "superspreader" event today. Another superspreader event that seemed impossible to restrict was Armistice Day (now called Veterans Day in the U.S.) on November 11, 1918, with enthusiastic crowds celebrating the end of WWI in the U.S., the U.K., and France.

The health mask became a symbol of compliance or protest. San Francisco was the first city to require masks being worn in public or pay a fine or face brief imprisonment (Hauser, 2020). While other cities mandated masks, many residents complied yet some balked. Suffragettes needed their voices to be heard and not muffled behind masks; cigar and cigarette smokers found masks a nuisance; and avid protestors formed anti-mask leagues.

Widely used communication tools

During the late 19th and early 20th centuries, daily and weekly newspapers were the primary sources on local news, current events, and official statements from government officials (Ewing, 2020). Wire services also transmitted reports within the U.S. and abroad, making it easier and faster for newspapers anywhere to share current events beyond local reports (Ewing, 2020). Founded in 1846 during the Mexican American War, the Associated Press is the oldest cooperative news wire service in the U.S. and is still the largest service in the U.S. (Editors of the Encyclopedia Britannica, n.d.). Students in journalism and public relations commonly call the wire service AP; its stylebook is one of the most popular writing references in the U.S.

Readers of archival newspapers and magazines will see many ads, many of which promoted elixirs that claimed to cure the influenza. Case study 2.4 addresses this topic in more detail. Other popular forms of written communication were magazines, posters, and brochures.

Before the pandemic spread in the U.S., movie theaters were frequented by viewers watching silent films and newsreels on WWI. During the pandemic, public health officials closed many movie theaters and other forms of amusement across the country. Movie theaters that remained open showed older film releases. The National Association of the Motion Picture Industry also had to curtail film productions temporarily for financial reasons (Kellem, 2022).

Although radio was used during WWI by the military, the first commercial radio station aired in 1920 in Pennsylvania, leading to a growth of stations across the U.S after the pandemic (PBS, n.d.).

Students of communications should be aware of President Wilson's Committee on Public Information (CPI) from April 1917 to August 1919, which is considered "the nation's first ministry of information" (Daly, 2017, para. 1), that took advantage of all communication resources available during this time for a strategic pro-war campaign. Wilson hired George Creel, a journalist with an interest in politics, as the "mastermind behind the U.S. government's propaganda campaign in the Great War" (Cull, n.d., para. 2). The CPI was also called the Creel Committee. Although the committee was not responsible for promoting public health, it had a vast influence on the advertising and public relations industry. Creel hired a team of many influential experts of the early 20th century in advertising, graphics, film, public relations, and other creative fields while undertaking multimedia tactics—a daily government-produced newspaper, guidelines on news reporting to journalists, 6,000 news releases, free ads in American print media, newsreels for movie theaters, and posters showcasing Americans and allies as heroes, Germans as evil beasts, and other patriotic illustrations (an iconic example includes the 1917 recruitment poster of Uncle Sam pointing at the viewer with the caption, "I Want YOU for U.S. Army," among other tactics) (Daly, 2017; Cull, n.d.).

Creel also understood the power of public opinion leaders and celebrities to speak on behalf of the committee's mission to generate positive sentiment about the war and to raise funds for savings bonds to support America's involvement with the war. He launched the "Four Minute Men," as a nod to the Minutemen during the American Revolutionary War, with a cohort of 75,000 men to spread positive messages at movie theaters nationwide during the average four-minute time limit it took the projectionist to change movie reels. The men later spoke at other public venues, such as churches and colleges, and at schools with a group of junior lecturers (Cull, n.d.; Daly, 2017).

George Creel's name remains controversial in the history of public relations and communications as does the legacy of the CPI for propaganda, media censorship, and prejudice against German Americans, as well as other issues.

Impact

A study by the National Bureau of Economic Research (Barro et al., 2020) found that the H1N1 influenza resulted in estimates of a real per capita reduction of 6% and a private consumption drop of 8% in many countries during that time. However, the U.S. fared better, with a respective decline of 1.5% and 2.1%. Other economic factors included inflation and lower economic activity, with stock returns sinking by 28 percentage points in countries with a 2.1% death rate. The U.S. experienced a mortality rate of 0.52%, resulting in the stock returns dropping by 7 percentage points.

Despite an atmosphere of sorrow and despair worsened by disruptions facing the public, institutions, and businesses, the pandemic motivated U.S. residents to volunteer in multiple capacities as drivers and healthcare workers, with the encouragement of the American Red Cross and public health agencies (Navarro, 2010). Case study 2.2 shows how a federal health agency and a nonprofit collaborated to reach the public on preventive measures and to motivate people to volunteer.

Although immigrants were blamed for the proliferation of earlier diseases by people born in the U.S., immigrants were not widely discriminated against for increasing the H1N1 influenza, except for an Italian community of immigrants in Denver who were criticized for spreading the influenza by ignoring health warnings and continuing to visit infected family and friends (Navarro, 2010).

German Americans, however, faced nativism after the U.S. declared war on Germany in 1917. At that time, German was the second most widely spoken language and the largest minority group as 9% of the total U.S. population and up to 25% to 35% in sections of the Midwest (Wuestenbecker, 2014). President Woodrow Wilson stoked prejudice against "hyphenated Americans," particularly German Americans (combined nationalities used to be written with a hyphen) of any religion during WWI, when he said, "And I want to say–I cannot say it too often–any man who carries a hyphen about with him carries a dagger that he is ready to plunge into the vitals of this Republic whenever he gets ready" (Voices of Democracy, n.d., para. 2). Places with German names were changed and even musical compositions by German musicians were not performed. German-language courses were dropped, German-language books were removed from library shelves, and German-language newspapers stopped publishing. Restaurant dishes were renamed from Sauerkraut to "Liberty Cabbage" (Kraut, 2010, p. 126). Several German American businesses and homes were vandalized while some German Americans were physically harmed by being tarred and feathered, and one was lynched in Illinois (Siegel & Silverman, 2017; Library of Congress, n.d.). Not surprisingly, some German American families anglicized their names to hide their German heritage.

These impacts were likely a result of various psychological factors (i.e., fear, stress, anxiety, etc.) that can create maladaptive coping mechanisms such as conspiracy theories, quackery, panic buying, resistance, intergroup conflict, and scapegoating, among others that we explore in other chapters (Freckleton, 2020; Jedwab et al., 2021; Taylor, 2019, 2022).

2.2 U.S. PUBLIC HEALTH SERVICE AND AMERICAN RED CROSS COLLABORATE: COMMUNICATING SAFETY MESSAGES DURING THE 1918–1919 INFLUENZA

Situation analysis

The pandemic itself occurred in three waves, each wave impacting local and national health systems (Centers for Disease Control and Prevention, 2018b). The first wave occurred in U.S. Army camps and France from

March to June 1918. War created epidemiological conditions that enabled the virus to spread globally (Byerly, 2010).

Recruits sent abroad to unfamiliar places were exposed to different germs and viral agents (Petit, 1976), climate changes, poor sanitation, overcrowding, and unfinished hospitals and barracks due to rapid expansion (Jester, Uyeki, Jernigan, & Tumpey, 2019). Respiratory illnesses developed and cases of pneumonia, grippe, and influenza spread in trenches and encampments, sickening roughly 30% of U.S. Army and Navy personnel (Byerly, 2010). Despite this level of occurrence, confusion existed among medical staff as some military personnel experienced mild symptoms with quick recovery, while others suffered complications and died. Additionally, influenza was not considered a reportable disease and, therefore, was not tracked by agencies (Barry, 2004). Gaps and inaccuracies in data muddled matters further resulting in limited public attention and a downplaying of severity (Jester et al., 2019; Petit, 1976).

The second wave of the pandemic is estimated to have occurred between August and November 1918 in the U.S. and proved to be the deadliest in terms of mortality curves for young adults, approximately 675,000 deaths out of the 20–50 million globally (Byerly, 2010; Jester et al., 2019). As troops returned home to various camps, the virus spread quickly into communities infecting 25% of the population (Bristow, n.d.). The rapid onslaught of illnesses overwhelmed the health care system for several reasons.

The influenza virus defied expectations of typical flu symptoms and shocked medical officers who witnessed unusually high fever, hemorrhage of lungs, cyanosis, and nausea among other effects associated with pneumonia (Byerly, 2010). No lab tests and no antiviral or antibiotics existed at that time to treat secondary infections (CDC, 2018a). The only available tools to control the spread of flu were largely limited to "non-pharmaceutical interventions such as isolation, quarantine, good personal hygiene, use of disinfectants, and limits on public gatherings" (CDC, 2018a, para. 3), which led to compliance challenges and "mask slackers" (Little, 2020; Navarro, 2020). Micro crises also developed within local communities resulting from shortages of nurses, physicians, medical personnel, hospital space, coffins, grave diggers, and burial spaces (Jones, 2010; Keeling, 2010).

The pandemic was also unfolding amid a backdrop of major changes in society. Efforts to combat influenza diverted labor and money from war efforts and vice versa, "under pressure from civil authorities who believed morale, and subsequently wartime productivity, could suffer" (Jester et al., 2019, p. 33). Surges in one's civic duty to volunteer and participate in missionary activities increased (Apfeldorf, 2020; Chilcote, 2016; Jones, 2010). Attitudes toward protecting consumers from fraudulent medicinal claims (Jester et al., 2019) and the effectiveness of alcohol as a cure were shifting as a precursor to Prohibition (Petit, 1976; U.S. Treasury Department, 1918). The U.S. government's role in intervening in public health matters was strained as more people fell ill. These gaps in information and resources left individuals and organizations fatigued (Martin, 2022) and confused with more questions than answers by the time the third wave hit as war ended. These conditions and contexts set the stage for the collaboration between the United States Public Health Service (USPHS) and the American Red Cross (ARC).

U. S. Public Health Service campaign

Communication programming and execution

USPHS was established over 130 years ago and has participated in most major public health crises. Its mission is "Protect, promote, and advance the health and safety of the nation" (Commissioned Corps of the U.S. Public Health Service, n.d., para. 2) and is the "preeminent public health asset called upon to solve public health challenges and address daily and emergency public health needs throughout the United States and globally." (U.S. Public Health Service Commissioned Corps, 2021, p. 2).

Under the leadership of Surgeon General Rupert Blue, the organization expanded its duties and responsibilities and became a centralized force in orchestrating large-scale influenza prevention efforts across federal, national, state, and local governments (Gernhart, 1999). Blue responded to the 1918–1919 pandemic with a four-part strategy (Bristow, n.d.; Gernhart, 1999; Morabia, 2021).

First, according to Gernhart (1999), public health departments were urged via telegram to provide daily, if not weekly, reports of local conditions; thus, *Public Health Reports* became an invaluable tool used to track the prevalence of the disease with state and municipal health departments. *Public Health Reports* volume 33, number 29 published on September 27, 1918, was the first to mention the prevalence of the "Spanish Influenza" in the United States and documented the number of cases across 26 states.

Secondly, Surgeon General Rupert Blue and the USPHS immediately followed up on September 28, 1918, by producing and circulating six million copies of an informational supplemental pamphlet (USPHS, 1918), in eight different languages, "*Spanish Influenza*" "*Three-Day Fever*" "*The Flu.*" This pamphlet contained public health advice and answers to these questions:

What is the Spanish Influenza? Is it something new? Does it come from Spain?
How can "Spanish influenza" be recognized?
What is the course of the disease? Do people die of it?

What causes the disease and how is it spread?
What should be done by those who catch the disease?
Will a person who has had influenza before catch the disease again?
How can one guard against influenza?

Other state and local health organizations assisted with the USPHS's efforts by distributing posters, ads, and cartoons with similar messaging (Tomes, 2010); placing streetcar signs; and publishing public service announcements in newspapers across the U.S. (Little, 2020).

The third part of the Surgeon General's strategy was the appointment of an influenza director to each state. This individual was responsible for coordinating the local disbursement of funds, a portion of the USD 1 million appropriated by Congress to combat the disease, whereas the chief health officer would coordinate the disbursement of human resources (physicians and nurses) to affected areas, more than 600 physicians to assistant surgeons, at a monthly stipend of USD 200, roughly USD 4 per day (Gernhart, 1999).

Once these funds were in place and the process more organized, the Surgeon General completed the fourth part of the campaign by ordering the suspension of public activities, and closing schools, churches, theaters, and other places of mass gatherings. This resulted in many communities posting or circulating various leaflets, additional public service announcements, cartoons, and other ads requiring citizens to wear masks as well as following anti-spitting ordinances (Gernhart, 1999; Navarro, 2020).

All these efforts focused on messaging that "emphasized that special health measures weren't just important because they kept the person who followed them safe. They were also important because they helped protect those around them" (Little, 2020, para. 11). Figure 2.1 features a poster and public notice produced by the U.S. Treasury Department and USPHS (1918), reminding individuals to cover their coughs, avoid crowds, and walk to work.

As more civilians and servicemen (a commonly used term in this time period) became infected and were confined to their homes or military camps, new challenges arose. Surgeon General Blue and USPHS established a network of emergency hospitals and a national system of soup kitchens to care for the sick and their families. They also conducted experiments with servicemen as subjects, "in the hopes of developing a vaccine" (Gernhart, 1999, p. 561). Lastly, in 1918, an Influenza Task Force was established with USPHS to document as accurately as possible how many people were affected and the rates of morbidity and mortality (Morabia, 2021). Led by PHS health officer Wade Hampton Frost, USPHS launched a house-to-house canvass survey of a representative group of 150,000 randomly persons across 18 localities (Morabia, 2021).

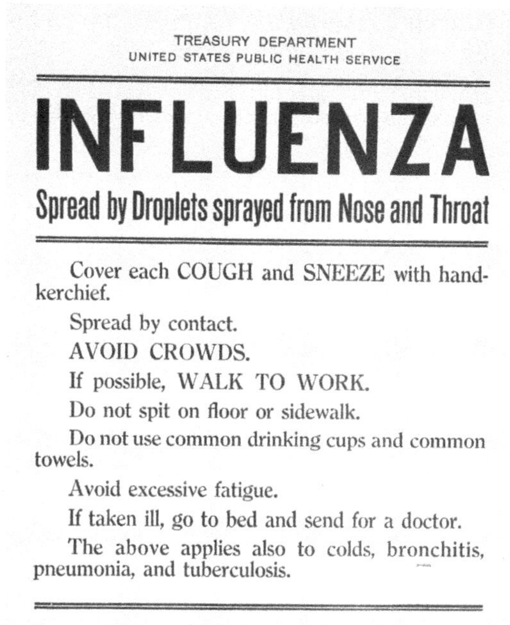

FIGURE 2.1 1918 influenza public health poster. U. S. Public Health Service, Treasury Department. National Library of Medicine. (Library of Congress, Rare Book and Special Collections Division, Printed Ephemera Collection. Public domain.)

Results and measurements of the Canvass Survey: Assessing the toll

Morabia (2021) chronicled the research activities of USPHS over a five-month period, documented the findings and discussed the relevance of this canvass survey to COVID-19 response. Beginning with research, survey technicians or "enumerators" conducted interviews with "the housewife or other responsible member of every household of the selected areas" (pp. 439–440). According to Edgar Sydenstricker, statistician for the USPHS in 1931, enumerators recorded basic demographic information (name, color, sex, age), housing details (number of rooms occupied), and economic status by four categories: "well-to-do," "moderate," "poor," and "very poor," based solely on their impressions (Sydenstricker & Lawrence, 2006, p. 191).

For each case of sickness, "the facts recorded were the nature of the illness (i.e., whether influenza, pneumonia, or 'doubtful'), date of onset, duration, and date of death, if death occurred" (Sydenstricker & Lawrence, 2006, p. 191).

Dr. Arthur J. Lawrence, assistant surgeon general and deputy assistant secretary for health (operations) for the USPHS in 1931, recognized that Sydenstricker's survey and analysis techniques were influential and innovative for the period, as he cross-referenced and triangulated data collected with age, economic status, morbidity, and locality. Significant findings included the concentration of incidences in the 25–29 age group, and the mortality rate which was "33 per cent [sic] greater in the class denoted as 'poor,' and was nearly three times as high among persons classified as 'very poor' (Sydenstricker & Lawrence, 2006, p. 195).

Morabia (2021) further acknowledged the indispensable nature of USPHS's efforts in tracking morbidity and mortality data, in real time and across localities and status, concluding that efforts to fight the current pandemic of COVID-19 could be accomplished better "than was done knocking on doors in 1918" (p. 445). Equally invaluable to the USPHS's campaign and house-to-house survey were the front-line contributions of nurses (Keeling, 2010) and collaborations with the American Red Cross.

American Red Cross campaign

Communication programming and execution

In 1881, almost 150 years ago, Clara Barton founded the U.S. chapter of the American Red Cross (ARC). The organization's mission during the 1918–1919 influenza pandemic was and remains today as follows:

> The American Red Cross prevents and alleviates human suffering the face of emergencies by mobilizing the power of volunteers and the generosity of donors.
>
> *(ARC, 2025, para. 1)*

This spirit of mobilizing a network of approximately 8 million female volunteers (Jones, 2010) prompted outreach from the Red Cross National Committee on Influenza, Surgeon General Rupert Blue, and United States Public Health Service to ARC. All recommended that ARC cooperate and participate in fighting influenza, more specifically to supply nursing personnel and equip hospitals with emergency supplies (Printing Office of the Tribune De Geneve, 1920).

Jones (2010) offers a case comparison of four ARC local responses in Boston, Pittsburgh, St. Louis, and Richmond to "demonstrate the importance of close, timely, and sustained coordination among local and state public health authorities and voluntary organizations before and during public health emergencies" (p. 92). ARC's organizational effectiveness varied widely but nonetheless served to underscore "the centrality and limits of voluntarism in American public health" (Jones, 2010, p. 92). Here is a summary of the coordinated efforts within each urban area.

Boston:

Before a national response to combating influenza was organized, the Red Cross chapter in Boston was the first to respond locally to the pandemic in mid-August 1918 by providing nurses to military and civilian hospitals through a recruiting campaign (posters and ads) and by coordinating activities with local and state authorities. The Boston chapter ignored national directives to provide nurses and supplies for war efforts, and instead

> redirected its volunteers from war work into influenza-related duties ... making gauze masks to protect those caring for influenza patients. Working for 17 days in a row, 537 volunteers produced 83,606 masks, which motor corps volunteers then delivered to hospitals, local organizations, and individual homes. The motor corps also transported items produced by the 484 volunteers in the sewing department, including 8,000 convalescent gowns, 500 pairs of pajamas, 100 nightgowns, and 40 sweaters for a children's hospital, as well as 70 flannel helmets, 70 pairs of hospital socks, [and] 30 sheets and pillowcases.
>
> *(Jones, 2010, p. 95)*

Further, the chapter and New England division of ARC launched a public health education and prevention campaign, producing and distributing circulars via social outreach to families of servicemen.

Pittsburgh:

In comparison, the primary mission of Pittsburgh's Red Cross chapter was to aid the war effort by observing a "clear hierarchy of priorities. Military hospitals and camps were to receive first priority, followed by coal plants and war production plants. Civilians' needs came last" (Jones, 2010, p. 96).

The chapter planned and coordinated activities with city health officials, departments, and committees "to collect and distribute hospital supplies, ensure fair prices and adequate distribution of drugs and vaccines, recruit and allocate nurses, provide transportation through its motor corps, and procure caskets and gravediggers" (Jones, 2010). This multifaceted approach was seen as a model for organized voluntarism as the chapter "operated as an effective complement to local health authorities" (Jones, 2010, p. 96).

St. Louis:

St. Louis' local ARC chapter represented a "well-coordinated partnership between volunteer and government sectors" (Jones, 2010, p. 100). Public health nurses and chapter volunteers worked together to serve more patients by efficiently organizing nurses, supplies, food, transportation, and information. The chapter printed and distributed over 1 million copies of the USPHS pamphlet and other flyers in various languages. In the end, St. Louis experienced the lowest rate of influenza, compared to other cities (Jones, 2010).

Richmond:

"The influenza response in Richmond contrasted sharply with those in St. Louis and Pittsburgh," (Jones, 2010, p. 100) as the ARC was one of several volunteer groups (Young Women's Christian Association, Boy Scouts and Campfire Girls, and Instructive Visiting Nurse Association) and individuals (doctors, local medical students, prominent local figures, and Catholic nuns) involved in caring for both civilian and military cases (Jones, 2010). While the chapter contributed funds, beds, pillowcases, toiletries and clothes, it was not the leader of the influenza efforts.

Jones (2010) concluded her case study analysis of the four cities and their influenza responses with this observation:

> The Richmond chapter's response to the influenza pandemic cannot be seen, however, as a failure. The chapter, in keeping with the ARC's wartime priorities, devoted its limited resources to aiding nearby servicemen and their families. But it lacked sufficient numbers of volunteers to fight a civilian epidemic as well. The fact that other voluntary groups stepped in to fill this gap—as they did in other cities—demonstrates that the ARC at the local level was not quite as irreplaceable as national headquarters insisted it was *(p. 101)*

Figure 2.2 shows one example of an American Red Cross poster (Ewing, 2015). This is not an exhaustive list of all that the ARC and its volunteers contributed but represents a general sampling across military camps and civilian efforts.

Results

As laudable as the ARC's overall efforts were, the narrow mission of the organization to supply need in matters of war time created contentions within national headquarters that wanted chapters "to do more than provide gauze masks, make soup and hospital garments: it had wanted them to coordinate

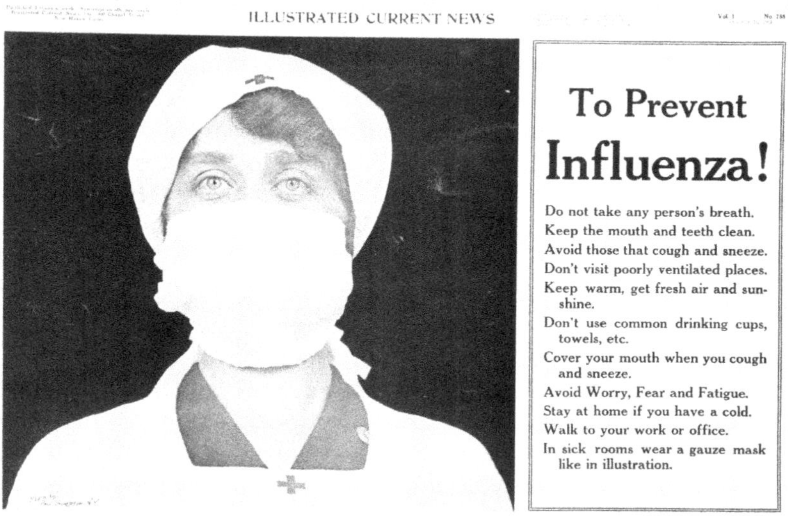

FIGURE 2.2 1918 newspaper included a poster of an American Red Cross nurse with tips on preventing the influenza. The National Library of Medicine. (Public domain.)

health care and health communications" (Jones, 2010, p. 101). The ARC was utilized and relied upon to distribute information, labor, and resources speaks to the prevalent ideology of volunteerism as an obligation of civic duty (Jones, 2010). Without the help of the ARC coordinating services at the local level, the USPHS would not have been as successful in fulfilling its duties.

Theoretical perspectives

Thompson & Schulz (2021) explored various theories from a health communication perspective to explain interpersonal, influence processes, and organization and societal phenomena. Underlying these theoretical perspectives are guiding principles that assist researchers in generating knowledge of health problems and how to control the spread of diseases: "Disease shapes communication. Communication shapes disease and other aspects of health. Social and cultural factors influence all aspects of health communication. How disease is defined and the manner in which we communicate about it determines how it is treated" (p. 11).

In this case study, the influenza pandemic divided the nation's resources as World War I occurred, thus shaping the communication about influenza as a dilemma or problem between keeping the nation safe from war or keeping the nation, its citizens and soldiers safe from influenza. All the pamphlets, flyers, newspaper ads, and other communications efforts from ARC and USPHS shaped how government agencies, organizations, and individuals responded to the pandemic through volunteerism and coordination of local and national efforts to prevent the spread of the disease as the four case studies by Jones (2010) illuminated.

Defining the pandemic as both a military and civilian problem "helps explicate cognitive processes and behaviors of health-related publics" (Krishna, 2021, p. 243), in particular volunteers. The Situational Theory of Publics originally developed and refined by James E. Grunig (1968, 1997) postulates

> that when faced with a decision, individuals tend to seek further information about the issue at hand to make the best possible decision. However, the degree to which individuals seek and attend to information depends on the extent to which the individual stops to think about the issue, i.e., problem recognition; how involved they are in the issue, i.e., involvement recognition; and the barriers they perceived in their path toward making a decision, i.e., constraint recognition.
>
> *(Krishna, 2021, p. 243)*

Volunteers, whether they worked with USPHS or ARC, were faced with decisions about how to help the efforts to prevent the spread of influenza and where to help, whether in military or civilian realms. The perceived barriers to volunteering included long hours, conflicting organizational priorities, working conditions, and exposure to influenza. They recognized a "gap between their expected and experienced state" and felt "motivated to do something about the problem and engage in a variety of active and passive communication behaviors in trying to address the problem" (Krishna, 2021, p. 248).

This theoretical perspective sheds light on the cognitive processes and reasons for why volunteers for the American Red Cross worked tirelessly in both military (expected) and civilian (experienced) arenas to raise funds, recruit nurses, cook, sew, and care for the families of affected individuals, especially against the backdrop of uncertainty regarding the origin of the influenza virus, its varied symptoms, the contagious pace at which the virus spread, and who was affected.

Key terms

American Red Cross
Clara Barton
Cyanosis
Enumerators

Grippe
Mask Slackers
Micro Crises
Non-Pharmaceutical Interventions (NPIs)
Prohibition
Situational Theory of Publics
Spanish Influenza
Surgeon General
United States Public Health Service (USPHS)
Wave Theory

Discussion questions

1 If you were alive in 1918, would you volunteer to work with the Red Cross?
2 Where do you fall on the continuum between keeping the nation safe from war or keeping the nation, its citizens and soldiers safe from influenza?
3 How might your perspective influence decisions made about resources?
4 This case study was about collaboration between a government agency and a nonprofit organization. What challenges did they face in collaborating? What advice would you provide for the organizations?

2.3 RINGING OFF THE HOOK: TELEPHONE COMPANIES CURB NON-ESSENTIAL PUBLIC USAGE OF PHONES DURING THE H1N1 INFLUENZA

Situation analysis

After Alexander Graham Bell received the first patent for his telephone invention in 1876, the telephone industry in the U.S. began to evolve. The first switchboard and telephone exchange launched in 1877–1878 with 49,000 telephones operational within three years. Twenty years later, 600,000 telephones were sold followed by 2.2 million telephones in 1905, and 5.8 million by 1910 (Elon University, n.d.). With an estimated 35% of U.S. households, mostly affluent, having telephones by 1920 (Statista, 2010), many people relied on communal telephones to make calls. In fact, Hartford was the home of the first coin-operated telephone in 1889 (Stamp, 2014), Chicago was the birthplace of the first prepay telephone station in 1898 (Hooks, 2017), (and Cincinnati was the location of the first street coin-operated telephone in 1905 (Hooks, 2017). However, the world's first public telephone booth was launched in Potsdamer Platz in Berlin, Germany, which required paper tickets to be handed to the telephone operator for brief calls in 1881 (Talkbox Booth, 2025).

Telephones at the time were referred to as candlesticks, sticks, or pole telephones, standing upright from a round base attached to a pole with a mouthpiece receiver on top along with a wire connecting an earpiece that hooked to the pole when not in use. Almost all telephones were analog systems dependent on operators connecting calls, without the caller being able to make a direct call to a person. Telephone operators, most of whom were young women, spent about a year training to learn the switchboard system and communicate with a neutral U.S. English accent with customers quickly and politely; "Number, please" was the opening dialogue with callers (Mogulescu, 2020, p. 4).

The New York Telephone Company positioned the telephone as a convenient way for people to stay in touch safely before the 1918–1919 influenza. In addition to easy social interaction, people of means used telephones to order groceries (Coleman & Mari, 2023) and to find out more about current events or even the correct time (McCracken, 2020) before and during the pandemic. During the pandemic, some schools closed by public officials, such as in Los Angeles, offered students instruction by telephone (Berger, 2020).

To provide the public with quick updates on major current events, some newspapers used stereopticons, which were slide projectors created in the mid-19th century with two lenses showing dissolving views of back-to-back images. Stereopticon bulletins projected news highlights, film excerpts, and imagery on large screens at the newspaper's offices or elsewhere. With these locations drawing large crowds, many stereopticons were not in service after the pandemic began, thereby putting an additional strain on both switchboard operators and newspapers receiving calls from the public for news updates, particularly during elections (McCracken, 2020).

To manage the increasing volume of callers, telephone companies nationwide had to encourage callers to curb usage due to a shortage of telephone operators. The scaled-down and overextended operators needed to connect necessary calls from doctors, nurses, pharmacists, and other emergency service personnel to save peoples' lives. With switchboard operators wearing gauzed masks, talking, and sitting just a few inches from their colleagues, infected operators still spread the influenza to their coworkers.

Debates also ensued about the dangers of telephones from how extremists believed telephones could spread diseases directly over the line to, more sensibly, how public call facilities could harbor germs with multiple callers without the telephones being regularly cleaned and disinfected (Coleman & Mari, 2023).

Communication programming and execution

Telephone services had to switch messaging from stimulating personal and trivial telephone usage to encouraging only essential calls for emergencies. Earlier pre-pandemic newspaper ads from various Bell

FIGURE 2.3 1910s Central Union Telephone Co. ad encouraging phone usage during quarantine. (Public domain.)

Telephone companies emphasized how telephones can help family and friends stay in touch safely during quarantine or any contagious illness. See Figure 2.3.

Vintage Everyday (2020) posted an example from the New York Telephone Company (NYTC) that ran on Thursday, November 17, 1910, from the *St. Louis Dispatch*. More examples can be found by searching within the database of the Library of Congress digital collection Chronicling America—Historic American Newspapers.

Switchboard operators were tied up connecting personal calls while facing a shortage of telephone operators infected with the virus and the urgent need to keep lines open for emergency services when the pandemic spread across the country. A third of the New York Telephone Company operators (2,000 employees) were too ill to work. The company curbed payphone usage by 50% and sent out mail to subscribers to keep lines open for emergencies (McCracken, 2020). A 1918 newspaper ad placed by the NYTC ran with the frank headline, "Don't telephone unless it is absolutely necessary" (NYTC, 1918a) and later ran an ad with the headline, "A Word of Appreciation" (NYTC, 1918b), to thank customers for their efforts in minimizing usage of personal calls. See Figure 2.4.

Examples of newspaper ads and notices from other telephone companies nationwide illustrated how they encouraged customers to cease

A WORD
of APPRECIATION

WHEN THE INFLUENZA EPIDEMIC was at its height, so many of our operators were absent that it was impossible to handle promptly all the telephone calls that were offered.

KNOWING that a word of explanation to the New York public would relieve the situation, we stated our case and asked our patrons to assist us by restricting their use of the telephone to *necessary* calls.

THE RESPONSE, as was expected, was immediate. Citizens' associations of all kinds, individual users both large and small, public telephone agents, in fact all classes of the telephone-using public gave us splendid cooperation.

THIS HELP was given cheerfully and willingly and the inconveniences were accepted with a good humor that greatly cheered those operators who were working so ably to carry the load during the absence of their fellow-workers.

WHILE MANY of our operators are still away and some restriction is still necessary on the general use of the telephone, the worst of a bad situation is now passed and we take this opportunity of expressing our appreciation of your kindly help.

THANK YOU!

NEW YORK TELEPHONE COMPANY

FIGURE 2.4 New York Telephone Company ad from *The Sun*, November 10, 1918. The New York Public Library, Astor, Lenox and Tilden Foundation. Chronicling America: Historic American Newspapers. Library of Congress. (Public domain.)

making nonessential calls. The writing style was direct yet with a polite tone and a clear call to action.

Piedmont Telephone & Telegraph Company's ad's headline stated, "To Telephone Users!," with the last paragraph reading:

> It is of the utmost importance that calls for doctors, drug stores, and all emergency calls arising from the epidemic be handled efficiently and it is the earnest desire of the company to do this. The public can assist by refraining from using the telephone except when necessary, so that prompt service can be given to the sick.
>
> *(Piedmont Telephone & Telegraph Company, 1918, para. x)*

The headline from Michigan State Telephone Co. read, "Telephone Users. Important Notice!" with the last paragraph stating, "Will you please restrict your use of the telephone to calls which are absolutely essential? If all telephone users will do this, it will be possible to handle with promptness and dispatch the essential business of the community" (McCracken, 2020, para 21).

The Bell Telephone Co. of Pennsylvania's notice headline stated, "Don't Telephone," with the first paragraph stating, "The gravity of the situation compels up to request all subscribers to refrain from making calls not required by sickness, war work or other absolute necessity" (Bell Telephone Co. of Pennsylvania, 1918).

Results and measurement

Before the pandemic ensued, the Department of Commerce—Bureau of the Census conducted a *Census of Electrical Industries:1917*, specifically for telephones in the continental U.S. (Department of Commerce—Bureau of the Census, 1920). Accordingly, here is a summary of the data collected by bureau clerks:

- Bell Telephone Systems (n=145) lines, compared to all systems and lines (n=53,234)
- Number of telephones for all systems and lines (n=11,716,520)
- Estimated number of messages and talks for all systems and lines (n=21,845,722,335)
- Number of female employees for all systems and lines (n=171,119), versus male employees (n=91,510) (Government Printing Office, 1920, p. 10)

The Census Bureau (n.d.) also recorded in *Historical statistics of the United States, Colonial Times to 1957* average daily calls by year for Bell

TABLE 2.1 Number of calls made on local exchanges and tolls (1918–1920)

Year	*Local Exchanges*	*Tolls*
1920	31,836	1,327
1919	29,286	1,167
1918	30,001	1,067

Telephone companies, in the thousands. For the years 1918–1920, the number of calls made on local exchanges and tolls are contained in Table 2.1.

We can infer from these numbers that the decrease in local exchanges calls in 1919 was the result of the various Bell Telephone companies' campaigns. The newspaper ad titled, "A Word of Appreciation" from the New York Telephone Company (1918b) indicated that callers followed instructions to restrict telephone usage: "THE RESPONSE, as was expected, was immediate. Citizens' associations of all kinds, individual users both large and small, public telephone agents, in fact all classes of the telephone-using public gave us splendid cooperation" (para. 3).

Market research was developed over the next decade. The first market research application is attributed to Daniel Starch who, in the 1920s, established a market research firm focusing on advertising effectiveness (Vasquez, 2011).

The telephone industry quickly resumed to normalcy post-pandemic, with the U.S. home to the world's largest network of telephone exchanges in 1920 (Mogulescu, 2020), while more innovations debuted in the 1920s, including the first three-way telephone call in 1921 and the first operational trans-Atlantic telephone call between New York and London in 1927 (Morris, n.d.). Moving forward in history, the last manual telephone switchboard was replaced in 1991 by computerized equipment for the Kerman Telephone Company located in a farming community near Fresno and managed by a sentimental owner (Hillinger, 1991).

Theoretical perspectives and assumptions

According to George Soper (1919), a member of the Sanitary Corps specializing in sanitation sciences and preventive medicine during WWI, the 1918–1919 influenza pandemic was the least understood in terms of cause and how to stop it. Because similarities existed between the H1N1 influenza with other respiratory diseases such as tuberculosis from the 1800s, people assumed it was no worse than the common cold.

Germ theory, developed and tested by many different contributors over 150 years prior to the pandemic, was a dominant force in explaining how germs and other microorganisms were responsible for other respiratory diseases and the communicable nature of influenza as it spread from person to person through sneezing.

As Soper explained, "There has been a good deal theorizing about these matters"—cause and prevention—"and some good research, but no common agreement has been reached with respect to them" (p. 501). Further, "the measures which were introduced for the control of the pandemic were based on the slenderest of theories" (p. 501) and assumptions that the disease could be stopped like other respiratory illnesses.

Theory can also be defined as a set of assumptions or accepted facts about the observed phenomenon. In the absence of a tested theory like germ theory, assumptions can provide useful insights into accepted facts operating at that time that impacted prevention:

1 People became indifferent because of the range of symptoms (mild to severe) of the respiratory infections.
2 Waste products (excretions) were not "deposited in a vessel or sewerage system where they can be dealt with as in typhoid" (p. 502) but instead were "projected in the air and allowed to pollute the hands, the food, the clothing, and, in fact the entire environment of the infected person" (p. 502).
3 In addition to the range of symptoms, the incubation periods varied as well, meaning "the disease may be transmittable before the patient himself is aware that he is attacked" (Soper, 1919, p. 502).

Employing similar methods to mitigate the spread of the disease, for example, using sanitary practices that killed other respiratory bacteria to try to eradicate the virus, isolating the infected individuals, self-protection, and administrative procedures (bans), ironically, failed to stop the spread of influenza (Soper, 1919; Tomes, 2010).

These methods were indicative of a lack of fundamental understanding of who was a virus producer, who was immune, the difference in isolating people in rural versus urban areas, the personal nature of individuals' health behaviors, and the high transmission rate that may happen without a person's knowledge. Also, it was not considered socially desirable to close establishments or require masks, unless necessary (Soper, 1919), which allowed the masses to continue to congregate. As Tomes (2010) laments,

> Perhaps the most important "lesson" taught by the pandemic was the realization that those measures that worked the best to control a highly infectious disease—bans on public gatherings, school closures, and strict quarantine and isolation—were precisely the ones most difficult to implement in a modern mass society.
>
> *(para. 3)*

Specific to this case study on the proliferation of telephones during this time, applications of germ theory adapted alongside the development of a mass society. Increases in mass transportation helped public health officials understand how people and germs comingled and traveled in crowded public places (Curiosity Collections, n.d.).

Increases in mass media and communication tools also helped public health authorities understand how information traveled in cities and rural areas. Radio and movie theaters were available communication tools at the time but did not have the same efficacy of usage as telephones. The technology of synchronous voice communication transported and connected people efficiently and quickly across distances, especially if one did not have an automobile. This allowed upper, middle, lower, urban, and rural communities to access information about symptoms, seek medical attention, report sickness, and connect socially with the sick and healthy in non-physical ways that were less risky (Coleman & Mari, 2023).

However, given the increased access and usage of public and communal telephones and inconsistent disinfecting procedures, telephones were also targeted as a contagion, reservoir of disease, and a fomite or transmitter of disease (Bonea, 2021; Coleman & Mari, 2023). A prominent public health belief developed around "fomite infection (transmission of germs via objects such as drinking glasses or books) and dust infection (transmission of dried germs mixed with common house dust and street dust)" (Tomes, 2010, p. 10).

Fear increased as public telephones expanded in Britain. Call boxes were deemed odorous, dirty, dusty, and unventilated spaces. Users "could inhale the dried sputum attached to mouthpieces and other instruments" (Bonea, 2021, p. 1071) deposited from infected individuals. This exposure stood in sharp contrast with the experiences of those who could afford private telephones at home (Coleman & Mari, 2023). Ultimately, the dust problem, originally proposed by Dr. George Homan (1906), as a potential explanation for how influenza was spread "would later be jettisoned" (Tomes, 2010, p. 50).

Key terms

Alexander Graham Bell
Bell Telephone Company
Fomite
Germ Theory
Stereopticon
Switchboard Operators

Discussion questions

1 Did any of your ancestors work as switchboard operators for telephone companies?
2 Do you or your family members have a land line telephone?
3 How does telephone usage during the first two decades of the 1900s differ from telephone usage during COVID-19? Or now?
4 What other fomites could explain the spread of diseases, like influenza?

2.4 PANIC PROFITEERS IN U.K. AND U.S.: HEALTH PRODUCTS PROLIFERATE WITH DUBIOUS PROMOTIONAL TACTICS AND CLAIMS TO PREVENT THE H1N1 INFLUENZA

Situation analysis

People around the world sought cures and rituals and revived ancient traditions to stop H1N1. In parts of Russia and elsewhere, black weddings (*shvartse khasene* in Yiddish) occurred when the least fortunate Jewish couples were married in cemeteries in the belief that the ritual would prevent diseases from spreading. Ancient herbal therapies were widely used in Asia while witch doctors native to India practiced their arts, and Chinese dragon figures marched through villages—all ways believed to dispel evil (Spinney, 2017).

Two unusual Western "remedies" were dishwasher appliances and gas fumes. According to the then U.S. Surgeon General, machine dishwashers reduced the transmission rates of H1N1 by two-thirds over regular dishwashing by hand. The reality was that electric dishwashers were rare for household use with only the wealthiest families able to afford them; mostly restaurants, hotels, and military kitchens used these appliances (Berger, 2020). In the U.K., some parents thought their ill children would be healed by breathing in chlorine fumes at gasworks, which were factories for manufacturing flammable gas produced by coal (Rogers, 2020).

Folk remedies included inhaling the aroma of raw onions as a method to soak up germs (National Onion Association, n.d.), a cure that goes back to the bubonic plague (known widely as the Black Death during the 14th century), while some people consumed lots of onion soup and other dishes with onions (Smith, 2021). Bloodletting, gargling with disinfectant, hanging garlic and camphor balls around one's neck, and consuming beef gravy, camphor oil, laxatives, aspirins, or alcohol were other "remedies" (Barry, 2021; Rogers, 2020; Smith, 2021).

Alcohol was widely debated as helpful to the ill or as detrimental to society at large. Although several doctors believed that alcohol had medicinal value, alcohol also was blamed as an evil scourge worthy of eradication for causing crime, poverty, dysfunctional families, and other social ills since the Temperance Movement in the 1830s. Dynamic figures such as Carrie Nation made news for wielding a hatchet and smashing up saloons in her home state of Kansas—and later the Woman's Christian Temperance Union, with their followers praying and singing hymns outside saloons while encouraging women to support alcohol bans.

The Anti-Saloon League made significant strides in transforming almost half of the U.S. from wet to dry, with no or limited sale of alcohol and saloon closures in 1913. It also encouraged most states to pass the Volstead Act in 1919 to support the Eighteenth Amendment, leading to Prohibition, a federal alcohol ban, in effect on January 17, 1920. In addition, the temporary Wartime Prohibition Act in 1918 stopped beer and wine manufacturing and lowered the alcohol percentages of liquor that could be sold (Lerner, 2011).

Temperance movements began in the 1830s in the U.K but never resulted in the government enacting prohibition of alcohol (Beckingham, 2023). A major change occurred, post-pandemic when, under the Intoxicating Liquor (Sale to Persons under Eighteen) Act 1923, it "became an offense to knowingly sell, or attempt to purchase, alcohol in a public house (pub) to, or by, anyone under the age of 18" (Feikert-Ahalt, 2023, para. 2). Beers and ciders, however, could be bought by 16- to 18-year-olds if they ate a meal at a property away from the bar. Before the Act, youth as young as 14 were able to purchase beer and wine (Feikert-Ahalt, 2023).

Residents in dry locations in the U.S. could ask doctors to prescribe whiskey for medicinal purposes to be picked up at drug stores. People could buy, at drugstores or through mail order, several elixirs containing alcohol and narcotics, primarily cocaine and morphine. In fact, the original Coke bottles contained traces of cocaine until 1929 (Hajar, 2016).

Government regulation of cosmetics, food products, medical prescriptions, and over-the-counter products were not fully developed at this time. The U.S. Food and Drug Administration (2023), more widely known as the FDA, is considered "the oldest comprehensive consumer protection agency in the U. S. federal government," (para. 1) since its inception in 1862 under the Department of Agriculture. Its focus during the pandemic was on the 1906 Food & Drugs Act to prevent the transportation of contaminated and mislabeled products from state to state (FDA, 2019). The Federal Trade Commission (FTC) was established in 1914 but focused on breaking up anti-competitive businesses. A few decades later, the FTC began to enforce stringent consumer protections for deceptive or misleading promotion and advertising of products (FTC, n.d.).

Other truth-in-advertising efforts focused on combatting deceptive advertising (Hess, 1922). In 1911, legal expert and author Harry D. Nims was commissioned by *Printers' Ink*, a weekly advertising trade magazine, to provide a legal opinion "as to what if any changes in the present laws are necessary or advisable ... to prevent effectually the publication of unfair, fraudulent and false advertisements" (Nims, 1911, p. 6). Editor of *Printers' Ink*, John Irving Romer, endorsed, recommended and printed Nims' model statute "for enactment in various states of the union as a working basis for the elimination of dishonest and misleading adverting":

> Any person, firm, corporation or association who, with intent to sell or in any wise dispose of merchandise, securities, service, or anything offered by such person, firm, corporation or association, directly or indirectly, to the public for sale or distribution, or with intent to increase the consumption thereof, or to induce the public in any manner to enter into any obligation relating thereto, or to acquire title thereto, or an interest therein, makes, publishes, disseminates, circulates, or places before the public, or causes, directly or indirectly, to be made, published, disseminated, circulated, or placed before the public, in this State, in a newspaper or other publication, or in the form of a book, notice, hand-bill, poster, bill, circular, pamphlet, or letter, or in any other way, an advertisement of any sort regarding merchandise, securities, service, or anything so offered to the public, which advertisement contains any assertion, representation or statement of fact which is untrue, deceptive or misleading, shall be guilty of a misdemeanor.
>
> *(Romer, 1911, p. 68)*

The magazine's editor contended that members of the Advertising Clubs of America (now called the American Advertising Federation) should serve as an industry self-regulatory model and be supportive of the statute enacted in many states to protect the industry against misleading advertising (Hoofnagle, n.d.). The Better Business Bureau and the National Vigilance Committee of the Associated Advertising Clubs of the World also collaborated to monitor infractions (Hess, 1922). Newspaper advertising revenues soared in the U.S.—from 44% in 1880 to 66.66% in 1919 (Petty, 2013; Stole, 2006). Advertising billings generated USD 30 million in 1880 and increased to USD 850 million 40 years later (Frederick, 1925; Petty, 2013).

In the U.K., strict regulations of accurate labels on consumer products were enacted with the Sale of Food Drug Act 1875 and later with the

Public Health Acts Amendment Act 1907 to help prevent adulteration of products and false claims of medicines concocted by quacks (O'Hagan, 2021). The False Royal Warrants recognize companies or individuals supplying goods or services to the royal family; foreign products masquerading as made in Britain were banned under the Merchandise Marks Act 1887. The advertising of falsehoods about products and services were addressed decades later in the Trade Descriptions Act 1968 (legislation.gov.uk, n.d.; O'Hagan, 2021).

Communication execution and programming

During the 1918–1919 influenza, advertisers in the U.S. and Britain dealt with limited advertising regulations and an exasperated public dealing with the conclusion of WWI and seeking health solutions and normalcy during the pandemic. The manufacturers' objectives were primarily to sell products and to promote elixirs. O'Hagan (2021) researched brand advertising of three major manufacturers in Britain—Chymol, Formamint, and Lifebuoy—during this pandemic and found that the attempts of advertisers to gain the trust of emotional consumers were "achieved by drawing on a combination of pseudoscientific evidence and visual cues to overstate the products' value and convince consumers that they were essential for preventing influenza" (p. 165).

Companies selling professed healing products during the 1918–1919 pandemic refocused their advertising from curing the common cold and other maladies to pandemic-specific messages, using fearmongering and misleading pseudoscientific assertions to claim influenza cures to persuade anxious consumers, mostly worried about surviving as the death toll rose, to buy their products.

Advertising messages shared a similar theme: "they all declared with confidence that there *was* a *way* to stop influenza, there was a *way* to survive" (Barry, 2021, p. 355). Some advertisers simply revamped older ads promoting common health purposes with pandemic-specific cures starting in 1918. For example, promotional copy for Hill's Cascara Quinine Bromide originally focused on how the product "cures colds, coughs and la grippe" (The Waring Historical Library, n.d.) and changed ads during the pandemic with headlines such as "Spanish Influenza can be prevented easier than it can be cured. At the first sign of a shiver or sneeze, take Hill's Cascara Quinine Bromide" (Hill's Cascara Quinine Bromide, 1918; Maden & Cassidy, 2020). Horlick's Malted Milk Company touted its product as "The Diet During and After Influenza" (Burg, 2020; Vital Signs, n.d.). A Gude's Pepto Mangan (1918) ad headline read "To regain health and strength after Spanish Influenza and pneumonia."

Originally touted as a blood builder, the now-defunct product was made of iron, manganese peptonate, and 16% alcohol (American Museum of National History, n.d.), containing more alcohol by volume than beer and wine.

Two examples of fearmongering include an ad by Neuffer's Lung Tonic (1919) with the headline: "500,000 DEAD: This is the Toll of Influenza During the Past Twelve Months ... MORE THAN DOUBLE OUR TOTAL War Casualties." The product apparently was successful until 1975 when the Federal Drug Administration banned it (Young, 2016).

A product in Britain called Formamint was made of "0.01 gram of formaldehyde combined with lactose; sugar, citric acid and flavoring matter" (Smithsonian, n.d., para. 2). Its influenza ad (see Figure 2.5) included an illustration of a street scene of well-dressed women surrounded by ratty-looking people coughing, with the headline, "Why catch their influenza?" Loeb (1994) and O'Hagan (2021) provided insight into the ad's cultural implications in Britain during 1918:

> We see working-class men in flat caps and plain coats mixed with middle-class men in homburg hats and tailored jackets, implying that high social status is not a barrier to influenza. However, paradoxically,

FIGURE 2.5 1918 Formamint ad promoting its tablets as a preventive measure for the 1918 influenza. Chronicle/Alamy Stock Photo.

amongst these men are smartly dressed women in furs, leather gloves and wide-brimmed straw hats, none of whom are suffering from influenza symptoms. The reason why becomes apparent when viewing the beautiful woman in the foreground who is looking over her shoulder at the crowd of sick people and furtively pulling out a bottle of Formamint to protect herself. The implication is clear: take Formamint when you are in a crowd and you will be safeguarded from influenza. Here, Formamint is not just promoting its product as a healthy food but also associating it with middle-class ideals of feminine beauty, high culture and material acquisitiveness.

(O'Hagan, 2021, p. 174)

The first usage of the word advertorial—the portmanteau of advertisement + editorial—appeared in *The Rotarian* magazine in 1914, according to the *Oxford English Dictionary* (2011). These ads look like editorial content with journalistic-style headlines and body copy with visuals adapted to the newspaper's editorial typeface and format.

University of North Carolina University's Gillings School of Global Public Health (2018) hosted a symposium titled *Going viral: Impact and implications of the 1918 Flu Pandemic.* The symposium offered various in-person and online events, including a virtual exhibition, developed by and housed within the University of North Carolina at Chapel Hill University Libraries. The online exhibition contains 10 sections, one of which titled *Profiting from the pandemic* (UNCL, 2018a), features six ads on Vick's VapoRub using an advertorial format. The ad copy provided broad content on taking precautions, seeking medical advice, and understanding symptoms and treatments, with each ad including a closing paragraph specifically on Vick's and its VapoRub product (like the boilerplate section of a news release). The headlines and subheads in the series read as follows:

Ad No. 1: Spanish Influenza–What It Is And How It Should Be Handled: Nothing New–Simply the Old Grip, or la Grippe, That Was Epidemic in 1889–90, Only Then It Came From Russia By Way of France and This Time By Way of Spain.

Ad No. 2: How To Use Vick's VapoRub In Treating Spanish Influenza: The Influenza Germs Attack the Lining of the Air Passages. When VapoRub is Applied Over Throat and Chest the Medicated Vapors Loosen the Phlegm, Open the Air Passages and Stimulate the Mucous Membrane to Throw Off the Germs.

Ad No. 3: Spanish Influenza—The Way To Treat It And Avoid It: Simply the Old-Fashioned Grip Masquerading Under a New Name.

Ad No. 4: Spanish Influenza—A New Name For An Old Familiar Disease: Simply the Same Old Grip That Has Swept Over the World Time and Again. The Last Epidemic in the United States Was in 1889–90.
Ad. No. 5: Spanish Influenza—Just Grip Camouflaged Under a New Name.
Ad. No. 6: The Way To Use VapoRub For Spanish Influenza: The Influenza Germs Attack the Lining of the Air Passages. When VapoRub is Applied Over Throat and Chest the Medicated Vapors Loosen the Phlegm, Open the Air Passages and Stimulate the Mucous Membrane to Throw Off the Germs (UNCL, 2018a).

Measurement and evaluation

With the most important goal to sell products, manufacturers evaluated results by the revenues generated from products sold. Newspaper advertising revenues rose from 1880 to 1919 from 44% to nearly 67% (Stole, 2006, p. 5), with U.S. dollar revenue estimates from USD 30 million to USD 850 million during the same time frame (Frederick, 1925; Petty, 2013). During the 1918–1919 pandemic, an estimated GBP20 million was spent by advertisers in Britain (O'Hagan, 2021).

For a specific example, Vicks VapoRub sales soared from USD 900,000 in 1918 to USD 2.9 million in 1919, requiring the Vicks manufacturing plant to stay open all day to meet the increasing consumer demand (Vicks, n.d.). Readers need to know that the field of market research to evaluate advertising effectiveness was not in existence until the 1920s (Vasquez, 2011).

Another barometer of success is longevity, with many of these products still for sale today while evolving over the years by complying with regulatory guidelines and changing consumer demographics and preferences. Brands in existence during the H1N1 influenza, such as Horlicks, Lifebuoy, Listerine, Lysol, Vaseline, and Vicks, remain on the market today.

Theoretical perspectives

William Stead, Jr. (1899) authored a booklet entitled *The Art of Advertising. Its Theory and Practice Fully Described.* Part I lays out five foundational principles that governed the theory of advertising; namely, its universality, its functions, the world in which advertising occurs, how advertising has evolved, and the emergence of an advertising agent.

According to Stead (1899), advertising was once looked down upon and relegated to the elite, privileged class but at the turn of the 19th century, it became a universal "systematized [sic] and regulated practice" (p.17) for all community members. As such, the process of advertising served two functions. The first was to inform and educate publics (Wagenseller,

1902) about specific products and advantages of one company's product over another:

> The most striking fact about the great mass of consumers is their dense ignorance. The ordinary man who has to earn his living, and the woman who has to look after the house, have no time to find out the best article on the market. They need to be educated.
>
> *(Stead, 1899, p. 21)*

The second function of advertising was to be a pipeline, the most efficient way for businesses, manufacturers, or retailers to supply consumers with goods. Advertisers were expected to appeal intelligently and without malice directly to "the housewife" and public (Stead, 1899, p. 20). In adopting the communication tools of the times, a new advertising world developed in which daily newspapers and other printed periodicals "commands an audience … reaches hundreds of thousands of readers … in the spot he is most susceptible, his home" (Stead, 1899, pp. 24–25). *Note that in the United Kingdom there were approximately 4,500 publications with an annual circulation of roughly 2.7 million, whereas in the United States there were more than 20,500 publications with an annual circulation of 3.3 million* (Stead, 1899).

As business increased and means of communication became cheaper roughly, USD 0.0023 per agate line per thousand circulation for evening newspaper ads (O'Mara & Ormsbee, 1920), an advertising agency needed to find new markets, study the market conditions, and ascertain facts to carefully map out a campaign of posting an ad in the newspaper, all the while approaching the public "in a fashion which will appeal to it and not disgust it" (Stead, 1899, p. 45).

Finding this tipping point and balance required an understanding of psychology. Professor Walter Dill Scott (1902) wrote *The psychology of advertising in theory and practice*. In it he describes the value of perception and how words and illustrations embody sensations in individuals, thereby enticing them to buy a specific product.

Another distinct feature of the psychology of advertising is the concept of apperception, which Scott (1902) defines as "the bringing to bear what has been retained of past experience in such a way as to interpret, to give weight to the new experience" (pp. 21–22). Advertisers used perception and apperception to call readers to action. The operating assumption was that advertisers were protectors, performing a social service to steer the public away from the likes of P.T. Barnum and the use of "bombast, hyperbole, and deceit … [to] hoodwink the public" into purchasing products for profit (p. 395).

As this case study illustrates, the war, influenza pandemic, increased newspaper usage, and changing social conditions contributed to publics' fears and vulnerabilities "about the causes of illness and governmental responses ... simplistic and unscientific misrepresentations about medications and devices which are claimed to prevent, treat or cure diseases. In turn, such vulnerability creates predatory opportunities for the unscrupulous" to take advantage (Freckleton, 2020, p. 1).

Manufacturers capitalized on these psychodynamics to create newspaper advertisements that educated publics and enticed buyers to purchase their products, by, as Long (2025) articulates:

- repurposing the product to boost immunity "to the threats of unnatural modern life: irregular habits, fatigue, sedentary jobs, and urban living, which lead to an enervated, ill body" (p. 108)
- preventing influenza using militaristic language by "being combatants in the war against disease" (p. 110)
- aiding in self-diagnosis and self-medicating, "enabling the public to have an increasing sense of agency regarding their health" (p. 103)
- living life free from worry which would "vaccinate the mind" (p. 104)

Looking back on the decisions of advertisers and manufacturers of products and political and legal consequences that emerged from some of their practices, Long (2025) reminds us that:

> we cannot assume that consumers purchasing products advertised in newspapers and magazines were making inappropriate choices—while advertising overpromised and was designed to sway, consumers were still attempting to make informed selections and were often following what was considered best practice at the time.
>
> *(p. 105)*

Key terms

Advertising Clubs of America (now American Advertising Federation)
Advertorial
Anti-Saloon League
Apperception
Food and Drug Administration
Fomite
Grippe
In-truth Advertising
Intoxicating Liquor (Sale to Persons under Eighteen) Act 1923
Printers' Ink Model Statute
Temperance Movement

Discussion questions

1 What are some folk remedies within your family? Are they effective?
2 Review ads from Lifebuoy, Vicks VapoRub, Horlicks, or Lysol during COVID-19. What similarities or differences from the ads during the 1918–1919 pandemic did you observe now as to how products were advertised?
3 How might you have combatted mis/disinformation back then? What are some suggestions for combatting mis/disinformation regarding medical claims and products now?

References

American Red Cross (2025). *Mission & values—Red Cross mission, vision, and fundamental principles*. https://www.redcross.org/about-us/who-we-are/mission-and-values.html

Apfeldorf, M. (2020, March 19). Pandemic and civic virtue: The American Red Cross and the influenza pandemic of 1918. *Library of Congress Blogs*. https://blogs.loc.gov/teachers/2020/03/pandemic-and-civic-virtue-the-american-red-cross-and-the-influenza-pandemic-of-1918/

Barro, R. J., Ursúa, J. F., & Weng, J. (2020, March). The coronavirus and the Great Influenza epidemic: Lessons from the "Spanish Flu" for the Coronavirus' potential effects on mortality and economic activity. *National Bureau of Economic Research*. [Working paper 26866]. https://www.nber.org/papers/w26866. DOI:10.3386/w26866

Barry, J. M. (2004, January 20). The site of origin of the 1918 influenza pandemic and its public health implications. *Journal of Translational Medicine*, *2*(3). DOI: 10.1186/1479-5876-2-3

Barry, J. M. (2021). *The great influenza: The story of the deadliest pandemic in history*. Penguin Books.

Beckingham, D. (2023, January 23.) A brief history of the temperance movement in Britain and Ireland. *BBC History Magazine*. https://www.historyextra.com/period/victorian/temperance-movement-history-when-start-britain-ireland/

Bell Telephone Co. of Pennsylvania. (1918, October 11). Don't telephone. [Ad]. Originally posted in the *Souderton Independent*. https://www.thereporteronline.com/2021/12/14/in-retrospect-news-from-the-dec-16-1921-and-dec-15-1971-souderton-independent/

Berger, K. (2020, October 9). How tech helped in the fight against the 1918 flu. *Cascade PBS*. https://www.cascadepbs.org/culture/2020/10/how-tech-helped-fight-against-1918-flu

Bonea, A. (2021). "Contagion by telephone": Print media and knowledge about infectious diseases in Britain, 1880s-1914. *Technology and Culture*, *62*(4), 1063–1086. https://doi.org/10.1353/tech.2021.0154

Bristow, N. (n.d.). Pandemic then and now: Lessons from the 1918 influenza. *The National WWI Museum and Memorial*. https://www.theworldwar.org/learn/about-wwi/pandemic-then-and-now

Burg, S. B. (2020, April 7). The virus that shut down Wisconsin: The Great Flu Pandemic of 1918. *PBS Wisconsin*. https://pbswisconsin.org/news-item/the-virus-that-shut-down-wisconsin-the-great-flu-pandemic-of-1918/

Byerly, C. R. (2010). The U.S. military and the influenza pandemic of 1918-1919. *Public Health Reports*, *125*(Supplement 3), 82–91. PMID: 20568570; PMCID: PMC2862337.

Census Bureau. (n.d.). *Historical statistics of the United States Colonial Time to 1957*. https://www2.census.gov/library/publications/1960/compendia/hist_stats_colonial-1957/hist_stats_colonial-1957-chR.pdf

Centers for Disease Control and Prevention. (2018a, March 21). *History of 1918 flu pandemic*. https://archive.cdc.gov/#/details?q=1918%20influenza&start=0&rows=10&url=https://www.cdc.gov/flu/pandemic-resources/1918-commemoration/1918-pandemic-history.htm

Centers for Disease Control and Prevention. (2018b, May 11). *1918 pandemic influenza: Three waves*. [CDC Archive]. https://archive.cdc.gov/#/details?q=1918%20spanish%20flu%20pandemic&start=0&rows=10&url=https://www.cdc.gov/flu/pandemic-resources/1918-commemoration/three-waves.htm

Centers for Disease Control and Prevention. (2019, March 20). *1918 Pandemic (H1N1 virus)*. [CDC Archive]. https://archive.cdc.gov/#/details?url=https://www.cdc.gov/flu/pandemic-resources/1918-pandemic-h1n1.html

Chandra, S., & Kassens-Noor, E. (2014, September 19). The evolution of pandemic influenza: Evidence from India, 1918–19. *BMC Infect Diseases*, *14*(510), 1–10. http://www.biomedcentral.com/1471-2334/14/510

Chilcote, J. (2016). *Epidemic and opportunity: American perceptions of the Spanish influenza epidemic*. [Doctoral dissertation, University of Kentucky]. Theses and Dissertations—History. http://dx.doi.org/10.13023/ETD.2016.338

Coleman, M. C., & Mari, W. (2023, May). Networks in motion: The alliances of information communication technologies and mobility technologies during the 1918 influenza pandemic. *Mobile Media Communication*, *11*(2), 156–173. DOI: 10.1177/20501579221148427

Commissioned Corps of the U.S. Public Health Service. (n.d.). *Who we are*. https://www.usphs.gov/about-us

Cull, N. J. (n.d.). Master of American propaganda—How George Creel sold the Great War to America, and America to the world. *PBS*. https://www.pbs.org/wgbh/americanexperience/features/the-great-war-master-of-american-propaganda/

Curiosity Collections. (n.d.). Contagion—historical views of diseases and epidemics: Germ theory. *Harvard Library*. https://curiosity.lib.harvard.edu/contagion/feature/germ-theory

Daly, C. B. (2017, April 28). How Woodrow Wilson's propaganda machine changed American journalism. *Smithsonian Magazine*. https://www.smithsonianmag.com/history/how-woodrow-wilsons-propaganda-machine-changed-american-journalism-180963082/

Davis, K. C. (2018, September 21). Philadelphia threw a WWI Parade that gave thousands of onlookers the flu. *Smithsonian Magazine*. https://www.smithsonianmag.com/history/philadelphia-threw-wwi-parade-gave-thousands-onlookers-flu-180970372/

Davis, S. C., Diegel, S. W., & Boundy, R. G. (2014, July). *Transportation energy data book*. (33rd ed.). Center for Transportation Analysis and Energy and Transportation Science Division. https://info.ornl.gov/sites/publications/files/pub50854.pdf

Department of Commerce—Bureau of the Census. (1920). *Census of electrical industries: 1917*. Government Printing Office. https://www2.census.gov/prod2/decennial/documents/1917telephones.pdf

Editors of the Encyclopedia Britannica. (n.d.). Associated Press—news agency. Britannica. https://www.britannica.com/topic/Associated-Press

Elon University. (n.d.) *1870s – 1940s: Telephone*. https://www.elon.edu/u/imagining/time-capsule/150-years/back-1870-1940/

Ewing, T. (2015, January 15). Influenza precautions, then and now. *National Library of Medicine* [Circulating Now Blog]. https://circulatingnow.nlm.nih.gov/2015/01/15/influenza-precautions-then-and-now/

Ewing, T. (2020, April 16). Researching epidemics in chronicling America newspapers. *Library of Congress Blogs*. https://blogs.loc.gov/headlinesandheroes/2020/04/researching-epidemics-in-chronicling-america-newspapers/

Fargey, K. M. (2019, Spring). The deadliest of enemy: The U.S. Army and influenza, 1918-1919. *Army History, 111*, 24–39. https://www.jstor.org/stable/26616953

Federal Trade Commission. (n.d.) *Our history*. https://www.ftc.gov/about-ftc/history

Feikert-Ahalt, C. (2023, November 20). *100 year anniversary of restrictions on alcohol in England and Wales for those under 18*. Library of Congress Blogs.[In Custodia Legis Law Librarians of Congress]. https://blogs.loc.gov/law/2023/11/100-year-anniversary-of-restrictions-on-alcohol-in-england-and-wales-for-those-under-18/

Freckleton, I. (2020). September-October). Covid-19: Fear, quackery, false representations and the law. *International Journal of Law and Psychiatry*, 72, 1–12. https://doi.org/10.1016/j.ijlp.2020.101611

Frederick, J. G. (1925). *Masters of advertising copy*. Frank-Maurice. https://babel.hathitrust.org/cgi/pt?id=uc1.b4502125&seq=9

Fujimura, S. F. (2003). Purple death: The great flu of 1918. *Perspectives in Health, 8*(3). https://www3.paho.org/English/DD/PIN/Number18_article5.htm

Gernhart, G. (1999, November/December). A forgotten enemy: PHS's fight against the 1918 influenza pandemic. *Public Health Reports*, 114, 559–561. DOI: 10.1093/phr/114.6.559.

Grunig, J. E. (1968). *Information, entrepreneurship, and economic development: A study of the decision making process of Colombian latifundistas* [Doctoral dissertation, University of Wisconsin Madison]. ProQuest Dissertations & Theses Global. https://www.proquest.com/pqdtglobal1/dissertations-theses/information-entrepreneurship-economic-development/docview/302379255/sem-2?accountid=11644

Grunig, J. E. (1997). A situational theory of publics: Conceptual history, recent challenges and new research. In D. Moss, T. MacManus, & D. Verĉiĉ (Eds.), *Public relations research: An international perspective* (pp. 3–46). London: International Thomson Business.

Gude's Pepto Mangan. (1918, November 5). *Lynchburg News- 1918 Nov5P3AD*. National Library of Medicine [Circulating Now Blog]. https://circulatingnow.nlm.nih.gov/2015/01/15/influenza-precautions-then-and-now/lynchburgnews-1918nov5p3-ad/

Hajar, R. (2016, January-March). Intoxicants in Society. *Heart Views, 17*(1), 42–48. DOI: 10.4103/1995-705X.182651

Hauser, C. (2020, December 10). The mask slackers of 1918. *The New York Times*. https://www.nytimes.com/2020/08/03/us/mask-protests-1918.html

Hess, H. W. (1922). History and present status of the "Truth-in-Advertising" movement as carried on by the Vigilance Committee of the Associated Advertising Clubs of the World. *The Annals of the American Academy of Political and Social Science, 101*, 211–220. http://www.jstor.org/stable/1014611

Hillinger, C. (1991, April 8). Pulling the plug: Phone company to replace last manual switchboard. *Los Angeles Times*. https://www.latimes.com/archives/la-xpm-1991-04-08-mn-130-story.html

Hill's Cascara Quinine Bromide. (1918, December 9). Advertisement for Hill's Cascara Quinine Bromide. *Evening Star* (Washington, D.C.). [Library of Congress Chronicling America database]. https://www.loc.gov/resource/sn83045462/1918-12-09/ed-1/?sp=14&q=spanish+influenza+can+be+prevented+easier+than+it+can+be+cured.++at+the+first+sign+of+a+shiver+or+sneeze+take&r=-0.212,0.13,0.996,0.852,0

Homan, G. (1906, September 15). The dust problem. In Dixon, S. G., Roberts, J., Gilchrist, A. W., Probst, C. O., & Homan, G. A Discussion On Tuberculosis. Opening Papers. *The British Medical Journal*, *2*(2385), 609–619. http://www.jstor.org/stable/20291154

Honigsbaum, M. (2013, April). Regulating the 1918-1919 pandemic: Flu, stoicism, and the Northcliffe Press. *Medical History*, *57*(2), 165–185. DOI:10.1017/mdh.2012.101

Hoofnagle, C. J. (n.d.). On the Printers' Ink Model Statute. *University of California, Berkeley School of Law*. https://hoofnagle.berkeley.edu/2014/09/24/on-the-printers-ink-model-statute/

Hooks, K. (2017, May 18). History of payphones ... you know, that thing you don't use anymore. *ABC10*. https://www.abc10.com/article/news/local/history-of-payphones-you-know-that-thing-you-dont-use-anymore/103-440924470

Humphries, M. O. (2014, January). Paths of infection: The first World War and the origins of the 1918 influenza pandemic. *War in History*, *21*(1), 55–81. DOI: 10.1177/0968344513504525

Jedwab, R., Khan, A. M., Russ, J., & Zaveri, E. D. (2021, July 17). Epidemics, pandemics, and social conflict: Lessons from the past and possible scenarios for COVID-19. *World Development*, *147*, 1–16. https://doi.org/10.1016/j.worlddev.2021.105629

Jester, B., Uyeki, T. M., Jernigan, D. B., & Tumpey, T. M. (2019). Historical and clinical aspects of the 1918 H1N1 pandemic in the United States. *Virology*, *527*, 32–37. doi.org/10.1016/j.virol.2018.10.019

Jones, M. M. (2010). The American Red Cross and local response to the 1918 influenza pandemic: A four-city case study. *Public Health Reports*, *125*(Supplement 3), 92–104. DOI: 10.1177/00333549101250S312

Keeling, A. W. (2010). "Alert to the necessities of the emergency": U.S. nursing during the 1918 influenza pandemic. *Public Health Reports*, *125*(Supplement 3), 105–112. https://www.jstor.org/stable/41435304

Kellem, B. G. (2022, January 31). The 1918 flu pandemic's impact on movie theaters. *JSTOR Daily*. https://daily.jstor.org/the-1918-flu-pandemics-impact-on-movie-theaters/

Kraut, A. M. (2010). Immigration, ethnicity, and the pandemic. *Public Health Reports*, *125*(Supplement 3), 123–133. DOI: 10.1177/00333549101250S315

Krishna, A. (2021). Theories of public relations. In T. L. Thompson & P. J. Schultz (Eds.), *Health communication theory*, (pp. 242–258). John Wiley & Sons Inc.

Legislation.gov.uk. (n.d.). *Trade Descriptions Act 1968*. https://www.legislation.gov.uk/ukpga/1968/29

Lerner, M. A. (2011, September/October). Going dry: The coming of Prohibition. *Humanities: The Magazine for the National Endowment of the Humanities*. https://www.neh.gov/humanities/2011/septemberoctober/feature/going-dry

Library of Congress. (n.d.) Shadows of war. https://www.loc.gov/classroom-materials/immigration/german/shadows-of-war/

Little, B. (2020, July 16). 'Mask Slackers' and 'Deadly' Spit: The 1918 flu campaigns to shame people into following new rules. *History—A & E Television Networks*. https://www.history.com/news/1918-pandemic-public-health-campaigns

Loeb, L. A. (1994). *Consuming angels: Advertising and Victorian women*. Oxford University Press.

Lofgren, E., Fefferman, N. H., Naumov, Y. N., Gorski, J., & Naumova, E. N. (2007). Influenza seasonality: Underlying causes and modeling theories. *Journal of Virology*, *81*(11), 5429–5436. DOI:10.1128/JVI.01680-06

Long, M. (2025). Immunity for sale: Depictions of immunity in British newspaper advertising, 1890-1940. *Medical History*, *69*(1), 99–118. DOI:10.1017/mdh.2024.26

Lovett, D. A. (2017, October 24). Ten famous people who survived the 1918 flu. *Smithsonian Magazine*. https://www.smithsonianmag.com/history/ten-famous-people-who-survived-1918-flu-180965336/
Maden, M., & Cassidy, P. (2020, March 26).1918 influenza outbreak wreaked havoc for months. *Jamestown Press*. https://www.jamestownpress.com/articles/1918-influenza-outbreak-wreaked-havoc-for-months/
Martin, E. (2022, March 4). The lessons learned from 1918 flu fatigue, according to historians. *National Geographic*. https://www.nationalgeographic.com/history/article/the-lessons-learned-from-1918-flu-fatigue-according-to-historians
National Museum of American History. (n.d.). *Gude's Pepto-Mangan bottle*. https://americanhistory.si.edu/collections/object/nmah_715780
McCracken, H. (2020, April 3). How the telephone failed its big test during 1918's Spanish flu pandemic. *Fast Company*. https://www.fastcompany.com/90484820/how-1918s-spanish-flu-outbreak-crushed-the-u-s-telephone-system
Mendenhall, E., Kohrt, B. A., Logie, C. H., & Tsai, A. C. (2022, July). Syndemics and clinical science. *Nature Medicine*, *28*, 1359–1362. https://www.nature.com/articles/s41591-022-01888-y
Merrill, S. (2009). *Introduction to syndemics: A critical systems approach to public and community health*. John Wiley & Sons, Incorporated.
Mogulescu, L. (2020, April 1). *How telephone operators helped people connect during the 1918 flu epidemic*. The New York Historical [Museum]. https://www.nyhistory.org/blogs/how-telephone-operators-helped-people-connect-during-the-1918-flu-epidemic
Morabia, A. (2021, March). The US Public Health Service house-to-house canvass survey of the morbidity and mortality of the 1918 influenza pandemic. *American Journal of Public Health*, *111*(3), 438–445. DOI: 10.2105/AJPH.2020.306025
Morris, J. (n.d.) The telephone: A brief history. *Independent Telecommunications Pioneer Association*. https://www.nationalitpa.com/history-of-telephone
Mougel, N. (2011). World War I casualties. (J. Gratz, Trans.). *REPERES- Module 1-1-1*. https://www.scribd.com/document/393675248/REPERES-Module-1-1-1-Explanatory-Notes-World-War-I-Casualties-En
National Onion Association. (n.d.). *Onions & flu*. https://www.onions-usa.org/tips-onion-myths-faqs/onions-flu/
Navarro, J. A. (2010). Influenza in 1918: An epidemic in images. *Public Health Reports*, *125*(Supplement 3), 9–14. DOI: 10.1177/00333549101250S304
Navarro, J. A. (2020, July 13). Mask resistance during a pandemic isn't new – in 1918 many Americans were 'slackers.' *The Conversation*. https://theconversation.com/mask-resistance-during-a-pandemic-isnt-new-in-1918-many-americans-were-slackers-141687
Neuffer's Lung Tonic. (1919, February 14). *The Abbeville Press and Banner* (Abbeville, S.C.). https://www.loc.gov/resource/sn84026853/1919-02-14/ed-1/?dl=page&q=influenza+advertisement&sp=4&st=text&r=-0.615,-0.054,2.23,1.712,0
New York Telephone Company. (1918a, October 18). Don't telephone unless it is absolutely necessary. [Ad]. *The Evening World*. https://www.loc.gov/resource/sn83030193/1918-10-18/ed-1/?sp=10&q=Spanish+Influenza&st=pdf&r=-0.149,-0.065,1.297,1.297,0
New York Telephone Company. (1918b, November 10). A Word of appreciation. [Ad]. *The Sun*. https://chroniclingamerica.loc.gov/lccn/sn83030431/1918-11-10/ed-1/seq-2/
Nims, H. D. (1911, November 16). Legal opinion of H. D. Nims. [Printed letter dated October 23, 1911]. *Printers' Ink*, *77*(7), 1–74. https://babel.hathitrust.org/cgi/pt?id=njp.32101066806009&seq=661&q1=Harry+D.+Nims

O'Hagan, L. A. (2021). Commercialising public health during the 1918-1919 Spanish flu pandemic in Britain. *Journal of Historical Research in Marketing, 13*(3/4), 161–187. https://doi.org/10.1108/JHRM-12-2020-0058
O'Mara & Ormsbee, Inc. (1920). *Attainable ideas in newspaper advertising.* https://www.loc.gov/item/20009657/
Oxford English Dictionary. (2011). *Advertorial.* https://www.oed.com/dictionary/advertorial_n?tab=factsheet#9721294
Paton, F. (2020, May 20). Nursing during the deadliest influenza pandemic of 1918. *Nurselabs.* https://nurseslabs.com/nursing-during-the-deadliest-influenza-pandemic-of-1918/
PBS. (n.d.). *The development of radio.* https://www.pbs.org/wgbh/americanexperience/features/rescue-development-radio/
Petit, D. A. (1976). *A cruel wind: America experiences pandemic influenza, 1918-1920 a social history.* [Doctoral dissertation, University of New Hampshire]. Doctoral Dissertations. 1145. https://scholars.unh.edu/cgi/viewcontent.cgi?article=2144&context=dissertation
Petty, R. D. (2013). From puffery to penalties: A historical analysis of US masked marketing public policy concerns. *Journal of Historical Research in Marketing, 5*(1), pp. 10–26. DOI: 10.1108/17557501311293334
Piedmont Telephone & Telegraph Company. (1918, October 18). To telephone users! [Ad]. *Gastonia Daily Gazette.* https://newspapers.digitalnc.org/lccn/sn93064764/1918-10-18/ed-1/seq-4/#words=Telephone+telephone+Users
Printing Office of the Tribune De Geneve. (1920). *The mobilization of the American National Red Cross during the influenza pandemic 1918-1919.* https://quod.lib.umich.edu/f/flu/7090flu.0014.907/–mobilisation-of-the-american-national-red-cross-during?view=text&seq=1&size=50
Rogers, K. (2020, October 17). Bloodletting and gas fumes: Quack treatments of the 1918 flu. *CNN.* https://www.cnn.com/2020/10/17/health/1918-flu-quack-cures-coronavirus-wellness/index.html
Romer, J. I. (1911, November 23). Legal repression of dishonest advertising. *Printers' Ink, 77*(8), 1–96. https://babel.hathitrust.org/cgi/pt?id=njp.32101066806009&seq=850&q1=model+statute
Scott, W. D. (1902). *The psychology of advertising in theory and practices. A simple exposition of the principles of psychology in their relation to successful advertising.* Small, Maynard & Company.
Siegel, R., & Silverman, A. (2017, April 7). During World War I, U.S. government propaganda erased German culture. *NPR—All Things Considered.* https://www.npr.org/2017/04/07/523044253/during-world-war-i-u-s-government-propaganda-erased-german-culture
Smith, K. N. (2021, February 28). 6 weird ways people tried to cure 1918 Influenza. *Forbes.* https://www.forbes.com/sites/kionasmith/2021/02/28/6-weird-ways-people-tried-to-cure-the-1918-influenza/?sh=4e8c380d98a5
Smithsonian. (n.d.). *Formamint.* National Museum of American History Behring Center Collection. https://americanhistory.si.edu/collections/object/nmah_715853
Soper, G. A. (1919, May 30). The lessons of the pandemic. *Science, 49*(1274), 501–506. DOI: 10.1126/science.49.1274.501.
Spanish Influenza Series. (2018). *UNC Libraries.* Richardson-Vicks, Inc., Records #4468, Southern Historical Collection, The Wilson Library, University of North Carolina at Chapel Hill. https://exhibits.lib.unc.edu/exhibits/show/going-viral/item/5576
Spinney, L. (2017). *Pale Rider: The Spanish flu of 1918 and how it changed the world.* Public Affairs/Hatchette Book Group.

Stamp, J. (2014, Sept. 18). The pay phone's journey from patent to urban relic. *Smithsonian Magazine*. https://www.smithsonianmag.com/history/first-and-last-pay-phone-180952727/
Statista. (2010). *Percentage of housing units with telephones in the United States from 1920 to 2008*. https://www.statista.com/statistics/189959/housing-units-with-telephones-in-the-united-states-since-1920/
Stead, W. Jr. (1899). *The art of advertising. Its theory and practice fully described*. T. B. Browne. https://archive.org/details/artofadvertising00stearich/page/10/mode/2up
Stern, A. M., Reilly, M. B., Cetron, M. S., & Markel, H. (2010, April). "Better Off in School": School medical inspection as a public health strategy during the 1918-1919 influenza pandemic in the United States. *Public Health Reports*, *125*(Supplement 3), 63–70. DOI:10.1177/00333549101250S309
Stole, I. (2006). *Advertising on trial: Consumer activism and corporate public relations in the 1930s*. University of Illinois Press.
Sydenstricker, E., & Lawrence, A. T. (2006). The incidence of influenza among persons of different economic status during the epidemic of 1918 (1931) [with commentary]. *Public Health Reports (1974-)*, *121*(Supplement 1: Historical collections 1878-2005), 190–204. https://www.jstor.org/stable/20057068
Talkbox Booth. (2025). *The full history of the phone booth*. https://www.talkboxbooth.com/post/history-phone-booth?srsltid=AfmBOooBVi4diib0kCJe4cl_sJUIU20R7F5jtDjMYCubT-5IO208w4ZS
Taubenberger, J. K., & Morens, D. M. (2006, January). 1918 Influenza: The mother of all pandemics. *Emerging Infectious Diseases*, *12*(1), 15–22. https://doi.org/10.3201/eid1201.050979
Taylor, S. (2019). *The psychology of pandemics: Preparing for the next global outbreak of infectious disease*. Cambridge Scholars Publishing.
Taylor, S. (2022). The psychology of pandemics. *Annual Review of Clinical Psychology*, *18*, 581–609. https://doi.org/10.1146/annurev-clinpsy-072720-020131
The Waring Historical Library. (n.d.). *Hill's bromide cascara quinine cures colds, coughs and la grippe*. [C. Wayne Weart Apothecary Trade Cards, 1870-1920, digital collection]. https://cdm16606.contentdm.oclc.org/digital/collection/weartatc/id/291
Thompson, T. L., & Schulz, P. J. (Eds.). (2021). *Health communication theory*. Wiley Blackwell.
Tomes, N. (2010). "Destroyer and teacher": Managing the masses during the 1918–1919 influenza pandemic. *Public Health Reports*, *125*(Supplement 3), 48–62. DOI: 10.1177/00333549101250S308
U.S. Food and Drug Administration. (2019, April 24). Part I: The 1906 Food and Drugs Act and its enforcement. https://www.fda.gov/about-fda/changes-science-law-and-regulatory-authorities/part-i-1906-food-and-drugs-act-and-its-enforcement
U.S. Food and Drug Administration. (2023, August 23). *A history of medical device regulation & oversight in the United States*. https://www.fda.gov/medical-devices/overview-device-regulation/history-medical-device-regulation-oversight-united-states
U.S. Public Health Service Commissioned Corps. (2021, January). *Doctrine In Officio Salutis*. https://dcp.psc.gov/ccmis/PDF_docs/USPHS%20Commissioned%20Corps%20Doctrine.pdf
U.S. Treasury Department—United States Public Health Service. (1918). *Influenza spread by droplets sprayed from nose and throat* [Pamphlet]. https://www.loc.gov/item/rbpe.24101900/
U.S. Public Health Service. (1918, September 25). *"Spanish Flu" "Three-Day Fever" "The Flu."* Government Printing Office. https://curiosity.lib.harvard.edu/contagion/feature/spanish-influenza-in-north-america-1918-1919

University of North Carolina Libraries. (2018a, April 4-6). *Profiting from the pandemic.* [Virtual exhibition]. https://exhibits.lib.unc.edu/exhibits/show/going-viral/profiting

University of North Carolina Libraries. (2018b, April 4-6). *Spanish influenza series.* [Virtual exhibition]. https://exhibits.lib.unc.edu/exhibits/show/going-viral/item/5576

University of North Carolina's Gillings School of Global Public Health. (2018, April 4-6). *Going viral: Impact and implications of the 1918 flu pandemic.* [Symposium]. Chapel Hill, North Carolina. https://exhibits.lib.unc.edu/exhibits/show/going-viral/going-viral

Vasquez, J. (2011, February 1). The history of marketing research. *Market Research World.* http://marketresearchworld.net/content/view/3754/49/

Vicks. (n.d.). *Vicks history.* https://prod.vicks.ca/en-ca/vicks-history

Vintage Everyday. (2020, April 15). *"When in Quarantine; People who are in quarantine are not isolated if they have a Bell Telephone" – Bell Telephone Ad, 1910.* https://www.vintag.es/2020/04/bell-telephone-ad-1910.html

Vital Signs. (n.d.). *01/19/1919: "The Diet During and After Influenza": Horlick's Malted Milk.* https://lib02.uwec.edu/Omeka/s/VitalSigns/item/4543#?c=&m=&s=&cv=&xywh=-27%2C-664%2C946%2C2413

Voices of Democracy—The U.S. Oratory Project. (n.d.). *Woodrow Wilson, "The pueblo speech" (25 September 1919).* https://voicesofdemocracy.umd.edu/wilson-the-pueblo-speech-speech-text/

Wagenseller, G. W. (1902). *Theory and practice of advertising* (2nd ed.). Wagenseller Publishing House. http://babel.hathitrust.org/cgi/pt?id=uiug.30112083843471&seq=7&q1=cent

Wuestenbecker, K. (2014, September 22). Percentage of Americans of German origin 1910. *Immigrant Entrepreneurship—1720 to the present.* https://www.immigrantentrepreneurship.org/documents/percentage-of-americans-of-german-origin/

Young, J. H. (2016, June 20.) Patent medicines. *South Carolina Encyclopedia* https://www.scencyclopedia.org/sce/entries/patent-medicines/

3

CASE STUDIES ON THE POLIO EPIDEMIC, 1927 TO PRESENT

3.1 INTRODUCTION

The polio epidemic in context

Poliomyelitis (commonly referred to as polio) was considered a "creeping mystery [that] instilled a sense of terror in the western world, particularly in America" (Bartlett, 2017, p. 44), with cases documented centuries ago in Ancient Greece, Rome, and Egypt, and with greater frequency since the 18th century in Europe and the U.S. followed by widespread outbreaks in the early 20th century. A polio epidemic broke out in New York City in 1916 resulting in 2,400 deaths, with 80% of children under 5, and 27,000 people died in the U.S. A few decades later, reported polio cases doubled every four years from 1940, from eight per 100,000 to 16 per 100,000 in 1944, and more than doubled again with the highest number reaching 37 per 100,000 in 1952, before an effective vaccine became available in 1955 (Oshinsky, 2005). Contracting polio could result in a complete recovery, lifelong paralysis, severe respiratory complications, or death. Children were the primary victims.

Before reviewing the various polio strains, readers need to understand the differences between elimination and eradication of a disease. Elimination means the cessation of a disease spreading within specific geographic areas, whereas eradication means the end of a disease worldwide. Polio exists in three distinctive variations:

1 Wild poliovirus type 1 (WPV1), the strain most widely causing paralysis, has been eliminated in most countries but not eradicated worldwide.

DOI: 10.4324/9781003434382-3

2 Wild poliovirus type 2 (WPV2) was the first strain to be eradicated in September 2015 after the last case in India.
3 Wild poliovirus type 3 (WPV3) was eradicated in October 2019, with the last case reported in November 2012 (CDC, 2024a).

Notable people who contracted polio include actors Alan Alda, Mia Farrow, Ida Lupino, and Marion Davies; science fiction writer Arthur C. Clark; film director Francis Ford Coppola; photographer Dorothea Lange; ballet dancer Tanaquil Le Clercq; singers/musicians Donovan, Neil Young, Judy Collins, Joni Mitchell, and Itzhak Perlman; artist Frida Kahlo; athletes Jack Nicklaus and Johnny Weissmuller; political figures Archbishop Desmond Tutu and President Franklin Delano Roosevelt (Disabled World, 2017).

A major public figure who became a public face for the crusade for a cure for polio was Franklin Delano Roosevelt (commonly referred to as FDR), the 32nd U.S. president and a polio survivor. His support led to the formation of the National Foundation for Infantile Paralysis (NFIP; later named the March of Dimes) through fundraising events nationwide. Case Study 3.2 covers the foundation's nationwide public relations initiatives that raised money for polio research.

Transmission and symptoms

The European Centre for Disease Prevention and Control (2023), known as the ECDC, created a comprehensive fact sheet about poliomyelitis—its pathology, clinical features, epidemiology, mode of transmission, how it is prevented, and what individuals can do to manage and treat the virus. Only infected people can transmit the polio virus to others by coughing or sneezing near a healthy person or by spreading miniscule pieces of feces by not handwashing after using the bathroom or changing diapers, thereby inadvertently contaminating cutlery, food, touched surfaces, swimming areas, and drinking water. People living in overcrowded environments with poor health services and sanitation are more susceptible than those who reside in sanitary conditions with good healthcare and access to vaccinations (ECDC, 2023).

Children under 5 years old and pregnant women are most susceptible to polio. Most infected people come down with symptoms within a week to 10 days; the incubation period can range from 3 to 35 days. People contracting abortive poliomyelitis, a mild form of polio, may experience temporary flu-like symptoms; those with moderate cases of non-paralytic polio may also get headaches and muscle spasms while feeling pain in their limbs, and sensitivity to light and touch. People suffering severe cases of spinal poliomyelitis may become paralyzed and unable to walk or use one's hands while those inflicted with bulbar poliomyelitis experience challenges breathing, swallowing, or talking. Both spinal and bulbar polio may result in lifelong disabilities or death (ECDC, 2023).

Treatments

Before vaccines were available in the mid-1950s, polio survivors used physical equipment, such as canes, leg braces, crutches, or wheelchairs, for mobility. Others with respiratory difficulties relied on ventilators. The largest ventilators called iron lungs were 7-foot-long steel cylinders with a few narrow windows and portholes, usually set upon a wheeled platform; patients were sealed into the machine with only their heads exposed while the machine helped them breathe. The artificial respirator functioned by External Negative Pressure Ventilation by forcing air into the patient's lungs causing the lungs to expand and then deflate while making a steady whooshing sound of the person breathing (Science Museum, 2018). Depending on the severity of polio, some patients needed weeks or months to breathe on their own and others required lifelong usage. The first iron lung was used in 1928. One of the last users, a lawyer and author, died at age 78 in 2024 after spending hours every day in the iron lung since he was 6 years old (Kindy, 2024).

Vaccinations reduced the fear of polio contagion and saved numerous people from a life of pain and disabilities since the first vaccine was introduced in the mid-1950s. In the 1980s, Rotary International and later the Global Polio Eradication Initiative (GPEI) led efforts to vaccinate 2.5 billion people (GPEI, n.d.a).

Widely used communication tools

A major change in mass media communication in the 1920s was the proliferation of radio for the public to hear news, music, sports, and entertainment programs. A Pittsburg station aired the first Election Day results in 1920 on radio, establishing itself as the first commercial radio station in the U.S. The radio host retrieved the election updates by telephone and shared the U.S. presidential winner, Warren Harding, with his listeners while non-listeners found out the election results hours later in the morning newspapers (Gunderman, 2020). Real-time coverage became a reality leading to many first broadcasts—baseball and football games in 1921, according to the Federal Communications Commission (FCC) (2023); radio advertisements in 1922 (Sterling & Skretvedt, 2025); presidential inauguration ceremony; and the premiere of the longest-running radio program with music and entertainment along with a live audience in 1925 (FCC, 2023). In 1925, 19% of U.S. households (5 million homes) owned a radio that almost doubled in 1929 to 35% to 40% of households with radios (Mintz, n.d.).

In the late 1930s, pools, schools, playgrounds, and other public spaces were shut down across the country. Chicago responded with a "radio school" experiment to teach roughly 315,000 elementary school children, collaborating with teachers, principals, and newspapers to air lessons via the radio until school resumed in September (Foss, 2020).

The "Golden Age of Radio" flourished with various entertainment format programs from the late 1920s to the early 1950s until television replicated popular radio shows into audiovisual formats with comedies and game shows to musical performances and soap operas (PBS, n.d.). Although the first rudimentary electronic television was demonstrated in 1927, RCA debuted the first regular television broadcasting system at the 1939 World's Fair where FDR became the first president to appear on TV (Fisher & Fink, 2025). Television's popularity grew in the 1950s with a greater choice of programs and stations. With the excessive cost of buying TVs—a few weeks' salary for the average worker—just 9% of American households owned television sets in 1950 (Allen & Thompson, 2025). As the prices declined with more TVs manufactured and more programs available across the country, 85.9% of American households had TVs in 1959 (Allen & Thompson, 2025), and 90% in 1960 (Library of Congress, n.d.).

United States Public Health Service (USPHS) broadcasted on radio and television networks in June 1955 *A Special Report on Polio* (United States Department of Health, Education and Welfare et al., 1955). U.S. Department of Health, Education, and Welfare Secretary Oveta Culp Hobby and Surgeon General Leonard Scheele used these media to "dispel fears about the safety of the new Salk vaccine ... and insure the vaccine's safety" (American History TV, 1955).

Impact

The major impact on public health worldwide was the development of effective vaccinations that required the cooperation of both the public and private sector. With polio research supported by NFIP, a polio vaccine became a reality in 1954 after one of the largest clinical trials of schoolchildren called "polio pioneers" in the U.S. took place. Two years later, children at public schools were vaccinated nationwide. Case study 3.3

explores the "polio pioneers" and subsequent vaccination campaign undertaken at public schools across the U.S.

GPEI (n.d.b.), founded in 1988, partnered with six organizations and individuals to eradicate polio:

- World Health Organization (WHO)
- Rotary International
- U.S Centers for Disease Control and Prevention (CDC)
- United Nations Children's Fund (UNICEF)
- Bill & Melinda Gates Foundation (now called the Gates Foundation)
- Gavi, the vaccine alliance

According to WHO (2025), reported global wild polio cases declined by over 99% from approximately 350,000 cases in over 125 countries experiencing epidemics since 1988 to two countries, Afghanistan and Pakistan. Without the vaccine, an estimated 20 million people who would have been paralyzed by polio are ambulatory. Case study 3.4 examines a comprehensive vaccination campaign in Africa called "Kick Polio Out of Africa" from the 1990s.

3.2 PRESIDENT FRANKLIN D. ROOSEVELT BECOMES THE FACE OF POLIO: FORMATION OF THE MARCH OF DIMES BUILDS AWARENESS OF POLIO NATIONWIDE

Situation analysis

About Franklin Delano Roosevelt (1882–1945), polio survivor and crusader

Reviewing highlights of FDR's accomplishments is essential to understand how he coped with polio yet functioned effectively as a political leader and as a crusader for funding polio research. Born to a wealthy family in Hyde Park, New York, FDR began his career as a lawyer in New York City before he pursued politics in 1910 when he served as a New York State senator (Democrat) for two terms and later became the assistant secretary of the Navy under President Woodrow Wilson's administration for seven years (FDR Presidential Library and Museum, 2016a).

As a hale and active individual, FDR faced disaster in 1921 while vacationing with his family in New Brunswick, Canada. He fell overboard his yacht into the freezing water of the Bay of Fundy and felt severely chilled. The next day, he and his three oldest children spent the day sailing, running, and swimming. After he returned home, he was exhausted and sat reading newspapers and responding to mail while wearing his wet bathing suit. He felt feverish and achy and went up a flight of stairs to bed, which was the last time he was able to walk on his own as he quickly succumbed to poliomyelitis (Gallagher, 1999; FDR Presidential Library and Museum, 2016b; Bartlett, 2017).

He took time out from politics for rehabilitation by exercising and swimming regularly to improve his health. He also spent time at a resort in Warm Springs, Georgia, which was known for its medicinal healing waters for polio victims. When Warm Springs faced financial problems and maintenance issues, FDR invested his own money and turned it into the Warm Springs Foundation as a nonprofit hydrotherapeutic center endorsed by the American Orthopedic Association in 1927. Today, it remains as the Roosevelt Warm Springs Institute for Rehabilitation (American Physical Therapy Association, 2023).

With the encouragement of his wife, Eleanor, and a political confidant, he continued his political career and was elected as governor of New York State in 1928 and campaigned for presidency during his second term as governor in 1930. He received seven million more votes than the Republic presidential contender Herbert Hoover in 1932 and was inaugurated as the 32nd president in 1933 during the height of the Great Depression, with rampant unemployment, business closures, and bank failures, among other bleak circumstances in the U.S. He led New Deal initiatives to revitalize the economy (FDR Presidential Library and Museum, 2016a)—one of his legacies was signing the Social Security Act in 1935. The Act spurred development of the Social Security Board, now known as the Social Security Administration (SSA), which remains today to provide financial support primarily to retirees, disabled people, and some of their dependents or survivors (Social Security Administration, n.d.). His other major challenge as president was War World II from 1939 to 1945, when he provided aid to countries, enforced a U.S. military draft, built up U.S. factories to produce ammunitions, and later took on the role as commander-in-chief of the U.S. Armed Forces and managed overseas military operations along with military advisers to end the war (FDR Presidential Library and Museum, 2016a).

Reelected for president in his fourth term, FDR was the longest-serving president in U.S. history (the U.S. Constitution's 22nd Amendment set two-term presidential limits in 1951). He died of a stroke the following year at age 63 in April 1945 before major events that year: military victories were declared in Europe in May, Japan surrendered in August, and WWII officially ended in September (Glass, 2019). He also created alliances with other allied nations through "The Declaration of the United Nations" (now called the United Nations) for post-war peacekeeping (FDR Presidential Library and Museum, 2016a).

Overcoming obstacles and discrimination

Hugh Gregory Gallagher, author of *FDR's Splendid Deception*, noted that only two photographs out of more than 35,000 images show him in a wheelchair at the FDR Library. No wheelchairs were seen in newsreels or drawn in cartoons of FDR. Gallagher (1999) explained how

> he was simply not perceived as being in any major sense disabled... This was not by accident. It was the result of a careful strategy of the President. The strategy served to minimize the extent of his handicap, to make it unnoticed when possible and palatable when it was noticed. The strategy was eminently successful, but it required substantial physical effort, ingenuity, and bravado.
>
> *(p. xiv)*

As a wealthy individual and political leader, FDR had access to the best medical care of his time. Although he never denied his condition, he was acutely aware of discrimination against people with polio—and attempted to hide his condition as much as possible.

FDR wore leg braces that enabled him to stand. Along with arm support of another person and a cane, FDR appeared to be able to walk briefly by taking a few steps by swinging his hips. Additionally, he designed his own wheelchair to fit in narrow spaces. FDR asked the press photographers to refrain from taking images of him in a weakened state; if not compliant, his Secret Service removed film from their cameras (FDR Library and Museum, 2016b). FDR also had access to a private train that traveled to the train track directly below the Waldorf-Astoria hotel on Park Avenue between 49th and 50th streets in Midtown Manhattan, which enabled aides to transport him discreetly through a private passage and elevator bringing him to his hotel room—without being seen by the public (Schlichting, 2001). To enable FDR to drive a car without using his legs, he had his personal cars customized with specialized hand controls that he used for leisure drives. His presidential auto fleet adhered to the Secret Service standards while some vehicles were more spacious and comfortable for a disabled person. FDR also had a presidential car fitted with his specifications (Mann, 2017).

Communication and execution

The President's Birthday Balls

Carl Byoir, founder of public relations agency Carl Byoir & Associates in New York City, played a significant role as the creator of the campaign to raise funds for FDR's Warm Springs Foundation through Byoir's client, Henry L. Doherty, a multimillionaire, entrepreneur, and oil and public utilities tycoon. Doherty was approached to donate to the foundation—and Byoir saw an opportunity to improve his client's controversial image by positioning him as a philanthropist aligned with FDR's nonprofit and polio research (PRMuseum, n.d.). Byoir envisioned a national birthday campaign to parlay on FDR's popularity and the support of public opinion leaders. Byoir served as executive director of fundraising promotion while Doherty initiated the National Committee for Birthday Balls (Cutlip, 1990).

The President's Birthday Balls debuted on FDR's birthday on January 30 in 1934, with 6,000 balls (Special to THE NEW YORK TIMES, 1934), from huge galas to small parties held nationwide; the tradition lasted until 1945, the year FDR died. The first series of balls raised funds exclusively for the Warm Springs Foundation; from 1935 to 1937, 70% of proceeds were allocated to local communities to help people with polio and to thank the local volunteers (Altamont Enterprise, 2018), while the rest of the funds went to the Warm Springs Foundation; and later switched to the new foundation (1938 to 1945).

The campaign's primary goal was to raise funds for polio; primary strategies were to build on the popularity of FDR, generate awareness and enthusiasm nationwide, employ multiple media communication tools, and engage third-party influencers (PRMuseum, n.d.). The following tactics were employed:

- Creation of the **slogan theme**, "Dance so that a child may walk," (Cutlip, 1990, p. 366) attributed to columnist Walter Winchell's (1937) news broadcast in which he urged listeners to attend the events for the President's birthday and "buy a ticket to dance, then some little child who can't even walk may be able to dance some day" (p. 42).
- **Promotional posters** and **billboards** on the balls. See Figure 3.1 as an example of a poster and Figure 3.2 of a billboard.
- **Involvement of leaders** of labor unions, business organizations, fraternal organizations (Elks, Masons), military veterans (American Legion), service organizations (National Exchange Club) (PRMuseum, n.d.).
- **Media relations**—Byoir personally telephoned newspaper publishers to select nominees to serve as local FDR Birthday Ball chairs, which also generated media exposure—and sent news releases to print and radio outlets (PRMuseum, n.d.).
- **Newsreels** about the balls were shown at movie theaters nationwide, featuring a song composed by George M. Cohan, a popular American entertainer of his time and composer of patriotic songs, such as *Yankee*

FIGURE 3.1 1939 poster for the President's Birthday Ball, an official event associated with the birthday of President Franklin D. Roosevelt to raise funds to fight infantile paralysis. Work Projects Administration Poster Collection, Library of Congress. (Public domain.)

Doodle Dandy, and performed by Lily Pons, a French-born American coloratura soprano (Larsen, 2012; PRMuseum, n.d.).

- **Birthday greeting telegrams** offered by Postal Telegraph and Western Union Telegram allowed people to add their names to the bottom of a huge telegram for 25 cents each for fundraising (Cutlip, 1990).
- **Radio broadcasts** of the president from the White House aired, with FDR declaring the first ball his most wonderful birthday.
- **Promotional fundraising** ad templates, along with news stories and images, in a 14-page newspaper called the *Bulletin* were sent to advertisers to promote the balls for additional fundraising streams (Cutlip, 1990).

FIGURE 3.2 1942 billboard sponsored by the National Foundation for Infantile Paralysis (later March of Dimes) in California. Franklin D. Roosevelt Presidential Library & Museum. (Public domain.)

Communication and execution

Launch of the National Foundation for Infantile Paralysis (March of Dimes)

To depoliticize the fundraising further and to squelch rumors about the balls serving as a "Democratic-backed movement," (Bartlett, 2017, p. 40) and as a way for FDR to pay off his personal debts at Georgia Springs (Cutlip, 1990), FDR founded a new nonprofit, the National Foundation for Infantile Paralysis (NFIP), in 1938, with Basil O'Connor, who was FDR's former law partner and president of the Warm Springs Foundation, serving as the first director. The new foundation was launched to provide a "three-pronged approach attack on polio: to promote research into its causes and cure; to care for patients struck by the disease; and to find a cure for the aftereffects of the paralysis" (Cutlip, 1990, p. 382). NFIP "signaled a major new direction in the history American medical philanthropy" (Brandt, 1978, p. 258) by building on the public relations efforts of the President Birthday Balls, employing multiple promotional tactics to convince people during trying economic times to donate and volunteer to the cause; and shifting focus to not just appealing to wealthy donors but to anyone.

In addition to the Birthday Balls, the new foundation's leaders and public relations team undertook other initiatives. Celebrity engagement became increasingly important with a focus on entertainment stars of the era, such as Jack Benny, Bing Crosby, Judy Garland, Jean Harlow, Helen Hayes, Mary Pickford, Ginger Rogers, and Rudy Vallee among others, who made appearances at Birthday Balls or talked about the foundation in media outlets (Bartlett, 2017; Larsen, 2012). One of the most popular comedians and entertainers, Eddie Cantor, coined the phrase "March of Dimes," a play on words of the well-known newsreel series shown in movie theaters, *March of Time*, to inspire people, many of whom were struggling during the Great Depression, to donate a dime (Larsen, 2012; Cutlip, 1990). A dime in 1938 would be worth about USD 2.28 in 2025. On his radio show, he encouraged people to send whatever they could afford to give, even a dime, to FDR at the White House. Ira Smith, who worked in the White House mail room in 1949, recalled what happened as letters with dimes arrived:

> We had been handling about 5000 letters a day at that time. We got 80,000 on the day the March of Dimes began producing. We got 50,000 the next day. We got 150,000 the third day. We kept on getting incredible numbers, and the Government of the United States darned near stopped functioning because we couldn't clear away enough dimes to find the official White House mail.
>
> *(Smith & Morris, 1949, p. 158)*

As an easier way to collect dimes, the Committee for the Celebration of the President's Birthday for NFIP created dime donation cards made of cardboard with slots to hold the dimes (Franklin, D. Roosevelt Presidential Library and Museum, n.d.). Various designs of dime donation cards continued for decades.

In addition, volunteers nationwide sought out donations in their neighborhoods, offices, bowling alleys, baseball games, and in other locations by using simple canisters to collect dimes that were given to the March of Dimes instead of mailing money to the White House (Cutlip, 1990).

Walt Disney also contributed to the fundraising efforts by producing an animated cartoon starring Mickey Mouse for movie theaters. Characters dressed like Mickey Mouse and his co-stars also led a marching band and sang "Hi Ho, Hi Ho, we'll lick polio" complemented the foundation's "Mile O' Dimes" competition to create the longest line of dimes in 1939. Well-known personalities like actor Helen Hayes, who lost her daughter to polio, also talked to the public about the foundation's importance (Cutlip, 1990; Larsen, 2012; Patterson, 2024).

Warner Brothers participated in raising funds for polio by producing short films on the polio crusade to be shown before movies began at theaters. When the lights went back on, movie ushers and volunteers collected donations. For example, *The Crippler* (1940), a short film shot like a horror film, staring a young foundation volunteer contending with an amorphous menacing monster spreading polio (Halliwell, 2021).

During WWII when men enlisted or were drafted, the March of Dimes created a new slogan, "Polio Wears No Party Label," to recruit women as volunteers in positions left open by men in the military. Former actress Mary Pickford was selected as the honorary director of this effort (Larsen, 2012, p. 50).

Outside of the foundation's own promotional efforts, the concept of the "Mothers' March on Polio" began in Wausau, Wisconsin (Cutlip, 1990), in 1950 as a practical way to deal with a short supply of canvassers to reach all homes and to avoid knocking on the doors of disinterested people. Residents interested in donating to the cause were asked to leave their porch lights on for an hour, usually from 7 to 8 p.m., to alert a March of Dimes volunteer to stop by their homes. This effective "Turn On Your Porch Light! Help Fight Polio Tonight!" approach was adopted nationwide by the foundation's headquarters (Cutlip, 1990; Larsen, 2012).

Results

The President's Birthday Balls and other fundraising initiatives generated extensive awareness in all media platforms to build awareness of polio. With one of the primary goals to raise money for polio support and research, the promotional efforts resulted in raising the following amounts:

- The President's Birthday Balls debuted in 1934 and raised exactly USD 1,016,443, (Larsen, 2012, originally cited in Walker, 1953) which would be approximately USD 24.3 million in 2025. The subsequent balls lasted until 1945, the year FDR died, in which USD 18.9 million was raised (Franklin D. Roosevelt Presidential Library and Museum, n.d.).
- Postal and Western Union telegraph services raised USD 11,343 (Cutlip, 1990).
- Commercial advertisers used the sponsored ads in the *Bulletin* and raised USD 1 million (Cutlip, 1990).
- Collections by volunteers during short films on polio shown in movie theaters raised USD 435,000 in 1941 (Larsen, 2012, originally cited in Smith, 1990).
- The "Mile O' Dimes" brought in USD 200,000 (Larsen, 2012, citing Cohn, 1965; Cutlip, 1990).
- The dime mailings to the White House included 2,680,000 dimes (USD 268,000) plus thousands more in checks and cash (Larsen, 2012; Cutlip, 1990).

Cutlip (1990), author of a book on fundraising in America, explained the importance of the NFIP (March of Dimes) fundraising:

> Because of its significance as the most successful money getter among health drives and because it demonstrates the influential role of public relations in today's philanthropy, the story of a fund-raising idea that, between 1934 and 1960, inclusive raised $618.5 million in pennies, dimes, and dollars deserves to be chronicled in detail.
>
> *(p. 352)*

In terms of building awareness, the American Institute of Public Opinion (now called Gallup, Inc.) reported in 1954 that 83% of the American public was familiar with the March of Dimes (Cutlip, 1990). The NFIP's Public Relations Department, with its staff growing to 30 professionals, proactively generated coverage in media outlets, with some stories ghost-written by the Department's staff. Patients in a doctor's waiting room anywhere in the U.S. could easily read stories on polio, particularly in the women's magazines, during the 1940s (Oshinsky, 2005).

With the success of fundraising for polio, the March of Dimes's shifted its focus to birth defects prevention. Now its stated mission is to "lead the fight for the health of all moms and babies," with goals "to end the preventable maternal health risks and deaths, end preventable preterm birth and infant death, and close the health equity gap" (March of Dimes, 2025, para. 1).

As a tribute to FDR's contribution to help victims of polio and polio research through the creation of the March of Dimes, the U.S. Mint released its FDR dime on his birthday in 1946, a year after he died. His profile is shown on the obverse side, and the reverse side illustrates a torch symbolizing liberty flanked by an olive branch for peace, and an oak branch for strength (U.S. Mint, 2025).

Theoretical perspective

The incredible story of FDR and his affliction with polio spurred the health information campaigns featured in this case study. These campaigns serve as an example of narrative engagement theory and the power of messaging "to describe and explain human behavior as well as a strategy to influence people and promote change," through the involvement and engagement with the audience in the process (Thompson, 2014, p. 910).

The most important audience these campaigns involved and engaged with was FDR. A "core polio narrative featuring FDR's triumph over disease and disability … would become a national myth" (Fairchild, 2001,

p. 488). FDR became the face of polio as he candidly and publicly described and explained his personal experiences with polio.

Frank (2013) identifies three specific narratives that wounded storytellers use in narrating their illness: restitution, chaos, and quest. Restitution posits that illnesses can be remedied, and an infected body can heal itself (Frank, 2013; Yamasaki, 2021). A healthy individual becomes ill and the illness represents a pivot in which the individual generates a story with good reasons for triumphantly defeating the illness and returning to a normal state. This was the cornerstone of FDR's image when he was first struck with polio and consistent with the prevailing theme that

> Polio could be defeated with good medical care and the right attitude … including a long period of rehabilitative therapy … was the first prerequisite to overcoming polio. However, hard work (by parents and patients), strong discipline, and the right attitude were the real keys to leaving the realm of the handicapped.
>
> *(Wilson, 1998, p. 476)*

FDR, with the help of his wealth, wife, aide, Warm Springs therapeutic services, and other individuals and organizations, attempted to gain the use of his legs again and overcome "obstacles that kept many polio survivors prisoners in their own homes" (Wilson, 1998, p. 478). However, the progressive nature of the disease soon turned into chaos narratives associated with loss of hope (Yamasaki, 2021), intimacy and autonomy (Fairchild, 2001) and lack of medical knowledge about polio, its cause, how to prevent paralysis (Wilson, 1998).

Eventually, wounded storytellers begin quest narratives by meeting the "suffering head on; they accept illness and seek to use it" (Frank, 2013, p. 115) to "guide and serve others who travel" parallel paths (Fairchild, 2001, p. 497). FDR was no exception:

> Driven by his own personal experience post paralysis, Roosevelt used his stature as a public figure to oversee both the medical success of Warm Springs and the financial success of the NFIP and affiliated polio care and research programs … he invested both time and energy in learning and developing methods for improving the conditions of polio sufferers. Roosevelt was the first American President to make a disease 'his disease.' His advisor made much of his transformation from polio victim to polio patron and featured his name, voice and boy in fundraising.
>
> *(Dorfman et al., 2018, pp. 161–163)*

The success of the President's Birthday Balls and launch of the NFIP are a direct result of narrative engagement as publics and organizations were influenced by FDR's experiences to change their behavior by donating dimes (Robinson et al., 2021).

Engagement did not stop with individuals donating dimes. Fairchild (2001) analyzed decades of polio narratives written by "servicemen, housewives, professors, librarians, musicians, writers, dancers" and students who "left a remarkable legacy of some four dozen published books and nationally circulating magazine accounts of their experiences" (p. 491) that represented a dialogue with the former president about the nature of disabilities. The first group of narratives (1930s to mid-1950s) focused on recovery. The second half of the 50s and beyond focused on coping with a chronic disability. Writers of the narratives who latched on to FDR "because he reflected an important change in the social construction of disability," (p. 534) looked up to him as a role model and idolized him as a hero.

A hero narrative serves "as a counter to the loss of control ... to highlight and model desired prosocial behaviors ... [and] its function of personifying a positive, proactive" response during a health crisis (Seeger & Sellnow, 2016, p. 113). The hero, usually a man, rises to a crisis with an inner strength and through personal qualities like taking responsibility for others while risking his own well-being impacts and influences history. The hero is acknowledged, recognized, and praised via a public tribute.

Narratives are the means by which individuals navigate their experiences with illness, health crises, disease, and pandemics (Sellnow & Seeger, 2021; Thompson & Schulz, 2021), and "underscore the importance of reciprocity for bearing witness to individual and community suffering and trauma" (Yamasaki, 2021, p. 49).

Key words

American Institute of Public Opinion
Basil O'Connor
Carl Byoir
Franklin Delano Roosevelt (FDR)
Gallup
March of Dimes
National Committee for Birthday Balls
National Foundation for Infantile Paralysis
New Deal
Polio

Roosevelt Warm Springs Institute for Rehabilitation
The Declaration of the United Nations (UN)
Warm Springs Foundation
Woodrow Wilson
World War II

Discussion questions

1. If the March of Dimes campaign were conducted now, would it be as effective? Would you donate a dime?
2. Why do you think FDR was open about polio, but went through great lengths to hide the complications? What value or purpose did this serve?
3. If you were planning a President's Birthday Ball for the current president of the United States as a fundraiser, how would you go about planning the event?
4. Are there other theoretical perspectives that might be applicable to this case study?

3.3 DR. SALK'S NEW VACCINE SEEKS "POLIO PIONEER" VOLUNTEERS FOR FIELD TRIALS: SUCCESS LEADS TO NATIONWIDE CAMPAIGN FOR MANDATORY POLIO VACCINES FOR U.S. SCHOOLCHILDREN

Situation analysis

In the 1950s, polio became one of the most infectious diseases affecting children in the U.S. Warm weather was dubbed "polio season," with the public fearful of swimming pools, children playing together, and public gatherings (Beaubien, 2012, para. 1). Almost 60,000 children contracted polio, with many paralyzed, and over 3,000 children perished during the worst polio outbreak in the U.S. in 1952 (Beaubien, 2012; WHO, 2025).

NFIP, which was commonly referred to as the March of Dimes before the official name change, enhanced its promotional efforts after the death of FDR in 1945, who was the original "face" of the nonprofit, to medical researchers while funds were being distributed for polio research for a new effective vaccine.

A major challenge for medical researchers engaged in trying to invent a new polio vaccine was the ability to grow the virus in laboratory cell culture. Three Harvard University doctors at Boston Children's Hospital made a breakthrough in 1949 when they cultivated viruses in test tubes in their laboratory. Dr. John Enders, Dr. Frederick Robbins, and Dr. Thomas Weller were the recipients of the Nobel Prize in Physiology or Medicine in 1954 for their accomplishments. At the award ceremony in Stockholm, Sweden, they were lauded for:

> their discovery of the capacity of the poliomyelitis virus to grow in test-tube cultures of various tissues. [Their] observations have found immediate practical application on vitally important medical problems, and it has made accessible new fields in the realm of theoretical virus research.
> *(Gard, 1954, para. 14)*

Enders, the virologist who led the research, was one of 15 U.S. scientists in *TIME* magazine's "Men of the Year" cover story in 1961. Enders, quoted in the article, stated: "As a rule, the scientist takes off from the manifold observations of his predecessors ... The one who places the last stone and steps across to the terra firma of accomplished discovery gets all the credit" (TIME, 1961, para. 1). He was referring to Dr. Jonas Salk who applied Enders and his team's research and became known as the first inventor of the polio vaccine.

Salk became the most prominent figure and the new "face" of the success of the March of Dimes' quest for an injected polio vaccine. As a professor at the University of Pittsburg School of Medicine, Salk tested his inactivated (killed) polio vaccine that provided protection for all three polio strains initially on monkeys and later humans—people with and without polio, and then on himself and his family. Salk and NFIP Director Basil O'Connor formed a solid relationship, and Salk was encouraged to undergo a medical trial with the NFIP's support, not without opposition from some of his research peers (Bartlett, 2017).

NIFP appointed Dr. Thomas Francis, epidemiology chair at the University of Michigan School of Public Health, to supervise Salk's trial. Francis earlier served as a professor at New York University' bacteriology department and previously mentored Salk when he was a student there and when Salk later conducted research at the University of Michigan with his first NFIP grant in immunology (Bartlett, 2017).

Meanwhile Salk's major rival, Dr. Albert Sabin conducted research at the University of Cincinnati. Unlike Salk, Sabin used a weakened live polio virus to create the first oral polio vaccine. Sabin tested his vaccine on animals before humans, including himself, his daughters, and young inmates at a nearby federal prison (Orsini & Martini, 2022). Sabin was publicly critical of Salk and "looked down on Salk and spoke out against the clinical trials of Salk's vaccine at every turn" (Bartlett, 2017, p. 57). With Salk conducting clinical trials in 1954, Sabin continued testing his vaccine on 77 million children in the then Soviet Union from 1959 to 1961, with high effectiveness (Orsini & Martini, 2022).

This case study focuses on two interrelated campaigns: 1) a nationwide effort called "polio pioneers" to encourage parents to allow their children to volunteer to be injected with Dr. Salk's experimental polio vaccine in a clinical field trial in 1954; and 2) the subsequent rollout of a vaccination campaign of the tested and approved polio vaccine at public schools nationwide in 1956.

Communication and programming

"Polio Pioneers"

NFIP funded the research and set up its Vaccine Advisory Committee of physicians and medical researchers in 1953 to establish guidelines and to supervise and approve the trial (Brandt, 1978) while its public relations staff undertook a nationwide media relations campaign to generate coverage in print and broadcast outlets on the process of developing a polio vaccine and the subsequent discovery of its sponsored polio vaccine. The goal of this campaign was to persuade parents to allow their young children at public schools to participate in vaccine trials in 1954, which were "among the largest and most publicized clinical trials ever undertaken" (Meldrum, 1998, p. 1233).

Strategies included positioning the trial as an opportunity to take part in a historic event, elevating Salk as a leader in polio research and as an American hero, conveying positive messages for children and their parents to contribute to research of a worthy cause to end polio now and for the future.

NFIP sought out schools with an established public health infrastructure and schools in locations that expressed interest in the trial. Other important audiences beyond parents were educators, parent-teacher associations, county health officials, and local politicians as authoritative sources to endorse the schools. NFIP's public relations staff created informative pamphlets on the trial for parents to secure consent for their children to participate. Carefully worded consent forms for parents to sign "underscored the idea that people were taking part in a positive endeavor with broad benefits, rather than an unwelcome imposition" (Ujifusa, 2021, para. 27).

NFIP used the term "Polio Pioneers" for the volunteers whether the children received the vaccine or a placebo. Children who participated in the first polio vaccine trials in 1954 received the following two "Polio Pioneer" branded items:

1 **Polio Pioneer circular pin** (about one inch in diameter) with an illustration of a red silhouette of a man looking into a microscope in a lab with

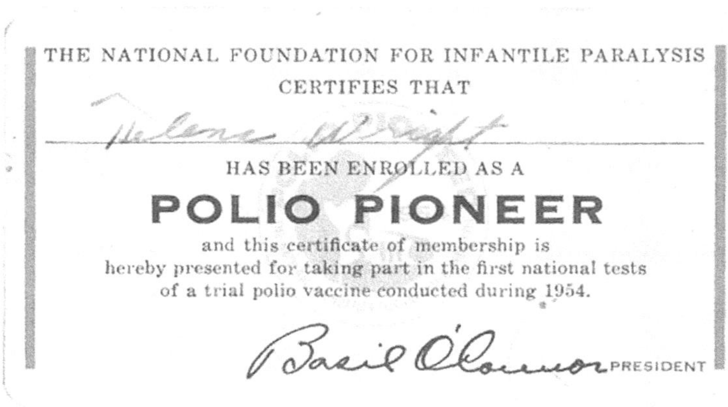
THE NATIONAL FOUNDATION FOR INFANTILE PARALYSIS
CERTIFIES THAT

HAS BEEN ENROLLED AS A
POLIO PIONEER
and this certificate of membership is
hereby presented for taking part in the first national tests
of a trial polio vaccine conducted during 1954.
PRESIDENT

FIGURE 3.3 Polio Pioneer membership certificate given to a participant in the 1954 polio vaccine field trials. Courtesy of the Division of Medicine and Science, National Museum of American History, Smithsonian Institution.

vials on an ivory background, and the words "Polio Pioneer, 1954" and "The National Foundation for Infantile Paralysis."

2 **Personalized Polio Pioneer certification card (2 1/2 inches × 4 1/2 inches): Front side** (See Figure 3.3)

Back side (no image available)

Black text reads: ATTESTED and includes fill-in-the-blanks for the name of the school, town or city, county, state, and date, and the chair's signature. The bottom line reads THE NATIONAL FOUNDATION FOR INFANTILE PARALYSIS.

The authors discovered that some participating children kept the items as mementos, donated them to historical societies and museums, or sold them on eBay and Etsy.

Results

NFIP persuaded many parents to volunteer their children. More than 1.8 million schoolchildren participated in 45 states in the polio vaccine trial. Over 600,000 schoolchildren in first, second, and third grades received three separate injections of the new vaccine (over 400,000 children) or a placebo of salt water (nearly 200,000 children, who were contacted later to get the real vaccine) over two months (Bartlett, 2017; Brandt, 1978; Meldrum,1998) while over a million children participated in observed control studies in 33 states (Dublin, 1955). With interest in polio vaccinations outside of the U.S., the trial also extended to three provinces in Canada and two small areas in Finland (Dublin, 1955).

Stories on Salk ran during the trial and during and after the vaccine effectiveness announcement in leading print and broadcast outlets worldwide. Salk's first TV interview was on Edward R. Murrow's *See It Now* (a TV program like the current *60 Minutes*), on April 12, 1955. When Murrow asked who owns the polio vaccine patent, Salk said: "The people. There is no patent. Could you patent the sun?" (Retro Report, 2016, paras. 17–18).

Although most media coverage was positive about the new vaccine, a few skeptics were vocal. Critic Walter Winchell, an influential columnist in print and broadcast media, was known for gossip. One of his popular quotes about Salk's vaccine has been widely cited as inducing panic and arousing local fears, according to Barcousky (2014), writer for the *Pittsburgh Post-Gazette*:

> "Good evening, Mr. and Mrs. America ... and all the ships at sea," Winchell said on his April 4 [1954] radio and television broadcast. "Attention everyone. In a few moments I will report on a new polio vaccine claimed to be a polio cure. It may be a killer" ... Winchell reported that the U.S. Public Health Services had found live polio viruses in seven of 10 vaccine batches it tested. "It killed several monkeys ... the United States Public Health Service will confirm this in about 10 days," he told viewers and listeners.
>
> *(para. 2–4)*

Algis Valiunas (2018), a contributing editor to the *New Atlantis* and a fellow at the Ethics and Public Policy Center, laments that the timing of Winchell's quote "three weeks before the scheduled trial, did all in Winchell's considerable power to induce mass hysteria ... Winchell had cunningly smudged the truth until it was unrecognizable" (p. 118).

NFIP quickly responded to allay public fears, and Salk's field trial began as originally slated a few weeks after Winchell's negative commentary. Sabin, Salk's rival, also spoke out against Winchell's misinformation (Valiunas, 2018).

Dr. Thomas Francis, director of the Poliomyelitis Vaccine Evaluation Center at the University of Michigan School of Public Health and supervisor of Salk's trial, addressed an audience of scientists and reporters on April 12, 1955—10 years after the death of FDR—at the university's Rackham Auditorium in Ann Arbor, Michigan. "Safe, effective, and potent"

(University of Michigan, 1955, para. 1) was the key message when Francis stated that his former student, Jonas Salk, successfully developed a polio vaccine that was about 90% effective in stopping paralytic polio. According to the news release distributed at this event and worldwide, the NFIP funded USD 7.5 million for the field trial and the subsequent evaluation (University of Michigan Information and News Services, 1955).

The news became the lead story as the "nation burst out in a mass expression of jubilation not seen since VJ Day [Victory Over Japan Day]" (Bartlett, 2017, p. 68). Many people across the country could hear church bells ringing, horns honking, and cheering people on the street. Later schoolchildren sent thank you letters to Salk and universities vied to present Salk with honorary degrees.

A Gallup Poll conducted in May 1954 found that more Americans were familiar with the field trials of Salk's polio vaccine than the full name of the 34th U.S. President David Dwight Eisenhower (Brandt, 1978; Carter, 1966; Oshinsky, 2005). It is important to note that people could have been confused by President Eisenhower's nickname "Ike." (*Note: The authors were not able to verify this result from this poll*). However, George Gallup reported in *Public Opinion News Service* on May 28, 1954, that 90% of persons questioned by Gallup reporters answered Yes to the question: "*Have you heard or read anything about the new vaccine to keep people from getting polio?*" (Gallup, 1954, para. 6). The same population were split (roughly 50/50) as to whether the vaccine will work (Gallup, 1954, para. 9).

Communication and programming

Nationwide vaccinations at U.S. public schools

After the Salk vaccine was determined to be effective in preventing paralytic polio, the U.S. rolled out a nationwide mandatory vaccination schedule for children in public schools beginning in 1956. Although the launch of the approved vaccine experienced glitches and criticism, multiple players from public health officials and K12 educators communicated positive messages on polio eradication to the public, particularly to parents, while schools began giving children vaccinations. The most tragic incident happened in April 1955 during the vaccine production, which created doubt for people unsure of the vaccine. Cutter Laboratories in California produced faulty batches that resulted in infecting 220,000 people, of which 70,000 experienced muscle weakness, 164 were paralyzed, and 10 died—and brought about new stringent federal regulations of vaccine production (Offit, 2005).

Stephen E. Mawdsley (2024), a historian of American medicine and vaccinations, explained the challenges of polio education:

> Perceptions of the polio vaccine, for example, were marred by prior research failures, scientific debates, manufacturing problems, sensationalist media coverage, and various social and cultural factors. Salk and the NFIP played a crucial role in defending and advancing the vaccine program, which led to a marked reduction in polio after April 1955.
>
> *(para. 15)*

The NFIP public relations team undertook the following tactics:

- Writing and distributing news releases with images, such as of children being vaccinated at their schools.
- Setting up interviews with Salk as the primary spokesperson with the media and presentations at conferences within the medical community.
- Discussing the vaccine benefits with health care professions to combat misinformation.
- Producing short educational films to be shown at movie theaters, such as *Unconditional Surrender,* that now can be viewed on YouTube, to extol vaccine benefits.
- Designing buttons with the message, "Get Salk Shots Now."
- Arranging focus groups to probe why people were experiencing vaccine hesitancy and grassroots activism (Mawdsley, 2024).

In addition, President David Eisenhower signed *An Act to extend through June 30, 1957, the duration of the Poliomyelitis Vaccination Assistance Act of 1955* (S. Res. 2990, 1955–1956) for mass vaccine distribution, thereby providing federal grants for states to buy the new vaccine and coordinate and host vaccinations for people under 20 and pregnant women (Anderson, 1955).

The burgeoning stardom of Elvis Presley also played a role in convincing youth, particularly teenagers, to get vaccinated for polio. After Presley's hit song, *Heartbreak Hotel*, the singer made his TV debut in 1956 on the *Ed Sullivan Show*, which was one of the most successful variety shows of the time; 60 million people tuned in, roughly 83% of the U.S. TV viewing audience (History.com Editors, 2019). Before Presley went on stage, photographers captured him getting an injection of the Salk vaccine (Anyiam-Osigwe, 2021). Presley also posed for pictures with Joanne Kelly (nee Wilson), one of the poster children of the March of Dimes, who made TV appearances and was photographed with many celebrities (Patterson, 2007). See Figure 3.4 of Kelly on a poster.

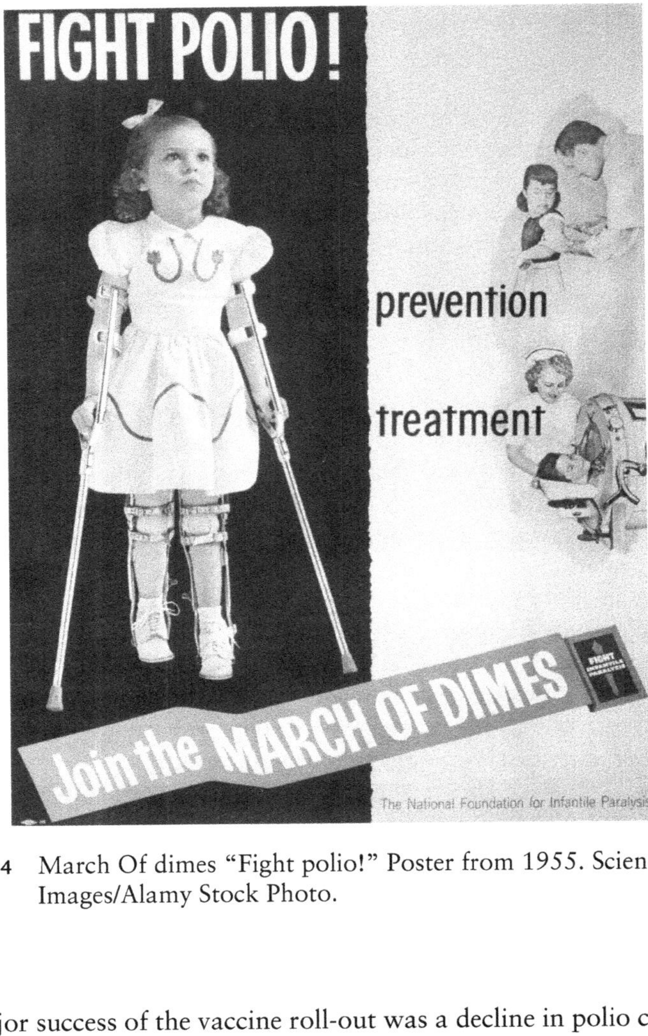

FIGURE 3.4 March Of dimes "Fight polio!" Poster from 1955. Science history Images/Alamy Stock Photo.

Results

The major success of the vaccine roll-out was a decline in polio cases. The death toll from polio plunged from over 15,000 cases per year in the early 1950s to under 100 cases annually in the 1960s and under 10 in the 1970s (National Foundation for Infectious Diseases, n.d.).

The Salk injected polio vaccine was eclipsed by Sabin's oral vaccine when it was approved in 1961. The American Medical Association (AMA) endorsed the oral vaccine in the U.S. since it was easier to administer, store, and ship (American Medical Association, 1961) President John F. Kennedy signed a Vaccine Assistance Act (H.R. Res. 10541, 1961–1962), "but his administration preferred Sabin's oral vaccine" (Halliwell, 2021, p. 168). However, Sabin's oral polio vaccine (OPV) was discontinued in the U.S. in 2000 while still being used abroad. Salk's inactivated polio vaccine (IPV), which is injected in the arm or leg, is the only one now used in the U.S. (CDC, 2024a).

Salk received extensive media exposure and kudos from President Eisenhower and Eleanor Roosevelt, among others, leading to a rise in public opinion. However, Sabin's frequent swipes against Salk damaged Salk's reputation in the scientific community; Salk was not invited to be part of the National Academy of Sciences (Brooks, 2015). In 1963, Salk set up the Salk Institute for Biological Studies in La Jolla, California, with support from the National Science Foundation and the March of Dimes (Salk Institute for Biological Studies, n.d.). Salk made lifestyle changes: he divorced his wife, married an artist who was Pablo Picasso's ex-partner and mother of three children (two with Picasso), and ditched his lab coats for turtlenecks and let his hair grow, possibly influenced by the 1960's countercultural movement. Salk then spent his last years trying to develop an AIDS vaccine and died in 1995 at age 80 without witnessing the renewed usage of his inactivated polio vaccine in the U.S. (Bartlett, 2017).

Theoretical perspectives

The two campaigns featured in this case study are central to understanding the ethics of communication during a health crisis, ethical dilemmas that can occur in public health campaigns, and ethics and morality of using humans as subjects for medical research during the 1950s.

Ethics of communication during a health crisis

From the perspective of crisis communication, five frameworks exist "as moral theories and function to describe, inform, and critique" ethical choices and behaviors: responsible communication, significant choice, the ethic of care, virtue ethics, and justice (Sellnow & Seeger, 2021, p. 272). "One of the most fundamental principles for assessing ethics is responsibility" (Sellnow & Seeger, 2021), to self and others. Being accountable is the cornerstone of the responsible communication, which is based on Max Weber's ideas of rational decisions and outcomes. Individuals are assumed to be morally obligated to "others and to ethical codes, standards and traditions" (Sellnow & Seeger, 2021, p. 278) for the sake of producing good outcomes (Guttman, 1997); "If someone freely made a choice that led to a particular consequence, then he or she is judged as responsible for the outcome" (Sellnow & Seeger, 2021, p. 278).

When applying these perspectives to a crisis, common ethical issues and questions arise when a decision is made that impacts others. A choice that violates a social norm or expectation can create risks and incite people to question "wrongdoing, intent, cause, blame, responsibility, victims, fairness and equality" (Sellnow & Seeger, 2021, p. 271). Ethical guidelines for carrying out medical decisions have evolved from the American Medical Association's *Principles of medical ethics* (1957) to include beneficence, non-maleficence, distributive justice, and autonomy (Strasser & Gallagher, 1994; Young & Wagner, 2024). Health professionals are to provide patients and research participants with informed consent, serve the patient's and participant's best interest by doing no harm and offering treatments to all who need it, and ensure that a patient and participant make decisions independently and of their own free will. Violating any of these principles can take away an individual's agency and ability to manage privacy regarding their health status (Petronio, 2002), increase their vulnerability to "sensationalism and scaremongering," (Strasser & Gallagher, 1994, p. 177), and subject individuals to manipulation and coercion (Faden, 1987).

Public health practitioners are concerned with improving the well-being of communities and minimizing threats "by maintaining a safe water supply, immunizing school children or engaging in epidemiologic research" (Kass, 2001, p. 1776). Choices such as the "need to tell patients and research subjects the truth [and] the patient's right to refuse care or research participation" made in the context of public health communication campaigns have the potential to create unintended short-term or long-term effects, outcomes, and consequences (Cho & Salmon, 2007). Cho and Salmon (2007) identified several typologies of these effects: confusion and misunderstanding, dissonance, boomerang, apprehension, desensitization, culpability, reinforcement distribution of social attitudes, and marginalization of unhealthy communities, among others.

These unintended outcomes may be mitigated with an ethical framework proposed by Kass (2001). This framework serves as an analytical tool for public health professionals to consider "ethical implications of proposed interventions, policy proposals, research initiatives and programs" (p. 1777). The tool includes questions that should be asked at the onset of a public health campaign regarding public health goals, effectiveness of the campaign to achieve the goals, any potential campaign burdens and whether they can be minimized, how fairly the campaign is implemented, and lastly, deciding "whether expected benefits justify the identified burdens" (p. 1781).

Public health campaigns and ethical dilemmas

Public health campaigns are designed to change a targeted populations' behaviors, attitudes, or beliefs about a specific health behavior, through an organized communication-based intervention (Snyder, 2007). Such campaigns are rooted in various theoretical models related to persuasion, how behaviors might change, and potential barriers; namely, theory of reasoned action, social cognitive theory, and stages of change, among others. These theoretical approaches may be used by campaign planners to craft campaign messages and develop goals for the campaign to maximize the adoption of a behavior or change in attitude (Snyder, 2007).

Public health campaigns generally follow the same guidelines as public relations campaigns in the sense that the objectives, strategies, and tactics are to be clear, specific, measurable, and evaluated. The specific mechanisms and activities used to "present complicated messages in order to increase the chance of people remembering the correct message [include] mnemonics or songs, or by selecting channels like reminder cards or refrigerator magnets ... credible spokespeople and organizations," (Snyder, 2007, p. S37) and "posters, handouts, public service announcements, discussion groups, workplace or clinic-based counseling and in-school presentations" (Snyder, 2007, p. S32) as well as the media of the time—television and radio. Additionally, two years after being formed in 1948, the Public Relations Society of America (PRSA) drafted its first code of professional ethical standards (Whitman & Guthrie, n.d.). During the 1950s, good character for a public relations professional meant "serving the public interest; avoiding conflict of interest; communicating honestly; avoiding misrepresentations to clients, employers and others," and continued professional development (Fitzpatrick, 2002, p. 90).

Within the realm of health communication, various ethical dilemmas emerge as well, especially regarding the design, implementation, and evaluation health campaigns. Guttman (1997) identifies four areas where dilemmas arise: strategy and content of messages, unexpected and negative outcomes, power and control (coercion and persuasion), and values. Guttman and Salmon (2004) further elucidate the ethical issues in public health communication interventions that can lead to guilt, fear, stigma, and knowledge gaps:

- Comprehension and literacy
- Who is responsible for informing individuals of consent
- Use of inflated data, emotional appeals, and strong visual imagery to increase motivation versus misusing or misrepresenting data to increase compliance
- Direct or indirect messages about potential risks

- Individual accountability and culpability for being healthy versus blaming individuals for not following the health intervention
- Labelling and stigmatizing individuals—"how does one reconcile the use of persuasive appeals that on the one hand scare people regarding potential hazards, and thus raise their motivation to avoid it [i.e. HIV], but on the other hand may present a negative image of those who have the disease?" [i.e., a child crippled with polio] (p. 547).

Ethics and morality of using humans in medical research during the 1950s

Dr. Jonas Salk, Dr. Albert Sabin, and NFIP were individually and collectively responsible for, and morally obligated to follow, the rules for using humans in scientific research. These public health campaigns occurred during a time when "there were no explicit, written codes of ethics for nontherapeutic human research for American civilian researchers prior to World War II" (Bateman-House, 2015, para. 4) nor government guidelines, licenses, or requirements for experimenting on humans, especially at-risk individuals (Brandt, 1978); however, operating ethical standards and responsible communication guidelines were implicit from previous polio vaccination efforts during the 1930s (Halpern, 2004), American Medical Association, and Nuremburg Code in 1947.

Halpern (2004) documented the morality and ethics of the polio vaccination efforts in 1934–1935. It was common scientific research to be conducted in colleague networks, which served as a "checks and balances" capacity by exerting pressures on its members to "conform to group norms and maintain the esteem of their colleagues [organizational sponsors]. Researchers who fail to confirm may find themselves ostracized or treated as marginal" (p. 42). At the time, the customary norms for clinical research testing included self and animal experimentation and "small-scale human testing to assess safety, followed by larger scale human trials to evaluate efficacy" (p. 49–50), and waiting to reveal results to the public before being vetted by the scientific community.

The American Medical Association in 1949 published its *Principles of medical ethics* book which outlined how a physician "assumes the obligation to conduct himself in accord with its ideals" (p. 3) such as:

- "The promise of radical cures or boasting of cures or of extraordinary skill or success is unethical" (p. 6).
- "A physician should expose, without fear or favor, incompetent or corrupt, dishonest or unethical conduct on the part of members of the profession" (p. 11), especially if there is a disagreement.

- "When an epidemic prevails, a physician must continue his labors without regard to the risk to his own health" (p. 24).
- "The ethical principles actuating and governing a group or clinic are exactly the same as those applicable to an individual" (p. 4).

The 1957 version was considerably shorter (two pages versus 36) yet contained similar standards of conduct, including when a physician should seek consultation if a case is difficult or if consultation will enhance the service.

The Nuremberg Code of 1947—Permissible Medical Experiments—was the result of a medical court case *U.S.A. vs. Karl Brandt et al.: The Doctor's Trial*, in which "twenty-three doctors and administrators accused of organizing and participating in war crimes and crimes against humanity in the form of medical experiments and medical procedures inflicted on prisoners and civilians" (Harvard Law School Library Nuremberg Trials Project, 2020, para. 1). The 10-point code provides the ethical, moral, and legal concepts that guide the justification of research experimentation on human subjects; namely, voluntary consent, results to improve society, animal experimentation, research facilities and preparations should protect participants from injury, suffering or death, "the degree of risk to be taken should never exceed that determined by the humanitarian importance of the problem to be solved by the experiment" (para 7), researchers should be scientifically qualified with knowledge of the disease, participants can withdraw from the experiment at any time, and, the scientist has the authority to end the experiment if a subject might be harmed.

The overall objective of this section on theory was to provide additional context in which these campaigns were operating. We as the authors did not want to impose an ethical judgment, but rather, we wanted readers to engage in dialog and debate regarding the choices that were made within the two interrelated campaigns.

Key words

Basil O'Connor
Cutter Laboratories
Dr. Albert Sabin
Dr. Thomas Francis
Gallup Poll
Inactive Polio Vaccine
Dr. Jonas Salk
March of Dimes
Medical Ethics
National Foundation for Infantile Paralysis (NFIP)
Oral Polio Vaccine

Polio Pioneers
Poliomyelitis Vaccine Evaluation Center
President Dwight D. Eisenhower
University of Michigan School of Public Health
VJ Day

Discussion questions

1 Has anyone in your family been diagnosed with poliomyelitis? If so, what are their recollections of being diagnosed and vaccinated?
2 What are the current debates surrounding required vaccinations for schoolchildren? Do you agree/disagree?
3 Given the success of the March of Dimes campaign and the Polio Pioneers in the 1950s, would a similar campaign be successful now? Why or why not?
4 Salk and Sabin were characterized as competitors within the medical community and criticized. What are the ethical issues surrounding the results of the trials? How would these ethical issues be resolved now?

3.4 MANDELA AND ROTARY CLUB LAUNCH "KICK POLIO OUT OF AFRICA": PAN-AFRICAN PUBLIC AWARENESS CAMPAIGN RALLIES FOOTBALL STARS AND PUBLIC AND PRIVATE SUPPORT TO ERADICATE POLIO

Situation analysis

In 1996, approximately 75,000 children each year were paralyzed by the wild polio virus in the African region. Efforts in Africa to eradicate polio were fragmented and necessitated a change to unite countries together through the Yaoundé Declaration and the launch of this Pan-African public awareness campaign "Kick Polio Out of Africa" (KPOA).

The World Health Organization-African Region (WHO-AR) and the Global Polio Eradication Initiative (GPEI) (n.d.a.) stated the campaign launched by Nelson Mandela represented "a watershed moment … [that] transformed attitudes, galvanized funding and mobilized entire governments and populations. Its impact was then, and remains today, unprecedented" (para. 1). This complex herculean effort to eradicate polio began in the 1980s and unfolded over 30 years. Achieving this goal required many strategies, campaigns, and initiatives.

The result of all these efforts averted 1.8 million wild polio cases averted, provided 9 billion oral polio vaccine doses provided, vaccinated 220 million children multiple times a year, and attracted 2 million volunteer vaccinators each year, according to WHO-AR and GPEI (n.d.b.). The next section outlines the extraordinary way that Rotary International and Nelson Mandela rallied football stars and public and private support to eradicate polio through the aims of the project, delivery of the project and the outcomes and evaluation.

Communication programming and execution

June Webber, the past district governor for Rotary International, has been actively involved with the Volunteer Service Organization arm of Rotary International for over 30 years. She is also a member of the Rotary Club of Waterfront in Cape Town, South Africa.

Dr. Chris Skinner is currently an independent public relations and communications professional. He is the former head of the Department in Public Relations at the Durban Institute of Technology in South Africa and one of the authors of the 9th edition of *Handbook of Public Relations* (Skinner et al., 2010).

Webber and Skinner published a chapter, Rotary International's Kick Polio Out of Africa Campaign, in Conrad and White's (2015) edited book *Sports-based Health Interventions: Case Studies from Around the World.* Webber and Skinner's case study provided a comprehensive summary of the aims of the project, how the project was established and implemented, and how the results were evaluated.

While the initial seed for this campaign was planted in 1996, Rotary International launched the four-month public awareness campaign, on its birthday, in the spring of 2010 in Cape Town, South Africa, where the FIFA World Cup Soccer Tournament was being held.

The goals were to increase awareness in donor countries, contribute to Rotary's Global End Polio Now efforts, while mobilizing polio-infected communities (Webber & Skinner, 2016). Other aims of the project included generating interest in other awareness events connected with the World Cup, inspiring Rotary members to host vaccination events for parents and children, and to educate the public about Rotary. Figure 3.5 shows the English-language logo of the campaign that includes the partners.

The central symbol for this campaign was a signed football that was to appear at various events in 23 countries where media would capture government and health officials endorsing the campaign and signing the ball, including Bill Gates (Synaptic Digital & Rotary International, 2010).

On February 23, 2010, retired professional goalkeeper and South African football personality, Hans Vonk, kicked the ball that had been signed by a polio victim—former Archbishop Desmond Tutu (Synaptic Digital & Rotary International, 2010).

The ball traveled throughout the continent via DHL Express, officially landing in Alexandria, Egypt, on June 12, 2010. Anyone with access to the internet and the KPOA WordPress blog (2010) could monitor the progress

FIGURE 3.5 "Kick polio out of Africa" (English) logo. Courtesy of the world health organization.

of the "ball's epic journey from country-to-country with detailed information, photos and videos," including the final event in which the ball was literally "kicked-out" of Africa (Webber & Skinner, 2016, p. 142). Additionally, other tactics included press releases, social media releases, paid placement ads starring African celebrities, parades, football games, telethons, and other special events, all featured in Webber & Skinner's 2016 chapter and on the KPOA blog.

Letoré (1998) also wrote about other strategies and tactics associated with the campaign such as radio interviews and public autograph sessions with members of the African Football Confederation, distribution of awareness posters, radio PSAs, National Immunization Days, door-to-door campaigns, establishment of surveillance procedures and labs, and others.

Results

Acclaimed as a "historic public health achievement," the wild poliovirus was eradicated from 47 African countries 24 years after the public health campaign began (Godoy, 2020, para. 1). The African Regional Commission for the Certification of Poliomyelitis Eradication declared on August 25 that the WHO African Region is certified free of wild poliovirus (King, 2020). This was one of many results of the collective efforts.

Webber and Skinner (2016) acknowledged the success of the KPOA campaign in producing unprecedented news coverage across 23 countries in which the ball appeared. This coverage in turn helped generate USD 200 million in Rotary fundraising and USD 350 million in matching contributions from the Bill & Melinda Gates Foundation. On the virtual ball blog site, 11,000 signatures were recorded in support of the campaign. Social media press releases, especially from Rotary International, received the highest record of 4,000 hits, which not only increased awareness of the organization but improved its public image.

Lastly, WHO-AR and GPEI (n.d.c.) identified "Seven Ways Polio Eradication Benefited Africa," on the Africa Kicks Out Wild Polio website. Not only had polio been certified as eradicated, but overall campaign efforts had also "contributed significantly to Africa's public health and outbreak response" (para. 2). These additional legacy results include:

- Establishment of a systematic data driven approach for polio and other disease interventions, such as COVID-19.
- Ability to reach and vaccinate children to accelerate the elimination of other diseases.
- Disease and epidemiological surveillance systems and laboratory networks for detecting and responding to any outbreak.
- Supplying Africa with skilled workers to fill the gaps in the health care system.
- Reduction of rumors and misinformation through targeted communication known as social mobilization.
- Increased capacity for outbreak response.
- Institute accountability frameworks "to ensure the timely allocation of resources and enhanced performance" (para. 25).

Theoretical frameworks

Public health in Africa

This campaign represents the difference in approach between the United States and Africa to tackling polio. Azevedo (2017) captured a theoretical framework of public health in Africa. From his perspective, public health in Africa is a complex mix of eight concepts: public versus global health, tropical medicine, health systems and culture, climates, and climate change that impact diseases, communicable versus non-communicable diseases, health disparities, globalization, and international health organizations. Azevedo's summary of these extensive and comprehensive concepts shall be pared down to the most applicable concepts related to polio eradication efforts.

The most important concept is a cultural understanding of health systems. Health systems either focus on the individual or the collective and the role of government in regulating, legislating, funding, monitoring, and protecting its citizens. African health systems are community, family, and population-based operating on the assumption that a "population-based approach is less expensive than a focus on individual disease cases and individual well-being" (Azevedo, 2017, p. 6). The role of government is also important to understand as governments vary across the different African countries. For example, the political and governmental system in Nigeria relies on communication and authority from community leaders and rulers who "have powers derived by both culture and religion … They rule through the traditional and the Islamic councils, under the supervision of the local government, having their received staff of office from the state government" (Jegede, 2007, p. 0420).

In 2003, Nigeria boycotted federal vaccination efforts due to lack of trust and rumors surrounding mass immunization efforts:

> The aggressive door-to-door mass immunizations that have slashed polio infections around the world also raise suspicions. From a Nigerian perspective, to be offered free medicine is about as unusual as a stranger's going door to door in America and handing over $100 bills. It doesn't make any sense in a country where people struggle to obtain the most basic medicines and treatments at local clinics.
>
> *(Murphy, 2004, para. 40)*

This is a specific example of an African communitarian approach to health in which the autonomy of individuals and community members are inseparable and reveals how state leaders in the Kano region of Nigeria were acting in the best interests of their people; but "unfortunately, they ended up disrupting national and global health agendas" (Jegede, 2007, p. 0420).

While this occurred in Nigeria, other countries in Africa were battling a different aspect of public health in Africa identified by Azevedo (2017)—health disparities as a result of contextual factors and infrastructural challenges unique to Africa, which requires a culture mastery to understand dynamics of health systems.

Culture Mastery

Christian Höferle, founder, president, and CEO of the Culture Mastery, LLC, defines culture mastery in his video introduction this way: "just because you are able to successfully lead, manage, and inspire people in one culture, that does not necessarily mean that you are able to do the same thing abroad in a different country, different culture, and different context" (The Culture Mastery, 2020).

Industrialized advances in virology, epidemiology, disease, vaccinations, and immunizations that worked in the United States, for example, the iron lung that relies on electricity or vaccines that needed refrigeration, would not be viable in an African country that lacked a health care infrastructure and access to public utilities. Efforts that relied on "posters, radio and television advertising to announce vaccination days … often failed to resonate in communities with low literacy or little access to media" (WHO-AR & GPEI, n.d.c., para. 14).

Scientists Salk and Sabin created two vaccines in the 1950s; however, with low vaccination rates "polio remained endemic across Africa" (WHO, 2020). Factors such as poor sanitation, war, competing ideologies, and inaccessible geographic landscapes presented logistical challenges to the GPEI. Such factors necessitated creative transportation solutions to reach remote nomadic communities. Mobile communities required mobile tactics such as helicopters, camels, motorbikes, boats, and mobile health teams traveling by foot for miles, painted messages on chimneys of brick kilns, and pop-up vaccination posts along borders and in bus and railway stations (Bartlett, 2017).

Everyone involved in eradicating polio needed to work within these conditions while considering the impact of "Africa's sheer size, cultural and linguistic diversity, and high levels of insecurity and migration," on eradication efforts (WHO-AR & GPEI, n.d.d., para 2). Additionally, involved parties needed to grasp the collective and community-based values of African culture. This is where soccer as an alternative sports metaphor for collaboration comes into play.

Soccer: Alternative sports metaphor for collaboration

The connection to sports ("football" in Africa and in most countries while called "soccer" in the U.S.)—is metaphorically significant to understanding the massive collaboration of 47 African countries in eradicating polio. As Nelson Mandela declared in his address at the launch of the campaign on August 2, 1996:

> We are calling on the continent's football players to bring their enormous influence to this campaign. Only unified efforts which galvanise whole societies towards these goals will succeed in **kicking this virus, that looks so much like a football,** [emphasis added] out of Africa and, eventually, out of the world.
>
> *(Nelson Mandela Foundation, 1996, para. 12)*

WHO's Africa Regional Director Matshidiso Moeti (2020) acknowledged the impact that Africans had as they responded to Mandela's plea and united, "setting in motion historic levels of international cooperation" to accomplish the perceived impossible (para. 5).

Using football and soccer as cultural metaphors (Two Chaps—Many Cultures, 2024), a YouTube video hosted by Christian Höferle and Brett Parry featured a segment with Michael Lehman, head of GEDIA Automotive North America. Lehman stated that football and soccer have nothing in common with each other; other than the fact that each sport uses a ball, the size and shape of the ball, the way the game is played, the actual players, and the rules that govern the game are different across and within countries.

Soccer as an alternative sports metaphor is useful for understanding organizational complexities of mobilizing individuals and organizations when applied to international cooperation (Bokeno, 2009). As a nonlinear system, soccer creates outcomes that "cannot be predicted from initial conditions along a straight or stable trajectory" (Bokeno, 2009, p. 3). As a game unfolds it becomes "chaordic," chaotic and orderly, as objectives and plans are interrupted by interferences (Bokeno, 2009, p. 3). Strategic adjustments need to be made to meet the specific challenges identified above to African countries (Mohammed et al., 2021). One such adjustment was made in communities where rumors and misinformation lead to lack of trust. The polio program developed social mobilization efforts or targeted communication strategies, such as using volunteers with a local community to "increase communities' acceptance of vaccines" (WHO-AR & GPEI, n.d.d., para. 16).

To combat the unpredictability and chaos of interruptions, collaborators also needed to check their assumptions (Bokeno, 2009). One unchallenged assumption manifested in a complication from Dr. Sabin's oral polio vaccine—reinfection. Despite immunization efforts, in places that had poor sanitation systems "fecal matter can enter the drinking water supply, and the virus is able to start spreading from person to person" (Godoy, 2020, para. 9); thus, communities became reinfected which prolonged the efforts at eradicating polio. As the virus continued to spread, collaborators needed to adapt to the changing conditions and create environmental and epidemiological surveillance to identify the virus in sewage.

Aside from soccer's nonlinear nature, the sport is holistic as there exists both a push and pull of individual agency and community/country identities (Bokeno, 2009). Unifying all 54 African countries to eradicate polio was challenging given the contextual factors above, but also because of individual countries' internal political dynamics and inability to contain polio outbreaks.

In 2003, the prevalence of polio was high in three northern states in Nigeria, which accounted for "45% of polio cases worldwide and 80% of cases reported from the African region" (Jegede, 2007, p. 0417). Political and religious leaders in these states halted immunization efforts through appeals to parents to not vaccinate their children, amid competing religious ideologies, rumors and distrust of vaccine contaminations (HIV and AIDS) and government fertility regulations (Jegede, 2007). This impasse was resolved in 2004 with the help of WHO and UNICEF—United Nation's Children Fund—and independent testing of the vaccine, and an "advocacy agenda to ensure that the right messages were delivered to the right people" (Jegede, 2007, p. 0420).

Bokeno (2009) identified that soccer as a sport is also emergent and engaged, related to player relationships and how they communicate with each other. These characteristics are helpful in understanding the success of the "Kick Polio Out of Africa" campaign, which was based on relationships of connection, stakeholder engagement (Mohammed et al., 2021), and support through communication.

Key words

African Regional Commission for the Certification of Poliomyelitis Eradication
Bill & Melinda Gates Foundation (now the Gates Foundation)
Eradication
Global Polio Eradication Initiative
KPOA
Poliomyelitis
Wild Polio
World Health Organization African Region
Yaoundé Declaration

Discussion questions

1 This chapter explores an African-centric approach to a health crisis. What aspects of culture are similar or different from a Western approach to health crises?
2 Are there other sports metaphors that could be used as a framework for understanding the "Kick Polio Out of Africa" campaign?
3 Other theoretical perspectives can be used to explain the extraordinary success of this campaign and global polio eradication efforts. What other theories can you identify?

References

Allen, S., & Thompson, R. J. (2025, January 29). *Television in the United States*. Encyclopedia Britannica. https://www.britannica.com/art/television-in-the-United-States

Altamont Enterprise. (2018, January 4). *A glimpse of Guilderland history. Three Roosevelt Birthday Balls brought swank times to Altamont in the depths of the*

Great Depression. https://altamontenterprise.com/01042018/glimpse-guilderland-history-three-roosevelt-birthday-balls-brought-swank-times-altamont

American History TV (1955, June 10). *A special report on polio*. https://www.c-span.org/program/american-history-tv/a-special-report-on-polio/585721

American Medical Association. (1957). *Principles of medical ethics*. https://babel.hathitrust.org/cgi/pt?id=ien.35558000040960&seq=3

American Medical Association. (1961, November 27–29). *Proceedings of the House of Delegates*. https://ama.nmtvault.com/jsp/PsImageViewer.jsp?doc_id=1ee24daa-2768-4bff-b792-e48599988fe94%2Fama_arch%2FHOD00001%2F00000071

American Physical Therapy Association. (2023). *1926—Franklin D. Roosevelt establishes the Georgia Warm Springs Foundation*. https://timeline.apta.org/timeline/franklin-d-roosevelt-establishes-the-georgia-warm-springs-foundation/

Anderson, O. L. (1955, October). The Polio Vaccine Assistance Act of 1955. *American Journal of Public Health*, *45*(10), 1349–1350. DOI: 10.2105/ajph.45.10.1349.

Anyiam-Osigwe, T. (2021, March 05). *A little less hesitation, a little more action—Elvis and the polio vaccine*. Vaccine Works [Digital platform hosted on Gavi]. https://www.gavi.org/vaccineswork/little-less-hesitation-little-more-action-elvis-and-polio-vaccine

Azevedo, M. J. (2017, February 1). Public health in Africa: Theoretical framework. *Historical Perspectives on the State of Health and Health Systems in Africa, 1*, 1–77. DOI: 10.1007/978-3-319-32461-6_1. PMCID: PMC7123320.

Barcousky, L. (2014, April 13). Eyewitness: 1954 Broadcaster Winchell warns of 'Killer' vaccine for polio. *Pittsburgh Post-Gazette,* A2. https://www.proquest.com/newspapers/eyewitness-1954-broadcaster-winchell-warns-killer/docview/1516126691/se-2

Bartlett, K. (2017). *The health of nations: The campaign to end Polio and eradicate epidemic diseases*. Oneworld. https://oneworld-publications.com/work/the-health-of-nations/

Bateman-House, A. (2015, June 9). Even without written codes, ethical standards for human research existed before World War II. *The Conversation*. https://theconversation.com/even-without-written-codes-ethical-standards-for-human-research-existed-before-world-war-ii-41219

Beaubien, J. (2012, October 15). Wiping out polio: How the U.S. snuffed out a killer. *NPR—All Things Considered*. [Radio recording and transcript].

Bokeno, M. (2009, June 30). An alternative sports metaphor for understanding teamwork as complex: Soccer. *Emergence: Complexity and Organization*, *11*(2), 1–7. DOI: 10.emerg/10.17357.efa1d765a1e756c6997561688fd3e9a8

Brandt, A. M. (1978). Polio, politics, publicity, and duplicity: Ethical aspects in the development of the Salk vaccine. *International Journal of Health Services*, *8*(2), 257–270. DOI: 10.2190/37T3-TDH8-GLRT-WU5W

Brooks, J. (2015, August 17). *Jonas Salk: Public hero, professional pariah*. KQED. https://www.kqed.org/stateofhealth/63035/jonas-salk-public-hero-professional-pariah

Carter, R. (1966). Breakthrough: The saga of Jonas Salk. Trident Press.

CDC. (2014, October 15). *Polio disease and poliovirus containment*. https://www.cdc.gov/poliovirus-containment/diseaseandvirus/index.html

CDC. (2024, July 9). *Polio vaccination*. https://www.cdc.gov/polio/vaccines/index.html#:~:text=Inactivated%20polio%20vaccine%20(IPV)%20is,is%20used%20in%20other%20countries

Cho, H., & Salmon, C. T. (2007). Unintended effects of health communication campaigns. *Journal of Communication*, *57*, 293–317. DOI:10.1111/j.1460-2466.2007.00344.x

Cutlip S. M. (1990). *Fundraising in the United States: Its role in American philanthropy*. Transaction Publishers.

Disabled World. (2017, November 10 - Last revised: 2025, May 22). Famous individuals who had Polio: A historical and modern list. *Disabled World (DW)*. https://www.disabledworld.com/disability/awareness/famous/polio.php

Dorfman, R. G., Orkaby, A., & Desai, S. P. (2018, Spring). Dr. Polio: Revisiting FDR's medical legacy. *Canadian Bulletin of Medical History*, *35*(1), 160–192. DOI: 10.3138/cbmh.192-122016

Dublin, T. D. (1955). 1954 poliomyelitis vaccine field trial plan, field observations, and follow- up observations. *JAMA*, *158*(14), 1258–1265. DOI:10.1001/jama.1955.02960140020003

ECDC. (2023, November 28). *Disease factsheet about poliomyelitis*. https://www.ecdc.europa.eu/en/poliomyelitis/facts

Faden, R. (1987). Ethical issues in government sponsored public health campaigns. *Health Education Quarterly*, *14*(1), 27–37.

Fairchild, A. L. (2001). The polio narratives: Dialogues with FDR. *Bulletin of the History of Medicine*, *75*, 488–534. DOI: 10.1353/bhm.2001.0115

FCC. (2023, October 17). *History of commercial radio*. https://www.fcc.gov/media/radio/history-of-commercial-radio

Fisher, M. J., & Fink, D. E. (2025, May 14). *Television*. Britannica. https://www.britannica.com/technology/television-technology

Fisher, W. (2021). *Human communication as narration: Toward a philosophy of reason, value, and action*. University of South Carolina Press.

Fitzpatrick, K. R. (2002). Evolving standards in public relations: A historical examination of PRSA's code of ethics. *Journal of Mass Media Ethics*, *17*(2), 89–110.

Foss, K. A. (2020, October 5). Remote learning isn't new: Radio instruction in the 1937 polio epidemic. *The Conversation*. https://theconversation.com/remote-learning-isnt-new-radio-instruction-in-the-1937-polio-epidemic-143797

Frank, A. W. (2013). *The wounded storyteller: Body, illness, and ethics* (2nd ed.). The University of Chicago Press.

Franklin D. Roosevelt Presidential Library and Museum. (2016a). *FDR biography*. https://www.fdrlibrary.org/fdr-biography

Franklin D. Roosevelt Presidential Library and Museum. (2016b). *FDR and Polio*. https://www.fdrlibrary.org/polio

Gallagher, H. G. (1999). *FDR's splendid deception: The moving story of Roosevelt's massive disability—and the efforts to conceal it from the public*. Vandamere Press.

Gallup, G. (1954, May 28). Public optimistic about new Salk polio vaccine. *Public Opinion News Service*. https://news.gallup.com/file/poll/320060/1954_05_29%20Public%20Optimistic%20About%20New%20Salk%20Polio%20Vaccine.pdf

Gard, S. (1954, December 10). Award ceremony speech/Nobel Prize in Physiology or Medicine 1954. *Nobel Prize*. https://www.nobelprize.org/prizes/medicine/1954/ceremony-speech/

Glass, A. (2019, April 12). *FDR dies at 63, April 12, 1945*. The FDR Foundation @ Adams House. https://fdrfoundation.org/fdr-dies-at-63-april-12-1945/

Global Polio Eradication Initiative. (n.d.a). *History of polio*. https://polioeradication.org/polio-today/history-of-polio/

Global Polio Eradication Initiative. (n.d.b.). *Who we are*. https://polioeradication.org/who-we-are/
Godoy, M. (2020, August 25). Africa declares wild polio is wiped out — Yet it persists in vaccine-derived cases. *NPR*. [Goats and Soda Blog]. https://www.npr.org/sections/goatsandsoda/2020/08/25/905884740/africa-declares-wild-polio-is-wiped-out-yet-it-persists-in-vaccine-derived-cases
Guerrini, A. (2023, January 19). Fighting through the fear: Lessons learned from the Polio Pioneers in an era of misinformation. *Distillations Magazine* [Science History Institute, Museum and Library]. https://www.sciencehistory.org/stories/magazine/fighting-through-the-fear/
Gunderman, R. (2020, November 2). How a 1920s radio broadcast changed politics forever. *Fast Company*. https://www.fastcompany.com/90570860/how-a-1920s-radio-broadcast-changed-politics-forever
Guttman, N. (1997). Ethical dilemmas in health campaigns. *Health Communication*, *9*(2), 155–190.
Guttman, N., & Salmon, T. (2004). Guilt, fear, stigma and knowledge gaps: Ethical issues in public health communication interventions. *Bioethics*, *18*(6), 531–552.
H.R. Res. 10541 — 87th Congress (1961-1962) (enacted). https://www.congress.gov/bill/87th-congress/house-bill/10541/text
Halliwell, M. (2021). *America health crisis: One hundred years of panic, planning, and politics*. University of California Press.
Halpern, S. A. (2004). *Lesser harms: The morality of risk in medical research*. University of Chicago Press.
Harvard Law School Library Nuremberg Trials Project. (2020, March). *NMT Case 1 U.S.A. v. Karl Brandt et al.: The Doctors' Trial*. https://nuremberg.law.harvard.edu/nmt_1_intro
History.com Editors. (2019, July 9). *Elvis Presley makes first appearance on the "Ed Sullivan Show."* https://www.history.com/this-day-in-history/september-9/elvis-presley-first-appearance-the-ed-sullivan-show
Jegede, A. S. (2007, March 20). What led to the Nigerian boycott of the polio vaccination campaign? *PLOS Medicine* *4*(3), 0417–0422. DOI: 10.1371/journal.pmed.0040073
Kass, N. E. (2001, November). An ethics framework for public health. *American Journal of Public Health*, *91*(11), 1776–1782.
Kick Polio out of Africa. (2010, February). *Archive for February 2010*. [WordPress blog]. https://kickpoliooutofafrica.wordpress.com/2010/02/
Kindy, D. (2024, March 13). Texas man who lived 70 years in an iron lung dies at 78: 'I never gave up.' *Smithsonian Magazine*. https://www.smithsonianmag.com/smart-news/texas-man-who-lived-70-years-iron-lung-dies-78-never-gave-up-180979008/
King, A. (2020, September 8). Certifying the interruption of wild poliovirus transmission in the WHO African region on the turbulent journey to a polio-free world. *Health Policy*, *8*(10), e1345–1351. https://doi.org/10.1016/S2214-109X(20)30382-X
Larsen, D. (2012, January/February). March of Dimes and vaccine advocacy. *American Journal of Health Education*, *43*(1), 47–54. https://doi.org/10.1080/19325037.2012.10599217
Letoré, D. (1998). Campaign to kick polio out of Africa. *Africa Recovery*, *12*(3), 18–19.
Library of Congress. (n.d.). *American women: Resources from the moving image collections*. [Research guide]. https://guides.loc.gov/american-women-moving-image/television

Mann, L. (2017, October 14). The "Sunshine Special": The presidential cars of Franklin D. Roosevelt. *The White House Historical Association*. https://www.whitehousehistory.org/franklin-roosevelts-presidential-cars-1
March of Dimes. (2025). *Home/About us*. https://www.marchofdimes.org/about-us/mission
Mawdsley, S. E. (2024, January 9). Hesitancy against hope: Reactions to the first polio vaccine. [Blog]. *Organization of American Historians*. https://www.oah.org/process/mawdsley-hesitancy-against-hope-reactions-to-the-first-polio-vaccine/#_ftnref17
Meldrum, M. (1998)., October 31). "A calculated risk": The Salk polio vaccine field trials of 1954. *British Medical Journal*, *317*(7167), 1233–1236. https://doi.org/10.1136/bmj.317.7167.1233
Mintz, S. (n.d.). *Statistics: The American economy during the 1920s*. The Gilder Lehrman Institute of American History. https://www.gilderlehrman.org/history-resources/teaching-resource/statistics-american-economy-during-1920s
Moeti, M. (2020, August 26). Africa's triumph over wild polio shows the power of regional unity. *The Guardian*. https://www.theguardian.com/global-development/2020/aug/26/africa-triumph-over-wild-polio-shows-the-power-of-regional-unity
Mohammed, A., Tomori, O., & Nkengasong, J. N. (2021, December). Lessons learned from the elimination of poliomyelitis in Africa. *Nature Reviews. Immunology*, *21*(12), 823–828. DOI: 10.1038/s41577-021-00640-w
Murphy, J. (2004, January 4). Distrust of U.S. foils effort to stop crippling disease. *Baltimore Sun*. https://www.baltimoresun.com/2004/01/04/distrust-of-us-foils-effort-to-stop-crippling-disease/
National Foundation for Infectious Diseases. (n.d.). *Polio*. https://www.nfid.org/infectious-disease/polio/
Nelson Mandela Foundation. (1996, August 2). *Address by President Nelson Mandela at the launch of the "Kick Polio Out of Africa" Campaign*. [Speech transcript]. http://www.mandela.gov.za/mandela_speeches/1996/960802_polio.htm
Offit, P. (2005). *The Cutter incident: How America's first polio vaccine led to the growing vaccine crisis*. New Haven, CT: Yale University Press.
Orsini, D., & Martini, M. (2022, March). Albert Bruce Sabin: The man who made the Oral polio vaccine. *Emerging Infectious Diseases*, *28*(3), 743–748. DOI: 10.3201/eid2803.204699; https://www.ncbi.nlm.nih.gov/pmc/articles/PMC8888238/
Oshinsky, D. M. (2005). *Polio: An American story*. Oxford University Press.
Patterson, N. (2007). Joanne Kelly, the March of Dimes poster girl who met (and kissed) *Elvis*. *Elvis Information Network*. https://elvisinfonet.com/interview_joannekelly.html
Patterson, S. (2024, December 31). The Mile O'Dimes. *St. Charles Avenue*. https://www.myneworleans.com/the-mile-o-dimes/
PBS. (n.d.). *The development of radio*. American Experience. https://www.pbs.org/wgbh/americanexperience/features/rescue-development-radio/
Petronio, S. (2002). *Boundaries of privacy: Dialectics of disclosure*. State University of New York Press.
PRMuseum. (n.d.). *The pioneer—Carl Byoir*. https://www.prmuseum.org/pioneer-carl-byoir
Public Relations Society of America. (n.d.). *About PRSA*. https://www.prsa.org/about
Retro Report. (2016, December 12). *Transcript: Could you patent the sun?* https://retroreport.org/transcript/transcript-could-you-patent-the-sun/

Robinson, J. D., Tian, Y., & Turner, J. W. (2021). Theories of message effects. In T. L. Thompson & P. J. Schulz, (Eds.). *Health communication theory*. (pp. 200–218). Wiley Blackwell.
S. Res. 2990—84th Congress. (1954-1956). (enacted). https://www.congress.gov/bill/84th- congress/senate-bill/2990/text
Salk Institute for Biological Studies. (n.d.). *History of Salk—About Jonas Salk*. https://www.salk.edu/about/history-of-salk/jonas-salk/
Schlichting, K. C. (2001). *Grand Central terminal: Railroads, engineering, and architecture in new York City*. Johns Hopkins University Press.
Science Museum. (2018, October 14). *The iron lung*. https://www.sciencemuseum.org.uk/objects-and-stories/medicine/iron-lung#how-did-the-iron-lung-work
Seeger, M. W., & Sellnow, T. L. (2016). *Narratives of crisis—Telling stories of ruin and renewal*. Stanford University Press.
Sellnow, T. L., & Seeger, M. W. (2021). *Theorizing crisis communication* (2nd ed.). Wiley Blackwell.
Skinner, C., von Essen, L., Mersham, G., & Motau, S. (2010). *Handbook of public relations*. Oxford University Press.
Smith, J. S. (1990). *Patenting the sun: Polio and the Salk vaccine*. William Morrow & Co.
Smith, I. R. T., & Morris, J. A. (1949). *The story of 50 years in the white house mail room*. Julian Messner Inc. https://archive.org/stream/dearmrpresident000583mbp/dearmrpresident000583mbp_djvu.txt
Snyder, L. B. (2007). Health communication campaigns and their impact on behavior. *Journal of Nutritional Education and Behavior*, *39*, S32–S40. DOI: 10.1016/j.jneb.2006.09.004
Social Security Administration. (n.d.). *Social Security history*. https://www.ssa.gov/history/orghist.html
Special to THE NEW YORK TIMES. (1934, January 31). Nation honors president at 6,000 birthday dinners; he voices sincere thanks: gets 300,000 greetings 100,000 are telegrams, one is 1,280 feet long signed by 40,000. Happy for Warm Springs Roosevelt expresses gratitude for the care funds will provide to the crippled. George V sends greeting president spends his usual busy day in his office, not leaving it until 6 p.m. messages flood the White House. *New York Times (1923)*. https://www.proquest.com/newspapers/nation-honors-president-at-6-000-birthday-dinners/docview/101069123/se-2
Sterling, C. H., & Skretvedt, R. (2025, March 29). *Radio*. Britannica. https://www.britannica.com/topic/radio/The-Golden-Age-of-American-radio
Strasser, T., & Gallagher, J. (1994). The ethics of health communication. *World Health Forum*, *15*, 175–177.
Synaptic Digital & Rotary International. (2010, June 15). Video from Synaptic Digital and Rotary International: Bill Gates in Nigeria to Kick Polio out of Africa. *PRNewswire*. https://www.prnewswire.com/news-releases/video-from-synaptic-digital-and-rotary-international-bill-gates-in-nigeria-to-kick-polio-out-of-africa-96372039.htm
The Culture Mastery, LLC. (2020). *The Culture Mastery—Why we do what we do*. [Video]. https://theculturemastery.com/#about
Thompson, T. L. (2014). Narrative engagement theory. In T. L. Thompson (Ed.) *Encyclopedia of health communication*. (Vol. 3, pp. 909–911). SAGE Publications, Inc., https://doi.org/10.4135/9781483346427.n354
Thompson, T. L., & Schulz, P. J. (Eds.). (2021). *Health communication theory*. Wiley Blackwell.

TIME. (1961, January 2). *Man of the Year: THE MEN ON THE COVER: U.S. Scientists.* https://time.com/archive/6830245/man-of-the-year-the-men-on-the-cover-u-s-scientists/

Two Chaps—Many Cultures. (2024, March 24). *Using football and soccer as cultural metaphors.* [Video]. https://www.youtube.com/watch?v=kKHiBLudeKc

United States Department of Health, Education, and Welfare, CBS Television Network, DuMont Television Network, NBC Television Network, Hobby, O. C., & Scheele, L. A. (1955, June 7). *A Special Report on Polio.* [Video]. Library of Congress. https://www.loc.gov/item/2023600419/

U.S. Mint. (2025). *Dime.* https://www.usmint.gov/learn/coins-and-medals/circulating-coins/dime#:~:text=The%20obverse%20(heads)%20shows%20Roosevelt's, find%20a%20cure%20for%20polio

Ujifusa, A. (2021, October 8). Schools helped defeat polio and diphtheria with vaccine efforts. Can they do it with COVID? *EducationWeek.* https://www.edweek.org/leadership/schools-helped-defeat-polio-and-diphtheria-with-vaccine-efforts-can-they-do-it-with-covid/2021/10

University of Michigan Information and News Service. (1955, April 12). *The first press release on polio vaccine evaluation results.* https://sph.umich.edu/polio/

University of Michigan School of Public Health. (1955, April 12). *1955 Polio vaccine trial announcement.* https://sph.umich.edu/polio/

Valiunas, A. (2018). Jonas Salk, the people's scientist. *The New Atlantis, 56,* 99–128. http://www.jstor.org/stable/26498248

Walker, T. (1953). *Roosevelt and the warm Springs story.* A. A. Wynn, Inc.

Webber, J., & Skinner, C. (2016). Rotary International's kick polio out of Africa campaign. In D. Conrad and A. White (Eds.), *Sports-based health interventions: Case studies from around the world,* (pp. 139–150). Springer. DOI: 10.1007/978-1-4614-5996-5_10

Whitman, B. J., & Guthrie, J. (n.d.). *PRSA & ethics: A history of our commitment to integrity and education.* https://www.prsa.org/docs/default-source/about/ethics/beps_handbook_2018.pdf

WHO. (2020, August 26). *History of polio and certification of wild poliovirus eradication.* [Video]. https://www.youtube.com/watch?v=SkSdFnzjNPs

WHO. (2025, April 2). *Poliomyelitis.* https://www.who.int/news-room/fact-sheets/detail/poliomyelitis

WHO-AR. (2020, August 25). *Africa kicks out wild polio virus, August 2020.* [Video]. https://www.youtube.com/watch?v=H4x59iskLM0

WHO-AR & GPEI. (n.d.a.). *Mandela: The leader who helped kick wild polio out of Africa.* https://www.africakicksoutwildpolio.com/mandela-the-leader-who-helped-kick-wild-polio-out-of-africa/

WHO-AR & GPEI. (n.d.b.). *Africa kicks out wild polio.* https://www.africakicksoutwildpolio.com/

WHO-AR & GPEI. (n.d.c.). *Seven ways polio eradication benefited Africa.* https://www.africakicksoutwildpolio.com/the-legacy-of-polio-eradication-in-africa/

WHO-AR & GPEI. (n.d.d.). *Immunization: How the Polio Programme reached every last child in the African region.* https://www.africakicksoutwildpolio.com/immunization-how-the-polio-programme-reached-every-last-child-in-the-african-region/

Wilson, D. J. (1998). A crippling fear: Experiencing polio in the era of FDR. *Bulletin of the History of Medicine,* 72(3), 464–495. https://dx.doi.org/10.1353/bhm.1998.0163.

Winchell, W. (1937, January). "Your New York correspondent." *The President's Birthday Magazine*. https://repository.tcu.edu/entities/publication/837091f1-be8c-4d4b-a9c4-bc38591ac350
Yamasaki, J. (2021). When theory and method intertwine. In T. L. Thompson & P. J. Schulz, (Eds.). *Health communication theory*. (pp. 42–63). Wiley Blackwell
Young, M., & Wagner, A. (2024, May 7). *Medical ethics*. National Library of Medicine [StatPearls Internet]. https://www.ncbi.nlm.nih.gov/books/NBK535361/

4

CASE STUDIES ON THE H2N2 "ASIAN FLU" PANDEMIC, 1957–1958, AND H3N2 "HONG KONG FLU" PANDEMIC, 1968–1969

4.1 INTRODUCTION

The H2N2 and H3N2 influenza pandemic in context

After the 1918 influenza, two other influenza pandemics occurred in the 20th century, the H2N2 (also called the "Asian flu" and hereafter used) from 1957 to 1958 and the H3N2 (also known as the "Hong Kong flu" and hereafter used) from 1968 to 1969 (WHO, 2024). Both pandemics were attributed to a new lethal strain caused from the genes of bird and animal flu strains mixing with human flu viruses. In addition, the way people travel shifted from rail and ocean liners to airlines, thereby spreading illnesses faster. Air travel eclipsed trains for the first time in 1955 for U.S. travelers, and airlines superseded ocean cruises as the most popular way to cross the Atlantic Ocean in 1957 (Smithsonian, n.d.).

The Asian flu apparently began in China and expanded throughout Asia and to other parts of the world due to the increase of air travel and infected soldiers returning home from the Vietnam War (1955–1975) (Saunders-Hastings & Krewski, 2016). The flu spread around the globe rapidly in 1957; it emerged in southern China and was first recorded in Singapore in the winter, followed by Hong Kong in the spring, U.S. coastal cities in the summer, and the U.K in the fall. The second phase occurred in 1958. The Asian flu left approximately 1.1 million people dead worldwide and 116,000 in the U.S. (CDC, 2019).

Descending from the Asian flu strain, the Hong Kong flu originated in China or Hong Kong in July 1968 and spread rapidly across Southeast

DOI: 10.4324/9781003434382-4

Asia, then south to Australia and over to Africa, north to Europe and south to South America. A cruise ship illustrated how easily the Hong Kong flu spread. The SS President Cleveland concluded its 18-days trans-Atlantic cruise in San Francisco after 96 of its passengers and crew were stricken with the Hong Kong flu (Special to The New York Times, 1957). U.S. Marine troops serving in the Vietnam War also brought this influenza to the U.S. when they arrived back home in fall 1968 (Tognotti, 2013). According to WHO (2024), "the H3N2 virus is still in circulation today as one of the viruses causing seasonal flu" (para. 5).

A few well-known survivors of the Asian flu included Brazilian President Juscelino Kubitschek, Italian opera singer Maria Callas, and Swedish American actor Ingrid Bergman (Kelly, 2020). CIA Director Allen Dulles and American actor Tallulah Bankhead both died from the Hong Kong flu (Peckham, 2020).

An estimated one million people died worldwide, including 100,000 people in the U.S., from the Hong Kong flu (CDC, 2019). The Hong Kong flu could have spread into outer space. In December 1968, President Lyndon B. Johnson greeted and congratulated the three astronauts before their Apollo 8 mission. No one knew and not even the president himself that he was infected with the Hong Kong influenza. Before the three astronauts boarded the spaceship as the first crewed ship to orbit the moon, they all were vaccinated to prevent the influenza. While in orbit, Colonel Frank Borman came down with the flu that was attributed widely to the Hong Kong flu—and debated to be "space adaptation syndrome" (Peckham, 2020, p. 451).

Back on earth, President Lyndon B. Johnson was hospitalized for the Hong Kong flu as Vice President Hubert Humphrey remained in bed with the same illness. Former President Harry S. Truman at 84 years old was hospitalized for the influenza the following year (Peckham, 2020).

Transmission and symptoms

The contagious airborne Asian flu usually lasted two days to a week after bed rest. Common symptoms were wobbly legs and chills that progressed to sores throats and coughs and later to aches and fevers. Children tended to get headaches, and boys usually experienced nose bleeding. More serious cases were exacerbated by people with pre-existing conditions, such as bronchitis, pneumonia, and cardiovascular disease (Jackson, 2009). People under 65 were the most susceptible since they had no immunity to this flu strain (Saunders-Hastings & Krewski, 2016).

The Hong Kong flu was highly contagious and transmitted by infected people spreading droplets from close contact, particularly when coughing or sneezing. Another way to catch the influenza was to touch an infected surface and then one's mouth (Kolhatkar, 2023). It typically lasted four to six days or about two weeks. Patients experienced upper respiratory flu symptoms, such as coughs, chills, fevers, muscle aches, nausea, and fatigue (Stanley, 2020). Adults 65 and older were the most vulnerable (Jester et al., 2020).

Treatments and preventive measures

Unlike the 1918–1919 influenza, both the Asian and Hong Kong flus were less severe, and the public in Western countries had access to antimicrobial medications and vaccinations (Tognotti, 2013). Preventive measures were limited; some countries closed public locations and stopped public events. During the Hong Kong influenza in the U.S., all 50 states experience elevated absenteeism in schools while some schools and universities closed in 23 states; 31 states also reported high industrial absenteeism (Sharrar, 1969). See Figure 4.1 of an ad for Musterole, dramatizing the need for a quick "Asian" flu remedy.

Widely used communication tools

Television became a popular and new communication tool during these pandemics. In 1950, the U.S. census added a question about television ownership for the first time and reported that 5 million U.S. households owned a television set. According to the U.S. Census Bureau (2023a), television usage soared over the next decade with over 46 million households (out of a total of 53 million households) having at least one television set in 1960. In fact, American households had more television sets than cars, telephones, washing machines, and air conditioners in 1960.

Looking at how presidents were presented on television illustrates its early evolution and increasing capabilities. FDR appeared on a prerecorded broadcast, becoming the first U.S. president seen on television at the opening ceremony of the 1939 New York World's Fair, which aired the segment at television sets up at the fair and around New York City. The first televised news conference from the White House was broadcast in October 1947 when President Harry S. Truman appealed to Americans to ration food for post-WWII Europe. Truman was the first president to have his inauguration aired on television nationwide in 1949. President Dwight D. Eisenhower also had two televised firsts: he welcomed camera crews to record his news conference from the White House in 1955 and was seen on a recorded color televised broadcast in 1958. Three years later, President John F. Kennedy held the first live

FIGURE 4.1 1950s Musterole ad. Shawshots/Alamy Stock Photos.

televised broadcast of his news conference at the White House (U.S. Census Bureau, 2023a).

Although television eclipsed radio as a major source of entertainment and news, radio adapted its programming to local information and music with disc jockeys, including "Top 40" countdowns and debuts of new talent, in the 1950s. Listeners no longer had to be at home or in their cars to listen to the radio when the invention of transistor radios made radio portable in 1954 (Digital Public Library of America, n.d.).

The estimated circulation of weekday print U.S. newspapers in circulation was 57.4 million in 1958 and 58.3 million in 1959; and increased during H3N2 with 62.5 million in 1968 and 62 million in 1969. To put these numbers into perspective, the estimated circulation of weekday print and digital U.S. newspapers in 2021 was 22.7 million (Pew Research Center, 2023).

Magazines thrived with the rise of special-interest publications in the 1950s and 1960s that contained original content, making them noncompetitive with television programming and advertising dollars at the time. The post-WWII economic boom resulted in greater wealth, a boom in college enrollment, and consumer interest in leisure and recreation. Special-interest magazines catered to the growing middle class and rising affluent and leisurely lifestyles (Abrahamson, 1992). A variety of new magazine titles emerged in the 1950s and 1960s: *Golf Digest* (1950), *Mad Magazine* (1952), *Sports Illustrated* (1954), *Bon Appétit* (1956), *Surfing World* (1962), *Cycle World* (1962), *Tennis* (1965), *Boating* (1966), and *Rolling Stone* (1967).

Impact

Major developments included the establishment of large-scale health organizations with extensive surveillance capabilities and databases. The World Health Organization (WHO), a United Nations agency, was founded in 1948 and the Communicable Disease Center (now called the Centers for Disease Control and Prevention or CDC) in 1946 (Saunders-Hastings & Krewski, 2016). WHO became the "first-ever global disease-tracking service" (WHO, n.d.a., para. 3) of epidemics, pandemics, and diseases around the world, using telex as the primary communication tool when it was launched. WHO also set up the Worldwide Influenza Centre in London in 1948, at the National Institute for Medical Research, which now is part of The Francis Crick Institute (WHO, n.d.b.).

Based in Atlanta, Georgia, CDC became a new division of the Bureau of State Services of the U.S. Public Health Service, with an initial mandate to stop the spread of malaria in the U.S. (CDC, 2023), and it has grown to become the leading public health resource in the U.S. that cooperates with the WHO. In 1952, WHO launched the Global Influenza Surveillance and Response System to keep track of influenzas and vaccines and to conduct research. CDC has overseen the WHO Collaborating Centre for Surveillance, Epidemiology, and Control of Influenza since 1956 as the "largest global resource and reference center supporting public health interventions to control and prevent pandemic and seasonal influenza" (CDC, 2024, para. 2).

With the two Asian-originated influenzas coinciding with China's Communist regime under Chairman Mao and the Vietnam War, public and media sentiment in the U.S. expressed xenophobia with racial and political commentary against Asians. A poster (Figure 4.2) created by an American

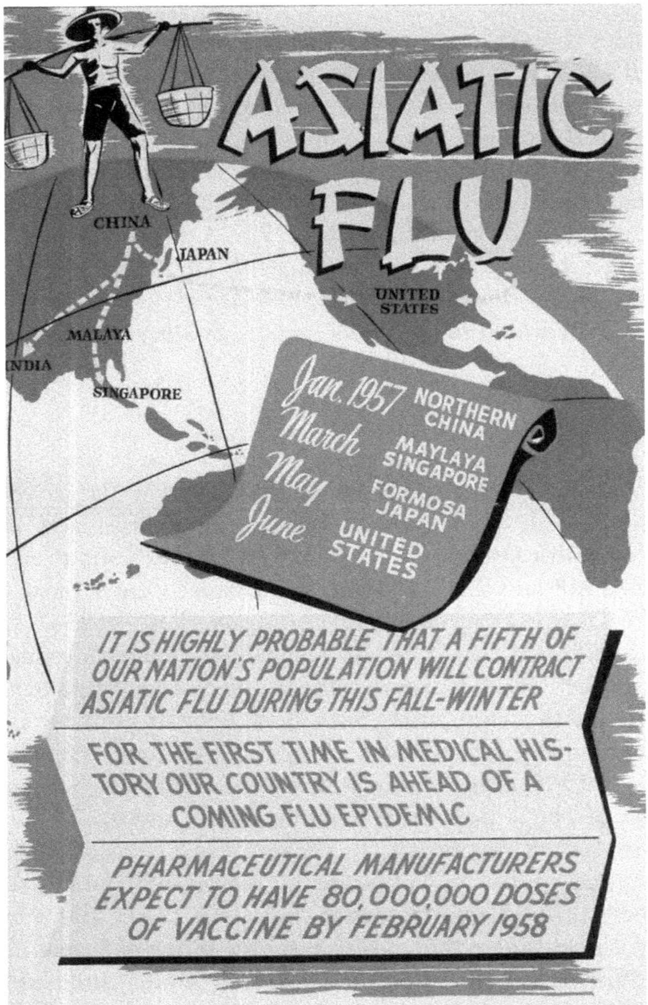

FIGURE 4.2 1957 influenza vaccine poster created by Frank Pinchak during the Asian flu. Contains racially stereotyped depictions of that time. Courtesy of the David J. Sencer CDC Museum.

pharmacist on the Asian flu in 1957 depicts a "racially stereotyped depiction of an Asian man stepping out from East Asia" (CDC Museum, 2025).

A billboard from 1968 shown in the CDC's digital museum stated, "Hong Kong Flu is UnAmerican! Catch something made in the U.S.A." (Bettman, 1968), and tabloids called it the "Mao Flu" (Honigsbaum, 2020), thereby illustrating the political sentiment of the time.

Historians refer to the Hong Kong flu as "the forgotten pandemic" (Honigsbaum, 2020) since the 1960s is remembered primarily for significant events: space exploration with the first moon landing; the Vietnam War and the U.S. draft; the Cold War with the Cuban Missile Crisis and the formation of the Berlin Wall; nuclear bomb fears; assassinations of John Fitzgerald Kennedy, Robert Francis Kennedy, and Martin Luther King Jr.; the Stonewall Uprising in New York City that sparked the gay rights movement; the civil rights movement for equal rights for African Americans; Woodstock, the rock music festival; and social unrest from the conservative 1950s to the more liberal 1960s. Some Americans were paranoid during the Cold War with fears of a nuclear war. For example, then Surgeon General Leroy Burney was asked if the new flu was the result of nuclear device testing in the Pacific region and if Communists were responsible for planting the virus, and replied no (Kelly, 2020).

4.2 U.S. PUBLIC HEALTH SERVICE AND OTHERS EDUCATE THE PUBLIC AND ENCOURAGE VACCINATIONS TO PREVENT INFLUENZAS: USING GROWTH OF TV FOR PUBLIC HEALTH MESSAGES

Situation analysis

In April 1957, Dr. Maurice Hilleman, chief of respiratory diseases at the Walter Reed Army Institute of Research based in Washington, D.C., was struck by reading a *New York Times* article about an epidemic in Hong Kong affecting infants—"cases that had escaped detection from the worldwide influenza surveillance systems" (Altman, 2005, para. 19). He realized that a pandemic was spreading and heading to the U.S: he was referring to the Asian flu (Streck-Havill, 2022).

Hilleman quickly acted by researching the virus, obtaining virus samples from Hong Kong, sending the samples to six U.S. pharmaceutical firms to develop the new vaccines, and issuing a news release from Walter Reed on the flu reaching the U.S. in September 1957. Vaccine manufacturers had produced flu vaccines earlier in the 1940s, which enabled them to work faster on developing the new flu vaccine. Hilleman also avoided the traditional channels of regulatory agencies to expedite the process (Little, 2020).

Ironically, another health expert connected the dots on a new outbreak from reading a newspaper article. In July 1968, the *Times of London* ran a story about a respiratory disease spreading in southeastern China. Charles Cockburn, an epidemiologist and chief medical officer for virus diseases at WHO, quickly understood the significance of the article. He was able to secure virus samples from a WHO representative in Hong Kong for testing at the Worldwide Influenza Centre in London, which announced the possibility of a new pandemic (Dehner, 2012). In the U.S., pharmaceutical labs began researching and testing a new vaccine to combat the Hong Kong flu while the CDC announced the vaccine's availability in late November 1968 (Blakely, 2001).

The USPHS, AMA, CDC, and other organizations educated the public about the Asian and Hong Kong flus and encouraged vaccinations. Some used the talent of the Ad Council for public service announcements. USPHS originated from the Marine Hospital Service, the first public health agency in the U.S. founded in 1798, which after a few name changes eventually became USPHS in 1912 (CDC, 2021). Today, it is part of the U.S. Department of Health and Human Services. Founded in 1847, AMA remains the largest association of U.S. medical professionals, societies, and stakeholders with its mission: "to promote the art and science of medicine and the betterment of public health" (AMA, 2025, para. 1).

Since the Ad Council was formed in 1942, it has played a significant role in WWII ad campaigns ("Buy War Bonds") to its longest-running advertising campaign, Smokey Bear, the iconic mascot fighting forest fires that is still commissioned by the U.S. Forest Service. The mission of the Ad Council "is to convene the best storytellers to educate, unite and uplift. By opening hearts and inspiring action, together we accelerate change" (Ad Council, 2025, para. 1) by creating public service announcements as part of social impact campaigns for nonprofits, nongovernmental organizations, and governmental departments.

Television became a new tool for communicators particularly during the Asian flu pandemic and the subsequent Hong Kong flu. According to the U.S. Census Bureau (2023a), television set ownership soared from 9% of American households in 1950 to 65% in 1960 and from 93% in 1965 to 95% in 1970. Another major change was the first mass-produced color television set manufactured by the Radio Corporation of America (RCA) in 1954 (RCA, n.d.). CBS aired the first televised color movie of *The Wizard of Oz* in 1956 when American households owned about 50,000 color television sets. Price was an issue when a 15-inch color television set retailed for over USD 1,000 (an equivalent of USD 32,000 in 2025). In 1960, American households had about 300,000 color televisions by 1960 and 20.9 million by 1970 (U.S. Census Bureau, 2023b).

Communication

This section focuses on the campaign undertaken in the U.S. for the Asian flu as more content was available on its communication activities. It concludes with the major similarities and differences between public communication of the Hong Kong and Asian flus.

The primary goal was public health education with two objectives: 1) to make the U.S. public aware of the Asian flu; and 2) and to encourage people to receive the new vaccine. Another secondary goal was to encourage cooperation with the private and public sectors on a global, national, state, and local level to share information. USPHS received a budget of USD 110,000 (approximately USD 1.25 million in 2025) for public health information and education (Hunter, 1958).

USPHS created 15 mailings of 14 radio, and four television and five newspaper PSAs for distribution to local public health and information officials across the country and to U.S. territories for easy adaptation and use in their local media. Another kit of print and broadcast PSAs was produced, on behalf of USPHS and AMA, by the Ad Council under the direction of Young & Rubicam, an advertising agency formed in 1923 that was acquired by WPP plc, a British advertising company, in 2000 (The Museum of Advertising, 2024). Television PSAs starred Edward R. Murrow, John Daly, and Dave Garroway, well-known broadcast journalists of the time, as narrators (Hunter, 1958).

Media relations was an important tactic to gain coverage in print and broadcast outlets widely read, seen, and heard by Americans. USPHS held news conferences, distributed news releases (more than once weekly between early June and December), and contacted journalists to pitch and develop stories (Hunter, 1958).

The increasing popularity of television played an important role in reaching the public with made-for-TV films, PSAs, and interviews with medical spokespeople on news programs. Here are a few examples:

- *The Silent Invader* (Coleman et al., 1957) was a 30-minute public service film for television produced by Westinghouse Broadcasting in Pittsburgh in collaboration with the AMA, USPHS, and the University of Pittsburgh in July 1957. The host, Dr. Carl Ide, made the following statement after a brief introduction from the sponsors, excerpted from the video transcription (National Library of Medicine, n.d.a.):

  > Throughout history, mankind has been forced to wage many battles in order to protect his family or nation against misfortune, disaster, or even possible extinction. Now sometimes these wars have been [pause] well they've been catastrophic. There was the

> catastrophe of 1918 when an influenza epidemic swept through our own nation as well as the entire world. Unlike the battles of nation-against-nation, or humanity against the forces of nature, when man has often had an opportunity to prepare himself, the battles against disease throughout the centuries have often found man in the unfortunate position of having to combat this enemy only after it had infiltrated his community and infected much of the population. Recently, you've become aware of a pandemic or a worldwide epidemic, which originated in the Far East and is now known as Asian influenza. Because of the alertness and efficiency of the United States Public Health Service, and the World Health Organization, a detection system similar to that of the aircraft spotting has been established throughout the world and has enabled us to recognize and follow the progress of Asian influenza as it circles the globe. Health authorities expect an outbreak this fall and winter in the United States. But not in such portions as in the 1918 epidemic.
>
> *(para. 2)*

The host then interviewed the following speakers in health, government, and medicine on their knowledge to provide the facts and medical advice to the public about the Asian flu: 1) Surgeon general Leroy Burney of the USPHS; 2) Associate dean of the University of Pittsburgh Graduate School of Public Health; 3) Associate director in charge of Research of the National Institute of Allergy and Infectious Diseases, USPHS; and 4) Secretary and general manager of the American Medical Association.

- *Asian Flu* (Poole et al., 1957), a 30-minute educational film for television, was filmed at WJZ TV in Baltimore, Maryland, for the ABC Television Network (Johns Hopkins File 7—Sheridan Library Collection at Johns Hopkins University) in November 1957. The lead spokesperson was the chief of the Division of Epidemiology and Communicable Diseases at the Maryland Department of Health, who discussed the vaccination program, the creator of the new vaccine for the Asian flu, characteristics of outbreaks, how virus strains are studied, preventive measures, and symptoms and treatments (Parsons, 2006).
- *Asian Influence Vaccination*, (CDC & USPHS, 1957) is the title of a series of four short PSAs for television to encourage families and workers to get vaccinated in 1957 (National Library of Medicine, n.d.b.).

The film, *Asian Flu*, served as "a virtual time capsule with its firsthand perspective of that pandemic" (Parsons, 2006, para. 4), which applies to all early public health television broadcasts. These films also illustrated the visual capabilities of television at that time.

Differences and similarities of communication during Asian and Hong Kong flus in the U.S.

The public health goals were the same: to build awareness of the flu and to get vaccinated while communicating with public health groups on multiple levels. A few major differences include the following:

- **Spokespeople and news sources**—During the Asian flu, news bureau operations, including news release distribution and spokespeople for media interviews, were from the USPHS and the surgeon general based in Washington, D.C. During the Hong Kong flu, the news bureau operations moved to Atlanta, Georgia, where the CDC with scientific experts is based (Blakely, 2001).
- **Narrative discourse**—"A theme of optimism and faith in science" (Blakely, 2001, p. 203) was prevalent during the Asian flu. News coverage focused on medical and scientific advancements. Blame and racial profiling were directed toward Communist China due to the Cold War and fear of communists. During the Hong Kong flu, science still maintained its importance yet a new narrative discourse frame emerged of "complacency, not control" (Blakely, 2001, p. 206), one that accepted that science and medicine have not conquered flus and believed more research is required as part of the natural occurrence of flu viruses.
- **Vaccinations**—Vaccine priorities shifted from the armed forces, people deemed essential by local public health administrators, and then the general public during the Asian flu to a medical approach prioritizing people who would benefit the most from vaccines, such as the elderly and ones with preexisting respiratory conditions, during the Hong Kong flu (Blakely, 2001).

Results

The Asian flu public health campaign achieved its goal on public education and objectives to make the public aware of the flu and to encourage vaccinations. The Gallup Poll conducted a survey in September 1957, which revealed that 92% of Americans were aware of the Asian flu, 79% knew a vaccine was available, and 65% were or wanted to get vaccinated (Hunter, 1958).

Proactive media relations led to stories in 32 national magazines and weekly news magazines plus other articles ran in trade outlets, regional and statewide publications, and medical and scientific journals. The *Journal of the American Medical Association* published 14 articles in fall 1957. *The Silent Invader*, the television program produced by Westinghouse Broadcasting. initially aired in five cities and on the University of Michigan's educational television network. Kinescope versions—the technique at that time to preserve a live broadcast before videotapes became standard—of the film footage was produced for other television networks to air the program. Near the end of fall 1957, 150 television stations in 41 states aired the film over 200 times. In addition, numerous health and medical experts were interviewed on television and radio programs (Hunter, 1958).

Vaccine availability for both the Asia and Hong Kong flus was far from successful due to time constraints and pharmaceutical production capabilities. Despite initiatives to accelerate the vaccine rollout in the U.S., the actual production only supplied 17% of the population, with 4 million dosages in August, 9 million in September, and 17 million in October when the Asian flu peaked (Henderson et al., 2009). George Dehner (2012), author of *Influenza: A Century of Science and Public Health Response*, provides an overview of the vaccine rollout and consequences:

> Ultimately, however, the vaccination campaign must be judged a failure, one that provides instructive lessons not only for the United States but for the global community. Above all else, this campaign failed because the pandemic spread far more quickly than manufacturers and others could prepare and distribute a protective vaccine. The new flu strain was not discovered until it was spreading epidemically, and by that time it was too late for 1950s technology to prepare vaccine in bulk. This problem of a speedy virus was exacerbated by a public health system both ill prepared [sic] and disinclined to undertake a large-scale vaccination campaign. The result displeased everyone involved. Members of the public could not gain access to vaccine when they needed it, public health officials were unable to protect their charges, and manufacturers were forced to absorb the cost of a large number of unsold vaccines. Although no one could know when the next influenza pandemic would occur, all parties needed to be better prepared.
>
> *(p. 90)*

During the Hong Kong flu, the first vaccines were available within 66 days, about a month faster than the Asian flu vaccine, and 5 million doses within 83 days, over a month faster than the production of the 1957 vaccine. However, the pandemic peaked in January 1969 in the U.S., leaving many vaccine doses unused (Dehner, 2012). Afterward, pharmaceutical manufacturers had to close down production while undistributed vaccines sat or were sent to countries in the Southern Hemisphere (Jester et al., 2020).

Theoretical perspective

A crisis is constitutive, meaning it is constructed in language and within social interactions. A health crisis or pandemic does not exist until someone labels it as such. In the case of the Asian flu, Dr. Maurice Hilleman stated in 1957, "This is the pandemic. It's here!" (Streck-Havill, 2022, para. 5). Similarly, Charles Cockburn and the Worldwide Influenza Centre in London announced the Hong Kong flu as another pandemic in 1968.

What accounts for the coincidence and parallel experience of sensing a crisis before it happened, ten years apart? The answer lies within the medical concept of a prodrome: "one or more symptoms that signal the impending onset of a disease or illness" (Merriam-Webster, 2025, para. 1). A prodrome in the context of a health crisis or a pandemic is a warning sign.

As medical professionals and researchers, Hilleman and Cockburn were familiar with the influenza virus, its prodromes, and available vaccines as information about physical symptoms was documented from the 1918–1919 Spanish flu and in newspaper stories about the virus in Hong Kong and China. In surveying the news about the cases of influenza in Asia and identifying the high incidences of people suffering as a warning, they had "the ability to intervene and avert the onset of the disease or reduce its severity" (Sellnow & Seeger, 2013, p. 34).

The term prodrome has also been used metaphorically and theoretically by Fink (1986) to describe how crises develop in stages over time, much like diseases; the first stage of a crisis being the prodromal stage (pre), followed by acute (onset), chronic (during), and resolution (post) stages. The pre-crisis or prodromal stage is "where various levels and forms of warning" are evident and can assist individuals in managing a crisis by preparing ahead of time "communication, such as the time of the release of information or the tone and content of a press release" (Sellnow & Seeger, 2021, p. 73). Prodromes or warnings when heeded can reduce the effects of a crisis and inform the strategic actions within the acute stage, the onset of the crisis is occurring.

Crisis communication scholars and theorists also explained warnings and how people "receive information about an immediate and impending threat, how that threat is interpreted and understood, and how it may impact individual decisions and actions" (Sellnow & Seeger, 2021, p. 33). Streck-Havill (2022) documents how Hilleman received information, interpreted and labelled it, and responded:

> When Hilleman saw the New York Times article, he knew a potential pandemic was headed for the United States. He acquired a sample of the virus from U.S. Navy doctors in Japan, and he and his colleagues identified the new strain and its potentially deadly effects. He instantly began to campaign for the U.S. military and U.S. public health officials to take notice.
>
> *(para. 5)*

Little (2020) noted how Hilleman "put out press releases announcing a new flu pandemic had arrived and would reach the United States by September 1957" (para. 9).

The chronic phase of a crisis is the longest lasting as individuals experience the crisis and organizations attempt to control the spread and reduce the effects by scanning the environment for threats and risks (Sellnow & Seeger, 2021). The Asian flu began in 1957 yet resurged in 1968. Individuals and organizations were vying to improve the vaccines as new strains developed.

The last and final of Fink's stages is the resolution phase in which the crisis is mitigated as quickly as possible. Hilleman "took swift action, and even as certain elements of the U.S. government were slow to recognize the pandemic, he sent virus samples to six American-based pharmaceutical companies" to produce 40 million vaccines ... "by September 1957. Through a massive vaccination campaign, and the fast action of Hilleman, potentially millions of lives were saved in the United States" (Streck-Havill, 2022, paras. 6–7). The swift manner in which the Asian flu was handled as it spread to the U.S. in 1957 is potentially a contributing factor to this forgotten pandemic (Honigsbaum, 2020; Pinkowski, 2021).

Key words

Ad Council
American Medical Association
Centers for Disease Control and Prevention
Global Influenza Surveillance and Response System
Maurice Hilleman
Public Service Announcements (PSAs)
The Francis Crick Institute's Worldwide Influenza Centre
The Silent Invader (made-for-TV film)
United States Public Health Service
WHO Collaborating Centre for the Surveillance, Epidemiology, and Control of Influenza

Discussion questions

1 What do you think accounts for the gap in time between the 1957 Asian flu and the 1968 Hong Kong flu?
2 As mentioned in this case study, the focus of this case study was on communication campaigns in the United States, rather than on campaigns within China and Hong Kong. What are the reasons for this? What might have impacted the authors' ability to find information about communication campaigns outside the U.S?

3 What do you think would have happened if Hilleman's and Cockburn's prodromal warnings had not been heeded?
4 During this time period, televisions and special interest magazines gained popularity and were used by individuals to get information about the influenza. Would other media (newspaper, radio, etc.) would have been just as effective? Why or why not?

4.3 HEALTH COMMUNICATION CAMPAIGN COMBATS SPREAD OF H2N2 IN SINGAPORE "NO MOVEMENT OF PERSONS – NO SPREAD OF INFLUENZA" BECOMES THE SLOGAN

Situational analysis

Loh and Hsu (2024), in *Pandemics in Singapore, 1819–2022: Lessons for the Age of COVID-19* assert "Singapore's influenza epidemic in 1957 was in many ways a repeat of 1918. But what is significant is it should not have been. The historical context was vastly different" (p. 180).

Historically, Singapore has evolved over centuries. As an island south of Malaysia that was once occupied by the Japanese, it was also a British Crown Colony, a separate self-governing state, a joint member of the Federation of Malaysia, an independent Republic of Singapore (One World Nations Online, n.d.) and a tropical, globally connected city (Lee et al., 2007). As such, the geographical, political, and cultural history of Singapore has evolved as well. With each historical era also came a structure and perspective related to health care and the role of government in matters of health for how infectious diseases like influenza were surveyed, identified, documented, and handled.

Geographically, Singapore is a tropical island country and city-state. Typically, tropical places have no defined influenza seasons like non-tropical cities, and yet, are none-the-less susceptible to influenza pandemics, due to a number of environmental and climate factors (Lee et al., 2007). As Ho (2022) laments "Three times the world coughed, and Singapore caught the bug" (para. 1) that ultimately became the pandemics of 1918, 1957, and 1968. Because Singapore does not have a defined influenza season, mortality rates from influenza for each pandemic are impacted (Lee et al., 2007). For example, the estimated number of influenza deaths for the 1918 influenza pandemic varied from the official record of 844, based on available data within archived colonial records (Registry of Births and Deaths), to approximately 3,500 based on statistical analyses, peer-reviewed journals, articles, and other government documents (Lee et al., 2008). Similarly, for the 1957 outbreak "the calculated excess deaths of 680 … exceeded the 28 recorded influenza deaths (Lee et al., 2007, p. 1054).

Singapore has been a major point of "intersection for influenza transmission throughout history" (Tambyah, 2006). As a major port city, viruses have traveled to and through Singapore as large movements of people, due to advances in transportation, have been allowed in and out of the city-state via ships and aircraft, thus impacting the locals and spreading the influenza worldwide (Payne, 1958). The Asian influenza virus of 1957 is thought to have spread in this manner: Hong Kong>Singapore> Russia> to the rest of the world. Within seven months, the entire world was infected with reports of 2 million deaths worldwide (Lee et al., 2007).

From a political perspective, Singapore has been subjected to many different forms of government. In 1918, Spanish influenza struck Singapore under British colonialism during World War I. During this time in the early 20th century, Singapore was less industrialized and lacked the space and infrastructure for managing contagious diseases. The prevailing cause of the influenza was attributed to "overcrowding, poor living conditions, and lack of public hygiene" (National Center for Infectious Diseases, 2021, p. 8). Singapore experienced a similar depravation of supplies when occupied by the Japanese during World War II, between 1942 and 1945 (Loh & Hsu, 2024).

After Britain returned to Singapore in 1945, the infrastructure of the healthcare system changed as the Medical Plan of 1948 was developed to "correct the public health ills of the war" over the next 10 years (Seng & Yang, 2018, para. 6). And yet, no official influenza policy was created when an extensive tuberculosis policy was adopted during the same time.

Politically during the 1950s, Singapore witnessed the rise of the Labour Front (LF) and People's Action Party (PAP) as steps toward self-governance and decolonization. Public health programs were implemented and supported with resources and technology (Loh & Hsu, 2024) Various officials were elected, including the Minister for Health, Armand Joseph Braga. Braga and other officials would ultimately respond to the 1957 pandemic (Loh & Hsu, 2024).

One other significant contextual factor in Singapore's history, and within the influenza pandemic of 1957, is culture and the influence it has on "definitions of disease and of disease in the creation of culture, and the role of the state in defining and responding to disease" (Rosenberg, 1989, p. 14). Culture is also an important context for understanding health communication theories that inform communication programming and execution of health campaigns (Ho & Sharf, 2021).

Communication programming and execution

Zhao (2020) discusses the important contributions of health communication campaigns in global public health and identifies general approaches and tasks. The general approach to health communication campaigns has been contextualized in educational interventions and/or social marketing programs. "Some educational interventions are carried out entirely in clinical or institutional settings without necessarily engaging in mass-reaching media" (p. S11), while social marketing focuses on incentives for changing health behaviors.

Additionally, Zhao notes that while health communication campaigns can support educational or social marketing initiatives, "not all health education and social marketing programs include communication campaign activities" (p. S12). Nonetheless, Zhao identifies broad tasks within health communication campaigns, similar to public relations campaigns: (1) objectives need to be identified, (2) messages need to be developed and delivered through channels to targeted audiences, and (3) the campaign needs to be evaluated.

Using Zhao's insights as a guide as well as the situational analysis help to frame the analysis provided here. Additionally, information was sourced from several documents, with facts and opinions, from the time period including available reports from Singaporean government archival documents, peer-reviewed academic articles and reports within medical journals, symposia and papers within published proceedings, historical and current books related to the influenza, and historical newspaper articles from *The Straits Times*. All documents were published in English.

Approach

The general approach for this health communication campaign was an educational intervention.

According to Tambyah (2006), "Singapore's medical and scientific leadership have always felt the responsibility to educate the community at large ... about the latest scientific and clinical developments in influenza" (p. 215). This is consistent with Zhao's (2020) observation that educational interventions can be carried out in clinical and institutional settings. Accordingly, "National and/or regional surveillance data based on probability samples are often helpful in identifying important demographic and behavioral characteristics of the targeted population" (Zhao, 2020, p. S12).

The first case of influenza in May 1957 was reported to the Health Division by a rural health officer when 30 individuals on the island Pulau Brani contracted the virus (Kanagaratnam, 1958; Marian, 2016; Singapore Parl Debates, 1957a). On May 5, according to Fearnley (2020), a telegram was sent to the WHO Influenza Centre in London exclaiming the extensive outbreak of influenza in Singapore that read "NOT NOTIFABLE DEFINITE STATISTICS UNKNOWN STOP STRAINS ISOLATED WILL FORWARD WORLD CENTRE" (p. 33).

Virologists at the University of Malaya could not identify the virus and had it sent to the World Health Organization Influenza Centre in London, where a new variant of type A was isolated, identified (typed) and named A/Singapore/1/1957, also known as the Singapore virus or Asian flu (Fearnley, 2020).

Lim et al. (1957) similarly studied an influenza outbreak on the Singapore Naval Base, from May 1 to May 20. There were approximately 18,400 workers and dependents at risk, primarily Asians, with a small percentage of Europeans (Communicable Disease Center, 1957). Lim et al. observed the symptoms, complications, and epidemiology of 298 influenza patients and revealed these results:

- "Influenza is not notifiable in the island and no reliable figures for overall incidence could be obtained" (p. 791)
- The outbreak spread from work to the family.
- Different ethnic groups (Chinese—80%, Indian, Malaysian, Indonesian) had higher attack rates (29%) than Europeans (6%), and workers of higher socio-economic class had fewer attack rates than lower socio-economic class workers.
- The virus strain at the Naval base was the same as the one Dr. Lim Kok Ann isolated at the University of Malaya and that was identified by the World Influenza Centre as A/Singapore/1/1957, also known as the Singapore virus or Asian flu.

The information gathered from this educational approach was published and used in official reports, proceedings, and academic journal articles to explain the epidemiology, clinical features (complications, demographics and racial incidence, deaths), and preventive and administrative measures. As Tambyah (2006) notes the "work of University and Government Clinician Scientists in documenting the Asian Flu outbreak in 1957 in leading medical journals exemplifies Singapore's integrated approach to medical research involving academics, scientists, clinicians across institutions and public health professionals" (p. 214).

Objectives and messages

Objectives are determined by understanding the specific behavior change and who is likely to be affected by the change (Zhao, 2020). Message strategies are either based on content (substance) or packaging of the content, and should take into consideration systemic structural elements as well and what channels work within the system (Zhao, 2020, p. S12)

In the 1918 influenza pandemic, the objective of the government was to prevent the spread of the virus by isolating infected individuals and advising them to seek treatment, disinfecting surfaces, avoiding crowded places, closing schools, and getting fresh air. Masks were required in other countries but were not required in Singapore.

Comparatively, the objective for the 1957 health communication campaign was focused on avoiding crowded places and safeguarding children. To that end, B. R. Sreenivasan (1957) professed a slogan to be used for avoiding crowed places: "No movement of persons—no spread of Influenza" (p. 214). No specific population is specified, other than schoolchildren.

According to the annual report for 1957 from Dr. Muthiah Doraisingham, director of Medical Services, Singapore to the Minister for Health, Singapore, Mr. A. J. Braga, people were warned through press and radio to avoid crowded places and 670 schools were closed mid-May. Mr. Braga in his parliamentary statement, *Influenza Epidemic in Singapore,* delivered May 22, 1957, declared three reasons for why schools were closed: high risk for the children as they traveled to and from school, spreading influenza to others, and how to teach if teachers were infected (Singapore Parl Debates, 1957b). In total, 262,000 students were affected (Lee et al., 2008). As straightforward as these objectives were, the messaging strategies were inconsistent related to other preventive and administrative measures.

The slogan, "no movement of people," did not include the movement of people in and out of the city state as influenza "is not a disease that called for quarantine measures against international travel" (Kanagaratnam, 1958, p. 145). Quarantine measures for passengers, ships, and planes were not instituted because they were not required by law but could be requested (Lee et al., 2007; Lee et al, 2008; Ministry of Health, 1959; Payne, 1958).

Because influenza was not a notifiable disease, like smallpox and tuberculosis, notifications by practitioners were not done (Kanagaratnam, 1958; Loh & Hsu, 2024; Ministry of Health, 1959). It was perceived as a mild epidemic: "The official discourse was that of a quickly passing event that posed little danger to the population at large" (Loh & Hsu, 2024, p. 186). Administrators concluded that because of the short duration of the pandemic, and that the pandemic was dwindling, very little could be done to prevent the spread, not even wearing masks ("Flu strikes Singapore: Hong Kong ships spread disease," 1957). This was in direct contrast to media headlines, which declared it as the worst ever pandemic in Colony history and documented high numbers of influenza cases (SPH Media Limited, Co., 2020).

Results/measurements/lessons learned

As Zhao (2020) noted, evaluation of campaign outcomes is often overlooked and challenging because of size but it is necessary. Because of the nature of the preventive measures and messages, little was done to assess the campaign's efforts. Many academics have written a variety of articles, essays, and papers about the lessons learned from revisiting the three pandemics that impacted Singapore. Briefly, the three major lessons are as follows: (1) the value of science in detecting, surveilling, and understanding the epidemiology of the virus, (2) the lack of prevention and being unprepared for a short-lived pandemic, and (3) the value of foresight in creating new and improved processes to handle pandemics in the future.

Value of science

WHO established global influenza surveillance sites in 1952, which has since become the Global Influenza Surveillance Response System (GISRS). The system fosters collaboration and sharing of data among 131 member states (World Health Organization, n.d.b.). These sites helped to clarify how the 1957 and 1968 pandemic strains of influenza were transmitted and spread. According to Tambyah (2006), "the major response to the 1957 Asian flu pandemic in Singapore was scientific. Careful surveillance in the segment of the population that was accessible to Western medical care was the cornerstone of case detection" (p. 213). This epidemiological information was helpful for understanding the difference in attack rates between Europeans and Asians, as Lim et al. (1957) discovered in their study. Further participation by Singapore as an epidemic intelligence point with the WHO surveillance system assisted the city-state in preparing for SARS and COVID-19 (Tambyah, 2006).

Lack of prevention

A number of perspectives exist on why there is a perception that the British government's response lacked preventive measures and left Singapore unprepared (Loh & Hsu, 2024; Sreenivasan, 1957). The virus, detected in 30 people on Pulau Brani island, was not initially seen as a threat (Loh & Hsu, 2024). The short period of time (the month of May) in which the virus hit Singapore and then left did not allow the ability to control the outbreak (Tambyah, 2006). Confusion existed as to the origin of the virus—Hong Kong or China—as scientists tried to identify the new strain. Ultimately, it was isolated in China (Payne, 1958). Dr. A. M. Payne (1958) states in proceedings of the Royal Society of Medicine from the *Symposium on the Asian influenza epidemic, 1957* that "It is unfortunate that this information did not reach the rest of the world until the epidemic was already spreading widely. If it had, we should have had two more months in which to prepare" (p. 1009).

Improved pandemic preparedness

Sreenivasan (1957) confers in his paper published in the *Proceedings of the Alumni Association, Malaya* that:

> This pandemic found us unprepared. The medical profession should have a machinery in whereby early in an epidemic, representatives of the profession can get together in order to decide:
>
> a how best the sick can be dealt with
> b what propaganda should be done to prevent the spread of the disease
> c how best the epidemic can be studied from the epidemiological, bacteriological, and clinical points of view ... Until this happens, the existing medical associations must give thought to the creation of such a machinery (p. 215).

Additionally, others have provided further recommendations for improving pandemic preparedness in Singapore (Lee et al., 2007, 2008; Loh & Hsu, 2024; Madhav et al., 2017; Ministry of Health, 2014; National Center for Infectious Diseases; 2021; Tambyah, 2006).

Theoretical framework

According to Ho and Sharf (2021), cultural theories of health communication can provide perspective on a specific variable such as race, provide insight into a broader understanding of health as it interacts with language, healing, and values, and offer a critique of institutional structures and political ideologies. More specifically, two particular theoretical perspectives are relevant in this case study: Social Determinants of Health (SDH) and Targeting and Tailoring.

SDH approach assumes that health care is complex and inequitable and tends to focus on behavioral causes of illnesses when the focus should be on the social, cultural, and material needs of sick individuals. The Targeting and Tailoring approach is concerned with how to craft "health messages to affect behavior change in target populations," that align with their core cultural values (Ho & Sharf, 2021, p. 283).

Within this case study then, the social determinants of health are related to British colonialism and a Western approach to healthcare amid a primarily Asian country (Chinese, Malay, Indian, and Eurasian) which favored non-Western approaches to health. These social determinants created challenges in targeting and tailoring health messages and treating affected individuals.

When the 1918 influenza epidemic hit, colonial administrators and doctors recommended prophylactic measures like rest and open air, various disinfectants for personal and public use, social distancing by avoiding crowded public places, and closing schools (Lee et al., 2007). However, they had difficulty enforcing these recommendations as "colonial measures to remove people from infected areas during an epidemic and to disinfect (or destroy) unclean shophouses and personal belongings disrupted the Asian's livelihood and social security," (Loh & Hsu, 2024, p. 11), breeding distrust between colonial government and its Asian subjects.

According to Loh and Hsu (2024), in 1957 amid the political turmoil of wanting independence from British rule, "locals were willing to undertake their own interventions to keep themselves well [and] ... turned to traditional [Chinese] remedies" like "Three Legs" brand of "fever powder," Guan Jilin tea, and carrots and olives as a way of managing the effects from the influenza virus (pp. 196–197). These social determinants of health and the tailoring and targeting of health messages were also prevalent within the health communication campaign in 1957.

Key words

Epidemic
Federation of Malaysia
Global Influenza Surveillance Response System (GISRS)
Labour Front (LF)
Minister of Health
People's Action Party (PAP)
Pulau Brani
Republic of Singapore
Smallpox
Social Determinants of Health
Tuberculosis
World Health Organization Surveillance System
World Influenza Centre

Discussion questions

1 The UNESCO Courier in 1958 provided a detailed map of how the Asian influenza traveled across countries. What techniques or technologies exist today that could do the same?
2 Using Zhao's recommendations for health communication campaigns, what recommendations would you make?
3 What are some other social determinants of health during pandemics and epidemics?

References

Abrahamson, D. (1992, May). *The rise of the special -interest magazine in 'The Other 1960s': An economic and sociocultural history.* [Doctoral dissertation, New York University]. ProQuest Dissertations & Theses Global. (303994846). https://www.proquest.com/dissertations-theses/rise-special-interest-magazine-other-1960s/docview/303994846/se-2

Ad Council. (2025). *Our history.* https://www.adcouncil.org/our-story/our-history

Altman, L. K. (2005, April 12). Maurice Hilleman, master in creating vaccines, dies at 85. *The New York Times.* https://www.nytimes.com/2005/04/12/us/maurice-hilleman-master-in-creating-vaccines-dies-at-85.html

AMA. (2025). *About.* https://www.ama-assn.org/about

Bettman. (1968). *Politically motivated sign, 1968.* [Photograph]. David J. Sencer CDC Museum. [Digital Exhibit]. https://cdcmuseum.org/items/show/926

Blakely, D. E. M. (2001). *Mass mediated disease: A case study analysis of news reporting and three influenza pandemics and public health policy.* [Doctoral dissertation, University of Southern Mississippi]. ProQuest Dissertations & Theses Global. (304724605). https://www.proquest.com/dissertations-theses/mass-mediated-disease-case-study-analysis-news/docview/304724605/se-2

CDC. (2019, January 30). *Influenza historic timeline 1930 and beyond.* https://archive.cdc.gov/www_cdc_gov/flu/pandemic-resources/pandemic-timeline-1930-and-beyond.htm

CDC. (2021, July 6). *The roots of public health and CDC.* David J. Sencer CDC Museum: In association with the Smithsonian Museum. https://www.cdc.gov/museum/online/story-of-cdc/roots/index.html

CDC. (2023, April 19). *Our history-our story.* David J. Sencer CDC Museum: In association with the Smithsonian Museum. https://www.cdc.gov/museum/history/our-story.html

CDC. (2024, September 12). *CDC's World Health Organization (WHO) Collaborating Center for surveillance, epidemiology and control of Influenza.* https://www.cdc.gov/flu/php/who-collaboration/index.html

CDC Museum. (2025). *Social stigma and naming the pandemic.* David J. Sencer CDC Museum: In association with the Smithsonian Museum. [Digital Exhibition]. https://cdcmuseum.org/exhibits/show/influenza/1957-pandemic/social-stigma-naming-pandemics

Coleman, T. (Writer), Wolfe, R. (Producer), & Simon, J. (Director). (1957). *The silent invader.* [Moving image]. Westinghouse Broadcast Company. https://collections.nlm.nih.gov/catalog/nlm:nlmuid-8800017A-vid

Communicable Disease Center. (U.S.). Influenza Surveillance Unit. (1957). *CDC influenza report no. 8, August 2, 1957.* https://stacks.cdc.gov/view/cdc/205

Dehner, G. (2012). *Influenza: A century of science and public health response.* University of Pittsburgh Press.

Digital Public Library of America. (n.d.). *Golden age of radio in the US.* [Exhibition]. https://dp.la/exhibitions/radio-golden-age/experiments-and-breakthroughs/entertainment-to-go?item=668

Fearnley, L. (2020). Chapter one: The origins of pandemics. In L. Fearnley *Virulent zones: Animal disease and global health at China's pandemic epicenter.* (pp. 27–47). Duke University Press. https://muse.jhu.edu/pub/4/monograph/book/78151

Fink, S. (1986). *Crisis management: Planning for the inevitable.* American Management Association.

"Flu strikes Singapore: Hong Kong ships spread disease." (1957, May 5). *The Straits Times.* https://eresources.nlb.gov.sg/newspapers/digitised/article/straitstimes19570505-1.2.2

Henderson, D. A., Courtney, B., Inglesby, T. V., Toner, E., & Nuzzo, J. B. (2009). Public health and medical responses to the 1957-1958 influenza pandemic. *Biosecurity and Bioterrorism: Biodefense Strategy, Practice, and Science*, *7*(3), 265–273. DOI: 10.1089/bsp.2009.0729

Ho, E. Y., & Sharf, B. F. (2021). Cultural theories of health communication. In T. L. Thompson & P. J. Schulz, (Eds.). (pp. 278–299). *Health communication theory* (1st ed.). Wiley Blackwell.

Ho, O. (2022, March 20). Three times that the world coughed, and Singapore caught the bug. *The Straits Times*. https://www.straitstimes.com/singapore/three-times-that-the-world-coughed-and-singapore-caught-the-bug

Honigsbaum, M. (2020, May 25). Revisiting the 1957 and 1968 influenza pandemics. *The Lancet*, 1824–1826. DOI: https://doi.org/10.1016/S0140-6736(20)31201-0

Hunter, J. S. (1958, February). Public information and education. *Public Health Reports (1896-1970)*, *73*(2), 149–153.

Jackson, C. (2009). History lessons: The Asian flu pandemic. *The British Journal of General Practice: The Journal of the Royal College of General Practitioners*, *59*(565), 622–623. https://doi.org/10.3399/bjgp09X453882

Jester, B. J., Uyeki, T. M., & Jernigan, D. B. (2020, May). Fifty years of influenza a(H3N2) following the pandemic of 1968. *American Journal of Public Health*, *110*(5), 669–676. DOI: 10.2105/AJPH.2019.305557

Kanagaratnam, K. (1958, April-September). Influenza epidemic in Singapore, 1957. *Public Health*, *72*(1-6), 143–146. https://doi.org/10.1016/S0033-3506(58)80032-3

Kelly, J. (2020, March 17). In 1957, a new flu appeared in Asia. The world watched and waited for it to spread. *The Washington Post (Online)*. WP Company LLC d/b/a The Washington Post. https://www.proquest.com/blogs-podcasts-websites/1957-new-flu-appeared-asia-world-watched-waited/docview/2377837507/se-2?accountid=11644

Kolhatkar, S. (2023, March 10). H3N2 Influenza Virus: Symptoms, treatment and all you need to know about 'Hong Kong' Flu. *NDTV|Profit*. https://www.ndtvprofit.com/nation/pfx-h3n2-influenza-virus-symptoms-treatment-and-all-you-need-to-know-about-hong-kong-flu

Lee, V. J., Chen, M. I., Chan, S. P., Wong, C. S., Cutter, J., Goh, K. T., & Tambyah, P. A. (2007). Influenza pandemics in Singapore, a tropical, globally connected city. *Emerging Infectious Diseases*, *13*(7), 1052–1057. DOI: 10.3201/eid1307.061313.

Lee, V. J., Wong, C. S., Tambyah, P. A., Cutter, J., Chen, M. I., & Goh, K. T. (2008). Twentieth century influenza pandemics in Singapore. *Annals of the Academy of Medicine, Singapore, 37(6)*, 470–476.

Lim, K. A., Smith, A., Hale, J. H., & Glass, J. (1957). Influenza outbreak in Singapore. *The Lancet*, *270*(6999), 791–797.

Little, B. (2020, March 18). *How the 1957 flu pandemic was stopped early in its path*. https://www.history.com/articles/1957-flu-pandemic-vaccine-hilleman

Loh, K. S., & Hsu, L. Y. (2024). *Pandemics in Singapore, 1819–2022: Lessons for the age of COVID-19*. Routledge.

Madhav, N., Oppenheim, B., Gallivan, M., Mulembakani, P., Rubin, E., & Wolfe, N. (2017). Chapter 17—Pandemics: Risks, impacts and mitigation. In. D.T. Jamison, H. Gelband, Horton, S. et al. (Eds.). *Disease control priorities: Improving health and reducing poverty*, (3rd ed.), (pp. 1–39). The World Bank. DOI: 10.1596/978-1-4648-0527-1_ch17

Marian, M. J. (2016). *Fever dreams: Infectious disease, epidemic events, and the making of Hong Kong*. [Doctoral thesis, The University of Toronto]. TSpace Repository. https://tspace.library.utoronto.ca/handle/1807/89282

Merriam-Webster. (2025). *Prodrome*. https://www.merriam-webster.com/dictionary/prodrome

Ministry of Health. (1959). *Influenza epidemic. In: Report of the ministry of health for the year ended 31st December 1957*. Government Printing Office. https://wellcomecollection.org/works/rh48utbd

Ministry of Health. (2014, April). *MOH pandemic readiness and response plan for influenza and other acute respiratory diseases*. https://silo.tips/download/moh-pandemic-readiness-and-response-plan-for-influenza-and-other-acute-respirato#

National Center for Infectious Diseases. (2021). *The road to pandemic preparedness in Singapore*. https://www.ncid.sg/For-General-Public/Documents/(NCID%20Yearbook%202021)%20The%20Road%20to%20Pandemic%20Preparedness%20in%20Singapore.pdf

National Library of Medicine. (n.d.a.). *The silent invader*. [Video transcript]. collections.nlm.nih.gov/transcript/nlm:nlmuid-8800017A-vid

National Library of Medicine. (n.d.b.). *Asian influenza vaccination*. [Moving image]. https://collections.nlm.nih.gov/catalog/nlm:nlmuid-8800001A-vid

One World Nations Online. (n.d.). *History of Singapore*. https://www.nationsonline.org/oneworld/History/Singapore-history.htm

Parsons, T. (2006, *February 22). Historic television program offers unique perspective of 1957 Asian flu pandemic*. Johns Hopkins Bloomberg School of Public Health. [Web article]. https://publichealth.jhu.edu/2006/1957-asian-flu

Payne, A. M. M. (1958, May 16). Symposium of the Asian influenza epidemic, 1957. *Proceedings of the Royal Society of Medicine51*, 29–38. https://journals.sagepub.com/doi/pdf/10.1177/003591575805101205https://journals.sagepub.com/doi/pdf/10.1177/003591575805101205

Peckham, R. (2020). Viral surveillance and the 1968 Hong Kong flu pandemic. *Journal of Global History*, *15*(3), 445–458. https://doi.org/10.1017/S1740022820000224

Pew Research Center. (2023, November 10). *Newspaper fact sheet*. https://www.pewresearch.org/journalism/fact-sheet/newspapers/

Pinkowski, J. (2021, January 7). The history of the forgotten pandemic. *Yale Insights*. https://insights.som.yale.edu/insights/the-history-of-the-forgotten-pandemic

Poole, L. (Producer), Calfee, K. (Director), & Benfield, B. (Writer). (1957). *Asian flu* [Videorecording]. WJZ Television Station, Baltimore. https://catalyst.library.jhu.edu/permalink/01JHU_INST/t3c16/alma991026980149707861

RCA. (n.d.). *100 years: A visual memoir of RCA—Radio Corporation of America*. https://www.rca.com/brand/rca-legacy

Rosenberg, C. E. (1989). Disease in history: Frames and framers. *The Milbank Quarterly*, *67*(Supplement 1), 1–15. https://www.jstor.org/stable/3350182

Saunders-Hastings, P. R., & Krewski, D.. (2016, December 6). Reviewing the history of pandemic influenza: Understanding patterns of emergence and transmission. *Pathogens*, *5*(66), 1–19. https://doi.org/10.3390/pathogens5040066

Sellnow, T., & Seeger, M. W. (Eds.). (2013). *Theorizing crisis communication* (1st eds.). Wiley Blackwell.

Sellnow, T., & Seeger, M. W. (Eds.). (2021). *Theorizing crisis communication* (2nd eds.). Wiley Blackwell.

Seng, L. K., & Yang, H. L. (2018, March 24). The disease that divides and unites. *Mediacorp Today*. https://www.todayonline.com/commentary/disease-divides-and-unites

Sharrar, R. G. (1969). National influenza experience in the USA, 1968-69. *Bulletin of the World Health Organization*, *41*, 361–366. https://iris.who.int/bitstream/handle/10665/262499/PMC2427724.pdf?sequence=1

Singapore Parl Debates; Vol. 3, Sitting No 11; Col 1938; [May 22, 1957a]. https://sprs.parl.gov.sg/search/topic?reportid=022_19570522_S0004_T0015
Singapore Parl Debates; Vol. 3, Sitting No 11; Col 1931; [May 22, 1957b]. https://sprs.parl.gov.sg/search/#/topic?reportid=014_19570522_S0006_T0023
SinoBiological. (n.d.). *Asian flu (1957 Influenza Pandemic)*. https://www.sinobiological.com/research/virus/1957-influenza-pandemic-asian-flu
Smithsonian. (n.d). *The evolution of the commercial flying experience 1914-today*. [Smithsonian Digital exhibition]. National Air and Space Museum. https://airandspace.si.edu/explore/stories/evolution-commercial-flying-experience
Special to The New York Times. (1957, June 9). 96 on cruise suffered Asian flu, liner reports on reaching coast. [Archived article]. *The New York Times*, p. 28. https://timesmachine.nytimes.com/timesmachine/1957/06/10/96025600.pdf?pdf_redirect=true&ip=0
SPH Media Limited, Co. (2020, April 19). From the archives: ST's coverage of past pandemics. *The Straits Times*. https://www.straitstimes.com/singapore/from-the-archives-sts-coverage-of-past-pandemics
Sreenivasan, B. R. (1957, September). The recent influenza epidemic in Singapore. *Proceedings of the Alumni Association Malaya*, *10*(3), 211–215.
Stanley, B. (2020, September 16). The forgotten history of the 1968 'Hong Kong Flu' pandemic. *OnlineMedEd*. https://www.onlinemeded.com/blog/history-repeats-the-forgotten-story-of-the-1968-hong-kong-flu-pandemic
Streck-Havill, T. (2022, August 25). Maurice Hilleman: The man who predicted a pandemic. *The Micrograph*. [National Museum of Health and Medicine]. https://medicalmuseum.health.mil/micrograph/index.cfm/posts/2022/maurice_hilleman
Tambyah, P. A. (2006). Singapore's efforts and experiences in influenza control. In P. Tambyah & P. Leung (Eds.), *Bird flu: A rising pandemic in Asia and beyond?* (pp. 211–220). World Scientific.
The Francis Crick Institute. (n.d.). *Worldwide Influenza Centre*. https://www.crick.ac.uk/research/platforms-and-facilities/worldwide-influenza-centre
The Museum of Advertising. (2024, January 8). *100 years: Young & Rubicam*. https://www.themuseumofadvertising.org/blog/2024/1/8/100-years-young-amp-rubicam
Tognotti, E. (2013). Lessons from the history of quarantine, from plague to influenza a. *Emerging Infectious Diseases*, *19*(2), 254–259. https://doi.org/10.3201/eid1902.120312
United States Census Bureau. (2023a, September). *U.S. Census Bureau history: Philo Farnsworth and the invention of television*. https://www.census.gov/about/history/stories/monthly/2023/september-2023.html
United States Census Bureau. (2023b, August 1). *History and the Census: The Wizard of Oz*. https://www.census.gov/about/history/stories/monthly/2023/august-2023.html
WHO. (n.d.a.). *Public health milestones through the years*. https://www.who.int/campaigns/75-years-of-improving-public-health/milestones#year-1945
WHO. (n.d.b.). *Global Influenza Surveillance and Response System (GISRS)*. https://www.who.int/initiatives/global-influenza-surveillance-and-response-system
WHO. (2024, March 30). *The burden of Influenza*. https://www.who.int/news-room/feature-stories/detail/the-burden-of-influenza
Zhao, X. (2020). Health communication campaigns: A brief introduction and call for dialogue. *International Journal of Nursing Sciences*, *7I*, S11–S15. https://doi.org/10.1016/j.ijnss.2020.04.009

5

CASE STUDIES ON MEASLES OUTBREAKS SINCE MMR VACCINE IN 1971

5.1 INTRODUCTION

Measles and the MMR vaccine in context

The earliest case of measles was documented in the 9th century by a Persian doctor and scholar, and nine centuries later, a Scottish physician discovered that measles was caused by a blood infection. Cases spread in frequency since the 16th century as sea exploration and colonization increased and introduced measles to isolated, susceptible communities with no prior exposure and immunity from the infection. The Faroe Islands, Hawaii, and Fiji, for example, faced deadly measles epidemics in the 1800s (WHO, n.d.).

The WHO (n.d.) considered measles to be "one of the most contagious diseases," (para. 1) indicated by high mortality rates worldwide, with an estimated 30 million cases and 2.6 million deaths annually until vaccination campaigns were undertaken in developing countries (WHO, 2024a). Measles became widespread in the U.S., with increasing death rates in the early- to mid-20th century until a vaccine was developed in 1953 and improved in 1971 to also prevent mumps and rubella. Before the vaccine became widely available in 1963, practically every child before the age of 15 became infected with measles (CDC, 2024a). CDC (2024a) estimated that three to four million children before 1963 contracted measles in the U.S., of which 400 to 500 died, 48,000 required hospitalizations, and about 1,000 contracted encephalitis (brain swelling), annually.

DOI: 10.4324/9781003434382-5

Transmission and symptoms

Measles is easily spread: one infected person can contaminate nine out of 10 unvaccinated people by coughing and sneezing in close contact or by touching surfaces that can harbor the virus. The virus can remain active within two hours (WHO, 2024a). Flu-like symptoms happen within one to two weeks after a person is infected. Initial symptoms include a high fever, cough, runny nose, and conjunctivitis, followed by Koplik spots on the inside of one's cheeks, leading to a rash of small red spots, sometimes with bumps, breaking out over the face, neck, upper body, legs, and feet, within three to five days (CDC, 2024b). The worst cases may cause encephalitis (swelling of the brain) resulting in hearing loss, intellectual disabilities, or death by pneumonia. The most susceptible people are children under 5, adults over 20, pregnant women, and those suffering from immunocompromising conditions from other illnesses (CDC, 2024b).

Treatments and preventive measures

The MMR vaccine and other measles vaccines can prevent contagion. The MMR vaccine stands for the measles, and the mumps and rubella, which are both contagious by respiratory droplets as measles but less serious than measles. Mumps results in puffy checks and swollen jaws caused by parotitis (inflammation of the parotid glands, the salivary glands between one's ears and jaw), while some people also experience cold-like symptoms, aches, and fatigue, and others have no symptoms. Recovery usually takes two weeks. Mumps rarely results in deaths or long-term effects for adults, except for such complications as inflammation of the testicles, ovaries, breast tissue, brain, tissue covering the brain and spinal cord, or in the pancreas. Deafness is another rare complication (CDC, 2024c).

Rubella, which is also referred to as "German measles," causes a red rash on the face and spreads to most of the body for up to three days. However, about 25% to 50% of infected people may not break out in a rash but remain contagious. Other symptoms may include headaches, conjunctivitis, and flu-like symptoms about one to five days before the rash. Unvaccinated pregnant women who become infected during the early months with rubella may experience miscarriages or death of the baby, or they may pass along measles to the newborns, resulting in birth defects known as congenital rubella syndrome. Approximately 70% of women—extremely rare in men and children—may feel arthritic discomfort for about a month (CDC, 2025a)

In the U.S., all states and the District of Columbia require two dosages of the MMR vaccines for children in childcare facilities and in kindergarten to 12th grade (requirements may change.) (Immunize.org, 2024a). Vaccine legislation for exemptions varies by state. All 50 states and the District of

Columbia have legislation requiring specified vaccines for students. Medical exemptions apply to all states and DC. Nonmedical exemptions differ from state to state for religious beliefs against vaccinations or for both religious and philosophical reasons while a few states only grant exemptions for medical reasons (Immunize.org, 2024b). Not all families or guardians have welcomed required vaccinations. Case study 5.2 examines an anti-vaccination movement spurred by disputes over the side effects of the MMR vaccine.

Widely used communication tools

Print and broadcast media were the most widely used communication tools when the MMR vaccine was launched. In 1971, the U.S. newspapers had print circulations of 62.2 million weekday editions and 49.7 million Sunday editions, whereas in 2022, total U.S. daily newspaper circulation (both print and digital weekday and Sunday editions) was approximately 20.9 million (Pew Research Center, 2023). With the U.S. in a recession from 1970 to 1971, consumers were forgoing nonessential products. An estimated 750 general magazines faced financial challenges with fewer readers and advertisers, resulting in a 1.5% drop in net profits and 5% in magazine revenues, stated Stephen E. Kelly, president of the Magazine Publishers Association (cited in Costello, 1971).

According to the U.S Census Bureau (2023), 95.5% of U.S. households (68.7 million units) reported that they owned at least one television set in 1970. The Consumer Technology Association reported that radio penetration by U.S. households reached 95% in 1971 and rose to 98% in 1978, holding steady until 2013, when it dropped back to 95% in 2016 (Inside Radio, 2016).

A significant invention leading to the Information Age took place in 1971 when the first email was sent on the Arpanet by a computer engineer in Cambridge, Massachusetts, who also created the @ symbol as email address identifiers (Left, 2002). The United States Department of Defense's Advanced Research Projects Agency Network (ARPANET) was developed in the 1960s for linking computers at research universities and institutions via telecommunications—and became the forerunner to today's internet.

Impact

Public health departments in cities, regions, states, and countries, along with the support of trans-governmental organizations and nongovernmental organizations, have strived to prevent the spread of measles with vaccination campaigns. Case study 5.3 covers two measles vaccinations conducted in an U.S. state and city, while case study 5.4 examines the world's largest MR vaccination campaign conducted in Bangladesh. The MMR vaccine offers the benefits of preventing mumps and rubella within two dosages of the vaccines, usually for infants at nine months where measles is an epidemic or between 12 and 15 months elsewhere, and the second dosage later around 4 to 6 years of age (WHO, 2024a).

Refugees and people living in remote low-income areas without easy access to adequate medical care face additional challenges. The WHO has established transnational initiatives to eliminate measles and rubella within specific regional targets. Gavi, the Vaccine Alliance, has collaborated with WHO African Region to help children in Africa. Gavi's Measles and Rubella Partnership claims to have prevented approximately 57 million deaths in Africa and within other countries supported by Gavi from 2000 to 2022. Despite its efforts, approximately 107,000 people worldwide died from the measles, mostly children under 5 who were unvaccinated or without the required second dosage, in 2023. The positive news is that 83% of the world's children aged 1 or under received the first measles dosage in 2023 (WHO, 2024a).

5.2 *THE LANCET* CLAIMS MMR VACCINES CAUSE AUTISM: ANTIVAXXERS SPREAD DOUBTS THEN AND NOW AFTER RESEARCH RETRACTION

Brief background on anti-vaccination movements

Anti-vaccination movements became prominent in the 19th century when the smallpox vaccine was introduced in England. The new vaccine met with some hesitancy in England due to religious objections, distrust in science and medicine, and personal liberty (College of Physicians of Philadelphia, 2022), particularly when the Vaccination Act of 1853 required infants to be vaccinated and, later in 1867, when the mandatory age for vaccines increased to14-year-olds or face penalties (a fine or jail time). Anti-vaccination groups and journals were quickly formed to combat the new laws, eventually leading up to the Vaccination Act of 1898 that softened penalties and compulsory terms and added a "conscientious objector" clause (Wolfe & Sharp, 2002, p. 325).

In the U.S., smallpox vaccines received quieter voices of opposition and were more widely accepted by the public and political leaders such as Thomas Jefferson, the third U.S. president, and James Madison, the fourth U.S. president. Under Madison's Administration, An Act to Encourage Vaccination—"the first federal endorsement of a medical practice in American history" (Lanzarotta & Ramos, 2018, p. 741)—was legislated in 1813 to encourage vaccines and distribute free vaccines by mail (Murphey, 2025).

With inspiration from British anti-vaccination advocacy groups, the Anti-Vaccination Society of America was established in the U.S. in 1879.

Other anti-vaccination leagues followed in New York City, New England, and elsewhere with the goal to repeal vaccination laws (Wolfe & Sharp, 2002). At the beginning of the 20th century, a board of health in Massachusetts mandated all people to be vaccinated after a smallpox resurgence. A resident of Massachusetts, Pastor Henning Jacobson, refused receiving smallpox vaccination and paying the fine for noncompliance and, subsequently, filed charges for violation of state and federal constitutions. He lost the case in the local court and again in the Supreme Court in *Jacobson v. Massachusetts* (Justia U.S. Supreme Court Center, n.d.) by a 7-2 majority in 1905, which set a precedent allowing a state to protect the public health of its residents over their individual liberties, such as compulsory vaccinations during an epidemic (Mosvick, 2024).

In the 1970s, a new DTP vaccine for Diphtheria (bacterial infection of nose and throat membranes), Tetanus (bacterial infection affecting the nervous system; also called lockjaw), and Pertussis (whooping cough) sparked anti-vaccination momentum in North America, Europe, Australia, and Asia, with claims that DTP vaccines could result in infants suffering from neurological complications (College of Physicians of Philadelphia, 2022; Kulenkampff et al., 1974). The Association of Parents of Vaccine Damaged Children (APVDC) was founded in 1973 by two English mothers whose children experienced brain damage purportedly caused by the DTP vaccine (Millward, 2017). APVDC proposed financial compensation from the government for vaccine victims and, in 1979, the Vaccine Damage Payments Act 1979 began offering financial benefits to children severely disabled from vaccinations (Millward, 2017).

Media exposure spread awareness of anti-vaccine sentiment of the DTP vaccine from the U.K. across the Atlantic to the U.S. A 1982 documentary aired initially on NBC-TV in Washington, D.C., *DPT: Vaccination Roulette* (Thompson, 1982), dramatically illustrated the supposed harmful side effects of the pertussis vaccine (Howson, Howe & Fineberg, 1991). The documentary resulted in a blitz of discussions on leading television talk shows and print media coverage. During the same year, Dissatisfied Parents Together, an anti-vaccination advocacy group, was established to put pressure on the government to report adverse reactions to vaccinations while some members proposed banning the vaccine (Howson, Howe & Fineberg, 1991). The American Academy of Pediatrics and other public health organizations held the position that the positive benefits of stopping the spread of diseases were greater than the rare risks of side effects from vaccines (Koplan & Hinman, 1987). In 1991, a book, *A Shot in the Dark*, on vaccine risks was co-authored by a co-founder of Dissatisfied Parents Together. The anti-DTP vaccine attention also led to lawsuits against DTP manufacturers (Koplan & Hinman, 1987).

Study linked MMR vaccine with autism

Small to large anti-vaccination movements got a boost in 1998 when *The Lancet,* a peer-reviewed international medical journal based in London, published research claiming that the MMR vaccine causes autism in children. See Figure 5.1 of a demonstration in London.

The lead author Dr. Andrew Wakefield et al. (1998), a British gastroenterologist, along with 12 co-authors, studied 12 children with

FIGURE 5.1 Demonstration outside Downing Street in Westminster—where the official residence and office of the British Prime Minister is located—of families concerned about the link between autism and MMR vaccine. Janine Wiedel photolibrary/Alamy Stock Photo.

gastroenterology issues and determined that eight of them developed autism after receiving the MMR vaccine. *The Lancet* (Editors of the Lancet, 2010) retracted the article 12 years later for faulty research, insufficient data, and conflict of interest. Except for Wakefield and two of his co-authors, the other 10 co-authors signed the retraction (Mayor, 2004). Wakefield subsequently lost his license to practice medicine. Despite the situation, Wakefield still stood by his research—and so did others who believed that the original Wakefield research provided a link between MMR vaccines and autism, which is also referred to as autism spectrum disorder (ASD). CDC (2025b) explains how people behave with ASD:

> People with ASD may behave, communicate, interact, and learn in ways that are different from most other people. There is often nothing about how they look that sets them apart from other people. The abilities of people with ASD can vary significantly. For example, some people with ASD may have advanced conversation skills whereas others may be nonverbal. Some people with ASD need a lot of help in their daily lives; others can work and live with little to no support.
>
> *(para. 1)*

Communication: Green Our Vaccines movement

Green Our Vaccines movement started in the U.S. in 1998. The advocacy group goals were to build awareness of different perspectives on the safety of vaccines for children, particularly linking the MMR vaccine with autism; to rid toxins from the manufacturing of vaccines, particularly thimerosal, despite authoritative scientists' claims of safety; and to provide a more flexible pediatric vaccine schedule. The Green Our Vaccines campaign's four major strategies were as follows: 1) to focus on celebrity appeal, 2) to develop a dialog on other points of view on vaccines, 3) to seek out high-profile platforms, and 4) to gain support from like-minded nonprofits.

Strategy 1: Focus on celebrity appeal

The movement was started by Jenny McCarthy who parlayed her cache as a celebrity, vaccine hesitancy advocate, and mother of a son with autism as the lead spokesperson. Other well-known people were involved with Green Our Vaccines, whether through media appearances and/or events, and they also have been vocal about vaccine safety on their own or through other groups.

- **Jenny McCarthy**, an actor, bestselling author, and former Playboy model, was the most prominent voice of the Green Our Vaccines movement through media coverage, public events, and social media. During numerous media interviews, she has shared a personal narrative of experiencing her son's health decline after the MMR vaccine that she believes led to an autism diagnosis. She wrote a series of books, including a few on autism—*Louder Than Words: A Mother's Journey in Healing Autism, Mother Warriors: A Nation of Parents Healing Autism Against All Odds*, and *Healing and Preventing Autism* (McCarthy, 2025).

- **Jim Carrey**, a well-known actor (*How the Grinch Stole Christmas, Sonic The Hedgehog, The Truman Show, Liar Liar*), was formerly involved with Jenny McCarthy and has supported her vaccination stances. In 2015, he tweeted that the California governor was a "corporate fascist" for a new state law making vaccinations compulsory for public schoolchildren, regardless of religious and personal beliefs, in the state shortly after the measles outbreak at Disneyland (Brait, 2015, para. 7).
- **Robert F. Kennedy Jr.** (also referred to as RFK Jr.) is a member of the prominent Kennedy family. He is the nephew of the 35th President John F. Kennedy, who was assassinated in 1963, and the son of Robert F. Kennedy, attorney general in President Kennedy's Cabinet, who was assassinated in 1968 shortly after winning California's Democratic primary as the presidential candidate. RFK Jr. has had a career with environmental and children's health nonprofits as an attorney for the Riverkeeper and later he co-founded the Waterkeeper Alliance (US-DHHS, 2025a). He was the founder, former chairman of the board, and former chief litigation counsel for the Children's Health Defense (2025), a nonprofit; its "mission is ending childhood health epidemics by eliminating toxic exposure" (para. 2). In 2023, he announced his candidacy for U.S. president initially as a Democrat and then as an Independent until he withdrew his candidacy and endorsed Trump. RFK Jr. was appointed as U.S. Secretary of Health and Human Services under the second Trump Administration in 2025.
- **Andrew Wakefield**, a British doctor who lost his license and right to practice after the retracted *The Lancet* study (Wakefield et al., 1998), relocated to the U.S. and established the Strategic Autism Initiative and the Autism Media Channel in Austin, Texas, in 2010. The same year, he published a book, *Callous Disregard: Autism and Vaccines – The Truth Behind a Tragedy*, with a foreword by Jenny McCarthy. He also directed *Vaxxed: From Cover-Up to Catastrophe*. a film about the father of a child with autism, which was released in 2016. He continues to be an active vaccine skeptic advocate (Boseley, 2018). Award-winning actor Robert De Niro, who has a son with autism, initially supported including *Vaxxed: From Cover-up to Conspiracy* during the 2016 Tribeca Film Festival until he was pressured to exclude Wakefield's film from the lineup (CBS News, 2016).

Strategy 2: Develop a dialogue on other points of view on vaccines

In interviews, McCarthy conveyed messages on how the Green Our Vaccinations movement is not anti-vaccination but a group that seeks changes for toxic ingredients in vaccines and for vaccine scheduling for children. In addition, she encouraged people, particularly mothers, to look at other perspectives on vaccinations for children. McCarthy, interviewed in 2010 for PBS-TV's *Frontline* (2015) exemplifies her messaging and informal conversational tone:

> We just want there to be some type of conversation, once. Sit down with our side, with our doctors and scientists, to take a look at what we're talking about. We're not an anti-vaccine movement. We're pro-safe-vaccine schedule. Until we have that conversation, people are going to think it's an anti- and pro- side.
>
> *(para. 50)*

McCarthy also shared her firsthand narrative about being a mother of an autistic son and her challenges witnessing her son's health after vaccinations and trying various diets and vitamins to improve his condition. She encouraged parents to search the internet for advice since she found support from Generation Rescue, a now defunct nonprofit claiming that environmental factors, including vaccines, can cause autism. She spoke about the value of a mother's instinct in tune with a child's health and wellbeing.

Strategy 3: Seek out high-profile platforms

Celebrities and high-profile individuals involved with Green our Vaccines were set up for interviews on high-impact print and broadcast outlets. Other media outreach included op-eds, trend stories on autism and vaccine hesitancy, and pro- and anti-vaccination debates.

The largest Green Our Vaccines event took place in Washington, D.C. at the Capitol Building and West Capitol Grounds on June 4, 2008. The keynote speaker was RFJ Jr., and speakers included McCarthy and Carrey, along with Dr. Boyd Haley, emeritus professor at the University of Kentucky with anti-vaccination views, and Dr. Jay Gordon, a pediatrician and advocate of vaccine hesitancy. The event attracted sponsors and volunteers, primarily Talking About Curing Autism, Generation Rescue, HEAL, Moms Against Mercury, and approximately 39 other nonprofits on autism and environmental concerns also participated. The event included a 1-mile march and rally followed by a news conference focusing on an increase in autism and the group's stances on vaccines (Talking About Curing Autism, 2008). Approximately 8,500 people—families, lawmakers, and advocates across the country attended the event (Boston Herald, 2018). Visual imagery on the event showed participants presenting a united visual front by wearing green T-shirts with Green Our Vaccines on the front and "Too Many, Too Soon," referring to its stance on vaccine scheduling for children, on the back side. Many participants carried signage with the movement's messages (Gorski, 2008).

An article in the *Washington Post* stated that, "McCarthy and Carrey took great pains, however, to make clear that their beef wasn't with vaccines themselves, but rather the quality, quantity and frequency" (Express, 2008, para. 8).

Strategy 4: Gain support form like-minded nonprofits on vaccine hesitancy

The Green Our Vaccine movement gained the attention of other like-minded nonprofits addressing autism, vaccine hesitancy, and environmental issues. Four autism advocacy nonprofits sponsored the Washington, D.C., event. The groups also drew on their supporters to attend the rally, and their websites and social media spread awareness of Green Our Vaccines. McCarthy developed a relationship and took on leadership roles of Generation Rescue, a nonprofit co-founded by J. B. Handley, entrepreneur and author, and his wife, who believe their son developed autism due to vaccines. Their nonprofit was designed to be a resourceful community for parents of children with autism who share the autism-vaccine link (Boghani, 2015). According to Generation Rescue's last tax return, the nonprofit ceased operations in December 2019 (Suozzo et al., 2025).

Results of Green Our Vaccines

The Green Our Vaccines movement met its goal to communicate its vaccine safety and hesitancy perspective nationwide through multimedia platforms. Its second goal, toxic-free vaccines was achieved to some degree.

Media coverage

The Green Our Vaccines campaign generated extensive media exposure in major broadcast and print outlets to build public awareness. Most stories were interviews with McCarthy, who had other story angles on her books and motherhood that could incorporate Green Our Vaccines messages, and other interviews were with McCarthy and Carrey, or debates with McCarthy and Wakefield among other medical and scientific experts who believe vaccines are safe (NPR, 2025). McCarthy and others appeared on some of the most popular television programs of the time—*Good Morning America*, *The Ellen DeGeneres Show*, *The Oprah Winfrey Show*, *Larry King Live*, and *The View* (which she also joined as a co-host from 2013 to 2014)—and television news channels, such as CNN and Fox News (McCraken, 2021). Numerous print media ran articles about Green Our Vaccines, such as *Time, Newsweek, People*, and *Redbook,* among other magazines and daily newspapers (ABC News, 2008; Kluger, 2009; Rones, 2008; Staff Author, 2009). Many of the personalities involved with the movement and other complementary nonprofits generated web and social media content.

Not all media exposure was positive, however, with comments on pseudo-science, unscientific misinformation, and conspiracy theories about McCarthy and other anti-hesitancy advocates and anti-vaccination groups. Here are a few examples:

- An article in the *Los Angeles Times* clearly articulated the author's point of view, who concluded:

> Still, as the state's leading regulator of physicians, the Medical Board [of California] should be in the forefront of the battle against anti-vaccination behavior by its licensees. So far, it isn't. By its inaction, it has ceded the stage to people like Jenny McCarthy.
> *(Hiltzik, 2015, para. 13)*

- An opinion piece on CNN's website stated, "Although her [McCarthy's] TV and movie career eventually stalled, her popularity among desperate parents, discredited scientists, sellers of snake oil, and conspiracy theorists has apparently propelled her back into the spotlight" (Perry, 2013, para. 11).

Vaccine sources that parents trust

Who do parents trust about vaccinations and what influence do celebrities have? Mahoney (2011) references two studies that investigated parental trust and vaccine safety information: Dr. Gary Freed et al. (2011) from the University of Michigan and Kirsten S. Vannice et al. (2011) of the U.S. Department of Health and Human Services (USDHHS). The major findings from both indicated:

- Most parents trusted their doctors (76%) and vaccine-safety sources from family and friends (67%).
- Sixty-five percent of participants somewhat trusted parents who believed their children were harmed by vaccines.
- Although "a lot" of trust in vaccine content shared by celebrities was only 2%; the "some" category was 24% of trust in celebrities.

- Mothers, unlike fathers, had more trust on vaccine safety content shared by parents, including celebrities, who believed that vaccines injured their children as discussed on television programs, magazines, and newspapers, if there was adequate time to review the information.
- Hispanic parents were more receptive to trust celebrities voicing opinions about vaccine safety than both white and Black parents.

Considered a dynamic and personable public speaker, McCarthy was able to conduct herself with confidence while debating with doctors and scientists, yet she can talk to parents with a relatable and warm maternal tone. As Samantha Gottlieb (2016), University of California, Berkeley, who researched vaccine skepticism and the "Jenny McCarthy effect," stated in her study: "Detractors attack McCarthy's lack of expertise, which her followers deliberately embrace. McCarthy's entitlement to ask questions about vaccine safety appeals to mothers who distrust medical authority" (p. 166).

Thimerosal and pediatric vaccine scheduling

In 2001, all vaccines for children were manufactured free of thimerosal (CDC, 2024d), while CDC and other parties evaluated vaccine scheduling. Although this was a goal of the Green Our Vaccines movement, its actual direct impact on changing vaccine production could be debated. This decision was prompted by the American Academy of Pediatrics, various public health agencies, and manufacturers of vaccines that recommended reducing or eliminating thimerosal as a precaution two years earlier (CDC, 2024d). According to the CDC (2024d), vaccines for MMR, varicella (chickenpox), inactivated polio, pneumococcal conjugate (PCVs) never contained thimerosal. Influenza vaccines are provided two ways: 1) with thimerosal for multi-dose vials, thereby preventing the growth of bacteria or fungi, and 2) free of thiomersal. In addition, the CDC supported the Immunization Safety Review report (Institute of Medicine, 2001) and other high-quality studies concluding no link exists between vaccines containing thimerosal and autism. Since thimerosal has been removed from all childhood vaccinations, autism rates continue to increase, according to a news release on an Autism and Developmental Disabilities Monitoring survey from the U.S. Department of Health and Human Services (2025b). When the survey first began in 2003, autism prevalence was 1 in 150 children and, in 2024, it was 1 in 31 children.

In terms of vaccine scheduling for children and adults, CDC's Advisory Committee on Immunization Practices traditionally has met three times annually to discuss recent medical and scientific research and provides the CDC with recommendation on any changes. Vaccine scheduling information can be found on CDC's (2025c) website.

Decline in vaccination rates

Vaccination hesitancy has been an issue in the U.S., a country that almost lost its elimination status of measles from WHO in 2019 due to approximately 1,300 cases of measles reported in 31 states (CDC, 2025d). Vaccination rates in U.S. kindergartens have declined overall from 95% in the 2019–2000 school year to under 93%, with the MMR vaccine at 92.7% during the 2023–2024 (Seither et al., 2024). Vaccine coverage of 95% or greater provides people with herd immunity (CDC, 2025e).

Dr. Gary L. Freed, chief of the Division of General Pediatrics and director of the Child Health Evaluation and Research Unit at University of Michigan, stated: "Even if only a fraction of parents receive, believe, and act on misinformation about vaccine safety provided by these different sources, individual children's health and the population's health may suffer because of vaccine preventable illnesses" (University of Michigan Health System, 2011, para. 11).

Theoretical framework

The decision to get vaccinated or not is a deeply personal one that is impacted by many contextual, ideological, socioeconomic, political, and psychographic factors (Quick, Reynolds-Tylus, Gonzalez, Al-Ghaithi, & Mackert, 2021). Health communication efforts at influencing an individual to adopt or perform one behavior, for example vaccination, over another such as hesitancy or anti-vaccination, is only effective when there is an understanding of the intended audiences' roots (Hornsey et al., 2018) and routes of persuasion (Petty & Cacioppo, 1986) likely to influence or guide their choice. This section will focus on two theoretical models to underscore the persuasive roots and routes of anti-vaccination related to the campaigns above.

Roots of persuasion

Researchers at the University of Queensland, Australia, used the attitude roots model—conspiratorial beliefs, disgust sensitivities, reactance, and individualism—hierarchy worldviews—to explore "the psychological factors that might motivate people to reject scientific consensus around vaccination" (Hornsey et al., 2018, p. 307). Here is a brief summary of these roots:

- **Conspiratorial beliefs**—people are motivated to believe Big Pharma conspiracy theories circulating on the internet that purportedly claim "pharmaceutical companies, regulators, politicians, and others are secretly working" to cover up "claims about the universal dangerousness" of pharmaceutical products and medical interventions (Blaskiewicz & Baldwin, 2013, p. 259).

- **Disgust** or phobias associated with "needles, hospitals and blood," gives people who experience this "permission to avoid the triggers for their disgust; for example ... a skepticism or hesitancy toward immunizations" (Hornsey et al., 2018, p. 308).
- **Reactance** to others who do not share the image you have of yourself as an anti-scientist or nonconformist; "To the extent that people nurture this self-image, they may be motivated to reject consensus views (like "immunization is good") as a short-hand way of communicating a nonconformist identity to the self and others" (Hornsey et al., 2018, p. 308).
- **Individualism-Hierarchy worldview** validates an individual's right to make decisions for themselves, without government intervention. The attitudinal link to vaccinations, according to Hornsey et al. (2018), is tenuous as individuals may be persuaded in possibly counterintuitive ways: "moral suspicion of ..."Big Pharma," which in turn would be associated with a skepticism or hesitancy toward vaccinations" (p. 309), or "immunization might be viewed as an excessive 'big government' initiative and so be treated with skepticism by those high in individualist and hierarchical worldviews" (p. 309).

These roots of persuasion are important to understand, regardless of whether one's personal decision is to vaccinate or not. The roots can provide professionals tools for developing an effective health communication campaign that can balance the rhetoric and discourse of any anti-vaccination movement, combat misinformation, and augment support for evidence-based policies (Trujillo et al., 2020) and increase the potential to prevent resurgences of contagious diseases (Benecke & DeYoung, 2019).

Routes of persuasion

Similar to the attitude root model used by Hornsey et al. (2018) is an older theoretical model of persuasive "communication-induced attitude change," (Petty & Cacioppo, 1986, p. 125) known as the Elaboration Likelihood Model based on two routes—central and peripheral—and a variety of experiences that are "capable of influencing or guiding behavioral, affective, and cognitive processes" (Petty & Cacioppo, 1986, p. 127).

Petty and Cacioppo (1986) define elaboration as the likelihood or extent to which a person is persuaded by a central or peripheral route.

A **central route** to persuasion involves a "careful and thoughtful consideration of the true merits of the information presented in support of an advocacy" (p. 125) and thinking or scrutinizing about "issue-relevant arguments contained in a message" (p. 128). The ability to consider information and analyze messages depends on message quality, credibility of the source, personal interests or values, and message processing (cognitive) and can lead to a positive or negative attitude change. For example, a mother is likely to be persuaded to get vaccinated if the information "contained content about the benefits of vaccinations" and was transparent and informative. Such a tactic would allow "confidence and trust around the practice to take hold" (Benecke & DeYoung, 2019, p. 3).

A peripheral route to persuasion occurs "without necessitating scrutiny of the true merits of the information presented" (p. 125) and when motivation to scrutinize is low and "a simple inference as to the validity of the message" is accepted (p. 132). Such a route triggers affective or emotional responses. For example, a mother is likely to be hesitant of getting a vaccination, through:

> anecdotes and highly emotional personal stories. These anecdotes involve the firsthand testimony of parents of autistic children who are convinced of the vaccination-autism link and use their own experiences to caution the audience against vaccination ... lay audiences often find them persuasive because of the sincerity of the featured parents and their seemingly common-sense arguments.
>
> *(Bricker & Justice, p. 6)*

Other tactics and tropes that provide insight into why an anti-vaccination movement can be convincing include: "skewing science, shifting hypotheses, censoring dissent, and attacking critics; also discussed are frequently made claims such as not being 'anti-vaccine' but 'pro-safe vaccines', that vaccines are toxic or unnatural, and more" (Kata, 2012, p. 3778).

The overall objective of this section on theory was to help readers discern "claims made by the anti-vaccination movement ... in order to critically evaluate the information and misinformation" (Kata, 2012, p. 3378). Use the discussion questions to identify the tropes used and the persuasive roots and routes of anti-vaccination related to the campaigns above.

Key words

An Act to Encourage Vaccination
Andrew Wakefield
Anti-vaccination Movements
Attitude Roots Model
Autism
Green Our Vaccines

Jenny McCarthy
Jim Carrey
MMR Vaccine
Robert F. Kennedy, Jr.
The Lancet
Thimerosal
Vaccine Hesitancy

Discussion questions:

1. What is your opinion regarding the claims made by Dr. Andrew Wakefield and the decision made by *The Lancet* to retract his research? Use a central or peripheral route to persuade someone to see your viewpoint.
2. Which root or route of persuasion was most effective within the "Green Our Vaccine" movement?
3. Which root or route of persuasion was evident within the anti-vaccination movement during COVID-19?

5.3 HOW A STATE AND A CITY GRAPPLE WITH MEASLES: "DUE BY TWO" CAMPAIGN IN OKLAHOMA AND "BOOSTER BOOSTER" PROGRAM IN PITTSBURGH AIM TO VACCINATE CHILDREN

Overall context

The rate of measles cases and outbreaks have decreased since the 1970s, due to the U.S. government's efforts to enact schoolwide state immunization requirements (Roper et al., 2021). However, some areas nationwide have had resurgences. *Morbidity and Mortality Weekly Report* reported 27,672 cases of measles across 49 states that represented a 50% increase in cases since 1989 (CDC, 1991).

Doctors affiliated with the National Center for Prevention Services, CDC in Atlanta, and New York University Medical Center documented the resurgence of measles in the U.S. from 1989–1990 (Atkinson et al., 1992). This resurgence yielded higher rates for morbidity and mortality in minorities and unvaccinated pre-school aged children. Their recommendation for preventing measles was for vaccination efforts to target pre-school aged children and "implementation of a two-dose measles strategy among school-aged children" (p. 451).

CDC in collaboration with the Advisory Committee on Immunization Practices are responsible for setting the immunization schedules for adults and children (Roper et al., 2021). These guidelines are updated periodically, and states are encouraged to keep their schedules updated as well.

The most current schedule for the measles, mumps, and rubella immunization shot calls for children to receive their first dose at 12 to 15 months, with a three-month interval before the second dose (CDC, 2021).

On November 3, 1990, President George W. Bush signed Public Law 101-502, otherwise known as the Vaccine and Immunization Amendments of 1990 Act. This law authorized funding through 1995 "to provide, without charge, immunizations against vaccine-preventable diseases to children not more than 2 years of age who reside in communities whose population includes a significant number of lower-income individuals" (Bush, 1991, Section 2, b 1-A). Oklahoma State Health Department received donations and other financial support to offset the cost of the vaccines as part of the "Due by Two" campaign.

In 2000, an historic public health achievement occurred as CDC (2000) stated measles was officially eliminated from the U.S. Additionally, all 50 states in the U.S. have school immunizations laws. However, each state has its own policies on how to enforce these laws and who or what agency is responsible for the enforcement. In Oklahoma, the State Board of Health prescribes and administers immunizations, while the Oklahoma State Department of Health (OSDH) enforces the required immunizations with assistance from the State Department of Education (OSDH, 2011). In Pennsylvania, school health personnel (superintendent, principal, or director) enforce the regulation requiring immunizations to attend school (Pennsylvania Department of Health, 2017).

"Due by Two Campaign" in Oklahoma

Communication programming and execution

The specific audience for this campaign was Oklahoma parents with children under the age of 2 who had not yet been vaccinated or vaccinated fully with both MMR shots. Oklahoma's First Lady Rhonda Walters who spearheaded the campaign identified that only 32% of this population had received the necessary immunizations (English, 1991).

The specific goal of the "Due by Two" campaign in the state of Oklahoma was tied to a nationwide initiative by the U.S. Department of Health and Human Services (USDHHS) *Healthy People 2000*, published in 1991. Within the nationwide effort, the specific risk reduction objective was to "increase immunization and prevent infectious diseases, by the year 2000" (p. 76). The specific strategies and tactics were to "Eliminate measles" and "Increase childhood immunization levels to at least 90% of 2 year-olds" (p. 76).

The specific time period for conducting this campaign was from October 1, 1991, through September 30, 1992.

As for campaign messages, Rhonda Walters consistently communicated the message that childhood immunizations are "Due by Two" via multiple media sources, including articles that were featured in *The Oklahoman, Tulsa World,* and *Five Star News*, print advertisements, television ads, radio spots, and in billboards and posters (Peck, 1994).

This central message was followed up with reminders that without the MMR shot, children are not fully immunized against the three diseases (English, 1993). To motivate parents further and reduce barriers, messages included:

> Immunization locations and special weekend activities aimed at producing mass immunizations. In addition, clinics stayed open in the early evening one night per week. The nominal fees charged for administering immunizations at state and local government health facilities were also dropped by the state legislature.
>
> *(Jones et al., 1996, p. 99)*

Regarding the cost of vaccines and the overall campaign, OSDH received financial support of almost USD 5,200,000. These funds came from various federal, state, and private sector sources, including a USD 440,000 donation from CDC in Atlanta and approximately USD 3,775,000 in donated public service advertising (Jones et al., 1996; Oklahoma State Department of Health, 1993; smokenews.com, 1991).

"Due by Two Campaign" in Oklahoma: Results

This campaign was successful. Not only did professors of marketing, business communication, and management evaluate the campaign's positive effect on how many children received the MMR shots (Jones et al., 1996), the "Due by Two" campaign received multiple awards. Rhonda Walters was honored in 1992 by the Oklahoma Kids organization for her stewardship as a spokesperson for Healthy Futures in promoting the well-being of children. "Due by Two' is one of the programs within Healthy Futures children's awareness campaign initiatives (English, 1992).

The "Due by Two" campaign also received the Lowe Runkle Distinguished Service Award from Oklahoma City Ad Club in 1992. The criteria included making a positive impact through public service initiatives or advertising and a dedication to human welfare, based on the values of the namesake Lowe Runkle, an advertising pioneer in Oklahoma (AAF Oklahoma, 2025).

President Clinton appointed Rhonda Walters to the Commission on Presidential Scholars, as a member, providing this reason: "As Oklahoma's First Lady, she promoted the Statewide Public Awareness Campaign on Children's

Issues which included the highly successful immunization campaign, 'Due by Two,' which helped spur a 40% increase in immunization in Oklahoma children under two years of age" (The White House, 1999, para. 2).

This campaign could serve as a model for other states to adopt in their approach to immunizing children (Jones et al., 1996). This campaign also represents the ability of government and state agencies to collaborate in solving a public health crisis like measles. The next case study was equally as successful 10 years later in assisting Pittsburgh Public Schools systems in vaccinating 11,000 students who were out of compliance with state vaccination requirements.

"Booster Booster" Program in Pittsburgh Public Schools

Communication programming and execution

The specific audiences for this campaign were parents and guardians of school-aged students, minority students, community influencers, and the media residing in Allegheny County Pennsylvania. Additional stakeholders included the University of Pittsburgh, Allegheny County Health Department (ACHD), Pittsburgh Public Schools (PPS) Superintendent John Thompson, and a consortium of community groups including churches, grocery stores, and the YMCA.

The University of Pittsburgh News Services (2001a) reported approximately 600,000 students across the state were at risk of being suspended for not providing documentation of their MMR vaccinations. Unvaccinated students are out of compliance with *28 Pa. Code§ 23.83* in Subchapter C Immunization (Commonwealth of Pennsylvania, 2017) referenced the *Procedural Manual School Immunization Records*, which states:

> All children at any grade, kindergarten through 12th, including all public, private, parochial or nonpublic school in this commonwealth, including vocational schools, intermediate units, and special education and home education programs, cyber and charter schools, **must show proof of immunization before they can attend school in this commonwealth.**
> *(emphasis added; Pennsylvania Department of Health, 2017, p. 4)*

Pennsylvania Department of Health (PDH) in 2017 published *Procedure Manual School Immunization Regulations* that contained all the revisions from the original 1983 manual. The relevant amendment for PPS occurred in 1997 and included "the requirement for all grades (K-12) for two doses of measles containing vaccine beginning in the 2000–2001 school year" (p. 3).

The deadline for students to provide documentation of their MMR booster vaccinations was April 30, 2001. In March 2001, approximately 11,000 students were still at risk of being suspended.

The Greater Pittsburgh Measles Immunization Task Force joined forces with the University of Pittsburgh's Graduate School of Public Health and Center for Minority Health and PPS to launch the program. "Booster Booster" became the overall theme and identity of the program, developed by the university, and included a logo used on letterhead, flyers, posters, and T-shirts—featured in Figure 5.2.

University Chancellor Mark Nordenberg stated at the launch of the program:

> It would be a shame if any child was [sic] suspended from school because of a failure to be immunized or to document that immunization. Our aim is ... to assist public health officials in maintaining full enrollment in the schools ... while also ensuring that their education is not interrupted.
>
> *(News Services, 2001a, para. 3–4)*

FIGURE 5.2 "Booster Booster" T-shirt. Courtesy of University of Pittsburgh and University of Pittsburgh Library System.

The ACHD's Director Dr. Bruce Dixon stated his willingness to work with families to update student immunization records and to accept a parent or guardian's double verbal consent in lieu of a signed consent form (News Services, 2001a).

The Public Relations Society of America (2002) provided a two-page summary of the situation, research, planning, and evaluation processes of the Greater Pittsburgh Measles Immunization Task Force. This summary is a campaign profile of an organization that received the Silver-Anvil Award of Excellence by PRSA. Here are highlights of the profile.

The Task Force began by conducting research to discover the issue in hesitation and noncompliance. Interviews were conducted with school and public health officials, yielding important insights: lack of response from letters sent through the mail; students needed parental permission; lack of access to health care; poorer schools had high percentages of nonresponses—especially from minority students; fear of getting the injection; and lack of awareness of new school vaccination requirements. The specific strategies were to:

- Tap into community leaders to drive the effort. Pastors were given scripts to communicate the need to immunize.
- Make use of grassroots community organizations and media to communicate consequences and encourage vaccinations. University basketball coaches were solicited to be spokespersons for radio and television interviews.
- Offer accessibility to vaccines. Free vaccination clinics were available at local businesses, including a chain grocery store, and the ADPH provided staffed mobile vaccination units. A hotline was set up and volunteers telephoned noncompliant families and answered questions.

To accomplish these strategies, the following objectives were established, in order of importance:

1 Bring into compliance the 11,000 students in danger of being suspended.
2 Increase media coverage with messages about the deadline and timely need for vaccination.
3 Position the University of Pittsburgh as a community health partner.

In executing this plan an initial press conference was conducted, followed by live television cut-ins, radio PSAs and live broadcasts, and print media coverage of the deadline and timely need for vaccination. The university published updates in press releases and donated its space within local newspapers to advertise clinics and raise awareness.

"Booster Booster" Program: Results

In evaluating the campaign, the University of Pittsburgh News Services (2001b) published that "Activities conducted under the auspices of the Greater Pittsburgh Measles Immunization Task Force's Booster Booster campaign have reduced the number of noncompliant students by more than 4,000, from 11,287 to 7,045" (para 1). Five days later, roughly 1,400 more students received the booster vaccinations or provided proof (News Services, 2001c, April 25, para 1). As of May 14, News Services (2001d) headlined in its press release that the Task Force reached a successful conclusion with 99% of public school students in compliance. A year later in June 2002, the Public Affairs Office of the University of Pittsburgh was recognized by PRSA and the international Council for Advancement and Support of Education, for the "Booster Booster" public awareness campaign (News Services, 2002, para.1).

Theoretical framework

The common factor across each of these campaigns is the need for children to be vaccinated without vaccine hesitancy. As children under the age of 2 cannot consent to being vaccinated, parents, schools, healthcare professionals at the city, county and state levels, and government officials are responsible for making the choice to prevent communicable diseases via immunizations.

In Oklahoma, the OSDH was the agency responsible for administering the "Due by Two" campaign and for increasing to 90% the number of children completely immunized by their second birthday (Jones et al., 1996, p. 99). A challenge was to understand why children were not receiving the second vaccination dose (English, 1993).

In Pittsburgh, the choice of whether to vaccinate a child was bound to being in compliance with state health regulations within the public school system. The city's challenge was the number of students facing suspension due to noncompliance with the vaccine requirement and understanding this hesitancy.

There are some theoretical considerations for health communication campaigns and underlying factors affecting adults' vaccine hesitancy (Kenzig & Mumford, 2022). Vaccine hesitancy refers to a "delay in acceptance or refusal of vaccination despite availability of vaccination services. Vaccine hesitancy is complex and context specific, varying across time, place and vaccines. It is influenced by factors such as complacency, convenience and confidence" (MacDonald & the MacDonald, 2015, p. 4161).

Vaccine communication is an important health communication topic, especially when it comes to challenges such as misinformation and fake news. When used effectively as part of a vaccination campaign, communication "can promote acceptance of vaccination … and influence vaccine uptake" (Greyson, 2021, pp. 2–3). Effectiveness depends on a communicator's ability to use specific, clear yet scientific words that are easily understandable. Additionally, communicators should "invoke positive connotations of immunity rather than the negative connotation of injections," and should do so in an ethical manner (Greyson, 2021, p. 3).

Kenzig and Mumford (2022) advocate for specific communication campaign strategies to address vaccine hesitancy. These strategies should take into consideration a specific target population and their needs and barriers to vaccination. Campaign messages are more effective with motivations, personal narratives, emotional anecdotes, and reliable information. The appeal of this strategic approach is that the strategies adjust as the targeted population's behavior adjusts; for example, when an individual moves from being vaccine hesitant to accepting the need for vaccination.

Key words

Advisory Committee on Immunization Practices
Booster
Commonwealth
Council for Advancement and Support of Education
Healthy People 2000
Measles
Mumps
First Lady Rhonda Walters
Rubella
Silver Anvil Award of Excellence
U.S. Department of Health and Human Services
Vaccine and Immunization Amendments of 1990 Act

Discussion questions:

1 Can you think of other reasons why parents would not vaccinate their children?
2 What are other barriers parents, children, or school officials might face in getting people to change their behavior?
3 How might vaccine hesitancy have been relevant during COVID-19?

5.4 BANGLADESH CONDUCTS WORLD'S LARGEST MR VACCINATION CAMPAIGN COUNTRYWIDE USING ADVOCACY COMMUNICATION STRATEGIES

Situational analysis

The Expanded Programme on Immunization (EPI) celebrated its 50th anniversary in 2024. Since its inception in 1974, EPI has had an evolving impact on prevention and protection of children against six illnesses, including measles and rubella (WHO, 2024b). Its success comes from collaborating with public health programs and international organizations like the Global Alliance for Vaccines and Immunizations (Gavi) to control outbreaks, enhance overall health and strive for equity in access, regardless of status and physical location (WHO, 2024b).

The mission of Gavi is "to save lives and protect people's health by increasing equitable and sustainable use of vaccines." The alliance boasts that it has helped vaccinate "more than 1 billion children in 78 lower-income countries, preventing more than 17.3 million future deaths" (Gavi, 2024, para. 1). To accomplish these feats, the alliance created a partnership model based on core strengths of governments, manufacturers, private sector organizations like the Bill & Melinda Gates Foundation, research agencies, and community/social/religious organizations to improve global health while increasing stability in poorer countries (Gavi, 2024). Both the EPI and Gavi were instrumental throughout Bangladesh's history of measles and rubella vaccination and eradication efforts by the Government of the People's Republic of Bangladesh (GPRB) and the Ministry of Health and Family Welfare (MoHFW).

Beginning in the mid-1980s, Bangladesh's immunization system needed much reform due to economic and infrastructural barriers. In general, immunization coverage for the densely populated country was approximately 2% (Al Amin, 2025) due to differential access to health care—urban versus rural—and a lack of adequate refrigeration also known as cold chain among other barriers. Cold chain is a set of guidelines to follow for storing and distributing vaccines, as the MR vaccine should be kept between –15 degrees and –25 degrees Celsius to ensure its effectiveness (PAHO, n.d.).

Several studies also identified other challenges and barriers, aside from cold chain issues, which impacted immunization efforts, such as political turmoil, finances, administrative delays with registration and funding (Sarma et al., 2019); lack of awareness of campaign efforts, sickness of children, and apprehension of side effects (Uddin et al., 2016); caretakers either not prioritizing or not remembering the vaccination schedule (Khanal et al., 2017); and programmatic barriers—staffing, capacity, and lack of infrastructure in rural areas, training, delivery and distribution logistics, and injection safety standards for disposal (GPRB, 2011). The cost of contracting measles (vaccinations, hospital stays, etc.) created an economic burden for caregivers equating to roughly 32% of their household income, and a total economic cost of USD 348,078 for 2,263 cases of measles (de Broucker et al., 2020). In today's exchange rates, this would equate to BDT 40, 790, 736.39 (Bangladeshi takas).

In 2006, measles ranked fifth as the leading cause of death in children because of the low vaccination rate and lower immunity rates (United Nations Foundation, 2006). This prompted the Bangladeshi government to launch the largest measles vaccination campaign in its history, as part of the Measles Initiative, involving WHO, UNICEF, and the CDC (Global Health Delivery Project, 2011). This initiative occurred in two phases—phase one in 2005 and phase two in 2006. Phase two was designed to vaccinate over 33 million children, ages nine months to 10 years, over a period of three weeks. This ambitious plan of action included controlling measles and reducing the number of measles-related deaths through a "catch-up" campaign in which educational institutions and EPI centers provided routine immunizations as well as the measles vaccine (United Nations Foundation, 2006). The plan was additionally supported by technical assistance from WHO and UNICEF for planning, implementing, and evaluating the campaign and financial assistance from the United Nations Foundation and American Red Cross (United Nations Foundation, 2006). After this campaign, the rate of coverage for measles was above 80% (Uddin et al., 2016).

Communication programming and execution

Aside from the efforts in 2006, the most influential and impactful campaign on MR vaccination coverage and routine immunization services was the *Comprehensive Multi-Year Plan of the National Immunization Program of Bangladesh 2011–2016* (GPRB, 2011). This plan provided a medium-term framework and advocacy approach to "reduce the burden of vaccine preventable diseases through high-quality immunization services ... in such a way so that the overall health system could be strengthened" (GPRB, 2011, page iv).

Objectives and key strategies

The mission of the immunization plan was guided by these principles:

1. *Quality and safety* – to *ensure* immunization services based on best practices.
2. *Maximal coverage and reach* – to overcome access barriers at all levels.
3. *Equity and gender equality* – to give priority to the underserved and hard-to-reach and high-risk groups.
4. *Sustainability through technical and financial capacity building.*
5. *Excellence in Program Management* – to ensure effective use of resources following result-based principles and evidence-based practices (emphasis in original; GPRB, 2011, p. iv).

The primary objectives were to achieve 95% measles coverage, nationally, and reaching elimination of measles by 2016, and to prevent and control other diseases with new and underutilized vaccines, namely rubella and congenital rubella syndrome (CSR).

Rubella and CSR can cause birth defects such as deafness, heart defects, lower birth rate, intellectual challenges, and hormone problems, among others (CDC, 2024e). Bangladesh had the greatest number of rubella cases (n= 3034) in 2012 in the South-East Asia Region (WHO Regional Office for South-East Asia, 2015) compared to 83 reported cases in 2006 (GPRB, 2011).

To combat and control both diseases, Bangladesh launched in 2014 the first and largest combined measles and rubella (MR) vaccination campaign that strove to reach 52 million vulnerable children under age 15 (reliefweb, 2014) by engaging thousands of community and religious leaders, vaccinators, and volunteers in 170,000 schools and 150,000 immunization centers over a three-week period (Sultana, 2014).

Other key strategies were concentrated on service delivery, advocacy and communication, surveillance, vaccine supply, quality and logistics, and program management. The activities associated with these strategies included, but were not limited to the following:

- Focusing on low coverage areas
- Strengthening communication and involvement with partners
- Improving timeliness and completeness of collecting, reporting, and surveillance procedures
- Updating logistics (forms, guidelines, transportation)
- Coordinating efforts (financial and capacity) for second dose injections for measles
- Training for managerial staff responsible for carrying out and monitoring implementation, especially for the second dose
- Introducing the other vaccines (pneumococcal, Rota, Hepatitis B, dT) and Rubella antigen
- "Involving community leaders linking community with immunization planning and implementation" (GPRB, 2011, p. 34)
- Directing communication strategies to mothers
- Training staff in interpersonal communication

These strategies and activities are consistent and align with the 2014–2020 *Strategic plan for Measles Elimination and Rubella and Congenital Rubella Syndrome Control in the South-East Asia Region* (WHO Regional Office for South-East Asia, 2015), in which Bangladesh was one of the countries monitored, surveilled, and supported financially.

Communication methods

To reach parents and influencers, the campaign employed a variety of communication and methods (Sarma et al., 2019). The MoHFW provided timely updates about the implementation process and funding to stakeholders via memos and letters.

The Ministry also developed, promoted, and implemented advocacy strategies across all levels: national, divisional, district, city, municipal, and upazillas (second-tier administrative divisions). These strategies included policy makers, media executives, professional organizations, and partners like the EPI, which provided information and educational materials. Additionally, EPI held advocacy meetings with the Bangladesh Medical Association, Pediatric Association, and "news editors from the press and electronic media to obtain their support for the publication of articles and message to help create favorable public awareness and counter instances of negative publicity" (Sarma et al., 2019, p. 8).

Other methods to reach parents and influencers included face-to-face interactions with community leaders and health assistants, National Immunization Days, and door-to-door registrations (Uddin et al., 2016). Because of the large Muslim community, announcements in mosques in more rural areas across the country were made, primarily to raise awareness, correct misinformation that circulated on SMS—short message service—and dispel misperceptions about the side effectives and effectiveness of the vaccines (Sarma et al., 2019).

Additionally, according to UNICEF and WHO, volunteers and other frontline workers targeted railway and bus stations, water terminals, and parks and footpaths in urban areas. In remote areas (districts and subdistricts or upazillas), they mobilized in small islands, marketplaces, mills for rice, brothels, or other areas where mothers and children resided (reliefweb, 2014).

With reference to communication with partners and stakeholders, WHO ensured availability of vaccines by providing refrigerated vehicles while EPI handled other cold chain logistics (storage, ice packs, and freezer tags) and managed stakeholder relations with local volunteers, social services, utility companies, ice cream factories, colleges, health institutions, and authorities (Sarma et al., 2019). EPI centers and schools were used as spaces to provide MR vaccines while WHO and UNICEF "enabled rapid identification of implementation problems and ability for EPI and partners to respond quickly with mitigating strategies" (Sarma et al., 2019, p. 8).

With reference to social media, much of the information about its usage during this time period and campaign was written in Bangla, the predominant language of Bangladesh, which was not recorded, or was sporadic across platforms with later dates.

Costs

The *Comprehensive Multi-Year Plan* of the National Immunization Program of Bangladesh 2011–2106 estimated the cost per country for supplementary immunization activities (SIA), outbreak response immunization (ORI), and MR surveillance. The total cost for Bangladesh was over USD 120,000,000 (WHO Regional Office for South-East Asia, 2015). Costs associated with vaccines for measles, measles second dose, and MR totaled one dollar per dose and supply costs associated with each injection totaled USD 0.20. WHO provided refrigerated vehicles used for distributing vaccines to rural districts (Sarma et al., 2019), estimated at USD 50,000 per vehicle. Total investment was estimated at USD 11 million (GPRB, 2011).

To help offset these costs, Gavi contributed 48% of financing over the course of five years from 2011 to 2015, which GPRB provided roughly 27%, with additional funding from WHO and UNICEF.

Outcomes and evaluation

Bangladesh's continued progress in its vaccination efforts as part of the Expanded Programme on Immunization earned GPRB the Gavi Alliance Award in 2009 and 2012, for reducing child mortality, one of the Millenium Development Goals (Sarkar et al., 2015).

The immunization efforts from 2011–2016 campaigns also garnered much success and have been formally assessed and evaluated by Uddin et al. (2016) before and after and by Gavi (2015) in its findings of a full evaluation of Bangladesh.

Within the pre-campaign survey, the rate of vaccinations was low but increased to 90% after the campaign, falling within the range of 90% to 95% coverage to ensure herd immunity (Uddin et al., 2016). The post campaign survey of 4,510 households revealed other useful and relevant data points and results:

- Lower levels (23%) of interpersonal communication in the registration process with caregivers, which is a potential reason why over 15% of caregivers who did not vaccinate their children did not know about the campaign.
- Children who attend school were more likely to get the vaccine (95% with some variation across regions).
- MR vaccination campaign positively impacted routine immunization services from EPI, strengthening storage and delivery systems.
- The campaign reshaped people's misperceptions.
- Door-to-door registrations improved communication between providers and caregivers.

- Logistics with the cold-chain process improved with repairs or new purchases.
- This large-scale program strengthened the coordination and integration of services across sectors and presented a future model for mobilizing other health interventions (Uddin et al., 2016).

Gavi (2015) and its partner organizations, in its full country analysis of Bangladesh, reported findings based on pre/post MR surveys, interviews, and session observations. Their report discovered a lack of education contributed to lower coverage rates in the more rural areas. Susceptibility to rubella was reduced significantly with high coverage rates and rubella antibody prevalence increased substantially to 93%. Public awareness and acceptance were increased, and health care workers used the campaign to provide catch-up vaccinations. Lastly, Gavi's findings suggested that administrative delays in funding campaign activities could be improved with more coordinated pre-planning efforts and incorporating the perspectives of stakeholders at various levels into decision-making processes. Overall, this combined MR mass vaccination campaign proved to be successful in 2014—and represents one of many efforts by GPRB in improving the lives of its people.

Theoretical framework

In order to understand the significance of this campaign, it is important to realize how health communication strategies have evolved to include advocacy, especially during a humanitarian crisis. Advocacy and communication strategies to address health crises and pandemics are based on several theoretical and applied aspects. These aspects represent an integration of social support and empowerment through cooperation with influencers (Forrester, 2024; Servaes & Malikhao, 2010).

First, a practitioner or government must acknowledge and recognize a public health problem and provide a rationale for behavioral change to combat the problem. This requires distinguishing the level of complexity of the health problem, the temporal nature of the problem—whether emergency, short term, or long term—and whether the approach to the problem is vertical or horizontal, tackling one disease at a time or tackling multiple diseases at the same time, respectively (Servaes & Malikhao, 2010).

In the case of Bangladesh, the approach to reducing cases of measles and preventing mortalities is a long-term problem, and it was a vertical problem until 2012 when rubella vaccines were introduced as part of national immunization efforts. In contrast, the 2020 campaign to vaccinate Rohingya refugees seeking political asylum from Myanmar in Bangladesh represented an emergent humanitarian, short-term, and horizontal problem. The displaced refugees who temporarily resided in Bangladesh needed other vaccinations besides measles and the campaign itself occurred just as the COVID-19 pandemic hit.

Second, communication with key stakeholders should be interpersonal—two-way, interactive, supportive, participatory, and engaged. This is to ensure that their voices and concerns are heard. The focus is not on pushing information out to stakeholders, but rather, listening to stakeholders and mobilizing the necessary resources to educate and effect change in vaccination uptakes (Servaes & Malikhao, 2010). Empathizing with key stakeholders also influences their ability to make decisions, especially related to public health policy.

The *Global Measles and Rubella Strategic Plan 2012–2020* offered recommendations and planned activities to engage and communicate with stakeholders, aiming for dialogue through various communication channels as well as training in message development, dissemination, and interpersonal communication (WHO, 2012). Bangladesh was identified as one of 47 high-priority countries with the highest disease burden and was offered technical and financial support from partners including Gavi.

Third, regarding the practice of advocacy, any message crafted must take into consideration contexts whether cultural, institutional, religious, socioeconomic, or emotional (Forrester, 2024).

For example, based on representative data from a Bangladesh Demographic Health Survey in 2007, a study was conducted to determine whether maternal education had an impact on measles vaccination coverage (Haque & Bari, 2013).

The study revealed that mothers play an essential role in ensuring the health and well-being of their children. The more mothers are educated about measles and rubella preventive measures, the more likely children are to get vaccinated (Haque & Bari, 2013). The same is true for vaccination behaviors. If a mother is vaccinated, the child will more likely be vaccinated.

Additionally, the study identified that over 60% of people surveyed lived in rural areas, had 81% of their children delivered in non-hospital settings with lower vaccination rates, and identified as Muslim (Haque & Bari, 2013). These factors suggest how health communication strategies can be designed to encourage community and religious leaders to advocate for the education of mothers (Haque & Bari, 2013).

The World Bank (2023) revealed that between 2010 and 2020, the literacy rate for Bangladeshi adults above age of 15 increased steadily from 60% to 75%, creating an additional context for the campaign. In relation to social media, in 2014, a digital culture was emerging with many prospects and problems (Hussain, 2015; Mozammel, Chowdhury, & Satter, 2012). Prospects included more than 7 million people using Facebook and more than 115 million using mobile phones, within a population of 150 million, for connecting with others (Hussain, 2015) while over 75% of ministries/divisions, departments/corporations, and academic institutions were connected to the internet (Mozammel, Chowdhury & Satter, 2012). Problems such as poor infrastructure and access to the internet, lack of policies, low levels of literacy and training, and high costs, among others were identified as well (Hussain, 2015; Mozammel, Chowdhury, & Satter, 2012).

In addressing the health crisis within the Rohingya refugee camps, GPRB needed to consider the differences in health beliefs and practices; for example, the belief that disease is linked to spirituality and that practices based on faith healing or herbal remedies align with this belief (Kapil et al., 2022). One can see the challenge of vaccination efforts, especially if these efforts are ineffective due to the differences in beliefs, language barriers, and substandard crowded housing.

Lastly, the keys to successful advocacy messages are in being relevant, timely, and easy to understand (Servaes & Malikhao, 2010). GPRB needed to act immediately to curb the spread of measles and rubella to the rest of its population while keeping the refugees safe.

Key words

Advocacy Communication Strategies
Bangladesh Medical Association
Bill & Melinda Gates Foundation (now known as the Gates Foundation)
Cold Chain
EPI
Gavi
Global Health Delivery Project
Government of the People's Republic of Bangladesh
Measles
Millenium Development Goals
Myanmar
Red Cross
Rohingya
Rubella
SEAR—Southeast Asian Region
UNICEF
Upazillas
WHO

Discussion questions

This case study illuminates the level of complexity of the health problem, the temporal nature of the problem—whether emergency, short term, or long term—and whether one culture's approach to the problem is vertical or horizontal. Given these dynamics, think about measles, mumps, and rubella here in the United States and answer these questions:

1 What are the complexities of this health problem?
2 With resurgences of measles and anti-vaccination movements, what is the temporal nature of this problem?
3 Is this problem a vertical or horizontal problem?
4 What can health practitioners learn from the way the people of Bangladesh approached the MR vaccine?

References

AAF Oklahoma. (2025). *Lowe Runkle Distinguished Service Award*. https://okcadclub.com/awards/

ABC News. (2008, June 3). *Celeb couple to lead 'Green Vaccine' Rally*. https://abcnews.go.com/GMA/OnCall/story?id=4987758

Al Amin, M. (2025, May 21). 50 years of progress: How Bangladesh chose health. *Gavi*. https://www.gavi.org/vaccineswork/50-years-progress-how-bangladesh-chose-health

Atkinson, W. L., Orenstein, W. A., & Krugman, S. (1992). The resurgence of measles in the United States, 1989-1990. *Annual Review of Medicine*, *43*, 451–463. https://doi.org/10.1146/annurev.me.43.020192.002315

Benecke, O., & DeYoung, S. E. (2019). Anti-vaccine decision making and the measles resurgence in the United States. *Global Pediatric Health*, *6*, 1–5. DOI: 10.1177/2333794X19862949

Blaskiewicz, R., & Baldwin, H. (2013). The Big Pharma conspiracy theory. *Medical Writing*, *22*(4), 259–261. DOI: 10.1179/2047480613Z.000000000142

Boghani, P. (2015, March 23). *J.B. Handley: No Study Shows "Vaccines Didn't Cause My Son's Autism."* PBS Frontline. [Interview transcript]. https://www.pbs.org/wgbh/frontline/article/j-b-handley-no-study-shows-vaccines-didnt-cause-my-sons-autism/

Boseley, S. (2018, July 18). How disgraced anti-vaxxer Andrew Wakefield was embraced by Trump's America. *The Guardian*. https://www.theguardian.com/society/2018/jul/18/how-disgraced-anti-vaxxer-andrew-wakefield-was-embraced-by-trumps-america

Boston Herald. (2018, November 17). All you need is love. *Boston Herald*. [Original story, June 5, 2008]. https://www.bostonherald.com/2008/06/05/all-you-need-is-love/

Brait, E. (2015, July 1). Jim Carrey calls California governor 'corporate fascist' over vaccine law. *The Guardian*. https://www.theguardian.com/society/2015/jul/01/jim-carrey-california-vaccine-law

Bricker, B., & Justice, J. (2018). The postmodern medical paradigm: A case study of anti-MMR vaccine arguments. *Western Journal of Communication*,1–18. DOI: 10.1080/10570314.2018.1510136

Bush, G. H. W. (1991, June 13). *Public papers: Remarks on childhood immunization*. George H. W. Bush Presidential Library & Museum. https://bush41library.tamu.edu/archives/public-papers/3091

CBS News. (2016, March 28). Anti-vaccination film pulled from Tribeca Film Festival. https://www.cbsnews.com/news/vaxxed-anti-vaccination-film-pulled-from-tribeca-film-festival-robert-de-niro/

CDC. (1991). Measles—United States, 1990. *Morbidity and Mortality Weekly Report*, *40*(22), 369–372. https://www.jstor.org/stable/41964631

CDC. (2000, February 17). *Elimination of endemic measles from the United States: Meeting*. https://www.federalregister.gov/documents/2000/02/24/00-4334/elimination-of-endemic-measles-from-the-united-states-meeting

CDC. (2021, January 26). *Routine measles, mumps, and rubella vaccination*. https://www.cdc.gov/vaccines/vpd/mmr/hcp/recommendations.html

CDC. (2024a, May 9). *History of measles*. https://www.cdc.gov/measles/about/history.html

CDC. (2024b, May 9). *Measles symptoms and complications*. https://www.cdc.gov/measles/signs-symptoms/index.html

CDC. (2024c, June 5). Signs & symptoms of mumps. https://www.cdc.gov/mumps/signs-symptoms/?CDC_AAref_Val=https://www.cdc.gov/mumps/about/signs-symptoms.html

CDC. (2024d, December 19). Thimerosal and vaccines. https://www.cdc.gov/vaccine-safety/about/thimerosal.html

CDC. (2024e, September 30). *Fast facts: Rubella and Congenital Rubella Syndrome (CRS)*. https://www.cdc.gov/global-rubella-vaccination/data-research/facts-stats/index.html

CDC. (2025a, January 17). *Rubella symptoms and complications*. https://www.cdc.gov/rubella/signs-symptoms/index.html

CDC. (2025b, April 15). *About autism spectrum disorder*/overview. https://www.cdc.gov/autism/about/index.html

CDC. (2025c). *Immunization schedules*. https://www.cdc.gov/vaccines/hcp/imz-schedules/index.html

CDC. (2025d, August 19). *Global measles outbreaks*. https://www.cdc.gov/global-measles-vaccination/data-research/global-measles-outbreaks/index.html

CDC. (2025e, August 27). *Measles cases and outbreaks*. https://www.cdc.gov/measles/data-research/index.html

Children's Health Defense. (2025). *The mission of Children's Health Defense*. https://childrenshealthdefense.org/about-us/childrens-health-defense-mission/

College of Physicians of Philadelphia. (n.d.). *Modern diphtheria vaccine*. https://historyofvaccines.org/history/diphtheria/timeline

College of Physicians of Philadelphia. (2022, April 20). *History of anti-vaccination movements*. https://historyofvaccines.org/vaccines-101/misconceptions-about-vaccines/history-anti-vaccination-movements

Commonwealth of Pennsylvania. (2017). *Title 28 Health and Safety, Chapter 23 School Health*. https://www.pacodeandbulletin.gov/Display/pacode?file=/secure/pacode/data/028/028toc.html&d=reduce

Costello, M. (1971, December 15). Magazine industry shake-out. In *CQ researcher*. CQ Press [Report]. DOI: https://doi.org/10.4135/cqresrre1971121500

de Broucker, G., Ahmed, S., Hasan, M. Z., Mehdi, G. G., Del Campo, J. M., Ali, M. W., Uddin, M. J., Constenla, D., & Patenaude, B. (2020). The economic burden of measles in children under five in Bangladesh. *BMC Health Services Research*, *20*, 1026–1035. https://doi.org/10.1186/s12913-020-05880-5

Editors of The Lancet. (2010, February 2). Retraction—Ileal-lymphoid-nodular hyperplasia, non-specific colitis, and pervasive developmental disorder in children. *The Lancet, 375*(9713), 445. DOI:10.1016/S0140-6736(10)60175-4.
English, P. (1991, September 20). Free shots available for tots. *The Oklahoman.* https://www.oklahoman.com/story/news/1991/09/20/free-shots-available-for-tots/62516417007/
English, P. (1992, September 26). Rhonda Walters honored. *The Oklahoman.* https://www.oklahoman.com/story/news/1992/09/26/rhonda-walters-honored/62481038007/
English, P. (1993, June 16). Child immunization rate improves across state. *The Oklahoman.* https://www.oklahoman.com/story/news/1993/06/16/child-immunization-rate-improves-across-state/62456262007/
Express. (2008, June 9). Autism action: Jenny McCarthy and Jim Carrey. *Washington Post.* https://www.washingtonpost.com/express/wp/2008/06/10/autism_action_jenny_mccarthy_and_jim_car/
Forrester, R. (2024, January 12). The role of advocacy in your communication strategy. *Forbes.* https://www.forbes.com/sites/forbescommunicationscouncil/2024/01/12/the-role-of-advocacy-in-your-communications-strategy/?sh=61d3e3b53875
Freed, G. L., Clark, S. J., Butchart, A. T., Singer, D. C., & Davis, M. M. (2011, May). Sources and perceived credibility of vaccine-safety information for parents. *Pediatrics, 127*(Supplement 1). S107–S112. https://doi.org/10.1542/peds.2010-1722P
Frontline. (2015, March 23). *Jenny McCarthy: "We're Not An Anti-Vaccine Movement ... We're Pro-Safe Vaccine."* PBS-TV. [Interview transcript]. https://www.pbs.org/wgbh/frontline/article/jenny-mccarthy-were-not-an-anti-vaccine-movement-were-pro-safe-vaccine/
Gavi. (2015). *Bangladesh—Findings from the 2014 Gavi full country evaluation.* https://www.healthdata.org/sites/default/files/files/Projects/GAVI/Gavi_Bangladesh_Handout_2015.pdf
Gavi. (2024). *About our alliance.* https://www.gavi.org/our-alliance/about
Global Health Delivery Project. (2011, April). *Cases in global health delivery: The Measles Initiative.* https://www.globalhealthdelivery.org/sites/projects.iq.harvard.edu/files/ghd/files/ghd-015_measles_initiative.pdf
Gorski, D. (2008, June 9). Jenny McCarthy, Jim Carrey, and "Green Our Vaccines": *Anti-* vaccine, *not* "pro-safe vaccine." *Science-Based Medicine.* https://sciencebasedmedicine.org/jenny-mccarthy-jim-carrey-and-green-our-vaccines-anti-vaccine-not-pro-safe-vaccine/
Gottlieb, S. D. (2016). Vaccine resistances reconsidered: Vaccine skeptics and the Jenny McCarthy effect. *BioSocieties, 11*(2), 152–174. https://doi.org/10.1057/biosoc.2015.30
GPRB. (2011). *Comprehensive multi-year plan of the national immunization program of Bangladesh 2011-2016.* https://www.gavi.org/sites/default/files/document/comprehensive-multi-year-plan-for-2011-2016pdf.pdf
Greyson, D. (2021). Challenges in vaccine communication. *Communication and Health: Media, Marketing, and Risk, 117.* https://scholarworks.umass.edu/communication_faculty_pubs/117
Haque, S. M. R., & Bari, W. (2013). Positive role of maternal education on measles vaccination coverage in Bangladesh. *International Journal of Psychology and Behavioral Sciences, 3*(1) 11–17. DOI: 10.5923/j.ijpbs.20130301.02
Hiltzik, M. (2015, January 27). Jenny McCarthy: Anti-vaxxer, public menace. *Los Angeles Times.* https://www.latimes.com/business/hiltzik/la-fi-mh-jenny-mccarthy-antivaxxer-public-menace-20150127-column.html

Hornsey, M. J., Harris, E. A., & Fielding, K. S. (2018). The psychological roots of anti- vaccination attitudes: A 24-nation investigation. *Health Psychology*, *37*(4), 307–315. https://doi.org/10.1037/hea0000586

Howson, C. P., Howe, C. J., & Fineberg, H. V. (Eds.). (1991). *Institute of medicine (US) committee to review the adverse consequences of pertussis and rubella vaccines*. National Academies Press. https://www.ncbi.nlm.nih.gov/books/NBK234365/

Hussain, R. (2015). The emerging digital culture of Bangladesh: Problems and prospects. *Journal of Philosophy, Culture and Religion*, *6*, 18–25. https://iiste.org/Journals/index.php/JPCR/article/view/20846/21106

Immunize.org. (2024a, July 11). *State MMR (Measles-Mumps-Rubella) vaccine requirements for childcare and school (K-12)*. https://www.immunize.org/official-guidance/state-policies/vaccine-requirements/mmr-childcare-school/

Immunize.org. (2024b, July 11). *State exemptions—Exemptions permitted for state childcare and school (K–12) as of May 2024*. https://www.immunize.org/official-guidance/state-policies/vaccine-requirements/exemptions-childcare-school/

Inside Radio. (2016, July 18). *Inside story: Radios in more U.S. homes now than in the 1950s*. https://www.insideradio.com/inside-story-radios-in-more-u-s-homes-now-than-in-the-1950s/article_8ed0712c-4cb5-11e6-a8c7-b3e12d86c826.html

Institute of Medicine. (2001). *Immunization safety review: Thimerosal-containing vaccines and neurodevelopmental disorders*. The National Academies Press. https://doi.org/10.17226/10208.

Jones, R. W., Marshall, C., & Bergman, T. P. (1996). Can a marketing campaign be used to achieve public policy goals? *Journal of Public Policy & Marketing*, *15*(1), 98–107. https://www.jstor.org/stable/30000339

Justia U.S. Supreme Court Center. (n.d.). *Jacobson v. Massachusetts*, 197 U.S. 11 (1905). https://supreme.justia.com/cases/federal/us/197/11/

Kapil, N., Bhatnagar, A., Alamgir, M., Osmani, A. G., Haque, M., & Rahman, S. M. (2022). Communication and community engagement to contain disease outbreaks and improve well-being: Rohingya refugee response, Bangladesh. In E. Manoncourt, R. Obergon & K. Chitnis (Eds.), *Communication and community engagement in disease outbreaks: Dealing with rights, culture, complexity and context*. (pp. 169–192). Springer International Publishing AG. https://doi.org/10.1007/978-3-030-92296-2 (eBook)

Kata, A. (2012). Anti-vaccine activists, web 2.0, and the postmodern paradigm – An overview of tactics and tropes used online by the anti-vaccination movement. *Vaccine*, *30*(25), 3778–3789. https://doi.org/10.1016/j.vaccine.2011.11.112

Kenzig, M. J., & Mumford, N. S. (2022). Theoretical considerations for communication campaigns to address vaccine hesitancy. *Health Promotion Practice*, *23*(1) 46–50. DOI: 10.1177/15248399211050415

Khanal, S., Bohara, R., Chacko, S., Sharifuzzaman, M., Shamsuzzaman, M., Goodson, J. L., Dabbagh, A., Kretsinger, K., Dhongde, D., Liyanage, J., Bahl, S., & Thapa, A. (2017, July 21). Progress toward measles elimination—Bangladesh, 2000–2016. *Morbidity and Mortality Weekly Report*, *66*(28) 753–757. DOI:10.15585/mmwr.mm6628a3

Kluger, J. (2009, April 1). Jenny McCarthy on Autism and vaccines. *Time*. https://time.com/archive/6933347/jenny-mccarthy-on-autism-and-vaccines/

Koplan, J. P., & Hinman, A. R. (1987). Decision analysis, public policy and pertussis: Are they compatible? *Medical Decision Making*, *7*(2), 71–73. DOI:10.1177/0272989X8700700201

Kulenkampff, M., Schwartzman, J. S., & Wilson, J. (1974). Neurological complications of pertussis inoculation. *Archives of Disease in Childhood*, *49(1)*, 46–49. https://doi.org/10.1136/adc.49.1.46

Lanzarotta, T., & Ramos, M. A. (2018). Mistrust in medicine: The rise and fall of America's first vaccine institute. *American Journal of Public Health*, *108*(6), 741–747. https://doi.org/10.2105/AJPH.2018.304348

Left, S. (2002, March 13). Email timeline. *The Guardian*. https://www.theguardian.com/technology/2002/mar/13/internetnews

Luies, S. K., Sultana, T., & Budden, A., et al. (2022). Partnerships in the introduction of new routine vaccines in Bangladesh: Evidence from a prospective process evaluation. *BMJ Open*, *12* e061742. DOI:10.1136/bmjopen-2022-061742

MacDonald, N. E. Sage Working Group on Vaccine Hesitancy (2015). Vaccine hesitancy: Definition, scope and determinants. *Vaccine*, *33*, 4161–4164. https://doi.org/10.1016/j.vaccine.2015.04.036

Mahoney, D. (2011, May). Vaccine safety info: Parents trust physicians. *Pediatric News*. https://cdn.mdedge.com/files/s3fs-public/issues/articles/70095_main_18.pdf

Mayor, S. (2004, March 13). Authors reject interpretation linking autism and MMR vaccine. *British Medical Journal*, *328*, 602. https://doi.org/10.1136/bmj.328.7440.602-c

McCarthy, J. (2025). *The official website of Jenny McCarthy—Bio*. https://www.jennymccarthy.com/jenny-mccarthy-bio/

McCracken, H. (2021, March 23). 17 moments in the long, turbulent history of vaccine skepticism. *Fast Company*. https://www.fastcompany.com/90610400/anti-vaccine-skepticism-timeline-history

Millward, G. (2017). A disability act? The vaccine damage payments act 1979 and the British Government's response to the pertussis vaccine scare. *Social History of Medicine: The Journal of The Society For The Social History of Medicine*, *30*(2), 429–447. https://doi.org/10.1093/shm/hkv140

Mosvick, N. (2024, February 20). *On this day, the supreme court rules on vaccines and public health*. National Constitution Center. https://constitutioncenter.org/blog/on-this-day-the-supreme-court-rules-on-vaccines-and-public-health

Mozammel, M., Chowdhury, H., & Satter, A. K. M. Z. (2012). *The role of E-Governance in creating digital Bangladesh*. https://www.semanticscholar.org/paper/The-Role-of-E-Governance-in-Creating-Digital-Mozammel-Chowdhury/b17fd90092ed27e1c0486a5409abdf5a2a511999

Murphey, H. L. (2025, January 29). The origins of the anti-vaccination movement. *Time*. https://time.com/7205900/anti-vaccination-movement-history/

News Services. (2001a, March 28). *Greater Pittsburgh measles immunization task force announces program to keep 30,000 kids in school*. [Press release]. University of Pittsburgh. https://www.news.pitt.edu/news/greater-pittsburgh-measles-immunization-task-force-announces-program-keep-30000-kids-school

News Services. (2001b, April 22). *Greater Pittsburgh measles immunization task force efforts benefit thousands of Pittsburgh students*. [Press release]. University of Pittsburgh. https://www.news.pitt.edu/news/greater-pittsburgh-measles-immunization-task-force-efforts-benefit-thousands-pittsburgh-student

News Services. (2001c, April 25). *Measles booster shots campaign passes halfway mark. Three more free clinics scheduled this weekend*. [Press release]. University of Pittsburgh. https://www.news.pitt.edu/news/measles-booster-shots-campaign-passes-halfway-mark-three-more-free-clinics-scheduled-weekend

News Services. (2001d, May 14). *Greater Pittsburgh measles immunization task force reaches successful conclusion, with 99 percent of Pittsburgh public school students in compliance more than 15,000 at-risk students aided in county*. [Press release]. University of Pittsburgh. https://www.news.pitt.edu/news/greater-pittsburgh-measles-immunization-task-force-reaches-successful-conclusion-99-percent-pit

News Services. (2002, June 21). *Pitt Public Affairs Office honors by two professional societies "Booster Booster" Awareness Program recognized as among the past year's best PR efforts nationwide.* [Press release]. University of Pittsburgh. https://www.news.pitt.edu/news/pitt-public-affairs-office-honored-two-professional-societies-booster-booster-awareness-program

NPR. (2025, February 13). *The Anti-vaccine movement.* [Throughline history podcast interview transcript]. https://www.npr.org/transcripts/1231104444

OSDH. (1993). *A report on the healthy futures media campaign.* [Unpublished report]. Oklahoma State Department of Health, Oklahoma City, OK

OSDH. (2011). *School administrator's guide to Oklahoma's Immunization Law.* https://oklahoma.gov/content/dam/ok/en/health/health2/documents/imm-school-administrators-guide-to-okla-immunization-law.pdf

PAHO. (n.d.). *Welcome to the Cold Chain Resource Center.* https://www.paho.org/en/immunization/cold-chain

PDH. (2017, March). *Procedural Manual School Immunization Regulations.* https://apps.health.pa.gov/silr/Docs/manual.pdf

Peck, M. G. (1994). *Improving urban MCH linkages: Highlights of the 1993 urban maternal and child health leadership conference.* CityMatCH at the University of Nebraska Medical Center. https://www.ojp.gov/ncjrs/virtual-library/abstracts/improving-urban-maternal-and-child-health-linkages-1993-urban-mch

Perry, D. M. (2013, July 17). Jenny McCarthy and fear-based parenting. *CNN.* https://www.cnn.com/2013/07/17/opinion/perry-jenny-mccarthy-autism

Petty, R. E., & Cacioppo, J. T. (1986). The elaboration likelihood model of persuasion. *Advances in experimental social psychology*, *19*, 123–205. Academic Press.

Pew Research Center. (2023, November 10). *Newspaper fact sheet.* https://www.pewresearch.org/journalism/fact-sheet/newspapers/

PRSA. (2002). *Silver Anvil Award of Excellence winner: Booster Booster: Greater Pittsburgh Measles Immunization Task Force.* https://www.prsa.org/

Quick, B. L., Reynolds-Tylus, T., Gonzalex, A. M., & Mackert, M. (2021). Segmenting priority audiences employing individual difference variables to improve health promotional efforts. In T. L. Thompson & P. J. Schulz (Eds.), *Health communication theory* (1st ed.), (pp. 19–41). John Wiley & Sons, Inc.

Regester, M., & Larkin, J. (2005). *Risk issues and crisis management: A casebook of best practice* (3rd ed.). Kogan Page Limited.

reliefweb. (2014, January 27). *Largest measles-rubella vaccination campaign underway in Bangladesh.* [Press release]. https://reliefweb.int/report/bangladesh/largest-measles-rubella-vaccination-campaign-underway-bangladesh

Rones, N. (September 1, 2008). "I'm on a mission to get my son better-and help others;" As Ryan faces new and frightening setbacks in his struggle with autism, his parents search for answers and find both purpose and peace in their new life. *Redbook.* https://www.redbookmag.com/life/mom-kids/advice/a3866/understanding-autism/

Roper, L., Hall, M. A. K., & Cohn, A. (2021). Overview of the United States' immunization program. *Journal of Infectious Diseases*, *224*(Supplement 4), S443–451. https://doi.org/10.1093/infdis/jiab310

Sarkar, P. K., Sarker, M. K., Doulah, S., & Bari, T. I. A. (2015). Expanded programme on immunization in Bangladesh: A success story. *Bangladesh Journal of Child Health*, *39*(2), 93–98. https://doi.org/10.3329/bjch.v39i2.31540

Sarma, H., Budden, A., Luies, S. K., Lim, S. S., Shamsuzzaman, M., Sultana, T., Rajaratnam, J. K., Craw, L., Banwell, C., Ali, M. W., & Uddin, M. J. (2019). Implementation of the world's largest measles-rubella mass vaccination campaign in Bangladesh: A process evaluation. *BMC Public Health*, *19*, 925–935. https://doi.org/10.1186/s12889-019-7176-4

Seither, R., Yusuf, O. B., & Dramann, D. et al. (2024, October 17). Coverage with selected vaccines and exemption rates among children in kindergarten — United States, 2023–24 school year. *Morbidity and Mortality Weekly Report*, *73*, 925–932. http://dx.doi.org/10.15585/mmwr.mm7341a3

Servaes, J., & Malikhao, P. (2010). Advocacy strategies for health communication. *Public Relations Review*, *36* 42–49. DOI:10.1016/j.pubrev.2009.08.017

smokenews.com. (1991, October 23). HEALTH DEPARTMENT: Immunizations given free to children: Rhonda Walters is sending parents the message that childhood immunizations are "Due by Two." *The Lawton Constitution*. https://www.swoknews.com/health-department-immunizations-given-free-to-children-rhonda-walters-is-sending-parents-the-message-that/article_2513376b-b47d-5eb4-b0e8-68fab53ec169.html

Staff Author. (2009, August 12). Jenny McCarthy maintains stance on more babies, more vaccines. *People*. https://people.com/parents/jenny-mccarthy-maintains-stance-on-more-babies-vaccines/

Sultana, M. (2014, February 19). *Bangladesh stages massive measles–rubella immunization campaign*. [Press release]. https://reliefweb.int/report/bangladesh/bangladesh-stages-massive-measles-rubella-immunization-campaign

Suozzo, A., Glassford, A., Ngu, A., & Roberts, B. (2025). *Generation Rescue Inc Form 990 for period ending December 2019*. Nonprofit Explorer [Tax return]. https://projects.propublica.org/nonprofits/display_990/202063267/01_2021_prefixes_20-22%2F202063267_201912_990_2021012117622846

Talk About Curing Autism. (2008, June 4). Green Our Vaccines rally with Jenny McCarthy & Jim Carrey & keynote address by Robert F. Kennedy Jr. *Fierce Healthcare*. [PRNewswire press release]. https://www.fiercehealthcare.com/healthcare/green-our-vaccines-rally-jenny-mccarthy-jim-carrey-keynote-address-by-robert-f-kennedy

The White House—Office of the Press Secretary. (1999, November 24). *President Clinton names Rhonda Walters as a member of the commission on presidential scholars* [Press release]. https://clintonwhitehouse6.archives.gov/1999/11/1999-11-24-walters-named-to-the-commission-on-presidential-scholars.html

Thompson, L. (Writer and Producer). (1982). *DPT: Vaccine roulette*. WRC-TV. https://search.worldcat.org/title/DPT-:-vaccine-roulette/oclc/9274001

Trujillo, K. L., Motta, M., Callahan, T., & Sylvester, S. (2020). Correcting misperceptions about the MMR vaccine: Using psychological risk factors to inform targeted communication strategies. *Political Research Quarterly*, 1–15. https://doi.org/10.1177/1065912920907695

Uddin, M. J., Adhikary, G., Ali, M. W., Ahmed, S., Shamsuzzaman, M., Odell, C., Hashiguchi, L., Lim, S., & Alam, N. (2016). Evaluation of impact of measles rubella campaign on vaccination coverage and routine immunization services in Bangladesh. *BMC Infectious Disease*, *16* 411–420. DOI: 10.1186/s12879-016-1758-x

United Nations Foundation. (2006, February 22). *Bangladesh launches largest ever measles vaccination campaign*. [Press release]. https://unfoundation.org/media/bangladesh-launches-largest-ever-measles-vaccination-campaign/

United States Census Bureau. (2023, September 1). *History and the Census: Philo Farnsworth and the invention of the television*. https://www.census.gov/about/history/stories/monthly/2023/september-2023.html

University of Michigan Health System. (2011, April 1). Parents trust doctors most when it comes to information about vaccine safety. *ScienceDaily*. www.sciencedaily.com/releases/2011/04/110401142857.htm

USDHHS. (1991). *Healthy people 2000: National Health Promotion and Disease Prevention Objectives*. Public Health Service. https://files.eric.ed.gov/fulltext/ED332957.pdf

USDHHS. (2025a, April 21). *Robert F. Kennedy, Jr.* https://www.hhs.gov/about/leadership/robert-kennedy.html

USDHHS. (2025b, April 15). 'Autism epidemic runs rampant,' New data shows 1 in 31 children afflicted. [News release]. https://www.hhs.gov/press-room/autism-epidemic-runs-rampant-new-data-shows-grants.html

Vaccine and Immunization Amendments of 1990 Act. 101st Congress§ Section Two (1990). https://www.congress.gov/101/statute/STATUTE-104/STATUTE-104-Pg1285.pdf

Vannice, K. S., Salmon, D. A., Shui, I., Omer, S. B., Kissner, J., Edwards, K. M., Sparks, R., Dekker, C. L., Klein, N. P., & Gust, D. A. (2011). Attitudes and beliefs of parents concerned about vaccines: Impact of timing of immunization information. *Pediatrics*, *127*(Supplement 1), S120–S126. https://doi.org/10.1542/peds.2010-1722R

Wakefield, A. J., Murch, S. H., Anthony, A., Linnel, J., Casson, D. M., Malik, M., Berelowitz, M., Dhillon, A. P., Thomson, M. A., Harvey, P., Valentine, A., Davies, S. E., & Walker- Smith, J. A. (1998, February 28). Ileal-lymphoid-nodular hyperplasia, non-specific colitis, and pervasive developmental disorder in children. *The Lancet*, *351*, 637–41. https://doi.org/10.1016/S0140-6736(97)11096-0

WHO. (n.d.). *History of the measles vaccine*. https://www.who.int/news-room/spotlight/history-of-vaccination/history-of-measles-vaccination

WHO. (2012). *Global measles and rubella strategic plan: 2012-2020*. https://iris.who.int/bitstream/handle/10665/44855/9789241503396_eng.pdf

WHO. (2024a, November 14). *Measles*. https://www.who.int/news-room/fact-sheets/detail/measles

WHO. (2024b, December 31). *50th anniversary of the Expanded Programme on Immunization (EPI)*. https://www.who.int/news-room/events/detail/2024/01/01/default-calendar/50th-anniversary-of-the-expanded-programme-on-immunization-(epi)

WHO Regional Office for South-East Asia. (2015). *Strategic plan for measles elimination and rubella and congenital rubella syndrome control in the South-East Asia region, 2014-2020*. WHO Regional Office for South-East Asia. https://iris.who.int/handle/10665/205923

Wolfe, R. M., & Sharp, L. K. (2002). Anti-vaccinationists past and present. *BMJ (Clinical Research Ed*, *325*(7361), 430–432. https://doi.org/10.1136/bmj.325.7361.430

World Bank. (2023, September 19). *Literacy rate, adult total (% of people ages 15 and above) - Bangladesh*. https://data.worldbank.org/indicator/SE.ADT.LITR.ZS?locations=BD

6

CASE STUDIES ON THE HIV/AIDS (HUMAN IMMUNODEFICIENCY VIRUS/ACQUIRED IMMUNODEFICIENCY SYNDROME) PANDEMIC, 1981 TO PRESENT

6.1 INTRODUCTION

HIV/AIDS in context

The early news coverage in 1981 on an unknown and mysterious illness, initially called the "gay cancer," (Wright, 2006, para. 1), appeared when healthy and young gay men in New York City and Los Angeles developed purple skin spots and swollen lymph nodes and passed away due to severe pneumonia or a type of cancer usually contracted by older people (Blakemore, 2017). Medical doctors and researchers were daunted by figuring out the cause and treatment of this unknown illness, particularly as 337 cases were reported, of which 130 patients perished before the end of the year (HIV.gov, n.d.). Doctors later identified Kaposi's Sarcoma, a cancer in the lining of the blood vessels and lymph nodes (American Cancer Society, n.d.), in advanced stages of HIV while the CDC published findings that Pneumocystis carinii pneumonia, a severe lung infection, was a cause, particularly for people with compromised immune systems (Blakemore, 2017).

Terms for the new diseases evolved since 1981. In 1982, medical professionals started to use the term Gay-Related Immune Deficiency (GRID), which "reflected homophobic ignorance and the dearth of epidemiologic evidence that existed at the time" (Ayala & Spieldenner, 2021, p. 1240). The term Acquired Immunodeficiency Syndrome (AIDS) was first used by the CDC (1982), defined as: "A disease at least moderately predictive of a defect in cell-mediated immunity, occurring in a person with no known cause for diminished resistance to that disease" (para. 6), which may cause

DOI: 10.4324/9781003434382-6

severe or deadly diseases, such as tuberculosis and cancer (WHO, 2025a). The International Committee on the Taxonomy of Viruses declared the term Human Immunodeficiency Virus (HIV), a virus that attacks white blood cells and weakens one's immunity system, as the official name for the virus that may lead to an advanced condition known as AIDS, in 1986 (HIV.gov, n.d.; WHO, 2025a).

The origin of HIV remains unknown. In 1959, the first confirmed HIV case came from a blood sample of a person residing in the Democratic Republic of Congo, but this person is unproven to be the first to contract HIV. Other apparent AIDS deaths occurred: a young man in St. Louis in 1969 and a Norwegian sailor in 1976 after being in Africa (Fitzsimons, 2018). A French Canadian flight attendant was mistakenly labeled as the first person with HIV, who contracted the virus in Africa or Haiti, and then spread it to gay men in the U.S. before his death in 1984. Further genetic analysis proved that the virus existed in New York City before the flight attendant traveled to that city (McNeil, 2016).

According to the World Health Organization (2025b), approximately 91.4 million people have contracted HIV, and 44.1 million people worldwide have lost their lives due to HIV since the epidemic's inception. The WHO African Region with 47 member states has been the most critically affected location, with one in every 30 adults living with HIV, comprising over two-thirds of the global population with HIV.

Two publicized announcements, among others, brought awareness that HIV can affect other types of people. Ryan White, age 13, from Indiana, contracted HIV from a blood transfusion in 1984, becoming one of the first children and hemophiliacs with HIV, but he also became a household name when his school banned his attendance until his mother battled in court for one-and-a-half years for his return to school. Ryan suffered discrimination with people claiming "God's punishment" for assuming he was gay. The family relocated, and Ryan went to another school and died a month before his high school graduation (HRSA, 2022). The other new face was Earvin "Magic" Johnson, a widely known basketball star of the Los Angeles Lakers, when he announced his HIV diagnosis and his retirement from basketball in 1991. As a heterosexual Black man, Magic "served as a catalyst in the United States for rapidly correcting the misperceptions of who was at risk for contracting HIV" (Cardazzi et al., 2023, p. 2048), thereby encouraging straight men to get tested for HIV and seek medical help.

A number of celebrities passed away due to AIDS, including tennis player Arthur Ashe; model Gia Carangi (one of the first women to die from AIDS); musicians Freddie Mercury of Queen, Eazy-E of NWA, Tom Fogerty of Creedence Clearwater Revival, and Liberace; fashion designers Perry Ellis and Halston; artist Keith Haring; actors Rock Hudson (considered the first Hollywood star to die from AIDS), Anthony Perkins, and Robert Reed; ballet dancer Rudolf Nureyev; and owner Steve Rubell of Studio 54 in New York City famous in the 1970s (Dobbins, 2021).

Other well-known people continue to live with HIV, such as Earvin "Magic" Johnson, former American National Basketball Association player who became an HIV/AIDS advocate and fundraiser; Greg Louganis, American Olympic Gold medalist in diving; Chuck Panozzo, American bass player for the band Styx; Charlie Sheen, American actor; and Jonathan Van Ness, American author, comedian, and TV personality of *Queer Eye* (Frysh, 2023).

Transmission and symptoms

HIV can be transmitted by body fluids from unprotected sex regardless of gender and needle sharing with people infected with the virus, as well as by infected medical tools for blood transfusions and other medical procedures. HIV-infected women can spread the infection to their unborn child during pregnancy and while breastfeeding the infant. During the early years of HIV, fears spread about the ways infection can be spread. HIV cannot be spread by healthy people touching, kissing, or sharing food and drinks with infected people (WHO, 2023).

During the first few weeks of contracting HIV, people may have no symptoms or experience flu-like symptoms, such as a fever, sore throat, and achiness. As the infection develops over a few months, people may also experience weight loss, a cough, and swollen lymph nodes. During the most severe cases, people without undergoing any treatments and those with preexisting infections (such as hepatitis C and hepatitis B) face a weakened immune system, making them vulnerable to other diseases (WHO, 2025a).

Prevention

President Ronald Reagan called AIDS "public health enemy No. 1" six years after the disease broke out in the U.S. (Ronald Reagan Presidential Library & Museum, 1987, para. 11) and appealed initially for monogamy or abstinence as solutions before a cure or treatment could be found (Gerstenzang, 1987). Condoms, primarily used by heterosexual couples before HIV for birth control, helped prevent HIV transmission between gay and straight couples, along with the added benefit of preventing other sexually transmitted infections. Overindulging in alcohol and taking drugs can allow lower resistance to condom-less sexual behavior or exchange of contaminated needles. Infected medical tools for blood transfusions and medical procedures also spread HIV. Other recommended preventive measures include voluntary male circumcisions (WHO, 2023) and rehabilitation services for people who inject drugs (UNODC, WHO, & UNAIDS, 2019).

The antibodies of HIV infection can be determined through self-tests, yet rapid diagnostic tests conducted by a health technician at a clinic confirm more accurate results. Most HIV-infected people acquire antibodies within four weeks, also referred to as the "so-called window period" when HIV may not yet be identified but infected people still can spread HIV to others. Positive test results require a retest to rule out errors (WHO, 2025a, para. 15).

At this time, no cure for HIV has been invented; however, antiretroviral therapy (ART) helps HIV-positive individuals—without evidence of HIV in their blood—strengthen their immune system to combat infections and prevent spreading HIV to others. ART can help pregnant women lessen the chance of HIV transmission to fetuses and to their infants while nursing (WHO, 2025a). With daily treatment, infected people can live normal lives.

Communication

A major development in television was CNN, the first TV channel providing 24/7 news coverage in 1980. Previously, TV viewers seeking national and international news had to rely on half-hour evening news programs on the three national networks (ABC, CBS, and NBC). The first nightly one-hour program on national news, *The MacNeil/Lehrer NewsHour*, aired on PBS in 1983, thereby "proving there existed both a need and a substantial audience for serious, long-form journalism" (PBS, n.d., para. 1). Co-host Robert MacNeil stated, "...the American public is smarter than they're often given credit for on television and they don't all need things in little bite-sized, candy-sized McNuggets of news" (Brown & Davenport, 2024, para. 12). These programs also offered more opportunities for public relations practitioners to pitch story ideas and to set up interviews for experts to provide more context on current events.

In 1981, 25% of U.S. households subscribed to cable TV. In addition to CNN, other cable networks available at that time were the Christian Broadcast Network (CBN), Nickelodeon, ESPN, BET, USA, and MTV, among others (Adgate, 2020). Total circulation of U.S. daily newspapers was high—before digital editions existed—61,431,000 million for weekday editions and 55,180,000 for Sunday editions in 1981 (Pew Research Center, 2023). Advertising revenues in magazines were flat in 1981 after a robust trend in the late 1970s (Kleinfield, 1981). A few women's and health-related magazines debuted the same year—*Health, Shape,* and *Woman's World* (Harvard Radcliffe Institute's Schlesinger Library, n.d.)

Impact

As HIV/AIDS spread worldwide, public health organizations, activist groups, and foundations became invested in raising awareness, dispelling panic, and communicating new medical treatments. In addition, the situation necessitated a conversation and subsequent changes about condoms when birth control could not be communicated in mass media.

The oldest HIV/AIDS activist group, the Gay Men's Health Crisis (now called GMHC), was founded in 1982 as the first community-based nonprofit on HIV/AIDS education. During its inaugural year, GMHC (n.d.) opened its office in Manhattan, started the first AIDS phone hotline in the world, launched a buddy system to support the needs of people with AIDS, and created free newsletters for medical professionals and the Library of Congress—years before the U.S. government became involved.

By summer 1985, the U.S. public was paying attention and 95% became familiar with the term AIDS, according to research conducted by the Gallup Organization (CDC, 1985). Although the CDC announced the virus worldwide in 1981, the first public health education campaign was launched in 1987 after the U.S. Surgeon General C. Everett Koop released his report on AIDS to Congress, resulting in 12 million copies shared with their constituents. The campaign needed to address five years of informational gaps that generated anxiety and misinformation about HIV/AIDS and infected people (Davis, 2006). Case study 6.2 explores early HIV/AIDS campaigns in the U.S.

Celebrities also played a significant role in helping to dispel myths and social stigma. For example, photos of a gloveless-Princess Diana shaking the hands of infected men in their hospital beds were transmitted around the globe to demonstrate that touching infected people would not spread the virus. While visiting the first HIV/AIDS hospital unit in London in 1987, Princess Diana stated: "HIV does not make people dangerous to know. You can shake their hands and give them a hug. Heaven knows they need it. What's more, you can share their homes, their workplaces, and their playgrounds and toys" (Green, 2021, para. 3). Celebrities, such as Magic Johnson and Elton John, set up foundations for HIV/AIDs awareness, treatment, and prevention as covered in case study 6.3.

With condoms being a significant and easily available preventive measure, advertisers and public relations practitioners had to contend with mass media restrictions on prophylactics—the "condom" word was not allowed. The word "protection" and other euphemisms could be used gingerly. The three major networks would not allow national airing of sex-related ads. HIV/AIDS activities supported by the U.S. Surgeon General persuaded local TV stations to show prophylactic ads, whether paid commercials or public service announcements, in 1987, mostly during late night hours. The caveat was that the station had to decide if the content would be acceptable or offensive to their local viewers. San Francisco's KRON was the first TV station to air ads of condoms (Chase, 1987). Before the inaugural World AIDS Day in 1988, the first AIDS public health campaign with TV PSAs and print ads appeared in the U.S. with the "condom" word (Davis, 2006). The U.S. was not unique with the advertising restrictions: the first condom ad aired on TV in the U.K. in 1987 (Toureille, 2017) and the first time the word "condom" appeared on a TV ad in Italy, a predominantly Catholic country, was in 2007 (Rusbridger & O'Leary, 2007). Case study 6.4 covers a condom campaign created in Germany.

Although HIV is far from over, with 40.8 million people infected at the end of 2024 (WHO, 2025a), people have greater access to testing and treatments. According to UNAIDS (2024a) approximately 86% of people worldwide with HIV were tested and knew their results in 2023. New HIV infections dropped by 38% in 2022 from 2010 and 59% since 1995. In 2022, 76% of people worldwide infected with HIV were undergoing antiretroviral therapy, and an estimated 630,000 people perished from AIDS-related deaths, unlike 2 million deaths in 2004 and 1.3 million deaths in 2010, meaning a reduction of 69% from its peak period in 2004 (UNAIDS, 2023). Despite the improving numbers and effective treatments, 14% of people around the globe are unaware if they have contacted HIV. Those living in geographic regions and communities facing poverty, famine, other diseases, unsanitary living conditions, wars, and natural disasters encounter greater challenges for medical needs.

UNAIDS (2022) addressed other challenges and the need for worldwide cooperation, as the COVID-19 pandemic "led to disruptions to key HIV treatment and prevention services, millions of girls out of school, and spikes in teenage pregnancies and gender-based violence" (p. 4). In addition, "HIV-related stigma and discrimination, together with other social inequalities and exclusion, continue to be key barriers, and our response to HIV/AIDS across the globe may be in jeopardy without continued commitment and strong partnerships" (HIV.gov, 2025a, para. 14)

6.2 FIRST U.S. FEDERAL GOVERNMENT HIV/AIDS CAMPAIGNS: "AMERICA RESPONDS TO AIDS" AND "UNDERSTAND AIDS" NATIONWIDE MAILER TO U.S. HOUSEHOLDS

Situation analysis

CDC (2024) determined that sexual contact and infected shared needles were the causes of HIV in 1981 and added infected blood transfusions the following year. Pervasive misinformation about the epidemic created fear among the public unaware of how the virus could be spread, resulting in discrimination against people infected with HIV, primarily the gay community. In addition, conservative politicians and religious groups spread anti-gay propaganda. The president's communications director described AIDS as "nature's revenge on gay men" (SPLC, 2005, para. 11) in 1981. During Reagan's presidency, the Family Protection Act (FPA) established in 1981 (introduced twice in the House and once in the Senate) described its goals in its subtitle: "States as the purposes of this Act the strengthening of the American family and the reversal of governmental policies which hinder its strength and prosperity" (H.R.311, 1981). The proposed bill contained explicit discrimination and prohibitions against the LGBTQ community (the term, "homosexuals," was widely used during that time):

> Prohibits the expenditure of Federal funds to any organization which presents male or female homosexuality as an acceptable alternative life style [sic] or which suggests that it can be an acceptable life style [sic]. Amends the Civil Rights Act of 1964 to provide that any action taken by an employer against a homosexual shall not be considered an unlawful employment practice. Prohibits any instrumentality of the Federal Government from seeking to enforce nondiscrimination with respect to homosexuals.
>
> *(H.R.311, 1981, para. 24)*

Despite the support of conservatives, the bill expired in committee and was never passed. Evangelical preacher and televangelist Jerry Falwell was one of the founders of the Moral Majority, a movement of conservative Christian voters who backed Reagan's presidency, which became the largest Christian advocacy group at the time (Biography, 2023; The Editors of Encyclopaedia Britannica, 2018). Their voices, particularly Falwell's on radio and TV, loudly expressed concerns about the gay community and women's equality (Equal Rights Amendment) among other issues they believed to be "unmoral" during Reagan's two presidential terms from 1981 to 1989 (Matzko, n.d.).

An important government figure in pushing for HIV/AIDS education was the U.S. Surgeon General C. Everett Koop who served from 1981 to 1989. In his obituary, *The New York Times* (Noble, 2013) stated that Koop "was widely regarded as the most influential surgeon general in American history and played a crucial role in changing public attitudes about smoking" (para. 1) and "almost single-handedly pushed the government into taking a more aggressive stand against AIDS" (para 4). One of Koop's major accomplishments in HIV/AIDS education was his report titled the *Surgeon General's Report on AIDS* released October 1986

(USPHS, 1986). His report appealed for a nationwide educational program on sex and AIDS that encouraged condom usage, dispelled myths on how HIV can be contracted (such as from mosquitoes), and provided facts on AIDS transmission and prevention (CDC, 2024). In an editorial in *Public Health Reports*, Koop (1987) stated:

> Controversial and sensitive issues are inherent in the subject of AIDS, and these issues are addressed in my report. Value judgments are absent. This is an objective health and medical report, which I would like every adult and adolescent to read. The impact of AIDS on our society is and will continue to be devastating.
>
> *(p. 1)*

Although Koop's report received backlash from conservatives, the report was well regarded with positive feedback from the public and media, welcoming "Koop's reframing of AIDS as a medical rather than moral issue, as well as his focus on facts rather than fear" (McKeever, 2021, p. 4). Koop's report sparked the U.S. government to undertake the first nationwide public health campaign on AIDS/HIV. Another impetus was when Congress mandated that CDC and USPHS send a mailer on AIDS to all American households by the end of June 1988 under Statute at Large 101 Stat. 1329–Public Law 100-202 (Davis, 1991; H. J. Res. 395, 1987).

"America responds to AIDS" and "Understanding AIDS" campaigns

In 1987, CDC hired Ogilvy & Mather (now called Ogilvy and part of WPP), a global creative agency with advertising and public relations services among others, to manage the "America responds to AIDS" (ARTA) communications campaign, the first public health communication campaign on AIDS in the U.S (PRSA, 1988), and to handle the 1988 "Understanding AIDS" pamphlet that set another milestone—the first time the federal government mailed a document on a public health issue to all U.S. residents (PRSA, 1989).

ARTA's objectives

ARTA's three broad goals were as follows (CDC, 2024):

- Build awareness of AIDS for people to understand the true facts about AIDS from transmission to treatment.
- Stop the spread of HIV infection by communicating precautionary measures.
- Urge people to find out information about testing, counseling, and seeking treatment, if infected.

The primary objectives of the "American Responds to AIDS" mailing were as follows:

- Prompt American households to read, think, and discuss topics in the brochure.
- Gain the support of a network of spokespersons by engaging important constituents in the process of creating the mailing.
- Encourage the media to become a part of the dialogue on AIDS and cover stories on the issues factually (PRSA, 1989).

Research

Initial research for developing the ARTA campaign included in-depth secondary research analysis of literature and data on HIV, AIDS, and public familiarity with the epidemic culled from CDC surveillance data, survey results from the National Center for Health Statistics, data from state-collected surveys, and national Roper and Gallup polls. A series of focus groups or meetings took place first with governmental and nongovernmental officials in national, state, regional, and local health departments, as well as with opinion leaders and professionals in AIDS prevention and education (PRSA,1988; Woods et al., 1991). The major findings were that few Americans had any investment in AIDS since it had not impacted their lives directly, and, consequently, they found the disease unrelatable and were uninterested in changing their personal behavior for themselves or their families (PRSA, 1988).

Research in fall 1987 undertaken for the "America Responds to AIDS" mailer included 10 focus groups in 10 high- and low-prevalence cities, 31 community meetings in 28 cities with over 600 leaders of various groups from Black and Latino and women and youth to health professionals and journalists in communications (Davis, 1991). The second phase of research in 1988 used 12 focus groups of individuals from diverse urban neighborhoods to review a prototype brochure in English and Spanish. In addition, health educators and AIDS prevention specialists provided feedback. The research findings of the prototype testing impacted the development of the final version of the mailer (Davis, 1991; PRSA, 1989).

Outside of CDC's research, Gallup conducted its own research on how Americans perceived AIDS (McCarthy, 2019). In 1983, Gallup reported that over three out of four Americans had knowledge of AIDS. However, Gallup discovered that 51% of Americans believed people contracted AIDS because it was their own fault and 43% to 44% agreed that AIDS could be attributed to God's retribution for sinful sexual behavior in responses respectively from two polls conducted in 1987 (McCarthy, 2019). The percentage of respondents in 1985 who indicated that they or another person they knew avoided places with gay men as a precautionary measure to prevent the disease was 28%. This number rose to 44% the following year. Additionally, 60% of Americans thought people with AIDS should carry an identification card when they contracted the virus, and 33% believed that employers should be able to dismiss employees with AIDS. On the positive side, many Americans (78%) believed that people with AIDS should receive compassion (McCarthy, 2019).

Five communication phases

ARTA campaign was structured in five phases, giving the communications team the opportunity to apply lessons learned with each phase (Woods et al., 1991). This case study focuses on the first four phases of the campaign launch and mailings from 1987 to 1989. The last phase was built on the previous four phases and moved into a different direction on educating the public.

Phase I: "General awareness: Humanizing AIDS"

The first phase began in fall 1987 to reach a general audience and to build awareness of AIDS while allaying fears of catching AIDS through casual contact, such as hugging, kissing, and sharing cutlery and linens. Since AIDS reached the U.S. in 1981, Americans had six years of formulating their own beliefs with limited information and plenty of misinformation. CDC was mandated to undertake an educational public relations campaign to provide information to the public and the media. The fall phase also aimed to provide answers to questions asked on the national AIDS Hotline, to encourage compassion for people with AIDS, and to "begin building a national consensus on AIDS" (PRSA, 1988, para. 4).

The first ARTA news conference was held with the secretary of Health and Human Services and other public health officials as spokespersons on the last day of September 1987, right before the new presidential proclamation, "AIDS Awareness Month," in October, with an audience of 50 reporters from leading print and broadcast media. Other tactics included a new ARTA logo for all materials; video news releases (brief pre-packaged broadcast-style stories for television usage); live and recorded satellite news interviews with public health experts; and print, radio, and television PSAs (Keiser, 1991; PRSA, 1988). PSAs were designed to meet AIDS healthcare professionals and volunteers who discuss their work over the previous six years and people with AIDS who share how they contracted the disease (PRSA, 1988).

Phase II: Understanding AIDS

During this phase, the *Understanding AIDS* educational brochure was created and mailed to the general public in 1988, as well as promoted through the media and events. CDC decided to send the same mailer to all Americans. The first challenge was preparing the written content to make complex information easy to understand and to address sensitive topics tactfully (Davis, 1991) as follows:

- The research showed that people found the term, "casual contact" unclear; preferred frank, understandable language instead of euphemisms (i.e., "body fluids"); and discuss people's behaviors rather than the names of high-risk groups ("drug addicts" and "gay") (p. 657).
- The readability level was tested on a seventh-grade level by using Gunning and SMOG Readability formulas (Readable, n.d.). The document was mailed to a population of various educational levels.
- The copy needed to be non-judgmental by using scientific terms.
- Scientific terms needed to be accurate yet clearly understandable. CDC writers and editors found obtaining consensus on how scientific content was worded since scientists were expanding and developing knowledge as their research on AIDS was underway.
- The encouragement of prophylactics or abstinence was problematic with various groups.

The approval process had to be streamlined to meet the distribution deadline. The then CDC director had the final approval and met daily with the staff members during the writing and design process. Based on findings from a focus group, Dr. Koop, the surgeon general, was identified as the government official with credibility on medical topics, thereby he was invited to review the final draft brochure and added changes to the texts. In addition, the Government Printing Office and U.S. Post Office ensured that the brochure's format conformed with printing and mailing coordination, expenditures, and deadlines. All mailings were addressed to "Postal Patron" and distributed through 455,000 postal carrier routes via 21 bulk mail centers. The mailing process of approximately English-language 126 million brochures was shipped in stages over two weeks. A Spanish-language brochure also was distributed throughout Puerto Rico (Davis, 1991).

One of the major events was a news conference in May featuring Dr. Koop, the secretary of the Department of Health and Human Services, CDC director, and other commentators. Approximately 8,000 AIDS commentators and journalists received briefing kits in advance with the brochure, background information, story ideas, and other details (Davis, 1991).

Other promotional tactics (PRSA,1989) included the following:

- A 90-minute interview video teleconference in a question-and-answer format for CDC experts to address any questions from physicians located at 1,600 hospitals nationwide.
- Four television PSAs (one in English, three in Spanish) and print PSAs placed in major publications.
- Video news releases distributed via satellite to almost 650 television stations.
- Five satellite news interviews highlighting federal health experts.
- Matte service articles (pre-packaged and pre-formatted news stories) bylined by Dr. Koop to weekly and daily newspapers nationwide.
- Point-of-purchase displays sent to pharmacies and health clubs among other locations.
- Posters were distributed to 11,000 post offices.

Phase III: "Women at Risk/Multiple Partners/ Sexually Active Adults"

This campaign phase later in 1988 aimed to curtail myths and stereotypes about Blacks and Hispanics as reported in the media in stories about higher rates of infections among Blacks and Hispanics. The CDC assistant secretary of Health and Human Services and the CDC director hosted national news conference to introduce the *Women at Risk and Multiple Partners/ Sexually Active Adults* mailer, which was attended by 24 broadcast and 18 print journalists. Other activities include a VNR, a press kit in Spanish mailed to over 400 Spanish-language media outlets, and a media reception in New York City with members of the Black community (Keiser, 1991).

Phase IV: "Parents and Youth"

CDC scientists and other scientific researchers were concerned about the rising number of teenagers being diagnosed with AIDS, which led to the fourth phase. The "AIDS Prevention Guide" was created in 1989 to reach concerned parents with advice on how to address this topic to their children. The guide also included handouts for teenagers and children to help them talk about the epidemic. A news conference was held to announce this phase with over 50 journalists in attendance, along with advance copies of the new brochure and a press kit distributed to 1,200 media outlets nationwide. The communications team sought endorsements of the guide from 28 national organizations, which were also included in the press kit. Other tactics included a VNR with Spanish-language translation, satellite news interviews with health officials, other media events and meetings, and three audio news releases, which are essentially news releases for radio with pre-taped audio of spokespersons and other sound effects as needed for a story (Keiser, 1991).

Phase V: "Preventing HIV Infection and AIDS: Taking the Next Steps"

Building on the four previous phases, this last phase in 1990 moved beyond basic facts, such as how AIDS is transmitted, to motivate people involved with risky behaviors to get tested, schedule meetings with counselors, and seek medical treatment (Woods et al., 1991).

Results

This case study covered public relations undertaken during the first four phases of the ARTA campaign from 1987 to 1989.

Phase I—With media relations being an important part of Phase I, media coverage included 222 published stories, achieving 49 million reader impressions, which means the estimated number of people who might have seen an article in this case, and the term also applies to those who heard a story on the radio, or watched it on television before social media. Broadcast media coverage spanned all network nightly news shows (NBC, CBC, ABC, and CNN) and leading public and private national radio outlets, while VNRs were used on approximately 66 television stations. (Keiser, 1991). The fall campaign also led to more than triple the number of calls to the National AIDS Hotline. Leadership forums, open discussion events, and campaign planning workshops led to helping to reach a national consensus on AIDS. The value of donated airtime of the PSAs exceeded USD 4 million (PRSA, 1988).

Phase II—The "Understanding AIDS" mailing was delivered by June 15, two weeks ahead of the mandate from Congress. According to Dr. David Davis (1991), writer-editor for the National AIDS Information and Education Program in the Office of the Deputy Director for HIV at CDC, three national telephone surveys conducted by the CDC, Gallup, and University of California, San Francisco indicated that 60% of the recipients remembered receiving the document. Whites, men, and high school graduates had greater recall of the brochure, and 80% read at least half of the document. This finding was interpreted to mean, by Davis (1991), "that almost 87 million adults read 'Understanding AIDS,' making it the most widely read publication in July 1998 (compared to the second most read publication that month, *Reader's Digest*, with 48.5 million readers)" (p. 660). Another significant finding was 40% to 50% of readers engaged in conversations on the topic with their family or friends and 30% discussed it with their children.

In addition, 29 leading AIDS-related organizations endorsed the mailing. The mailing was covered in over 1,300 print media, with millions of media impressions—350 million general audience, 16.7 million Black readers, and almost 10 million Latino readers—and broadcast media generated 742 million media impressions. Print PSAs ran in major Spanish-language and English-language publications, and broadcast PSAs generated USD 3.7 million of complimentary airtime (PRSA, 1989).

Phase III—According to Niki Hutton Keiser (1991), AIDS communications specialist with the Centers for Disease Control's National AIDS Information and Education Program, important lessons were learned within this phase:

> The media coverage of this phase of the campaign, while positive in content, was the lowest in volume of any phase to date. However, articles were carried by Jet magazine, the Associated Press, and the Miami Times, partially due to the special efforts to involve media predominately serving racial or ethnic minority audiences. Important lessons were learned from this phase. Unlike the previous phases, this one offered varying messages for different target audiences. There was no central theme for the media to grasp and present in a clear story. Without a single "hook," the result was less coverage.
>
> *(p. 625)*

Phase IV—Broadcast media results were particularly successful during this phase (Keiser, 1991). Television evening new shows, including shows on ABC, PBS, and CNN, reached 38 million viewers while satellite news interviews reached 2.4 million people. A nationally syndicated television show popular during this time, "*Geraldo!,*" featured the AIDS brochure and information, attributing to almost 6,775 calls on the National AIDS hotline on the same day the show aired. Leading radio networks joined the news conference and filed stories with their affiliates nationwide. The VNRs were viewed by approximately 2.5 million potential viewers, and audio news releases aired on 127 stations in 38 states, potentially reaching 5.5 million potential listeners. Highlights of print media included 400 articles with 154+ million reader impressions (Keiser, 1991).

These two campaigns won the Silver Anvil Award of Excellence from PRSA in 1988 and 1989. Figure 6.1 shows an example of poster from the "Let's Stop HIV Together" campaign that started in 2012.

FIGURE 6.1 Example of poster from "Let's Stop HIV Together" campaign launched in July 2012. Courtesy of Centers for Disease Control and Prevention.

Theoretical considerations

Much of the success of the ARTA campaign can be attributed to Surgeon General Dr. C. Everett Koop, hereafter referred to as Koop. Cameron (2025) referred to him as "'Influencer General' based on his persona, credibility, candor, authenticity, and "his reputation for refusing to be silenced or co-opted" (p. 3). What accounts for Koop's success as an influencer in this campaign? Two theoretical concepts, "The 'opinion leader' is one of these.

Together with its companion concept, the 'two-step flow'," are relevant to understanding his influence in the fight against AIDS (Katz, 2015, p. 1023).

The two-step flow of communication hypothesis was originally conceived by Lazarfeld, Berelson, and Gaudet (1944). The general understanding is that information flows in two-steps—from the mass media to opinion leaders and from opinion leaders, "who are active media users and who collect, interpret, and diffuse the meaning of media messages" out to their social networks who consume less media (Postelnicu, 2016, para. 1). These two steps imply a linear process—point A to point B and point B to C.

Because the "president and others in the administration were not communicating about this deadly disease," Koop broke the silence on HIV/AIDS by releasing the first report on AIDS to the media and public. This launched Koop's media advocacy efforts to "advance public health goals by working strategically with those who help shape media content" (McKeever, 2021, p. 2). Two years after the report was issued to the media, the eight-page mailer was sent to over 100 million households in the U.S. (McKeever, 2021).

Koops' decision represented a shift in the two-step flow process wherein the process is not as straightforward and linear. Information can flow in multiple directions from an opinion leader to the mass media and then back again to publics.

Media alone, however, does not have the power to be persuasive "because there is considerable resistance (apathy) among various publics against being moved away from their comfortable indifference to many public issues" (Mendelsohn, 1973, p. 61). Katz (1957) modified the two-step flow process to clarify that interpersonal relationships impact the decision-making process in two different ways:

> serving as networks of communication, interpersonal relations are also sources of pressure to conform to to the group's way of thinking and acting, as well as sources of social support. The workings of group pressure are clearly evident in the homogeneity of opinion and action observed ... among doctors in situations of unclarity or uncertainty. The social support that comes from being integrated in the medical community may give a doctor the confidence required to carry out a resolution.
>
> *(p. 77)*

Opinion leaders are able to persuade many people to alter or change their behaviors and attitudes through leveraging their social networks and interpersonal abilities (Thompson, 2014). Opinion leaders also share these traits:

> high interest in a particular topic ... greater access to and use of the mass media, particular communication skills such as persuasiveness or

> perspective taking, credibility on a topic with their peers, and being well connected … bridging many social groups.
>
> *(Thompson, 2014, p. 43)*

Koop, as a medical doctor, had a high interest in keeping the focus on information and education and the science behind how the disease was spread and how it could be prevented. He had greater access to media, kept them informed, and reminded them of his stance on "behaviors and prevention, rather than people and lifestyles" (McKeever, 2021, p. 4). Koop directly addressed the public with the mailer and addressed media and other influential organizations through press conferences to inform "the audience how they can request a copy of [his] report, providing mobilizing information and a clear call to action for the readers" (McKeever, p. 4).

Koop was also a communicator, government employee, and spokesperson, but never considered himself a public relations practitioner. Instead, he became an opinion leader who leveraged media and his social networks to push an "aggressive agenda of education and government action" in spite of "working in opposition to many of his conservative counterparts" (McKeever, 2021, p. 6).

He took the perspective of reframing AIDS as a community effort, "a medical epidemic, rather than a moral debate," and by shifting the focus away "from *whom* to *what* causes AIDS" (McKeever, p. 3–4). His efforts as an opinion leader and efforts as a media advocate helped "change perceptions, norms, and public health" (McKeever, 2021, p. 7). His impact is best summarized here:

> Koop was an influencer before Instagram, before YouTube, almost before the internet itself. He built his influence through scientific credibility, and a gravitas that carefully cultivated public trust … His legacy offers a blueprint for public health communication in the 21st century.
>
> *(Cameron, 2025, p. 3)*

Key words

America Responds to AIDS
Family Protection Act
Gallup
Jerry Falwell
Moral Majority
Ogilvy & Mather
Surgeon General C. Everett Koop
Video News Release

Discussion questions

1 If you received an eight-page "Understanding AIDS" mailer, would you read it? Why or why not?
2 Thinking about available modes of communication today, what would you use to educate people about AIDS today?
3 Who is a current opinion leader regarding AIDS?
4 What AIDS Public Service Announcements have you seen recently?

6.3 STAR POWER: MAGIC JOHNSON AND SIR ELTON JOHN FORM FOUNDATIONS TO EDUCATE THE PUBLIC ABOUT HIV/AIDS

Situational analysis

For decades, musicians, actors, sports icons, dignitaries, and philanthropists have been supporting charities associated with HIV/AIDS focusing on advocacy, raising funds, and donations. The efforts from Bill Gates, Princess Diana, and other celebrities have spearheaded many foundations, funded educational programs to raise awareness, provided resources and access to those infected, informed policies, and helped destigmatize the disease through compassion. While HIV/AIDS has impacted millions worldwide, in the U.S. the toll from the epidemic has disproportionally hit the arts and fashion worlds as well as communities of color (HIV.gov, 2025b; Noland, Marchall, Goodale, & Schlecht, 2009; Rahimi, 2005). Outside the U.S., sub-Saharan Africa and Asia are the hardest hit regions (KFF, 2024).

Magic Johnson and his Magic Johnson Foundation

American basketball player Earvin Johnson, Jr. was born in Michigan in 1959. His high school nickname "Magic" was bestowed upon him for his "creative and entertaining ballhandling … innovative no-look and bounce passes and a knack for making big plays in the clutch" (Editors of Encyclopedia Britannica, 2024, para. 2–3). He was the first rookie to win NBA's Most Valuable Player award, after leading the Lakers into five championships in the 1980s.

Standing at 6 feet, 9 inches tall, Magic Johnson had a successful domestic and international sports career from 1979 to 1991. He was inducted into the College Basketball and Basketball Halls of Fame, won various awards, received the *Sports Illustrated* Sportsman of the Year legacy award, became a singer and writer, and medaled in the 1992 Olympic Games (Magic Johnson Enterprises, n.d.a.).

Amid all this fame, in 1991 Earvin "Magic" Johnson announced he was retiring due to his HIV diagnosis. This announcement brought attention to the fact that heterosexual sex (without a condom) with an infected person can result in HIV. At that time, the general belief was that only gay men and intravenous drug users were susceptible. As a way to combat this stigma, he vowed to become a spokesperson (Uenuma, 2021). Magic Johnson set up a nonprofit foundation, Magic Johnson Foundation (MJF), headquartered in Los Angeles, California, in 1991 in his name to lessen new HIV diagnoses among African Americans, who were experiencing almost 50% of new infections (PRSA, 2007). MJF has since been rebranded as "an investment conglomerate that provides high-quality products and services that focus primarily on ethnically diverse and underserved urban communities" (Magic Johnson Enterprises, n.d.b.).

In 2006, public relations agency Fleishman Hillard Inc. teamed up with Magic Johnson, the Magic Johnson Foundation and Abbott Laboratories to create the solution-oriented "I Stand with Magic—Campaign to End Black AIDS", "with a bold goal to reduce the amount of new HIV infections among African Americans by half over the next five years" (PRSA, 2007, para. 1).

Sir Elton John and the Elton John AIDS Foundation

According to his website, www.eltonjohn.com, the Grammy-winning superstar was born in 1947 as Reginald Kenneth Dwight in Middlesex, England. A child prodigy, Sir Elton John began playing the piano at the age of 3. At age 11 he received a scholarship to the Royal Academy of Music, which helped nurture his eclectic talent for "assimilating and blending diverse pop and rock styles into a propulsive, streamlined sound that was extroverted [and] energetic" (Holden, 2024, para. 3). His fashion sense and closet filled with a flamboyant wardrobe was equally eclectic as he rocked gaudy, over-the-top costumes of sequins and feathers on stage throughout the 1970s and 1980s (Christie's, 2024).

Sir Elton John's passion for music is legendary, followed by sports (Elton, n.d.). He is an acclaimed and successful solo artist with two diamond, 43 platinum, and 26 gold albums, over 70 top 40 hits with 300 million records sold worldwide, numerous awards, 4,600 performances, and knight status conferred by Queen Elizabeth. He is self-proclaimed as having a fearless commitment to overcoming the stigma associated with HIV/AIDS (EJAF, 2025).

In the early 1990s, Sir Elton John was the first male pop icon to disclose that he was gay (Holden, 2024). Shortly after, his persona and life's mission drastically shifted when friends and teen Ryan White died of AIDS. The shock and "helpless, suffocating feeling as one after another succumbed [are] memories etched on my soul" (Ellis, 2023, para. 5), which prompted his sobriety and philanthropic efforts. Sir Elton John stated that he was the luckiest person to not have contracted the virus when his friends Freddie Mercury and Rock Hudson died from it (Seward, 2012).

In 1992, the nonprofit Elton John AIDS Foundation (EJAF) was created in the United States and has since then been "driven by a clear mission: to be a powerful force in ending the AIDS epidemic," (EJAF, 2024, p. 12) raising over USD 650 million for HIV/AIDS programs in 55 countries (Lifson, 2021). Within the United Kingdom, the Foundation was incorporated in 1993 to empower people "infected, affected and at risk of HIV/AIDS, to alleviate their physical, emotional and financial hardship, enabling them to improve their quality of life, live with dignity and exercise self determination [sic]" (Charity Commission for England and Wales, n.d. para.1). The foundation sponsored several partnerships in the U.S., U.K., and Africa, Academy Award parties, annual Enduring Vision galas, and other campaign events. In addition, Sir Elton John and his husband, David Furnish, created pop-up charity shops, called Elton's Closet or Rocket Man Resale, in different locations to sell their clothing and memorabilia on behalf of the EJAF. Figure 6.2 is an exterior shot of Elton's Closet in Rockefeller Center in New York City.

The yearlong 2022–2023 EJAF Rocket Fund campaign with Saks Fifth Avenue and its unveiling of the company's holiday window display culminated his *Farewell Yellow Brick Road* tour in New York City and ignited the partnership with the luxury retailer.

FIGURE 6.2 Sir Elton John and David Furnish opened Elton's Closet to benefit the Elton John AIDS Foundation. Photo (April 2006) from Rockefeller Center of the shop's exterior during a five-day public sale of their personal wardrobes. GTCRFOTO/Alamy Stock Photo.

"I Stand With Magic" Campaign (2007)

Communication programming and execution:

The specific case study features Magic Johnson Foundation's campaign with multiple promotional activities to educate primarily the African American community. Much of the information about the research, planning, execution, and evaluation of this campaign was available in the PRSA's (2007) profile for which the Foundation won the Silver Anvil Award of Excellence.

Research

Beginning with research, CDC's *Morbidity and Mortality Weekly Report* (*MMWR*) in 2006 revealed just over 1 million people were living with HIV/AIDS and that African Americans constituted roughly 46% of cases (CDC, 2008). This coupled with high death rates, a lack of "access to health care, stigma, denial of sexual preference, and being unaware of HIV status are among the factors and barriers to HIV prevention" (PRSA, 2007, para. 3) especially for African American men and women.

Because of the high percentage and multiple barriers, the major challenges for the "I Stand with Magic" campaign were based around how to: a) reach vulnerable populations with credible, positive messaging via Johnson in a competitive news environment, b) break the taboo of HIV/AIDS so peers can engage in conversations, c) improve testing so people can get immediate results of their status, and d) meet the campaign goal of 50% reduction at the national level (PRSA, 2007).

Planning

These challenges provided insight into "what drives African Americans to take action against health risks" and helped shape the public relations planning process (PRSA, 2007, para. 7).

The "I Stand with Magic" campaign unfolded over a two-month time period (October to December) to culminate in World AIDS Day launch on Friday, December 1, 2006. Without advertising and within a budget of USD 150,000, the campaign sought to meet these objectives:

- Establish, build, and increase national visibility of the campaign messaging about the importance of awareness and testing in preventing HIV, among African Americans, specifically in Los Angeles.
- Connect and mobilize the community with credible informational resources and awareness of testing.

To meet these objectives, the following strategies were executed:

- The campaign launched on World AIDS Day via a press conference with key influencers (doctors, Mayor Villaraigosa, Congresswomen Waters, State of California Supervisor Burke, Executive Director Wilson of the Black AIDS Institute, and Muhammad Ali and his daughter, among other celebrities) in the African American community.
- These key influencers led grassroots initiatives, targeting "Black radio, colleges prisons and churches to get the message out" (Williams, 2007, para. 8).
- Campaign recipients were asked to "stand" with Magic and get tested.
- Free, mobile, and confidential rapid testing (20 minutes) was offered in Los Angeles County on World AIDS Day via partnerships with AIDS service organizations.
- From a media relations perspective, an interactive website was created for people to pledge to stand with Magic, an announcement was previewed about Magic Johnson and his wife, Cookie, appearing on *The Oprah Winfrey Show* to share his story of living with HIV, and the messaging was picked up nationwide in African American consumer and trade media outlets (PRSA, 2007). Additionally, a Facebook group and two PSAs directed by Spike Lee were created in conjunction with National HIV Testing Day as part of the campaign's initiative to end Black HIV/AIDS (Abbott, 2008).

Outcomes and evaluation

Over 9 million people tuned into Oprah's show with Magic and Cookie Johnson to learn about the campaign. On launch day, over 110 million media impressions were obtained, with a 45% "core message pull through" (PRSA, 2007, para. 13). The grassroots efforts generated approximately 8,200 visits to the campaign website, over 50 scholars agreed to participate, almost 80 key influencers received information about the campaign, and over 6,500 brochures and DVDs were distributed (PRSA, 2007). In regard to HIV/AIDS testing, just short of 1,200 tests were completed in Los Angeles.

From an academic perspective, studies and reports were conducted about the positive impact Magic Johnson's disclosure had on risk behaviors (Black AIDS Institute, 2011; Brown & Basil, 1995; Cardazzi et al., 2023; Clarke, 2006; Francis et al., 2019) and how he "redefined the perception of the disease in the minds of many" (UNAIDS, 2015, p. 85), from a disease of the "other, or guilty, i.e., homosexuals and (poor) drug injectors … [to] a disease of machismo and heterosexuality" (Clarke, 2006, p. 320).

Saks debuts holiday campaign supporting the Elton John AIDS Foundation (2022)

Communication programming and execution

During the holiday season of 2022, the EJAF teamed up with the luxury North American retailer Saks Fifth Avenue, hereafter referred to as Saks, to raise funds, with a light show and holiday window display unveiling at its New York's store, along with a concert by Sir Elton John, and the launch of a multi-vendor collection of products for sale from over 60 designers donating to the Elton John AIDS Foundation's Rocket Fund. This successful campaign received the 15th Annual Shorty Awards (n.d.) for its multiple platforms. Criteria from the award and supplemental research of press releases and news articles about the campaign were used in summarizing the objectives, strategies and execution, and results.

Objectives

The objectives for this campaign were focused around supporting both the missions of Saks and EJAF. Saks (n.d.) is driven to help customers express themselves through inspiring style and aims to deliver "one-of-a-kind shopping experiences, featuring an expertly curated assortment of fashion and highly personalized customer service" (para 1), while EJAF's mission is simple, being a powerful force in the fight to end AIDS (EJAF, 2024, p. 12).

Goals and strategies

The goals and strategies of the campaign were as follows:

- Continue Saks' annual holiday tradition of lighting the window displays, engage customers, drive traffic to its stores, and support a worthy cause.
- Create an integrated partnership with the EJAF's Rocket Fund and Saks to align values and bolster brand recognition.
- Share the passion for self-expression, creativity, fashion, and giving back—including a USD 1 million donation to the Rocket Fund
- Co-curate a multi-vendor merchandise collection (60 designers) and showcase the collection in three dedicated windows at the Saks Fifth Avenue New York Flagship store between 49th and 50th streets, with USD 500,000 from proceeds regardless of sales to be donated to the Rocket Fund (Saks, 2022).

Execution

The window unveiling, for the first time, featured rocket ships and kaleidoscopes and 600,000 individual points of LED lights, making the experience "more colorful, vibrant and immersive than ever before" (Saks, 2022, para 7). Saks aimed to create the heartwarming spirit of the holiday reminding everyone that "While it's the happiest time of the year for many, we mustn't forget about the billions of people around the world for whom safety, respect, and dignity are not guaranteed" (Saks, 2022, para. 6), and of the Rocket Fund's mission to end stigma and discrimination of affected individuals.

Sir Elton John and his husband, David Furnish, chairman of EJAF and CEO of Rocket Entertainment Group, participated in live Saks events to discuss the mission of the Foundation with Gucci's former Creative Director Alessandro Michele and Versace's Chief Creative Officer Donatella Versace about friendship, fashion, and philanthropy (Saks, 2022).

Sir Elton John, wearing "head-to-toe Gucci red-and-blue tracksuit, Gucci x Adidas sneakers and a tailored match-a-green blazer with his name emblazoned on the breast pocket" (Puckett-Pope, 2022, para. 1), rolled in on a "pink golf cart ... [and] took his seat at his piano, which had been wheeled out directly onto Fifth Avenue, where traffic was temporarily stopped" (Vogue World Parties, 2022, para. 2), to sing his medley of Christmas and other recognized songs like *Your Song*.

Other tactics included online Q&A sessions on social media channels (Instagram, TikTok, Facebook, YouTube), and an editorial hub, The Edit, was created for fashion news and style inspiration (Saks, 2022).

Results

Here are highlights of results from the Shorty Awards (n.d.):

- An estimated 400,000 visitors attended the spectacle in person while four million people tuned in on Saks social media platforms.
- 36.7 million likes on Instagram, which broke the record for most liked posts of all time while the TikTok video featuring Sir Elton John was one of the highest viewed videos for Saks.
- 7 billion media impressions overall, with 30,000 visits to Saks.com, and 36,000 views of the Saks Live.

Overall, this campaign, which unfolded over a year, was successful in meeting the missions of both Saks and Elton John AIDS Foundation, but also in raising funds for and awareness of the AIDS epidemic.

Theoretical perspectives

Many theories are associated with disclosure from a variety of disciplines including interpersonal communication, mass communication, or health communication. These theories attempt to explain why someone would choose to disclose in person or online a private matter like HIV/AIDS status. From a theoretical perspective, several factors influenced the public revelation of Magic Johnson's HIV positive status and Sir Elton John's negative status: the diagnosis, their celebrity identity, private health information and media coverage, and calculated risks/consequences.

Once people are diagnosed, their health irrevocably changes as symptoms can appear as the disease progresses. Such physical manifestations make it difficult for one to hide an illness and necessitate not only acceptance but also disclosure to reduce risk to others. This is the impetus behind the Disease Progression Theory or DPT (Serovich, 2001). DPT goes hand-in-hand with the Consequence Theory or CT (Serovich, 2001). As a disease progresses, disclosure progresses as well based on the outcome, cost, or consequence of the disclosure. Aside from disclosure, other theoretical considerations within this case study include Social Cognitive Theory (SCT) and the "celebrification" of HIV/AIDS (Noland et al., 2009, p. 194).

From a social cognitive perspective, SCT suggests that recipients of health-related messages will likely imitate a celebrity's healthy behaviors, for example HIV testing, based on observations and ethos of the celebrity as a role model (Ike, 2024). Additionally, "attitudes and belief change regarding sexual behavior" are promoted by the emotional connection to celebrities and how they are the "personification of the message" (Brown & Basil, 1995, p. 364).

The celebrification of HIV/AIDS is not a new phenomenon, as celebrity endorsements of public health campaigns have been a successful brand and marketing strategy for decades, whether cause related, customer engagement, or product based (Jun et al., 2023). However, when examined over a 25-year period of celebrities and their involvement in HIV/AIDS movement, the relationship between the media and celebrities emerged as three distinct generations (Noland et al., 2009).

The first and longest generation of nearly 20 years (1981–1999) began as the epidemic emerged. During this time period when Magic Johnson was diagnosed and Sir Elton John came out, the relationship between media and celebrities was "modalized around fear: fear of HIV/AIDS' deadliness and possible contagion and fear to be associated publicly with … a marginalized lifestyle and sexual orientation" (Noland et al., 2009, p. 200) and modalized around a slow disclosure of statuses. Celebrities emerged as leaders in prevention, awareness, and support.

The second and shortest generation of five years (2000–2006) yielded more mainstream media coverage of HIV/AIDS in developing countries as it became fashionable for celebrities to raise awareness and funds

(Noland et al., 2009). Celebrities, as non-medical personnel and proxies for their audiences, embody more personalized and affective messaging to reach the public via the media. The third generation (2007 to present) of celebrity HIV/AIDS endorsements has inspired celebrities to affect change on a broader and deeper level in the political arena (Noland et al., 2009).

As high-profile figures constantly in the spotlight of the media, Magic Johnson's and Sir Elton John's public disclosures had the potential to impact their careers negatively as well as their social networks due to anxiety and uncertainty—self and other imposed—fears, rejection, stigmatization, ostracism, isolation, anger, denial, and other emotional experiences (Serovich, 2001). Equally, disclosures can have positive outcomes and consequences including social and emotional support, compassion and empathy, and access to resources to improve one's health. As an example, within 24 hours of Johnson's disclosure, CDC National AIDS hotline fielded almost 120,000 phone calls of people seeking AIDS-related information (Hoffman et al., 2017) and for months continued to receive 30,000 calls a week (The Henry J. Kaiser Family Foundation, 2006), a testament to his personality and status.

Magic Johnson's choice to disclose was prompted by the diagnosis. Sir Elton John's choice to disclose aligned with its "potential role in prevention ... and crucial step towards ending stigma and discrimination against people living with HIV and AIDS" and advocacy trajectory (Obermeyer et al., 2011, p. 1011). Their choices had profound positive consequences within their campaign efforts.

Key words

Core Message Pull Through
Disease Progression Theory and Consequence Theory
Elton John AIDS Foundation
Elton John's Closet and the Rocket Man Resale
Ethos
Facebook Group
Grassroots
HBCUs—Historically Black Colleges and Universities
Magic Johnson Foundation, now Magic Johnson Enterprises
PSA—Public Service Announcement
Saks
Social Cognitive Theory
Shorty Awards
World AIDS Day

Discussion questions

1 If you were in a position to collaborate with a celebrity to raise funds for HIV/AIDS, which organization would you choose, and which celebrity? Be prepared to justify your choices.
2 Within the last year, what other celebrity-endorsed HIV/AIDS campaigns have you been exposed to?
3 What or who would motivate you to get tested for HIV?

6.4 GERMANY'S "GIB AIDS KEINE CHANCE" (DON'T GIVE AIDS A CHANCE) CAMPAIGN: EDUCATING THE PUBLIC ABOUT CONDOM USE AND RISKY BEHAVIOR

Situation analysis

As part of the Ministry of Health in Germany, its Bundeszentrale für gesundheitliche Aufklärung (Federal Center for Health Education), known as BZgA, operated as the central coordination center for AIDS prevention and other health topics such as family planning, nutrition and physical exercise, addiction, and organ and blood donations. This case study focuses on an AIDS public health communication campaign that started in 1987 before the reunification of a united Germany of the former German Democratic Republic (East Germany) and the Federal Republic of Germany (official name of Germany since the reunification; former name of West Germany) in October 1990. The terms, Germany and Berlin, remain, but readers need to be aware that they may refer to West Germany or West Berlin before reunification based on the year.

The first reported case of AIDS occurred in 1982 (Marcus & Starker, 2006), leading to the first AIDS registry of cases in Germany set up by the Robert Koch Institute, "the central federal institution responsible for disease prevention and control in Germany" (European Center for Disease and Prevention Control, 2025, para. 1), which is like the CDC in the U.S. In 1983, Germany's leading news magazine, *Der Spiegel*, published a cover story titled, "*AIDS:* The Puzzling Illness," thereby bringing more attention to the epidemic. Between 1983 and 1985, several AIDS support groups were established by activists and organizers initially in urban areas, and the Deutsche Aidshilfe (German AIDS Federation), an independent nonprofit association serving as an umbrella to other organizations committed to AIDS prevention and advocacy, was founded in Berlin (BZgA, 2009). In 1985, tests became mandatory for HIV antibodies in blood products. During the same year, BZgA sent out an AIDS informational brochure titled

"AIDS: What You Should Know About AIDS" to all 27 million German households (BZgA, 2009a).

According to Dr. Henning Tümmers (2013), a professor at the University Hospital of Tübingen, AIDS polarized German politicians and the public. In 1987, Federal Health Minister Rita Süssmuth was against mandatory HIV testing, reporting, and isolation, while the State Secretary in the Bavarian Ministry of the Interior Peter Gauweiler supported restrictive measures in Bavaria. Faculty at Essen University Hospital clamored for restrictions on citizens' basic rights to protect the general public. The same year, BZgA (2010) researched public awareness of AIDS and found that two-thirds of the German population over age 16 rated AIDS as one of the most dangerous diseases, and the responses from 16- to 20-year-olds were higher at 85%. These indicators prompted the government to undertake a comprehensive AIDS education campaign.

> Readers in the U.S. may be surprised how sexuality is freely expressed in Germany and many other European countries. Well-known travel writer, Rick Steves (2005), stated: "Europe's light and easygoing approach to sex and nudity can provide some shocking moments for U.S. travelers" (para. 1). He wrote about seeing businesspeople in Munich take off their clothes, lay out their blankets, and sunbathe fully nude in a public park. He also commented on co-ed mineral spas and nudity shown on billboards in Germany. This case study covers visual imagery and copy produced in Germany's HIV/AIDS prevention campaign that would most likely be censored in the U.S.

Communications

The campaign's primary goals (BZgA, 2012) were threefold: 1) to prevent an increase of HIV infections and other sexually transmitted infections (STIs); 2) to provide advice and care services; and 3) to collaborate with national and international organizations.

The campaign's strategies were as follows:

- Keep the public informed frequently about risks of infections and protective options about HIV/AIDS and other sexually transmitted infections.
- Urge the public to use condoms, particularly in risky sexual situations.
- Encourage the public to take responsibility for their own health and the health of their sexual partners.

The campaign's target audiences (BZgA, 2012) were broad to reach the population overall about AIDS prevention. Germany's epidemiological data identified the following at-risk groups for more in-depth education:

- Men who have sex with men (MSM) and their sexual partners. CDC (2022) stated, "The term, 'MSM," often is used clinically to refer to sexual behavior alone, regardless of sexual orientation" (para. 1).
- People who live in areas where HIV is endemic and their sexual partners.
- Intravenous drug users and their sexual partners.

Other identified at-risk audiences were people in non-monogamous lifestyles:

- People working in the sex industry and their clients.
- People traveling to locations where HIV is prevalent and people seeking sexual partners in these areas.
- People having spontaneous sexual relations with people unknown to them.
- Young people who are becoming sexually active.

The campaign's communication-didactic approach was to treat the difficult subject of AIDS, a deadly disease, with empathy and humor, instead of employing dramatic shock tactics. BZgA examined other campaigns using shock imagery and messaging and found that sparking fear would be ineffective with its target audiences and would stigmatize affected people with HIV/AIDS. The campaign illustrated how people can stay safe. Under the "Gib AIDS keine Chance" ("Don't Give AIDS a Chance") umbrella theme, the campaign was designed to maintain consistency of messaging throughout all multimedia platforms. BZgA also evaluated its campaign through surveys to determine effectiveness and best methods to optimize communication initiatives. Tactics, such as posters and TV and cinema spots, were tested in focus groups to evaluate perceptions, comprehension, and acceptance of the creative (BZgA, 2012). The campaign was structured in the following thematic series: *"mach's mit"* ("do it"...with a condom) debuting in 1993; *"Liebesorte"* ("places for love") series starting in 1999; and *"Wissen und Kondom"* ("Knowledge and Condom") series beginning in 2012.

Thematic series, "mach's mit" (do it...with a condom) debuting in 1993

BZgA survey findings revealed that people aged 16 to 45 paid limited attention to AIDS/HIV informational communications, which prompted

BZgA to create a new strategy to reach this group in 1993. The first series of posters with huge condoms as the motif were the outcome of a creative project for university students in design and communications. With the support of the German Outdoor Advertising Association, the association's members displayed about 100,000 posters on a complimentary basis to BZgA (BZgA, 2012).

The whimsical visual images showed condoms flat out of the packaging as circles in different shapes and colors. For examples, the poster, "Für Engelchen und Teufelchen" (HORIZONT, 2012) translated as "For the Little Angels and the Little Devils" showed an angel depicted as a yellow condom with a drawn halo while the devil was a red condom with drawn pointy ears. The poster, "Frühlingsgefühle" (HORIZONT, 2012) translated as "Spring Fever" illustrated a butterfly made of four condoms in green and yellow as the wings with the rest of its body and antennae simply drawn in black ink. The poster of "Gummi, Bärchen," (Chisholm Larsson Gallery, 2025a) translated directly as "Gummy Bears" or more colloquially as "Condom, Sweetheart," depicted a gummy bear made of two large condoms for the body along with seven smaller condoms forming the face, ears and paws.

The posters received lots of sensational attention initially. This poster series evolved into a multimedia integrated communications campaign. Three other national creative competitions were conducted in 1999, one with a cinema chain, another on BZgA's website (which no longer exists), and another with art and graphic design schools in 2005. The winning creative submission was a series of six images with fruits and vegetables adorned with condoms along with amusing captions. The imagery could be seen all over Germany on 75,000 large poster spaces starting in May 2006. In 2007, six more motifs followed, and in 2008, the food imagery series concluded with six new motifs. BZgA was able to obtain free printing and placements of its posters from the Association of German Private Healthcare Insurers, which made a significant contribution to the fame and success of the entire campaign (BZgA, 2012).

The food posters featured photographs of fruits or vegetables "wearing" prophylactics. An image of a group of vegetables was titled, "Sicher querbeet" (Security all over!,) (Calisphere, n.d.), another showed a lemon with the caption, "Sicher Macht Lustig!" ("Safety Makes It More Fun!") (Chisolm Larsson Gallery, 2025b), and three cucumbers in varied sizes was titled, "Passt Auf Jede Gurke!" ("Watch Out For Every Cucumber!") (BZgA, 2012).

All posters and visual materials in the condom series included the logo of "Gib AIDS keine Chance" in the lower left corner and BZgA's telephone number and website on the bottom right.

Thematic "Liebesorte" ("places for love") series starting in 2009

With condom sales rising in 2008 and 2009 to 215 million condoms for each year (BZgA, 2009b), BZgA changed its approach in spring 2009 when it revised its "mach's mit" concept to "Liebesorte" ("places for love") with photos of staged scenes where people can or could have sex—brothel beds, secluded lake spots, hotel rooms, the kitchen table, and others. The images deliberately were devoid of people, with hopes that viewers could create their own fantasies. Media platforms included postcards, posters, TV and cinema spots, and others. For example, one image showed a large fluffy rug in front of a roaring fireplace with the caption, "Mit der feuer spielen, AIDS riskieren" translated as "When you play with fire…you risk aids" (HORIZONT, 2012). BZgA (2012) explained:

> Every motif was developed through careful research in the respective target groups and tells a different "love" story. The message of this series: falling in love, having fun, and giving away your heart and much more is desirable and permissible, but risking AIDS is not. That is why none of the posters are lacking the most important utensil: the condom! *(p. 26)*

Thematic "Wissen und Kondom" ("Knowledge and Condom") series beginning in 2012

This series showcased visual imagery of real people from teens to older people stating how they "express their individual notions of sexuality" BZgA (2025, p. 30): "I want it tenderly," and "I want it with pleasure" (translated from the original German copy) among other racier comments. The updated tagline reads "mach's! aber mach's mit" ("Do it! But do it with"), which means use a condom for protection from HIV and STIs. The people's appearances and their comments were deliberately contradictory—a heavily tattooed muscular man wanted tenderness and a well-dressed and proper-looking woman over 60 expressed a desire for lust (BZgA, 2012). These posters also contained a QR code to BZgA's website. Promotional activities included postcards, billboards, social media, and online videos of some of the people who posed for the posters, among others (BZgA, 2012).

Beyond the themes, BZgA undertook other promotional activities including television and cinema spots, each 30 or 60 seconds in length, with many starring German celebrities in 1987, and a variety of promotional materials and events during World AIDS Day. A series of radio spots featuring the voices of celebrities began in 1987. In addition, BZgA held events, such as "Join-in Circuits" targeting young people across the country, and "Country Circuits' in five countries, and "Youth Film Days" in over 270 German towns (BZgA, 2012).

Results

In Germany, the Federal Government and the Federal Ministry of Health made HIV/AIDS and STIs important priorities in health prevention and education since the mid-1980s. This campaign can be measured by whether its goals were fulfilled.

To prevent an increase of HIV infections and other sexually transmitted infections (STIs)

The number of Germans impacted by HIV/AIDS has been low in Western Europe and around the globe. A report by the European Centre for Disease Prevention and Control (2010) found that Germany and Finland had the lowest numbers of confirmed new cases per 100,000 population by country in 2009. UNAIDS (2024b) reported 68,000 Germans of all ages were living with HIV of which 75% were receiving antiretroviral therapy in 2012. From 2004 to 2009, over 4,000 Germans died of AIDS and over 37,000 were infected with HIV from 2000 to 2012 (European Centre for Disease Prevention and Control, 2010).

According to BZgA's research, condom use increased from 58% to 73% in 1997, declined slightly in 1998 while remaining consistent until 2004 and rose to 69% in 2005, and later a significant increase to 80% in 2010 and 2011 (BZgA, 2012). Another BZgA survey found that 97% to 98% of Germans recalled at least one mass medium from 2003 to 2008 (BZgA, 2009a).

An area of improvement noted by BZgA for future health prevention campaigns was awareness of STIs when the research indicated few people were aware of the range of STIs (BZgA, 2012).

To provide advice and care services

An important personal communication measure was telephone counseling (and later also on its website) on an anonymous and personal basis every day of the week. Topics covered HIV, AIDS, and STIs. BZgA estimated that 20,000 conversations and online dialogues took place every year. Non-German speakers were able to seek advice at another number. BZgA also participated in a variety of events that enabled interaction and insightful experience with people and BZgA representatives. Its mobile and interactive exhibition called "Liebesleben" ("Love Life"), which started in 1994 and was revamped in 2003, received 10,000 visitors during a day at each event held in central squares in small towns and big cities around four times a year for 10 days. Its "AIDS-Rallye" began in 1992 and attracted 20,000 teenagers and young adults in 50 locations every year (BZgA, 2012).

To collaborate with national and international organizations

BZgA collaborated with a wide variety of public and private organizations and individuals involved with them from health counselors, teachers, and medical doctors. These organizations have helped BZgA's AIDS prevention campaign gain greater promotional reach and financial support for promotional tactics and coordination. A new relationship with the Association of German Private Healthcare Insurers in 2005 provided generous support of EUR3.4 million per year for at least five years by covering expenses for newspaper advertisements, posters, billboards, and cinema spots. The German Outdoor Advertising Association covered expenses for posters and billboards for World AIDS Day, an international event, and provided over 100,000 free poster spaces. The association spent EUR 1.5 million in 2009 in support of BZgA. These financial boosts also enabled BZgA to reach more of the general population and high-risk audiences (BZgA, 2012).

Theoretical framework

Public health communication campaigns and information campaigns, like this one from the German government, can be both effective and successful based on a number of theoretical approaches and concepts. The concepts explored within this section include campaign messages as input with positive outcomes, how audience members are exposed to these messages through humorous appeals, whether the audience is receptive to humor, and the structure of a didactic campaign.

Heinz Bonfadelli (2022), Department of Communication and Media Research, University of Zurich, Switzerland, explored several theoretical approaches to the effectiveness of public health campaigns. Relevant to this case study is Bonfadelli's model of campaign messages as input, followed by exposure, receptivity, and the various cognitive, attitudinal, and behavioral effects the messages have on individuals and potentially society as a whole. Campaign messages when framed as an input with positive outcomes will inspire individuals to behave accordingly, same with negatively framed outcomes. What impacts the outcomes and the reception of the messages is the mechanism or medium of the input—whether the message is communicated as a story, by a celebrity endorser, use of emotions like humor or fear appeals, entertainment-education, or by the "concept of transportation," (emphasis added, p. 65). How individuals are exposed to a health communication campaign is theoretically dependent on whether individuals are actively seeking health information, have been selectively exposed to campaign messages (cognitive process), and are activated or aroused by stimuli (emotional process).

Researchers affiliated with the University of South Dakota, Struckman-Johnson et al. (1994), identified and analyzed five appeals within PSAs to persuade a selected audience to change their behavior, especially related to AIDS and condoms: fear arousal-no sex/condom theme; fear arousal-sex/condom theme; erotic; humorous; and factual. In their study on college students, they discovered that all five types of appeals can be effective, acknowledging that the participants' perception of humor drove their intent to change their behavior, and further recommend "combining appeals (e.g., fear with erotic) and emphasizing the positive features of condom use" (p. 2223).

Elise Stevens (2018), Journalism & Mass Communication, University of North Carolina, Chapel Hill, added an additional persuasive appeal—emotions—in her study of viewer engagement with condom advertisements in online video PSAs. She uncovered that "PSAs with humor appeals received more viewer attention in terms of views, comments, and ratings than humorous advertisements" (p. 18). Similarly, the blog *Say it with a condom* explores the psychology of condom advertising and other research studies conducted on positive appeals and positive message design, among others, concluding: "Condoms with a custom message can make a major impact—especially when that message is funny or educational. Any customized condom will be memorable, but research suggests that humorous or informative ones can also help increase condom use" (Say it with a condom, 2024, para. 1).

How likely individuals are to be receptive to the message is theoretically dependent on a number of factors:

- Complexity of the message and the ability to process the information contained within a message (limited capacity).
- Persuasiveness of the message (elaboration likelihood model).
- How individuals make sense of the messages and construct meaning.
- Level of empathy, identification and interaction individuals are to have with the characters featured in the campaign—in person or mediated (Bonfadelli, 2022).

Another factor that can affect an audience's receptivity to health messages is humor. Borden and Suggs (2019) assert that humor will be more receptive when it "is understood by an audience without a college education and is commonly concerned with subject matters that are a part of everyday life," for example sex (p. 194). Using simple humor can minimize competing narratives regarding behavior, for example having sex versus abstinence versus using a condom, so that a campaign's health behavior message is heard more easily. Secondly, humor can also endear "an audience to the messenger and [reduce] tensions around a contentious issue" (p. 193), which helps individuals make sense of messages and construct the intended meaning.

Mendelsohn (1973), whom Bonfadelli (2022) references, identifies some other reasons why information campaigns can be effective and succeed. These reasons include:

- The use of mass media to reach publics and change their attitudes is not enough. Communicators should collaborate with social scientists to determine "appropriate targets, themes, appeals, and media vehicles ... in achieving carefully delimited goals" (p. 50).
- Using a "didactic approach, which simply tries to inform people" with a judgment about their behavior, "that they may be bad drivers, would be met with audience resistance." Instead, communicators should craft messages or develop programming that would provide insight in their "deficiencies without offending them" (p. 53).
- "The major task facing the communicator ... is to recognize, understand and attempt" (p. 53) to overcome the message recipients' apathy—whether toward the health issue, health message, behavior change, or the media.

In this case, the German government identified an appropriate target audience, young people 16- to 20-year-olds who were becoming sexually active, those at risk (MSM, intravenous drug users) and their sexual partners, and sex workers and clients, among others. The campaign was divided into three themes over two decades, focusing on condom use, places for love, and people's knowledge of condoms. Within each theme, humor, an often applied strategy in social marketing, (Borden & Suggs, 2019) was utilized to "connect a product [condoms] or service to an audience, shock viewers to attract attention [not scare] and increase word of mouth and broaden an audience to those not previously targeted" (Borden & Suggs, 2019, p. 194), and over time, the humor evolved with what segmented and targeted audiences found funny. The media vehicles ranged from posters, postcards, TV and cinema spots, billboards, social media, and online videos. The delimited goals were to educate, inform, and persuade individuals to use condoms, and to encourage responsibility to self and others. The campaign's didactic approach was to treat the difficult subject of AIDS, a deadly disease, with empathy and humor, in such a way to acknowledge that individuals are having sex, but that they should do so safely. Using multiple media channels in a humorous manner achieved "high reach" (Rossman, 2015, p. 411), which had a positive influence on the effectiveness of strategic health communication campaigns, especially when the campaign's objective was to "introduce a new behavior," condom use during sex, which "is higher as compared to changing existing … recurring habitualized behavior" like sex (p. 411).

Key words

Bundeszentrale für gesundheitliche Aufklärung (Federal Center for Health Education), known as BZgA
Communication-Didactic Approach
Elaboration Likelihood Model
EUR
Federal Republic of Germany (official name of Germany since the reunification of East and West Germany in 1990; former name of West Germany)
German Democratic Republic (former name of East Germany)
MSM
Sexually Transmitted Infections (STIs)
Social Marketing
World AIDS Day

Discussion questions

1 Was the humor in this campaign effective? Were you persuaded? Discuss your answers.
2 Would this campaign be effective here in the U.S., as a government-led initiative? Please explain.
3 If you were hired to create a similar campaign in the U.S., how would you use humor to create messages? What barriers might you encounter in people receiving the intended message?

References

Abbott. (2008, June 27). Earvin "Magic" Johnson and Abbott bring "I Stand with Magic" Program: Part of the campaign to end Black HIV/AIDS to Facebook community. *3BL CSR Wire*. https://www.csrwire.com/press_releases/26849-earvin-magic-johnson-and-abbott-bring-i-stand-with-magic-program-part-of-the-campaign-to-end-black-hiv-aids-to-facebook-community

Adgate, B. (2020, November 2). *The rise and fall of cable television. Forbes.* https://www.forbes.com/sites/bradadgate/2020/11/02/the-rise-and-fall-of-cable-television/
American Cancer Society. (n.d.). *About Kaposi Sarcoma.* https://www.cancer.org/cancer/types/kaposi-sarcoma/about/what-is-kaposi-sarcoma.html
Ayala, G., & Spieldenner, A. (2021). HIV is a story first written on the bodies of gay and bisexual men. *American Journal of Public Health*, *111*(7), 1240–1242. https://doi.org/10.2105/AJPH.2021.306348
Biography. (2023, November 29). *Jerry Falwell.* https://www.biography.com/religious-figures/a45986619/jerry-falwell
Black AIDS Institute. (2011). *AIDS—30 years is enuf!* https://blackaids.org/wp-content/uploads/2020/09/30-Years-Is-Enuf-BAI-Report-June-2011.pdf
Blakemore, E. (2017, July 3). This was the first major news article on HIV/AIDS. *Smithsonian Magazine.* https://www.smithsonianmag.com/smart-news/was-first-major-news-article-hivaids-180963913/
Bonfadelli, H. (2022). Theoretical approaches of health campaigns and practical applications to COVID-19 campaigns. *Science Journal of Public Health*, *10*(1), 60–72. https://doi.org/10.11648/j.sjph.20221001.17
Borden, D. S., & Suggs, L. S. (2019). Strategically leveraging humor in social marketing campaigns. *Social Marketing Quarterly*, *25*(3), 193–208. https://doi.org/10.1177/1524500419854068
Brown, J., & Davenport, A. A. (2024, April 12). Renowned journalist and NewsHour co-founder Robert MacNeil dies at 93. [Video transcript]. *PBS.* https://www.pbs.org/newshour/show/renowned-journalist-and-newshour-co-founder-robert-macneil-dies-at-93
Brown, W. J., & Basil, M. D. (1995). Media celebrities and public health: Responses to "Magic" Johnson's HIV disclosure and its impact on AIDS risk and high-risk behaviors. *Health Communication*, *7*(4), 345–370. https://doi.org/10.1207/s15327027hc0704_4
BZgA. (2009a). *The AIDS prevention campaign. 1985-2009 report.* [Brochure].
BZgA. (2009b, May) *Public awareness of AIDS in the Federal Republic of Germany 2008 Knowledge, attitudes and behaviour relating to protection against AIDS.* https://www.bioeg.de/fileadmin/user_upload/PDF/studien/aids_2008_short_gb--b4b98d93f64922a224a1641abe9a0d6c.pdf
BZgA. (2010, May). *Public awareness of AIDS in the Federal Republic of Germany 2009: Knowledge, attitudes and behaviour relating to protection against AIDS.* https://www.bioeg.de/fileadmin/user_upload/PDF/studien/aids_2010_short_gb--ff3166f609421ca7f69189fc68d31bb1.pdf
BZgA. (2012). *25 years, 1987 to 2012: Documentation of 25 years of the AIDS prevention campaign in Germany.* https://www.liebesleben.de/media/englische-inhalte/Doku_GAKC_2013_Englisch.pdf
Calisphere. (n.d.) Image/Sicher querbeet! [inscribed]. *University of California Los Angeles.* https://calisphere.org/item/ark:/21198/zz001zzpmt/
Cameron, N. M. D. S. (2025, July 1). The power of the 'Influencer General.' https://thehill.com/opinion/healthcare/5377666-surgeon-general-influencer-predecessor/
Cardazzi, A., Martin, J. C., & Rodriguez, Z. (2023). Information shocks and celebrity exposure: The effect of "Magic" Johnson on AIDS diagnoses and mortality in the U.S. *Health Economics*, *32*(9), 2047–2079. https://doi.org/10.1002/hec.4712
CDC. (1982, September 24). Current trends update on Acquired Immune Deficiency Syndrome (AIDS)—United States. *Morbidity and Mortality Weekly Report*, *31*(37), 507–508. https://www.cdc.gov/mmwr/preview/mmwrhtml/00001163.htm

CDC. (1985, August 23). Results of a Gallup Poll on Acquired Immunodeficiency Syndrome– New York City, United States, 1985. *Morbidity and Mortality Weekly Report*, *34*(33), 513–514. https://www.cdc.gov/mmwr/preview/mmwrhtml/00000597.htm

CDC. (2008, October 3). HIV prevalence estimates—United States, 2006. *MMWR*, *57*(39), 1073–1079. https://www.cdc.gov/mmwr/preview/mmwrhtml/mm5739a2.htm

CDC. (2022). *Men Who Have Sex with Men (MSM)*. https://www.cdc.gov/std/treatment-guidelines/msm.htm

CDC. (2024, July 8). *The AIDS epidemic in the United States, 1981-early 1990s*. https://www.cdc.gov/museum/online/story-of-cdc/aids/index.html

Charity Commission for England and Wales. (n.d.). *The Elton John AIDS Foundation*. https://register-of-charities.charitycommission.gov.uk/charity-search/-/charity-details/1017336/charity-overview

Chase, M. (1987, January 20). Condom ads to air on San Francisco Television Station—KRON is first major outlet to accept commercials in AIDS education effort. *Wall Street Journal*, 1.

Chisholm Larsson Gallery. (2025a). *Original vintage poster: Gib AIDS Keine Chance (8) Gummi, Barchen mach's mit*. https://www.chisholm-poster.com/posters/CL76252.html?srsltid=AfmBOopQyrVXXFFXtQi2HR2Nvz0M1m-HerlDjrrkai24PfL6CTU61MPj./

Chisholm Larsson Gallery. (2025b). *Original Vintage Poster: Gib AIDS Keine Chance (4) Sicher Macht Lustig!* https://www.chisholm-poster.com/posters/CL74345.html?srsltid=AfmBOoosx9hAB3qCg-BeCF76PJdZzkRnLup1VnpUzXP-4PH5e3kf07rS

Christie's. (2024, February). *The collection of Sir Elton John: Out of the closet*. https://onlineonly.christies.com/s/collection-sir-elton-john-out-closet/lots/3449

Clarke, J. N. (2006, December). Homophobia out of the closet in the media portrayal of HIV/AIDS 1991, 1996 and 2001: Celebrity, heterosexism and the silent victims. *Critical Public Health*, *16*(4) 317–330. DOI: 10.1080/09581590601091620

Davis, D. (1991). Understanding AIDS—The national AIDS mailer. *Public Health Reports*, *106*(6), 656–662. https://www.jstor.org/stable/4597032

Davis, J. (2006, June.). Evolution of an epidemic: 25 Years of HIV/AIDS media campaigns in the U.S. *Kaiser Family Foundation*. https://www.kff.org/wp-content/uploads/2013/01/7515.pdf

Deutsche Aidshilfe. (n.d.). *Our mission statement*. https://en.aidshilfe.de/mission-statement#acc-626725

Dobbins, L. (2021, November 11). 23 celebrities who lost their battle with AIDS. *HIV Plus Magazine*. https://www.hivplusmag.com/people/2021/11/11/celebrities-famous-died-death-aids-hiv#rebelltitem1

ECDC. (2010). *HIV/AIDS surveillance in Europe 2009*. https://www.ecdc.europa.eu/sites/default/files/media/en/publications/Publications/hiv-aids-surveillance-report-2012-20131127.pdf

ECDC. (2025). *Robert Koch Institute*. https://www.ecdc.europa.eu/en/robert-koch-institute-1

Editors of Encyclopedia Britannica. (2024, June 5). *Magic Johnson American basketball player*. https://www.britannica.com/biography/Magic-Johnson

EJAF. (2024). *Annual report 2024*. https://www.eltonjohnaidsfoundation.org/wp-content/uploads/2025/07/Elton-John-AIDS-Foundation_Annual-Report_2024-Digital.pdf

EJAF. (2025). *About us—Speaking up for those who need it most*. https://www.eltonjohnaidsfoundation.org/about-us/our-mission/

Ellis, D. (2023, November 30). Elton John welcomes expansion of opt-out testing for HIV to 46 Accident & Emergency sites across England and calls on all political leaders to do more to end AIDS in a speech at Speaker's House. *News Medical Life Sciences*. https://www.news-medical.net/news/20231130/Elton-John-welcomes-expansion-of-opt-out-testing-for-HIV-to-46-Accident-Emergency-sites-across-England-and-calls-on-all-political-leaders-to-do-more-to-end-AIDS-in-a-speech-at-Speakers-House.aspx

Elton. (n.d.). *A multiple Grammy-winning legend and flamboyant superstar, Elton is the most enduringly successful singer/songwriter of his generation*. https://www.eltonjohn.com/elton-john

Fitzsimons, T. (2018, October 15). LGBTQ history month: The early days of America's AIDS crisis. *NBC News*. https://www.nbcnews.com/feature/nbc-out/lgbtq-history-month-early-days-america-s-aids-crisis-n919701

Francis, D. B., Stevens, E. M., Noar, S. M., & Widman, L. (2019). Public reactions to and impact of celebrity health announcements: Understanding the Charlie Sheen effect. *Howard Journal of Communication*, *30*(5), 479–494. https://doi.org/10.1080/10646175.2018.1532852

Frysh, P. (2023, October 10). Famous faces of HIV and AIDS. *WebMD.com* https://www.webmd.com/hiv-aids/ss/slideshow-celebrities-hiv-aids

Gerstenzang, J. (1987, April 1). Reagan calls AIDS Enemy No. 1, advises abstinence. *Los Angeles Times*. https://www.latimes.com/la-reagan-aids-story-story.html

GMHC. (n.d.). *History*. https://www.gmhc.org/history

Green, I. (2021, June 30). How Princess Diana challenged HIV stigma with every hug. *Terrence Higgins Trust*. https://www.tht.org.uk/news/how-princess-diana-challenged-hiv-stigma-every-hug

H. J. Res. 395—100th Congress. (1987-1988): A joint resolution making further continuing appropriations for the fiscal year 1988, and for other purposes. (1987, December 22). https://www.congress.gov/bill/100th-congress/house-joint-resolution/395/text

H. R. 311 - 97th Congress. (1981-1982): A bill to strengthen the American family and promote the virtues of family life through education, tax assistance, and related measures. (1981, March 10). https://www.congress.gov/bill/97th-congress/house-bill/311

Harvard Radcliffe Institute's Schlesinger Library. (n.d.). *Magazines in chronological order*. https://guides.library.harvard.edu/c.php?g=310573&p=2088135

HIV.gov. (n.d.). *A timeline of HIV and AIDS*. https://www.hiv.gov/hiv-basics/overview/history/hiv-and-aids-timeline#year-1986

HIV.gov. (2025a, February 7). *The global HIV and AIDS epidemic*. https://www.hiv.gov/federal-response/pepfar-global-aids/global-hiv-aids-overview

HIV.gov. (2025b, February 20). *Minority HIV/AIDS Fund in action*. https://www.hiv.gov/federal-response/smaif/smaif-in-action

Hoffman, S. J., Mansoor, Y., Natt, N., Sritharan, L., Belluz, J., Caulfield, T., Freedhoff, Y., Lavis, J. N., & Sharma, A. M. (2017). Celebrities' impact on health-related knowledge, attitudes, behaviors, and status outcomes: protocol for a systematic review, meta-analysis, and meta-regression analysis. *Systematic Reviews*, *6*(1), 13–13. https://doi.org/10.1186/s13643-016-0395-1

Holden, S. (2024, May 25). Elton John. *Encyclopedia Britannica*. https://www.britannica.com/biography/Elton-John

HORIZONT. (2012, November 16). *25 Jahre Anti-Aids-Kampagne: Wie sich die Werbung über die Zeit verändert hat*. https://www.horizont.net/marketing/nachrichten/-25-Jahre-Anti-Aids-Kampagne-Wie-sich-die-Werbung-ueber-die-Zeit-veraendert-hat-111382

HRSA. (2022, February). Who was Ryan White? *Ryan White HIV/AIDS Program*. https://ryanwhite.hrsa.gov/about/ryan-white

Ike, C. (2024). Celebrity endorsements in public health campaigns. *International Journal of Public Relation and Communication*, *1*(1), 1–13. https://forthworth-journals.org/journals/index.php/IJPRC/article/view/56

Jun, M., Han, J., Zhou, Z., & Eisingerich, A. B. (2023). When is celebrity endorsement effective? Exploring the role of celebrity endorsers in enhancing key brand associations. *Journal of Business Research*, *164*, 113951. https://doi.org/10.1016/j.jbusres.2023.113951

Katz, E. (1957, Spring). The two-step flow of communication: An up-to-date report on an hypothesis. *The Public Opinion Quarterly*, *21*(1), 61–78. http://www.jstor.org/stable/2746790

Katz, E. (2015). Where are opinion leaders leading us? *International Journal of Communication*, *9*, 1023–1028.

Keiser, N. H. (1991). Strategies of media marketing for "America Responds to AIDS" and applying lessons learned. *Public Health Reports*, *106*(6), 623–627.

KFF. (2024, July 25). *The global HIV/AIDS epidemic*. https://www.kff.org/global-health-policy/fact-sheet/the-global-hiv-aids-epidemic/

Kleinfield, N. R. (1981, May 5). Major magazines losing ad pages. *The New York Times*. https://www.nytimes.com/1981/05/05/business/major-magazines-losing-ad-pages.html

Koop, C. E. (1987, January-February). Editorials—Surgeon General's Report on Acquired Immune Deficiency Syndrome. *Public Health Reports*, *102*(1), 1–3. https://pmc.ncbi.nlm.nih.gov/articles/PMC1477712/pdf/pubhealthrep00179-0003.pdf

Lazarsfeld, P. F., Berelson, B., & Gaudet, H. (1944). *The people's choice. How the voter makes up his mind in a presidential campaign*. Duell, Sloan and Pearce.

Lifson, A. (2021). Elton John—National Humanities Medal 2021. *National Endowment for the Humanities*. https://www.neh.gov/award/elton-john

Magic Johnson Enterprises. (n.d.a.). *Earvin "Magic" Johnson- Accomplishments*. https://magicjohnson.com/magic

Magic Johnson Enterprises. (n.d.b.). *Our executive team—Earvin Johnson Chairman and Chief Executive Officer*. https://magicjohnson.com/company

Marcus, U., & Starker, A. (2006). Heft 31HIV und AIDS. Gesundheitsberichter stattung des Bundes. *Robert Kock-Institut*.

Matzko, P. (n.d.). Jerry Falwell helps found the Moral Majority - Timeline Event. *The Association of Religion Data Archives*. https://www.thearda.com/us-religion/history/timelines/entry?etype=1&eid=46

McCarthy, J. (2019, June 28). Anxiety during the 1980s AIDS crisis. *Gallup*. https://news.gallup.com/vault/259643/gallup-vault-fear-anxiety-during-1980s-aids-crisis.aspx

McKeever, B. W. (2021). Public relations and public health: The importance of leadership and other lessons learned from "Understanding AIDS" in the 1980s. *Public Relations Review*, *47*(1), 1–9. https://doi.org/10.1016/j.pubrev.2020.102007

McNeil, D. G. Jr. (2016, Oct. 26). H.I.V. arrived in the U.S. long before 'patient zero.' *The New York Times*. https://www.nytimes.com/2016/10/27/health/hiv-patient-zero-genetic-analysis.html

Mendelsohn, H. (1973). Some reasons why information campaigns can succeed. *The Public Opinion Quarterly*, *37*(1), 50–61. https://www.jstor.org/stable/2747814

Noble, H. B. (2013, February 25). Everett Koop, forceful U.S. surgeon general, dies at 96 https://www.nytimes.com/2013/02/26/us/c-everett-koop-forceful-surgeon-general-dies-at-96.html

Noland, C. M., Goodale, G. G., Marshall, P. D., & Schlecht, H. P. (2009). Summer/Fall). An exploration of the impact of celebrity on the HIV/AIDS pandemic. *Journal of Health & Mass Communication*, *1*(3/4), 194–210. http://hdl.handle.net/10536/DRO/DU:30050337

Obermeyer, C. M., Baijal, P., & Pergurri, E. (2011, June). Facilitating HIV disclosure across diverse settings: A review. *American Journal of Public Health*, *101*(6) 1011–1023. DOI: 10.2105/AJPH.2010.300102

PBS. (n.d.). PBS News Hour history. https://www.pbs.org/newshour/about/history

Pew Research Center. (2023, November 10). Newspapers fact sheet. https://www.pewresearch.org/journalism/fact-sheet/newspapers/

Postelnicu, M. (2016, November 28). *Two-step flow model of communication. Encyclopedia Britannica*. https://www.britannica.com/topic/two-step-flow-model-of-communication

PRSA. (1988). *Silver Anvil Award of Excellence winner: America responds to AIDS*. https://www.prsa.org/

PRSA. (1989). *Silver Anvil Award of Excellence winner: The national AIDS mailing*. https://www.prsa.org/

PRSA. (2007). *Silver Anvil Award of Excellence winner: I Stand with Magic campaign to end Black AIDS*. https://www.prsa.org/

Puckett-Pope, L. (2022, November 23). Partying with Sir Elton John at the Saks Fifth Avenue holiday show. *Elle on AOL*. https://www.aol.com/partying-sir-elton-john-saks-215400790.html

Rahimi, S. (2005, November 10). An enduring ribbon of stars. *The New York Times*, p. B1–B5. https://www.proquest.com/historical-newspapers/enduring-ribbon-stars/docview/92914349/se-2

Readable. (n.d.). *The Gunning Fog Index*. https://readable.com/readability/gunning-fog-index/

Ronald Reagan Presidential Library & Museum. (1987, April 1). *Remarks at a luncheon for members of the College of Physicians in Philadelphia, Pennsylvania*. [Speech transcript]. https://www.reaganlibrary.gov/archives/speech/remarks-luncheon-members-college-physicians-philadelphia-pennsylvania

Rossman, C. (2015). Strategic health communication: Theory- and evidence-based campaign development. In D. Holtzhausen & A. Zerfass (Eds.). *The Routledge handbook of strategic communication*, (pp. 409–423). Routledge.

Rusbridger, L., & O'Leary, E. (2007, November 22). AIDS ad breaks Italy taboo over using word 'condom.' *Reuters*. https://www.reuters.com/article/idUSL22610889/

Saks. (n.d.). *About Saks Fifth Avenue*. https://ca.saks.com/en-ca/about-us/company-information

Saks. (2022, November 23). Saks debuts 2022 holiday campaign supporting the Elton John AIDS Foundation. [Press release]. *PR Newswire*. https://www.prnewswire.com/news-releases/saks-debuts-2022-holiday-campaign-supporting-the-elton-john-aids-foundation-301686179.html

Say It with a Condom. (2024, March 20). *The psychology of condom advertising*. [Blog] https://www.sayitwithacondom.com/blog/the-psychology-of-condom-advertising/

Serovich, J. M. (2001). A test of two HIV disclosure theories. *AIDS Educ Prev*, *13*(4), 355–364. https://www.ncbi.nlm.nih.gov/pmc/articles/PMC1237028/pdf/nihms-3713.pdf

Seward, C. (2012, July 17). Elton John: Lucky to be HIV-free. *The Atlanta Constitution*. https://www.ajc.com/entertainment/celebrity-news/elton-john-lucky-hiv-free/vSTgJIcDI6vuuWY0TICDDI/

Shorty Awards. (n.d.). *Saks holiday campaign: Elton John AIDS Foundation*. https://shortyawards.com/15th/saks-holiday-campaign-elton-john-aids-foundation

SPLC. (2005, April 28). History of the anti-gay movement since 1977. *The Intelligence Report.* https://www.splcenter.org/fighting-hate/intelligence-report/2005/history-anti-gay-movement-1977

Stevens, E. (2018, February). What's so appealing? An examination of emotional appeals and viewer engagement in safe-sex PSAs and condom advertisements. *Health Marketing Quarterly, 35*(1), 18-31. https://doi.org/10.1080/07359683.2017.1375241

Steves, R. (2005, August 25). Prudishness is one thing; censorship quite another. *USA Today*, 13A. https://link-gale-com.ezproxy.ithaca.edu/apps/doc/A135485452/AONE?u=nysl_sc_ithaca&sid=bookmark-AONE&xid=af19e2f8

Struckman-Johnson, C., Struckman-Johnson, D., Gilliland, R. C., & Ausman, A. (1994). Effect of persuasive appeals in aids psas and condom commercials on intentions to use condoms. *Journal of Applied Psychology, 24*(24), 2223–2244. https://doi.org/10.1111/j.1559-1816.1994.tb02381.x

The Editors of Encyclopaedia Britannica. (2018, February 12). *Moral Majority. Encyclopedia Britannica.* https://www.britannica.com/topic/Moral-Majority

The Henry J. Kaiser Family Foundation. (2006, June). Evolution of an epidemic: 25 years of HIV/AIDS media campaigns in the U.S. https://www.kff.org/wp-content/uploads/2013/01/7515.pdf

Thompson, T. L. (Ed.). (2014). *Encyclopedia of health communication.* SAGE Publications, Incorporated.

Toureille, C. (2017, November 13). 30 years on, remembering the day the UK aired its first TV ad campaign for condoms. *International Business Times.* https://www.ibtimes.co.uk/30-years-remembering-day-uk-aired-its-first-tv-ad-campaign-condoms-1646823

Tümmers, H. (2013). "GIB AIDS KEINE CHANCE": A message of prevention in two German states. *Zeithistorische Forschungen/Studies in Contemporary History* [Online edition], *10*(3), 491–501. DOI: https://doi.org/10.14765/zzf.dok-1502

Uenuma, F. (2021, November 4). Magic Johnson's HIV disclosure helped to shatter stigmas. But 30 years later, disparities in treatment remain. *Time.* https://time.com/6113046/magic-johnson-hiv-aids-impact/

UNAIDS. (2015, July 14). *How AIDS changed everything—MDG6: 15 years, 15 lessons of hope from the AIDS response.* https://www.unaids.org/en/resources/documents/2015/MDG6_15years-15lessonsfromtheAIDSresponse

UNAIDS. (2022). *Full report—In Danger: UNAIDS Global AIDS Update 2022* https://www.unaids.org/en/resources/documents/2022/in-danger-global-aids-update

UNAIDS. (2023). *Fact sheet 2023—Global HIV statistics.* https://www.humanitarianlibrary.org/sites/default/files/2023/10/UNAIDS_FactSheet_en.pdf

UNAIDS. (2024a, July 22). *2024 global AIDS report—The urgency of now: AIDS at a crossroads.* https://www.unaids.org/en/resources/documents/2024/global-aids-update-2024

UNAIDS. (2024b). *Germany.* https://www.unaids.org/en/regionscountries/countries/germany

UNODC, WHO, & UNAIDS. (2019). *HIV prevention, treatment, care and support for people who use stimulant drugs.* https://cdn.who.int/media/docs/default-source/hq-hiv-hepatitis-and-stis-library/hiv-prevention-treatment-care-and-support-for-people-who-use-stimulant-drugs.pdf?sfvrsn=d162259_0

USPHS. (1986). *Surgeon General's report on Acquired Immune Deficiency Syndrome.* https://files.eric.ed.gov/fulltext/ED277672.pdf

Vogue World Parties. (2022, November 23). With a performance on Fifth Avenue, Sir Elton John helped Saks ring in the holidays. *Vogue.* https://www.vogue.com/slideshow/saks-holiday-windows-sir-elton-john-2022

WHO. (2023, October 2). Voluntary medical male circumcision shown to be highly cost- effective, highlighting the need to intensify scale up and sustainability. https://www.who.int/news/item/02-10-2023-voluntary-medical-male-circumcision-shown-to-be-highly-cost-effective--highlighting-the-need-to-intensify-scale-up-and-sustainability

WHO. (2025a, July 15). *HIV and AIDS*. https://www.who.int/news-room/fact-sheets/detail/hiv-aids

WHO. (2025b). *The Global Health Observatory: HIV*. https://www.who.int/data/gho/data/themes/hiv-aids

Williams, T. (2007, May 19-May 25). "I Stand with Magic." Afro - American https://www.proquest.com/newspapers/i-stand-with-magic/docview/367490247/se-2

Woods, D. R., Davis, D., & Westover, B. J. (1991). "America Responds to AIDS": Its content, development process, and outcome. *Public Health Reports*, *106*(6), 615–622. https://www.jstor.org/stable/4597025

Wright, J. (2006, May 8). Remembering the early days of 'gay cancer.' *NPR*. https://www.npr.org/2006/05/08/5391495/remembering-the-early-days-of-gay-cancer

7

CASE STUDIES ON MAD COW DISEASE (BOVINE SPONGIFORM ENCEPHALOPATHY), 1986 TO PRESENT

7.1 INTRODUCTION: BSE IN CONTEXT

Bovine Spongiform Encephalopathy is commonly referred to as BSE: Bovine stands for cows; Spongiform for the spongy appearance of a cow's brain tissue under a microscope; and Encephalopathy for brain disease. BSE is also known as "mad cow disease" due to the impaired behavior of infected cows staggering and acting nervously from this fatal neurological disease (FDA, 2020). BSE was first identified in Britain in 1986 and later was discovered in cows in 23 other countries, including the U.S., Canada, and Japan (CDC, 2025). An estimated 4.4 million cows were destroyed in the U.K. alone (Finnegan, 2015). The human variant of BSE called Variant Creutzfeldt-Jakob Disease (vCJD) first occurred in the U.K. in 1996. Since then, the disease has infected 233 people worldwide, with most deaths occurring in the U.K. and four in the U.S. (CDC, 2024).

Many scientists and medical researchers believe BSE is caused by an abnormal protein called a prion that incubates for four to six years before a cow shows symptoms. Cows contract BSE from feed ingredients containing parts of a contaminated cow (FDA, 2020). Although cows are herbivores, they were being transformed "into carnivores, indeed, cannibals" (Best, 2001, p. 31) by cost-saving measures of rendering all parts of dead animals for various purposes. Before industry practices changed due to BSE, cow feed used to include parts of cows not consumed by people—"heads, brains, stomachs, intestines, spinal cords, feet, hooves, tails, and blood" (Best, 2001, p. 33)—transformed into a powder added as a protein supplement to animal feed. No test to determine BSE in a live cow exists

DOI: 10.4324/9781003434382-7

at this time; only brain tissues of dead cows can be examined under the microscope to identify BSE (FDA, 2020).

Transmission and symptoms

BSE is only transmitted by cows eating contaminated meat-and-bone meal feed comprised of parts of BSE-infected cows. As a rare neurodegenerative disease, BSE causes cows to lose their physical coordination and develop nervous and aggressive behaviors, eventually leading to the destruction of their central nervous systems. Mostly young cows, about a year old, contract the disease with symptoms occurring years later due to BSE's four- to six-year incubation period. Once symptoms begin, cows usually die within two weeks to six months. BSE cannot be spread by infected cows or humans with vCJD in contact with a healthy cow (FDA, 2020).

Variant Creutzfeldt-Jakob Disease (vCJD), the human equivalent of BSE, is extremely rare and only a few people become infected with this deadly neurodegenerative disorder. Humans can contract vCJD by eating beef products containing meat from BSE-infected cattle (CDC, 2024). According to the National Health Service (NHS) (2021) in the U.K., five people developed vCJD from blood transfusions from a donor who later became ill with the disorder; however, the victims could have come down with vCJD from eating contaminated beef. The disease is not contagious by being near cows or spread by respiratory droplets from an infected person sneezing or coughing next to a healthy person. In addition, humans cannot contract vCJD from consuming milk and other dairy products from infected cows (FDA, 2020). The primary symptoms of vCJD are diminished mental abilities, such as memory loss and impaired decision-making like dementia. Infected people may experience problems with their vision, sleeping, swallowing, and physical coordination that cause death usually within a year or two from heart or lung conditions, pneumonia, or other medical issues (NHS, 2021). Spinal fluid tests can help identify vCJD while the infected person is alive, but the most effective test to confirm the disease is a brain biopsy undertaken during an autopsy (Mayo Clinic, 2023).

Treatments and preventive measures

BSE has no vaccines or cures currently. Infected cows were slaughtered as a safety precaution. Preventive measures include bans of cattle livestock and cattle feed containing parts of cows (CDC, 2025). Like BSE, no medical treatments are available for vCJD. Supportive measures and palliative care can keep infected people as comfortable as possible as their symptoms progress before they pass away (Mayo Clinic, 2023). In addition, the industry took on preventive methods, such as tests and enhanced surveillance, to monitor the health of cattle and to set up guidelines on handling infected cattle (World Organisation for Animal Health, 2023).

In 1989, Britain banned selling certain organ meats to humans, and the U.S. banned imports of bovine livestock from Britain. In 1993, Britain banned meat and bone meal as feed to animals and as farm fertilizers when the situation worsened with 120,000 BSE-infected cattle. In the mid-1990s, the following initiatives took place:

- Britain banned meat-and-bone meal feed to livestock and its use as farm fertilizers.
- Approximately 4.5 million cattle were slaughtered in Britain when more vCJD cases occurred.
- Japan banned imports of British meat-and-bone feed for animal.
- European Union banned both beef and beef-related products from Britain (Center for Food Safey, n.d.).

In 1997, the U.S. Food and Drug Administration banned animal feed containing proteins from cows, sheep, deer, and other animals. In 2003, the U.S. Department of Agriculture banned sick and injured cows and cattle of all ages and stopped adding cattle brains and other parts from cattle over age 2.5 years to meat products for humans. Import bans have been lifted since 1999 (Center for Food Safety, n.d.).

Widely used communication

Newspapers, magazines, television, and radio were the primary media in the mid-80s while newer technology was becoming more popular and commercially available. Print newspapers still had high circulations in 1986—62,502,000 weekly newspapers and 58,925,000 Sunday newspapers—before their decline started in the 1990s (Pew Research Center, 2023). New magazines debuted in the mid-and late-1980s, such as *Parenting, Men's Health, Cooking Light, Country, First, Traditional Home*, *Midwest Living, PC/World, Computer Word,* and *Macworld* (PSA Research, n.d.). Fewer people relied on the radio for news reports; only one all-news radio station remained, and other radio programs cut back on news programming. Reasons for the decline of radio news included budget cuts, television viewership of news, and Federal Communications Commission's radio deregulations on required hours of non-entertainment content (Stuart, 1986). Cable television was growing in popularity in the mid-1980s; 48.1% of U.S. households (42 million households) had cable in 1986, an increase of 4.1% (2.3 million households) over the previous year (Associated Press, 1986). Television was facing a new strong competitor—85% of U.S. households contained at minimum one videocassette recorder or player in 1995, a rise of 28% from a decade earlier (Chicago Tribune, 2021).

Newer facsimile (fax) machines became a popular communication tool in many offices, including newsrooms and PR and advertising agencies, and at hotels for business travelers across the U.S. and in other countries in the 1980s. Retail sales of fax machines in the U.S. expanded from USD 238 million in 1982 to USD 914 million in 1987. Unlike older models of fax machines, newer equipment could transmit documents from one office to another anywhere in the world within 20 seconds, making faxes cheaper and faster than messengers or courier services (Sims, 1988). Today, faxes still exist primarily for security purposes in sending confidential documents over phone lines versus the internet.

An early and rudimentary version of email, MCI Mail, debuted in 1983 and failed quickly since the product was unable to attract customers, primarily due to the growth of fax machines that delivered documents faster and competitors, such as USPS, which created its own email systems (Hagley Museum, n.d.). The first personal computers debuted in the mid-1980s. Today, computer users would consider the older models extremely limited in speed, memory, graphics, portability, and range of features and capabilities. In 1984, 8.2% of U.S. households owned computers; the number almost doubled to 15% in 1989 (U.S. Department of Commerce Bureau of the Census, 1991) The first handheld portable cellphone, Motorola DynaTAC 8000X, was launched in 1984 for commercial use. Its capabilities would be considered inadequate in comparison to today's mobiles; the Motorola model weighed almost three pounds and required 10 hours to recharge for 30 minutes of talk time (Mobile Phone Museum, n.d.). The size also was bulky: 1.75 inches wide, 13 inches high, and 3.5 inches in depth (Radiomuseum, n.d.). The market price was steep–USD 4,000 (Mobile Phone Museum, n.d.), which would cost around USD 12,418 in 2025.

Impact

The risk of BSE changed livestock industry practices with bans on specific animal feed and fertilizers containing remnants of cows and other animals. Livestock farmers, meat processors, and feed producers were financially impacted due to the destruction of livestock, bans on specific cattle organs sold to people, and restrictions on cattle imports (World Organisation for Animal Health, 2023).

The Meat and Livestock Commission went into crisis mode, particularly in 1996, as the BSE epidemic continued to spread throughout the U.K. Slaughters of livestock and deaths of people resulted in plunging public confidence in consuming beef and trade bans enforced by the European Union. The media also exacerbated the situation with scary stories provoking public hysteria even while the industry made major improvements in its safety standards The U.K. experienced not only a drop in domestic beef sales but also exports due to bans of its beef products. The economic loss in the U.K. was estimated to be USD 980 million during 1986, the first year of the BSE outbreak, while domestic beef consumption dropped by 20% (Carter & Huie, 2004). In 2004, the U.S. beef industry estimated USD 200 million was spent on BSE-associated expenditures (Coffey et al., 2005). The European Union reported an 11% decline in beef consumption, costing the EU USD 5 billion in beef industry subsidies (Leiss et al., 2004). After BSE infected cows in Canada in May 2003, the country was prohibited from transporting live cattle and beef products to the U.S. and other countries, causing Canadian cattle producers to face direct and indirect economic losses of approximately CAD 5.3 billion by December 2004 (Statistics Canada, 2006).

Sit-down restaurants, supermarkets, and fast-food restaurant chains also contended with losses due to BSE. The stock market, for example, reacted quickly to the first reported BSE case in the U.S. and the subsequent recall of 100,000 pounds of U.S. beef in 2003. Stocks dropped for fast food restaurant chains (McDonald's and Wendy's), steakhouses (Outback Steakhouse and Lone Star Steakhouse) (Associated Press, 2003), and meat processors (Tyson and Smithfield) (Moss et al., 2004), while cattle futures dropped in the Chicago Mercantile Exchange (called CME Group since 2007) (Associated Press, 2003).

Widespread fear of consuming beef spread primarily in the U.K. and U.S., and in other countries. Communication efforts in the U.K. and U.S. received criticism for underplaying the health crisis. Authors of the book, *Mad Cow USA,* stated, "U.S. assurances of safety were based on public relations and public deception, not science or adequate regulatory safeguards" (Rampton & Stauber, 2003, p. 1). Another book, written by Leiss et al. (2004), *Mad Cows and Mother's Milk,* starts with its first chapter titled, "Mad Cows or Crazy Communications?," claiming inconsistent information from governmental officials and the media on the level of risk for people consuming beef. The then U.K. Agricultural Minister John Gummer staged a news conference with himself and his reluctant 4-year-old daughter eating hamburgers to demonstrate that people should not fear vCJD. In fact, his daughter was not in the mood for eating a hamburger, so Gummer took a bite out of her burger for the publicity photo.

BBC News World Edition (2000) wrote Gummer is "Probably the most derided politician to emerge out of the BSE scandal" (para. 1). Photos of the event have been widely used in stories about BSE. *Mad Cow USA* authors stated: "It was a photo opportunity that would come back to haunt him in subsequent years, becoming a symbol of the government's shameless eagerness to flack for beef despite mounting evidence of human danger" (Rampton & Stauber, p. 131).

7.2 NATIONAL CATTLEMEN'S BEEF ASSOCIATION STAMPEDES TO PROTECT INDUSTRY: BEEF CHECKOFF PROGRAM COMMUNICATES BEEF SAFETY IN THE U.S.

Situation analysis

The Economic Research Service within the United States Department of Agriculture (USDA, 2025) reported that cattle production is the most significant sector of the U.S. agricultural industry, "consistently accounting for the largest share of total cash receipts for agricultural commodities" (para. 1), receiving an estimated 22% of USD 515 billion in cash receipts for all agricultural commodities in 2024. The U.S. has been the largest producer of beef and home to the greatest number of consumers of beef products (by total volume) since the USDA's economic research series started in 1960. In addition, the U.S. ranked as the second largest importer of beef due to consumer demand (USDA, 2025) and ranked third as the largest exporter of beef worldwide with Australia closely ranking fourth while Brazil ranked No. 1 followed by India (water buffalo) in 2023 (Fleck, 2024).

About National Cattlemen's Beef Association and Beef Checkoff

As the oldest and largest U.S. trade association for the cattle industry, the National Cattlemen's Beef Association (NCBA) was founded in 1898 and continues to serve as the marketing trade association for cattle farmers and ranchers from its offices in Denver and Washington, D.C. Its vision is "To be the trusted leader and definitive voice of the U.S. cattle and beef industry," and its mission is "To serve the cattle and beef industry by improving the business climate, growing beef demand and increasing the world's access to U.S. beef" (NCBA, 2025, para. 2).

NCBA oversees the funding for the Beef Checkoff Program that was established in 1985 as part of the Food Security Act of 1985 (also referred to as the Farm Bill) that set up the Cattlemen's Beef Promotion and Research Board and the Beef Promotion Operating Committee under the Beef Promotion and Research Act of 1985 (Agricultural Marketing

Service, 1985). The program "assesses $1 per head on the sale of live domestic and imported cattle, in addition to a comparable assessment on imported beef and beef products" (Beef Checkoff, 2025, para. 1), which means that its budget varies based on beef sales. It is responsible for creating initiatives to stimulate sales of beef products to restaurants, food retailers, and consumers in the U.S. and abroad. The program conducts research, explores new product development, and develops and oversees advertising and public relations campaigns. However, the program is unable by law to use its funding for lobbying for government policies, controlling prices, or owning cattle, packing plants, or any type of retail outlet (Beef Checkoff, 2025).

The Beef Checkoff Program's iconic "Beef. It's What's For Dinner" campaign started in 1992 with television and radio advertisements featuring celebrity narrations and Aaron Copland's "Hoe-Down" music from the ballet *Rodeo* and showing scenes of people from cities to rural areas enjoying beef served different ways (Beef Checkoff, 2020a). The campaign has evolved to appeal to changing eating habits and lifestyles of consumers on digital platforms. For example, in 2010, the campaign's new tagline became "29 Lean Cuts. One Powerful Protein" to promote the nutritional value of leaner beef cuts (NCBA, 2010) and, in 2023, the tagline changed to "Together We Bring More" to celebrate special occasions and milestones with memorable meals (Beef Checkoff, 2023). Its website provides recipes, nutritional facts, and news releases. See Figure 7.1 of an infographic on grilling tips.

The first "Beef. It's What's for Dinner" campaign had a research, public relations, and advertising budget of approximately USD 80 million to USD 90 million. In 2017, the promotional budget was nearly USD 30 million due to a drop in beef sales, which was attributed to rising beef prices, health concerns about consuming red meat, and higher consumption of chicken products (Bruell, 2017).

BSE cases in North America

The first North American case of BSE was identified in 1993 in a cow in Alberta, Canada, imported from Britain, and the second case of BSE was a Canadian-born cow in 2003 (Canadian Food Inspection Agency, 2025). A 37-year-old Canadian citizen who took multiple trips to Britain died from the human version of BSE, Variant Creutzfeldt-Jakob Disease (vCJD), in 2002 (Ehman, 2002). In the U.S., the first BSE case was a dairy cow from Canada that tested positive in Washington state in 2003, and the first diagnosed case of vCJD in the U.S. was a 22-year-old British woman living in Florida in 2002 (Center for Food Safety, n.d.).

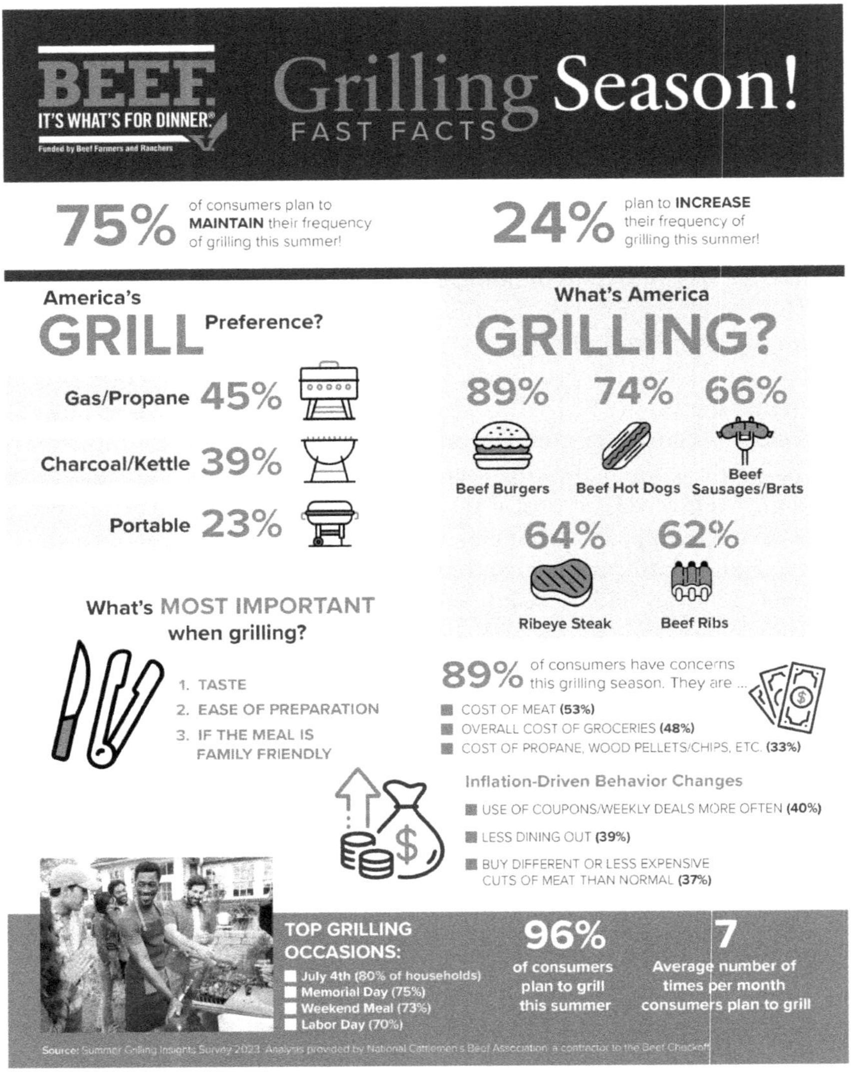

FIGURE 7.1 Infographic on "Grilling Season! Fast Facts." Courtesy of Beef. It's What's For Dinner. www.beefitswhatsfordinner.com.

Communication and execution

This communication section and part of the results section come from the Public Relations Society of America's summary of a Silver-Anvil Award winner, "Protecting Consumer Confidence in U.S. Beef: A Success Story" by the NCBA in 2005. The campaign took place from December 23, 2003, to October 1, 2004. Unless otherwise noted, PRSA (2005) is the source.

On the same day, the BSE-infected cow was found in the U.S. on December 23, 2003, NCBA and the Beef Checkoff put its BSE Crisis Response Plan into action, along with the support of state beef organizations. The plan was previously developed when the BSE epidemic was spreading in the U.K. in 1996 and refined as the crisis evolved. The goal was to restore and sustain U.S. consumer confidence in the safety of U.S. beef products. To achieve the goal, the plan's three primary strategies included the following:

1 Ensuring consumers had widely available accurate and scientific information on beef products to help with the decision-making process of purchasing beef products.
2 Presenting a cohesive and respective voice on behalf of the U.S. beef industry.
3 Correcting misinformation on multiple platforms.

NCBA was able to acquire insight in developing its strategies from market research conducted since 1996. The research findings based on focus groups, 29 quantitative tracking surveys, and media monitoring and analysis of BSE news coverage provided the following actions:

- Emphasize scientific spokespersons.
- Ensure focused messages for effectiveness.
- Accentuate local BSE response plans at the state level in cooperation with state beef councils and state cattle ranchers' organizations.
- Undertake proactive media relations to pique consumers' interests.
- Develop a response strategy to correct inaccurate information quickly.

The target audiences spanned a variety of people and organizations:

- Consumers, particularly ones who were uncertain about BSE and its impact on them.
- The media, spanning consumer, agriculture, and industry trade outlets; realizing that some journalists disseminated potentially inaccurate information to report on a new BSE story on a tight deadline.
- State and industry beef-related organizations invested in reassuring consumers and beef industry constituents.
- U.S. government agencies, primarily those that the public trusts for safety expertise and knowledge.
- U.S. beef export markets that may be concerned about the confidence levels of their consumers and pressured by their local beef industry.
- Beef marketers, such as retailers, food service operations, and wholesalers, who are dedicated to satisfying their customers' choices, not necessarily defending the beef industry.

NCBA undertook a variety of tactics immediately after BSE was reported in the U.S., resulting in lead stories in the media; afterward, secondary stories on broader topics related to BSE. Here are highlights of the tactics used:

- **Media relations**—focused on communicating that BSE is not a health risk in the U.S.
  - Setting up telephone news conferences—15 minutes after the USDA's announcement on the first case of BSE in the U.S.—with 160 consumer and trade journalists, and later throughout the campaign to convey updates and facts.
  - Training NCBA executives to be spokespersons for hundreds of media interviews within a few days of the announcement.
  - Briefing third-party experts on the facts to share during their media interviews.
  - Distributing photos and videos on the accurate state of the beef industry.
- **Crisis website**—activated to serve as the major source of information for the media, consumers, the beef industry, and governments.
- **Email advisories**—sent to beef and beef-related industry stakeholders with science-based information.
- **Password-protected extranet**—served as an information clearinghouse for state and allied associations.
- **Government interaction**—encouraged officials to maintain a transparent process and provide science-driven facts.
- **Internet monitoring**—corrected online misinformation quickly and ensured accurate information was widely available.

Results

The NCBA evaluated the results of the BSE Management plan in four categories:

1. Consumer demand—Beef demand increased 7.74% in 2004, the most significant increase in decades.
2. Confidence—A NCBA tracking survey from January 2005 revealed that 93% of consumers were confident in consuming beef. In 13 of the NCBA's tracking surveys, consumer confidence remained stable. A CNN/USA Today/Gallup survey from January 2–5, 2004 showed that only one in six Americans worried that they or their families might contract vCJD while 17% stated that they have reduced or stopped consuming meat (Moore, 2004).
3. Consumer spending—CattleFax is "the single source for all information on the beef and agricultural industries" (para. 1). CattleFax presented

a research report on the state of the beef industry to the Range Beef Cow Symposium at the University of Nebraska, Lincoln, highlighting consumer spending was almost USD 71 billion: in 2004 and USD 71.3 billion in 2005.

4 Media coverage—BSE was covered in approximately 5,400 articles in 154 major consumer media outlets, almost four times the number of BSE articles monitored by the NCBA the previous year. Media monitoring also found that USDA and NCBA officials were the most widely quoted sources on BSE.

The PRSA Silver Anvil award-winning entry concluded with a summary: "Together with the Cattlemen's Beef Board, state organizations and producer leaders, NCBA maintained consumer confidence in beef safety and demand for beef" (PRSA, 2005, p. 3).

Although this PR campaign focused on U.S. consumer consumption of beef products, the U.S. beef industry dealt with other challenges. The first BSE case in the U.S., even though the cow was from Canada, resulted in restriction of U.S. beef exports during 2004 to 2007. Several countries in 2004 decided to resume trading when they were certain that U.S regulations and industry supervision restored the safety of U.S. beef. Japan and Korea, however, maintained their restrictions, causing approximately 86% "of the lost export sales caused by BSE-related restrictions and of potential export gains if tariffs and TRQs [tariff-rate quotas] were removed," (p. xvii), according to USITC—the U.S. International Trade Commission (2008).

The global beef trade: Effects of animal health, sanitary, food safety, and other measures on U.S. beef exports report describes the financial losses the U.S. faced:

> During 2004–07, BSE-related restrictions were a major barrier to U.S. beef exports; these restrictions cost the U.S. beef industry $1.5–2.7 billion in lost revenue annually. A loss in annual export sales ranging from $3.1 billion in 2004 to $2.5 billion in 2007 was offset in part by additional sales in the domestic market. Annual losses were greatest in 2004 and have since declined, as some countries have eased restrictions and U.S. exporters have developed alternative markets (albeit at lower prices).
>
> *(USITC, 2008, p. xvi)*

Theoretical framework

This case study provides more insight into a specific concept associated with crisis and risk management approaches within the food industry: issues management. This crisis communication and public relations practice is an important factor that allowed NCBA and Beef Checkoff Program to act swiftly in addressing the BSE crisis.

First, it is important to identify the concept of issues management. Elizabeth Dougall, Ph.D., (2008) posted an article about issues management on the Institute of Public Relations website. Accordingly, "Issue management is an anticipatory, strategic management process that helps organizations detect and respond appropriately to emerging trends or changes in the socio-political environment" (para. 5). Organizations engage in this process during a crisis to get a pulse on how stakeholder perceptions and expectations of an issue shift, which can indicate important consequences for an organization. This knowledge informs organizational efforts to repair relationships with stakeholders and rebuild trust and confidence. Within the food industry, consumer perceptions of risk are important because they are "often very different from those of the professionals and, at times, there is a complete disconnect between consumers' views and the true risks associated with a product or a process" (Wall & Chen, 2018, p. 2).

From the perspective of the NCBA (2023), "the issue management team is responsible for developing beef-specific ... resources, including crisis plans at national and state levels, talking points, market research insights and fact sheets and social media resources," along with "day-to-day issues monitoring" (p. 2). The organization prides itself on the proactive measures it took to establish "an emergency plan in place for nearly 10 years in the event of such a crisis," which allowed NCBA to not be "caught flat-footed" (Henderson, 2020, para. 5).

Organizations face several issues within the food industry that need to be monitored and managed regarding BSE so that a crisis has less of an opportunity to erupt. Yasmine Motarjemi (2014), food safety consultant, Nyon, Switzerland, identified these issues that have the potential to create a crisis in the food industry: advances in science and technology, emergence of new hazards like mad cow disease, human error, product tampering or failure. John Sofos (2014), professor emeritus, Colorado State University, adds to this list:

- allergens
- bacteria and other pathogens, pesticides, chemicals or other additives
- "system failures or abuses during food animal production, product processing and distribution, and preparation for consumption, as well as by consumption habits" (p. 156)
- changing consumer preferences
- regulatory requirements and policy changes
- inadequate training/education in food handling and storage
- media savvy consumers

- sanitation challenges
- "bone chips and foreign bodies such as metal, glass, wood, plastic, stones, etc." (p. 157).

Managing and monitoring these issues are important because multiple stakeholders require different messages for each issue (Wall & Chen, 2018). For example, Motarjemi (2014) points out that organizations should understand the consequences of such issues for consumers, businesses (e.g., grocery stores, restaurants, and contractors) and public health and regulatory agencies (USDA, WHO, CDC).

For consumers who may lose confidence in the food supply if they have been exposed to something harmful, "preparing response measures in advance would free up valuable time during a crisis to focus on consumers and communicate accurate information so that they can continue to confidently purchase beef" (Beef Checkoff, 2020b, para. 6). Motarjemi (2014) identifies some public expectations for organizations: transparency in communication, prioritization of health over profits/losses, and more information on the source of food and traceability, an issue important for consumers (Petitt, 2001). Traceability is a regulation enacted after BSE "to access specific information about a food product that has been captured and integrated within the product's recorded identification throughout the supply chain" (Islam & Cullen, 2021, p. 4).

Jenn Tilliss, executive director of the issues management and media relations team at NCBA, identified two actions that Beef Checkoff (2020b) took to meet these expectations of consumers: "Minimize consumer confusion and concern through quick dissemination of information," and "Educate industry partners and stakeholders with aligned messaging at state and local levels through clear channels of communication" (para. 6).

For businesses, issue management is essential to repairing an organization's image and mitigating economic consequences associated with "product recall and waste of produced food… loss of market shares and loss of trust of their customers and the regulatory authorities" (Motarjemi, 2014, p. 1099). Messages should ensure that partners and "the entire beef industry [have] access to the resources and information needed to maintain consumer confidence and demand when issues and crises arise" (NCBA, 2023, p. 2).

Regarding public health and regulatory agencies and issues management, organizations must comply with new controls that "were unimagined prior to the identification of bovine spongiform encephalopathy (BSE) in the late 1980s" (Petitt, 2001, p. 584). Messages should ensure that organizations like Beef Checkoff and NCBA remind audiences that "America's beef producers take food seriously, as do the government agencies that regulate and monitor production in the United States. To suggest otherwise is false and irresponsible" (Henderson, 2020, p. 3).

Key words

BSE—Bovine Spongiform Encephalopathy
Beef Checkoff Program
Beef, It's What's for Dinner campaign
National Cattlemen's Beef Association (NCBA)
Tariffs
United States Department of Agriculture (USDA)
USDA's economic research series
Variant Creutzfeldt-Jakob Disease (vCJD)

Discussion questions

1 Have you seen the "Beef. It's still what's for dinner" campaign on social media?
2 Do you read labels of beef products to know the country of origin?
3 This chapter was about the beef industry's approach to handling mad cow disease/BSE. Imagine if you were in a position to create a campaign for cattle farmers? How would you approach the campaign?

7.3 BSE TAKES A BITE OUT OF BURGERS: MCDONALD'S BEEFS UP ITS PUBLIC IMAGE AND HEALTH COMMUNICATION

Situational analysis

A brief history of McDonald's Corporation

According to the historical timeline on its website, McDonald's began in 1940 in San Bernardino, California. Brothers Dick and Mac McDonald who owned a Bar-B-Q restaurant transformed it into a self-service drive-in establishment in 1948. They successfully grew the business to nine franchises, using their Speedee Service System, and limited menu that included 15 cent hamburgers, shakes, and fries (McDonald's, n.d.a.).

Fascinated by the McDonald brothers' operation and Speedee system, Ray Kroc opened his first restaurant in 1955 in Des Plaines, Illinois, and acquired the rights of the McDonald brothers' company in 1961. As global opportunities opened, Kroc expanded into international markets yielding over 36,000 McDonald's restaurants in over 100 nations (McDonald's, n.d.a).

Since April 1994, "when it stopped updating the number .... McDonald's has sold a lot of burgers. Billions of burgers. Or as the company likes to say: billions of billions of burgers" (Kasperkevic, 2017, paras. 3–5). In terms of overall sales from franchised restaurants, between 2006 and 2023, McDonald's had just under USD 120 billion in sales (Statista, 2024). As such, McDonald's was the largest purchaser of beef and pork in the U.S. (SEC, 2023), buying close to one billion pounds (Tribune News Services, 2003).

In its *Purpose & Impact Progress Summary 2022–2023*, the publicly traded fast food restaurant's success is a result of its **M**arketing, their **C**ore menu, and the three **D**s: digital, delivery, and drive-thru personalized experiences for customers (emphasis added). "Behind the Golden Arches is a global community of crew, farmers, suppliers, Franchisees and countless others who make up who we are as a brand" with approximately 150,000 employees worldwide, of which 70% are employed outside the U.S. (McDonald's Corporation, 2022–2023, p. 5).

Over the years, McDonald's has enjoyed both highs and lows in terms of reputation. In 2023, it rose to number five in the Kantar BrandZ Most Valuable Global Brands ranking overall, and number one in the fast-food category (Hluska, 2023), and number one in leading restaurant brands in 2025, by brand value (Statista, 2024).

The company has also faced a consumer perception battle regarding an unhealthy image of its food (Sutton, 2015). Domestic and international consumers of McDonald's have become concerned with obesity and its link to a "host of health problems including arthritis, cancer, cardiovascular disease, diabetes, high cholesterol, and hypertension," via processed ingredients that are "calorically dense and fiber-poor" (Spencer et al., 2005, p. 380) and high in carbs and sugar.

Other company blunders included failed menu items and alliances with other fast-food corporations, poor communication with franchisees, and turnover in leadership (Johnson, 2021). The company has also dealt with a lawsuit over coffee that was too hot and a "McLibel case" regarding its environmental, health and labor practices in the U.K. (Wikipedia, 2024).

Despite the fact that it follows stringent international safety standards for its beef set by the USDA and the World Organization for Animal Health (2023), McDonald's was hit to its core as confidence in British beef plummeted in the late 1990s. McDonald's banned British beef in burgers across its stores in the U.K. (Devi, 1996). The concerns over the safety of beef persisted into the early 2000s, as:

> All those nightly newscasts of massive cattle burnings didn't do much to drive hamburger sales ... European sales at McDonald's in January and February fell by 10 percent, no small amount considering the

> company derives as much as 36 percent of its overall operating income from the continent ... and the stock quickly fell to its lowest in three years—at $27.55 a share, the price was almost half of its all-time peak of $50 in 1999 ... The future of its staple product, the hamburger, is increasingly periled.
>
> *(Lindsey, 2001, paras. 5–7)*

Navigating these reputational crises has enabled McDonald's (n.d.b.) to become a "trusted brand for generations to come by being resilient and agile" (para.1), through its award-winning public relations campaigns, "evolving enterprise risk management (ERM) framework, business continuity governance, crisis management processes" (para. 2).

McDonald's Corporation: A leader in beef safety campaign

Communication programming and execution

Research

This section comes from the Public Relations Society of America's campaign profile, which is a summary of a Silver-Anvil Award winner, "McDonald's Corporation: A Leader in Beef Safety." The campaign took place in 2004. Unless otherwise noted, PRSA (2004) is the source.

One of the corporation's retired senior executives once said about how the company would respond to a crisis, "We find six of the smartest people in the building, sit down and work out a solution. Our collective experience will point us in the right direction" (quoted in O'Rourke & Smith, 2023, p. 7).

From a research standpoint, this approach had not changed much in 2004, when a cross-functional corporate team—Communications/Media, Government Relations, Marketing, Operations, Supply Chain, and Senior Management—was assembled to conduct **primary** research regarding the following:

1 Updates on the BSE situation, in order to identify critical issues, establish accountabilities and create deliverables.
2 External validation that its safety policies and standards meet or exceed government regulations. "McDonald's invented or was an early adopter of every significant beef safety measure used in the beef industry today. Immediate communication with consumers and internal audiences" was paramount (para. 1).
3 Consumer reactions to BSE, used to develop "targeted, relevant communication strategies and materials based on feedback" (para. 2).

4 Employees' effectiveness and understanding of BSE communications through an online survey.
5 Media coverage and analysis.
6 Types of inquiries and perceptions from consumers who called the 800 number.
7 Restaurant manager perceptions and impacts, through daily reports within McDonald's Operations Resource Center.

Secondary research included reviewing the already created crisis contingency plan, and "what if" scenarios from what the corporation did previously about BSE in Europe and Canada.

Planning

The data collected by the cross-functional team shaped the planning of five objectives for this campaign, to be delivered in phases:

1 Consumers needed to be reassured of the safety of U.S. beef supply.
2 As a crisis can cause significant damage to an organization and its employees, O'Rourke & Smith (2023) advocate for a proactive framework for managing a crisis so as to "minimize any business interruptions/sales impact" (para. 4)—the second objective of this plan.
3 In addition to consumers, employees need to be reminded that their employer has the highest food safety and quality control standards in the industry and is recognized as a leader.
4 These ongoing standards need to be promoted to protect the McDonald's brand.
5 Promoting high standards of policy and procedures using McDonald's established leader position can help prevent further incidents.

The overarching strategy for reaching these objectives "was to differentiate McDonald's in the minds of consumers by telling McDonald's story and showing that the Northwest case of BSE had no effect on McDonald's restaurants" (para. 5), before the competition.

On Christmas, one day after the announcement of the first U.S. case, CNN International (2003) reported that both McDonald's and Wendy's stated "their supply chains were not linked" to the case in Washington state (para. 8). Burger King is following suit "walking a delicate line in their marketing and communication efforts ... to inform consumers that their individual products have not been tainted" (Day, 2004, para. 5).

The specific tactics or steps/actions for this campaign were deployed in phases (O'Rourke & Smith, 2023).

Phase One occurred within 24 hours of the identification of BSE in the U.S. During this phase, consumer research began. The online Employee Beef Safety Communications survey was administered. Key media statements and fact sheets were created and distributed. Communication between headquarters, divisional presidents, and SME (subject matter experts) was coordinated daily via conference calls. A hotline was created for managers to provide updates. Customer service representatives provided additional training and coaching on how employees handle customer calls about BSE.

Phase Two occurred in the next 48 hours as a Marketing Communications/Public Relations Resource kit was developed for affected markets. Key public figures and the International Scientific Advisory Council (ISAC) were mobilized to help manage the BSE crisis while employees were equipped with key messages and procedures for handling customer inquiries.

Phase Three at 72 hours and beyond focused on designing a centralized internal BSE website to house all BSE posts and information, which was used in responding to media requests.

Execution: Internal and external processes

To execute the planning required careful coordination of both internal and external processes designed to influence the organization's performance and enhance competence (Svyantek, 2022).

Internally, McDonald's Corporation provided employees with a resource kit, sample response letter for customers, list of FAQs, glossary of key terms, and a CD-ROM: *What you need to know about McDonald's Beef Safety*. CD-ROMs, created in the early 1980s and popularized in the 90s, provided an easy technological way to back up and store a lot of information so it could be distributed and used by multiple people easily (Suzuki, 2022).

Externally, the plan was executed using multiple key media statements, fact sheets with local impacts and beef safety details, backgrounders on McDonald's standard for quality, food, and safety, and McDonald's spokespersons and third-party influencers. Before McDonald's was active on social media in 2008 (Singh & Perepu, 2014), these influencers acted as representatives and spoke on behalf of the company.

Results: Outcomes and evaluation

According to PRSA (2004), all objectives were met and exceeded. Table 7.1 documents the metrics and measurements of success.

TABLE 7.1 Metrics and measurements of success

	Objective	*Outcome and Results*
1	Consumers needed to be reassured of the safety of U.S. beef supply.	Over two-thirds of consumer participants surveyed rated McDonald's as having high standards and stringent protocols in the restaurant industry, exceeding government regulations. Almost three-quarters of consumers believed that there was no connection between the BSE case in Washington and McDonald's or its suppliers. And, over half felt the McDonald's provided steady BSE leadership over the years.
2	Interruptions to business/sales were minimized through proactive management of the issue.	No negative sales impacts, only positive—increase 12%.
3	Employees needed to be reminded that their employer has the highest food safety and quality control standards in the industry and is recognized as a leader.	Nearly 100% answered that they received enough information to appropriately respond to BSE questions, and over 90% felt they were well informed brand ambassadors.
4	Promote and protect the McDonald's brand.	**Internally:** 99% of employees surveyed felt they received enough communication regarding Beef Safety, and 98% felt confident in McDonald's beef safety practices. **Externally:** McDonald's was successful in telling its story consistently in the media, which helped to differentiate the company from its competitors.
5	Promote high standards of policy and procedures using McDonald's established leader position that can help prevent further incidents.	McDonald's had already established itself as having long-standing practices regarding Advanced Meat Recovery and Specific Risk Materials (SRMs).

As Richard Edelman, CEO of Edelman, a global public relations firm based in New York City, stated in the forward to the book *Strategic Crisis Communications* "companies who got it right made tough decisions that usually meant taking actions that would have at least a short-term financial toll. They spoke to their issues and went about solving them openly and transparently" (O'Rourke & Smith, 2023, p. x).

McDonald's got it right and was appropriately bestowed PRSA's (2004) Silver Anvil Award of Excellence. The corporation, through a swift enactment of its strategic crisis communication plan, was able to keep consumer confidence in the safety of its beef, minimize the impact of BSE to the business, and maintain a strong brand image internally and externally.

Theoretical perspectives

Phases of crises

Crises in general have three distinct phases—pre, during, and post (Coombs, 2019). Within the pre-crisis stage, organizations may receive warning signs or prodromes. These signs may occur as spikes in sentiment or activity on social media, in the physical or social environment (i.e., climate change), and within or outside the organization. For example, in terms of Mad Cow disease (BSE), the first reported incident in 1985 of the disease in cattle in the U.K. was a prodrome for any institution or industry associated with beef, such as agriculture, slaughterhouses, restaurants like McDonald's, food processing plants, and grocery stores, among others.

Organizations during the pre-crisis phase may also engage in issue, risk and reputation management to prevent the crisis from happening. They may also prepare for a crisis by identifying a crisis management team and creating a crisis management plan with strategies for communicating to stakeholders (Coombs, 2019).

As a risk-reducing measure to keep the U.S. free from BSE, McDonald's took preemptive steps in April 2001 to hold U.S. meatpackers accountable to federal feed rules. As spokesperson Walt Riker told the *Wall Street Journal*, "We could do better from a prevention standpoint. Because of the [mad cow] issue in Europe, we thought it was absolutely prudent and common sense" (Lindsey, 2001, para. 13). The Food and Drug Administration reported that "hundreds of feed makers had failed to comply" (Associated Press, 2001, para. 1) with the rules revealing gaps in the beef safety system (Bonné, 2003).

From a reputational standpoint, McDonald's set out to change its image and revitalize the brand to address concerns over BSE and cater to health-conscious consumers. Near the end of September into October 2003, it launched a new "and for the first time, global—marketing strategy in Germany ... around the motto 'i'm lovin' it'" (Knowledge at Wharton Staff, 2003, para. 10), as a way of creating a consistent identity, regardless of cultural location.

Once a crisis occurs—the second phase—it is labeled as such and the crisis management plan is enacted (Coombs, 2019). Even though McDonald's was facing a crisis as the fears of BSE and vCJD spread throughout countries where it operates—UK, France, Germany, Italy, Japan, and

Canada—these events were not identified as a crisis in the U.S. until Christmas Eve, December 24, 2003.

Just before Christmas, when families were gathering around a table with traditional roasted meats, the U.S. Department of Agriculture reported the first incident of BSE in a Holstein from Washington state (Tribune News Services, 2003). McDonald's responded with a public relations and crisis communication campaign to "differentiate [it] in the minds of consumers by telling [its] story and showing that the Northwest case of BSE had no effect on McDonald's restaurants" (PRSA, 2004, para. 4) and that it "does not use downed cows or animal parts [spinal cord and brain] that have been known to transmit mad cow disease" (Day, 2004, para. 12).

When a crisis has abated and been declared over, organizations enter the post-crisis phase, in which they learn about what worked or did not work by gathering feedback and making changes in policy or procedures (Sellnow & Seeger, 2021). McDonald's had already dealt with Mad Cow/ BSE, learning how "to detect problems with incredible speed and then make tweaks to the system in other countries to avoid the replication of controversies or risks that could adversely impact its market" (Lindsey, 2001, para, 23). Another outcome of the post-crisis phase is the generation of new knowledge about the interplay between crises and pandemics, especially after COVID-19.

Nested or cascading crises

Crises, depending upon the type, can be isolated incidents for organizations or they can develop within a pandemic. When a pandemic produces additional crises, this creates a cascading or nested effect in which "decisions and outcomes at the one-level spill over and have repercussions on the others" (Blavoukos & Bourantonis, 2017, p. 314).

The interdependent nature of a crisis with a pandemic impacts multiple systems, for example: community resilience (Hyvärinen & Vos, 2016), crisis management (Thielsch et al., 2021), educational systems (Kaukko et al., 2021), environmental and animal industrial complex (Adams, 1997), political relations (Blavoukos & Bourantonis, 2017), and social media and employment (Robinson et al., 2021), among others.

Mad Cow disease was a nested, cascading, complex pandemic that created crises in many industries across many different countries and could "neither be handled by individuals nor by any single municipality, organization or even country alone" (Thielsch et al., 2021, p. 150). As such, organizations needed to adapt, learn, and cooperate with other organizations to improve their crisis management capabilities during the BSE pandemic.

Key words

Advanced Meat Recovery
Business Continuity
Creutzfeldt-Jakob (vCJD)
Enterprise Risk Management (ERM)
Food and Drug Administration
Future Trends Monitoring
Golden Arches Logo
McLibel Case
Prodrome
Specific Risk Materials
Speedee Service System
United States Department of Agriculture (USDA)
World Organisation for Animal Health

Discussion questions

1 McDonald's was an early adopter of beef safety standards, yet, waited until 2008 to adopt social media into its communication efforts. Discuss the reasons behind this decision.
2 McDonald's battled BSE in Europe and other countries before the crisis came to the U.S. What are some of the challenges McDonald's faced in its crisis management efforts when the pandemic was in its early stage?
3 Do you, any of your family members, or friends fear eating beef? If so, why?

References

Adams, C. J. (1997). "Mad Cow" disease and the animal industrial complex: An ecofeminist analysis. *Organization & Environment*, *10*(1), 26–51. https://www.jstor.org/stable/26161653
Agricultural Marketing Service. (1985). Beef Research Information Act (Beef Promotion and Research Act of 1985). *USDA* [7 U.S.C. 2901-2911]. https://www.ams.usda.gov/sites/default/files/media/Beef%20Act.pdf
Associated Press. (1986, December 12). U.S. cable households on rise. *Los Angeles Times*. https://www.latimes.com/archives/la-xpm-1986-12-12-ca-2519-story.html
Associated Press. (2001, March 14). McDonald's acts to keep mad cow from U.S. *Los Angeles Times*. https://www.latimes.com/archives/la-xpm-2001-mar-14-fi-37522-story.html
Associated Press. (2003, December 24). Mad cow case hits food stocks. *NBC News*. https://www.nbcnews.com/id/wbna3800570
BBC News World Edition. (2000, October 11). *John Gummer: Beef eater*. http://news.bbc.co.uk/2/hi/uk_news/369625.stm
Beef Checkoff. (2020a, July 30). *Beef. It's still what's for dinner*. https://www.beefboard.org/2020/07/30/beef-its-still-whats-for-dinner/

Beef Checkoff. (2020b, April 14). *How the Beef Checkoff prepares for a beef crisis.* https://www.beefboard.org/2020/04/14/how-the-beef-checkoff-prepares-for-a-beef-crisis/

Beef Checkoff. (2023, July 5). *New beef campaign celebrates the milestones in life.* https://www.beefboard.org/2023/07/05/together-we-bring-more/

Beef Checkoff. (2025). *About the Checkoff.* https://www.beefboard.org/checkoff/about-checkoff/

Best, S. (2001). Cows, capitalism, and cover-ups: The politics and economics of mad cow disease. *Tamara: Journal of Critical Postmodern Organization Science, Suppl. Inaugural Issue, 1*(1), 31. https://www.proquest.com/scholarly-journals/cows-capitalism-cover-ups-politics-economics-mad/docview/204436184/se-2

Blavoukos, S., & Bourantonis, D. (2017). Nested institutions. In R. Biermann, J.A. Koops (Eds.), *Palgrave handbook of inter-organizational relations in world politics.* (pp. 303–317). Palgrave Macmillan UK. DOI 10.1057/978-1-137-36039-7_14

Bonné, J. (2003, December 24). Does the food safety net work? *NBC News.* https://www.nbcnews.com/id/wbna3802544

Bruell, A. (2017). *Beef is back for dinner as marketers woo nostalgic millennials: 'Beef. It's What's for Dinner' slogan returns in social-media campaign.* Dow Jones & Company Inc.

Canadian Food Inspection Agency. (2025, March 23). *Bovine spongiform encephalopathy.* https://inspection.canada.ca/en/animal-health/terrestrial-animals/diseases/reportable/bovine-spongiform-encephalopathy

Carter, C. A., & Huie, J. (2004, September/October). Market effects of searching for mad cows. *Agricultural and Resource Economics Update, 8*(1) 5–7. [University of California Giannini Foundation of Agricultural Economics]. https://giannini.ucop.edu/publications/are-update/issues/2004/8/1/market-effects-of-searchi/

CattleFax. (2025). *Who we are.* https://www.cattlefax.com/#!/about/who-we-are

CattleFax. (2005, December). *State of the beef industry and cattle market situation and outlook.* https://digitalcommons.unl.edu/cgi/viewcontent.cgi?article=1050&context=rangebeefcowsymp

CDC. (2024, May 13). *About Variant Creutzfeldt-Jakob Disease (vCJD).* https://www.cdc.gov/variant-creutzfeldt-jakob/about/index.html

CDC. (2025, July 7). *Bovine Spongiform Encephalopathy (BSE).* https://www.cdc.gov/mad-cow/php/animal-health/index.html?CDC_AAref_Val=https://www.cdc.gov/prions/bse/bse-north-america.html

Center for Food Safety. (n.d.). *Timeline of Mad Cow Disease.* https://www.centerforfoodsafety.org/issues/1040/mad-cow-disease/timeline-mad-cow-disease-outbreaks

Chicago Tribune. (2021, August 9). *Report finds VCR becoming the appliance of the 1980s.* https://www.chicagotribune.com/1986/06/13/report-finds-vcr-becoming-the-appliance-of-the-80s/

CNN International. (2003, December 25). *World Business: Mad cow slams U.S. restaurants.* https://www.cnn.com/2003/BUSINESS/12/25/stocks.madcow/index.html

Coffey, B., Minert, J., Fox, S., Schroeder, T., & Valentin, L. (2005, April). *The economic impact of BSE on the U.S. Beef industry: Product value losses, regulatory costs, and consumer reactions. Kansas State University.* [Agricultural Experiment Station and Cooperative Extension Service; Document MF-2678]. https://krex.k-state.edu/server/api/core/bitstreams/0a47761f-9709-47a5-8779-83a65539403d/content

Coombs, W. T. (2019). *Ongoing crisis communication: Planning, managing, and responding* (5th ed.). Sage.

Day, S. (2004, July 1). A time for finesse: Marketing beef after a mad cow discovery. *The New York Times*. https://www.nytimes.com/2004/01/01/business/a-time-for-finesse-marketing-beef-after-a-mad-cow-discovery.html

Devi, S. (1996, March 24). McDonald's bans British beef in burgers. *UPI*. https://www.upi.com/Archives/1996/03/24/McDonalds-bans-British-beef-in-burgers/9295827643600/

Dougall, E. (2008, December 12). *Issues management*. Institute for Public Relations. https://instituteforpr.org/author/elizabeth-dougall-ph-d/

Ehman, A. J. (2002). Threat from Canada's first vCJD case minimal: MDs. *Canadian Medical Association Journal*, *167*(6), 680. https://pmc.ncbi.nlm.nih.gov/articles/PMC122044/

FDA. (2020, July 2023). *All about BSE (Mad Cow Disease)*. https://www.fda.gov/animal-veterinary/animal-health-literacy/all-about-bse-mad-cow-disease

Finnegan, G. (2015, January 29). The Mad Cow Disease crisis - how Europe's health research came of age. *Horizon: The EU Research and Innovation Magazine*. https://projects.research-and-innovation.ec.europa.eu/en/horizon-magazine/mad-cow-disease-crisis-how-europes-health-research-came-age

Fleck, A. (2024, March 1). Meat: The biggest exporters of beef in the world. *Statista*. https://www.statista.com/chart/19122/biggest-exporters-of-beef/GBIB&xid=2f576100

Hagley Museum. (n.d.). *William G. McGowan's MCI*. https://www.hagley.org/research/digital-exhibits/information-age

Henderson, G. (2020, November 12). BSE crisis averted—Thanks Beef Checkoff. *Drovers*. https://www.drovers.com/opinion/bse-crisis-averted-thanks-beef-checkoff

Hluska, D. (2023, August 30). McDonald's rises in the ranks, landing in the top 5 most valuable global brands. *Kantar*. https://www.kantar.com/north-america/inspiration/brands/mcdonalds-rises-in-the-ranks-landing-in-the-top-5-most-valuable-global-brands

Hyvärinen, J., & Vos, M. (2016). Communication concerning disasters and pandemics: Coproducing community resilience and crisis response. In A. Schwarz, M. W. Seeger, & C. Auer (Eds.), *The handbook of international crisis communication research*. (pp. 96–107). Wiley Blackwell.

Islam, S., & Cullen, J. M. (2021). Food traceability: A generic theoretical framework. *Food Control*, *123* 1–14. https://www.sciencedirect.com/science/article/abs/pii/S0956713520307647?via%3Dihub

Johnson, D. D. (Ed.). (2021). McDonald's corporation. [Company overview]. *International directory of company histories*, *238*. Gale, part of Cengage Group. https://go-gale-com.ezproxy.ithaca.edu/ps/i.do?p=GBIB&u=nysl_sc_ithaca&id=GALE%7CI2501326404&v=2.1&it=r&sid=bookmark-GBIB&asid=2f576100

Kasperkevic, J. (2017, March 26). I've always wondered … how many burgers has McDonald's actually sold? *Marketplace*. https://www.marketplace.org/2017/05/26/how-many-burgers-has-mcdonalds-actually-sold/

Kaukko, M., Kemmis, S., Heikkinen, H. L. T., Kiilakoski, T., & Haswell, N. (2021). Learning to survive amidst nested crises: Can the coronavirus pandemic help us change educational practices to prepare for the impending eco-crisis? *Environmental Education Research*, *27*(11), 1559–1573. https://doi.org/10.1080/13504622.2021.1962809

Knowledge at Wharton Staff. (2003, October 22). McDonald's sets out to conquer the world by changing its image. *Knowledge at Wharton—A business journal from the Wharton School of the University of Pennsylvania*. https://

knowledge.wharton.upenn.edu/article/mcdonalds-sets-out-to-conquer-the-world-by-changing-its-image/
Leiss, W., Powell, D., & Whitfield, A. (2004). Mad cows or crazy communications? In W. Leiss & D. Powell. *Mad cows and mother's milk: The perils of poor risk communication*, (2nd ed.). (pp. 3–25). McGill-Queen's University Press.
Lindsey, D. (2001, March 26). Will mad cows kill the Big Mac? *Salon*. https://www.salon.com/2001/03/26/mcdonalds_2/
Mayo Clinic. (2023, January 28). *Creutzfeldt-Jakob disease*. https://www.mayoclinic.org/diseases-conditions/creutzfeldt-jakob-disease/diagnosis-treatment/drc-20371230
McDonald's. (n.d.a.). *McDonald's history*. https://corporate.mcdonalds.com/corpmcd/our-company/who-we-are/our-history.html
McDonald's. (n.d.a). *Business resilience*. https://corporate.mcdonalds.com/corpmcd/our-purpose-and-impact/impact-strategy-and-reporting/business-resilience.html
McDonald's Corporation. (2022-2023). *McDonald's Corporation Purpose & Impact Progress Summary 2022-2023*. https://corporate.mcdonalds.com/content/dam/sites/corp/nfl/pdf/McDonalds_PurposeImpact_ProgressSummary_2022_2023.pdf
Mobile Phone Museum. (n.d.) *Motorola DynaTAC 8000X*. https://www.mobilephonemuseum.com/phone-detail/dynatac-8000x
Moore, D. W. (2004, January 9). Little concern about Mad Cow disease. By 2-to-1 margin, Americans say problem is minor. *Gallup News Service*. https://news.gallup.com/poll/10165/little-concern-about-mad-cow-disease.aspx
Moss, M., Oppel, R. A. Jr., & Romero, S. (2004, January 5). Mad Cow forces beef industry to change course. *The New York Times*. https://www.nytimes.com/2004/01/05/us/mad-cow-forces-beef-industry-to-change-course.html
Motarjemi, Y. (2014). Crisis management. In Y. Motarjemi & H. Lelieveld (Eds.). *Food safety management: A practical guide for the food industry* [e-book]. (pp. 1097–1126). Elsevier Science & Technology.
National Health Service. (2021, September 7). *Prevention -Creutzfeldt-Jakob disease*. https://www.nhs.uk/conditions/creutzfeldt-jakob-disease-cjd/prevention/
NCBA. (2010). New 'Beef. It's What's For Dinner.' advertising features popular lean beef cuts. *PR Newswire*. [News release]. https://www.prnewswire.com/news-releases/new-beef-its-whats-for-dinner-advertising-features-popular-lean-beef-cuts-92974229.html
NCBA. (2023). *Issues & crisis management, beef advocacy, training & engagement, beef quality assurance*. [AR# 2433-11]. https://www.beefboard.org/wpcontent/uploads/2023/10/NCBA_2433-II_FINAL.pdf
NCBA. (2025). *About*. https://www.ncba.org/about
O'Rourke, J. S. IV, & Smith, J. A. (2023). *Strategic crisis communication* (1st ed.). Routledge.
Petitt, R. G. (2001, August). Traceability in the food and animal industry and supermarket chains. *Revue Scientifique et Technique—Office international des épizooties*, *20*(2) 584–597.
Pew Research Center. (2023, November 10). *Newspapers fact sheet*. https://www.pewresearch.org/journalism/fact-sheet/newspapers/
PRSA. (2004). *Silver Anvil Award of Excellence winner: McDonald's Corporation: A leader in beef safety*. https://www.prsa.org/
PRSA. (2005). *Silver Anvil Award of Excellence winner: Protecting consumer confidence in U.S. Beef: A success story*. https://www.prsa.org/
PSA Research. (n.d.). *Top U.S. magazines by circulation*. http://www1.psaresearch.com/images/TOPMAGAZINES.pdf

Radiomuseum. (n.d.) *Cellular "Brick" Phone DynaTAC 8000X*. https://www.radiomuseum.org/r/motorola_cellularbric_phone_dynat.html

Rampton, S., & Stauber, J. C. (2003). *Mad cow U.S.A.* Common Courage Press.

Robinson, L., et al. (2021). Cascading crises: Society in the age of COVID-19. *American Behavioral Scientist*, *65*(12) 1608–1622. DOI: 10.1177/00027642211003156

SEC. (2023). *Shareholder proposal No. 5 on McDonald's Corporation. 2023 Proxy Statement*. https://www.sec.gov/Archives/edgar/data/63908/000121465923005605/r418230px14a6g.htm

Sellnow, T. L., & Seeger, M. W. (2021). *Theorizing crisis communication* (2nd ed.). Wiley Blackwell.

Sims, C. (1988, May 6). Coast-to-coast in 20 seconds: Fax machines alter business. *The New York Times*. https://www.nytimes.com/1988/05/06/business/coast-to-coast-in-20-seconds-fax-machines-alter-business.html

Singh, G., & Perepu, I. (2014). *McDonald's: Using social media to connect with customers*. [Case study]. IBS Center for Management Research. https://www.thecasecentre.org/products/view?id=122514

Sofos, J. N. (2014). Meat and meat products. In Y. Motarjemi & H. Lelieveld (Eds.). *Food safety management: A practical guide for the food industry* [e-book]. (pp. 105–202). Elsevier Science & Technology.

Spencer, E. H., Frank, E., & McIntosh, N. F. (2005). Potential effects of the next 100 billion hamburgers sold by McDonald's. *American Journal of Preventative Medicine*, *28*(4) 379–381. DOI:10.1016/j.amepre.2005.01.009

Statista. (2024). *Companies & products—McDonald's*. [Report]. https://www-statista-com.ezproxy.ithaca.edu/study/14355/mcdonalds-statista-dossier/

Statistics Canada. (2006, June 28). *Canada's beef industry and BSE*. https://www150.statcan.gc.ca/n1/pub/11-402-x/2006/0920/ceb0920_001-eng.htm

Stuart, R. (1986, December 28). Fewer radio listeners are hearing the news. *The New York Times*. https://www.nytimes.com/1986/12/28/weekinreview/fewer-radio-listeners-are-hearing-the-news.html

Sutton, D. (2015, May 16). McDonald's unhealthy image and why it can't shake it. *Deseret News*. https://www.deseret.com/2015/5/16/20564909/mcdonald-s-unhealthy-image-and-why-it-can-t-shake-it/

Suzuki, E. (2022, October 13). *The history of the CD-ROM*. Autodesk. https://www.autodesk.com/products/fusion-360/blog/cd-rom/

Svyantek, D. J. (Ed.). (2022). *Crisis, chaos, and organizations: The coronavirus and lessons for organizational theory*. Information Age Publishing, Inc.

Thielsch, M. T., Röseler, S., Kirsch, J., Lamers, C., & Hertel, G. (2021). Managing pandemics— Demands, resources, and effective behaviors within crisis management teams. *Applied Psychology: An International Review*, *70*(1) 150–187. DOI: 10.1111/apps.12303

Tribune News Services. (2003, December 24). Mad cow hits McDonald's shares. *Chicago Tribune News*. https://www.chicagotribune.com/2003/12/24/mad-cow-case-hits-mcdonalds-shares/

U.S. Department of Commerce Bureau of the Census. (1991). Computer use in the United States: 1989. *Current Population Reports—Special Studies*. [Series P-23, No. 171]. https://www2.census.gov/library/publications/1991/demographics/p23-171.pdf

U.S. International Trade Commission. (2008, September). *Global Beef Trade: Effects of Animal Health, Sanitary, Food Safety, and Other Measures on U.S. Beef Exports*. [Investigation No. 332-488; Publication 4033]. https://www.usitc.gov/publications/332/pub4033.pdf

USDA. (2025, May 22). *Cattle & beef - Sector at a glance.* https://www.ers.usda.gov/topics/animal-products/cattle-beef/sector-at-a-glance
Wall, P. G., & Chen, J. (2018). Moving from risk communication to food information communication and consumer engagement. *NPJ Science of Food*, 2(21) 1–5. https://doi.org/10.1038/s41538-018-0031-7
Wikipedia. (2024, June 2). *Criticisms of McDonald's.* https://en.wikipedia.org/wiki/Criticism_of_McDonald%27s
World Organisation for Animal Health. (2023, July). *Guidelines for targeted BSE surveillance.* https://www.woah.org/app/uploads/2023/07/ang-book-bse-guidelines-07072023-final.pdf

8

CASE STUDIES ON SARS (SEVERE ACUTE RESPIRATORY SYNDROME), 2002–2003, AND MERS (MIDDLE EAST RESPIRATORY SYNDROME), 2012 TO PRESENT

8.1 INTRODUCTION: SARS AND MERS IN CONTEXT

This chapter focuses on two coronaviruses before COVID-19: Severe Acute Respiratory Syndrome (referred to as SARS) produced by the Severe Acute Respiratory Syndrome Coronavirus (SARS-CoV) and the Middle East Respiratory Syndrome (called MERS) triggered by the Middle East Respiratory Syndrome Coronavirus (MERS-CoV). According to the CDC (n.d.), most people during the fall or winter become infected with common human coronaviruses, which may be as mild as catching a cold. The SARS pandemic and MERS epidemic, however, could result in severe or deadly respiratory complications. WHO explained the context of SARS, "It was the first severe and readily transmissible new disease to emerge in the 21st century and spread along respiratory routes and cause [sic] an epidemic through international air travel of people to other countries outside of its originating country". (WHO, n.d.a., para. 2). With a case fatality ratio of 9.6%, the SARS pandemic resulted in approximately 8,098 probable cases and 774 deaths in 29 countries from November 2002 to July 2003 (CDC, 2003). Beijing became the city with the greatest number of infected people, with 2,521 cases, while the country of China experienced the highest number of cases and deaths worldwide, with 5,327 cases and 349 deaths (Abraham, 2004). WHO reported 29 cases in the U.S. from SARS (Abraham, 2004). Most people who contracted SARS were adults in good health from ages 25 to 70 (WHO, n.d.).

The first SARS case was reported in Guangzhou, China, in 2002 when an ambulance driver filled in for a bereaved co-worker and became the

DOI: 10.4324/9781003434382-8

first medical employee to succumb to SARS. The ambulance driver quickly became ill, unresponsive to antibiotics, and died six days later in the hospital while infecting almost a hundred hospital workers, patients, and family members (Abraham, 2004). Frontline medical workers worldwide were highly vulnerable; more than 1,700 became infected with SARS worldwide (Abraham, 2004). The WHO (2003a) issued a press release in July declaring containment of SARS worldwide.

In 2012, MERS emerged in Jordan and Saudi Arabia and quickly spread throughout the Middle East and the Arabian Gulf, and to other parts of the globe. Saudi Arabia experienced the largest number of total cases at 84% while South Korea reported the largest number of cases and deaths outside the Middle East and Arabian Peninsula (CEPI, n.d.). The common denominator of people becoming infected with MERS was geographic location: carriers were individuals visiting or living in countries in the Arabian Peninsula or nearby. People 50 to 59 years old were at the greatest risk for MERS, followed by people 30 to 39; however, people 70 to 79 experienced the highest case-fatality ratio (WHO Regional Office for the Eastern Mediterranean, 2018).

WHO-Eastern Mediterranean Region (2025) reported a total of 2,627 laboratory-confirmed cases and 947 deaths of MERS worldwide, a case fatality ratio of 36% in 27 countries from April 2012 to April 2024. In 2014, the CDC Office of Readiness and Response (2014) confirmed two U.S. cases of MERS-infected people who worked in the healthcare industry temporarily in Saudi Arabia and survived after returning home and being treated in U.S. hospitals.

Medical experts identified infected camels as carriers of the disease, prompting the Saudi Ministry of Agriculture to issue a warning for residents to avoid camel milk unless boiled and camel meat except canned, as well as being near camels; those who needed to be with camels were encouraged to wear masks and gloves and wash hands before and after as preventive measures (Westall, 2014). This announcement resulted in backlash from camel owners and farmers in a region with approximately 17 million camels (bin Saud, 2024), where the camel is a traditional part of life, if not one's livelihood or beloved pet. Case study 8.4 reviews how the Saudi Arabia Ministry of Health's "We Can Stop It" public health campaign on MERS educated the public about camels.

WHO (2022) advised people to protect themselves from MERS by washing their hands thoroughly before or after petting camels; avoiding consumption of raw camel milk and camel meat, as well as other raw meats; keeping away from markets, farms, and other locations with camels; and avoiding being near camels if people have preexisting illnesses putting them at higher risk of contracting MERS.

Transmission and symptoms

SARS, a contagious airborne respiratory infection, could be spread by a healthy person breathing droplets of saliva from an infected person in close proximity or by touching surfaces previously handled by an infected person. A major challenge was the growth of air travel enabling passengers in close contact with other passengers and crew to spread SARS while on the plane and after they arrived at their destinations. Common SARS symptoms were like the seasonal flu, pneumonia, and other diseases. During the onset of the infection, people experienced a high fever, coughs, aches, and breathing difficulties, but blood tests were effective only after people developed full-blown symptoms (Abraham, 2004).

Unlike SARS, MERS is a zoonotic virus; MERS is believed to be spread from animals, primarily dromedary camels (camels with one hump), to people within close contact. Although less frequently, humans also could spread the infection to other people, mostly while being patients in hospitals. Individuals infected with MERS suffered from flu-like symptoms and developed breathing problems. Some infected patients later developed pneumonia or kidney problems. Most people who perished had preexisting health conditions (WHO, 2022).

Treatment and preventive measures

At the time of writing, no vaccines or treatments are available to prevent SARS and MERS. The WHO (n.d.) recommended guidelines to prevent SARS by frequent and thorough handwashing with soap or using hand disinfectants and wearing masks. Efforts to contain outbreaks included reporting cases through public health surveillance networks, such as WHO and CDC, tracking the source of contact causing the infection, and quarantining for 10 days, among others.

Communication tools

For both SARS and MERS, public health communication played a significant role, particularly on the internet, with soaring usage rates worldwide. During SARS, 9.4% of individuals worldwide used the internet in 2002 and 11% in 2003 (Global Policy Forum, n.d.). In the U.S., almost 59% of the population had internet access in 2002 and almost 62% the following year (Statista, 2024). Usage rose dramatically during MERS, with 33% and 35% worldwide penetration in 2012 and 2013 respectively and almost 75% and over 71% in the U.S. during the same period (Statista, 2024).

The first social networking site, Six Degrees, debuted in 1997 and shut down in 2001. During SARS, two sites were launched, Friendster and

LinkedIn, in 2002, followed by MySpace in 2003. More social networking sites were introduced after MySpace and toward the end of MERS in 2014, such as Facebook in 2004, YouTube and Reddit in 2005, Twitter (now called X) in 2006, Instagram and Pinterest in 2010, and Snapchat in 2011, among others (Hutchinson, 2019). On the negative side, social media made it simple for anyone to share content—without it being verified and fact-checked by professional editors.

Concurrently, the term "infodemic" arose during SARS when it was coined by author and foreign and political affairs analyst David J. Rothkopf (2003), as a portmanteau of information and epidemic or pandemic in a *Washington Post* op-ed, in which he defines an infodemic:

> An infodemic is not the rapid spread of simple news via the media, nor is it simply the rumor mill on steroids. Rather, as with SARS, it is a complex phenomenon caused by the interaction of mainstream media, specialist media and internet sites; and "informal" media, which is to say wireless phones, text messaging, pagers, faxes and e-mail, all transmitting some combination of fact, rumor, interpretation and propaganda. It can be rendered more difficult to understand by multiple languages, cultures and attitudes toward the free and open flow of information. It involves consumers of information ranging from officials to private citizens who have varying abilities to see the whole information picture, varying degrees of sophistication about what to do with the information they have, little opportunity to authenticate data before acting on it, and little if any training in understanding or controlling the rapidly changing information picture.
> *(para. 7)*

SARS also provided "valuable lessons on how to fight new global diseases," (Abraham, 2004, p. 143) with expedient virus reporting and collaboration among scientists, doctors, and public health officials to prevent the outbreak locally and globally. Sharing accurate public educational content became essential to coping with the rapidly spreading SARS pandemic in 2003, with faster and easier-to-update content on its websites and social media—and combatting inaccurate information. The CDC describes itself as "the nation's leading science-based, data-driven, service organization that protects public health" (CDC, 2024, para. 1). During SARS, CDC became a sought-after hub for frequent updates, facts, and travel alerts about SARS on its website and social media. In addition, CDC created a response and communication plan for public health agencies on a local, state, and federal basis to contain future SARS outbreaks. Despite the U.S. being CDC's target market, international audiences viewed one-third of its website content (Arguin et al., 2004).

Impact

The public and private sectors in areas most impacted by SARS cooperated with each other to communicate health messages and updates to residents, tourists, and business travelers. In early 2003, for example, SARS spread to Singapore and prompted both the public (Health Promotion Board and Ministry of Education, among others) and private sector (Singapore Tourism Board, Singapore Airlines, and others) to collaborate and create an integrated communications plan to contain the disease for its residents and visitors and to protect the country's economy. The theme, "Fighting SARS Together!," was used to share educational messages on personal hygiene and social responsibility while conveying positive messages about citizens working together to help Singaporeans and the country at large in four languages (Karan et al., 2007). This chapter includes SARS communication campaigns from Toronto, Canada, (case study 8.2) and Hong Kong (case study 8.3).

SARS widely affected the tourism industry. Airports became quiet, flights were canceled or flew almost empty, and hotel occupancy rates plummeted in SARS-infected countries. The economy globally experienced a loss of approximately USD 30 billion, mostly in Asia (Abraham, 2004). Two areas heavily impacted by SARS, China and Hong Kong, suffered with the greatest economic losses in inward and outward investment and tourism-related industries. Canada and East Asia countries also experienced economic downturns (Keogh-Brown & Smith, 2008). The International Air Transport Association reported that airlines serving routes in the Asia Pacific lost approximately 8% annually, resulting in an estimated loss of USD 6 billion in revenues (Wyman, 2020)

MERS primarily resulted in per capita GDP declines in countries in the Arabian Peninsula; 32% in Kuwait, 25% in Qatar, 16% in Saudi Arabia, and 12% in the United Arab Emirates (Ceylan & Ozkan, 2020). South Korea experienced the greatest economic impact from MERS outside of the Arabian Peninsula; the country lost approximately USD 2.6 billion in international tourism (Joo et al., 2019).

8.2 "TORONTO: YOU BELONG HERE" POST-SARS CAMPAIGN: TURNING TORONTONIANS INTO TOURISTS TO REENERGIZE ECONOMY AND REVITALIZE TOURISM

Situational analysis

Located on the southwestern shore of Lake Ontario, Toronto is Canada's most populous city and has been a popular place for visitors from the U.S. and around the globe. It is home to a vibrant cultural scene with theaters, festivals, and museums, along with the scenic beauty of parks, ravines, and the waterfront, along with diverse neighborhoods, restaurants, and nightlife. English and French are the country's official languages while almost three out of 10 Canadians speak another language; the most commonly used non-official languages are Spanish, Mandarin, and Punjabi (Statistics Canada, 2025). The Toronto Travel Guide on the website of *Conde Nast Traveler* (n.d.) describes Toronto's multicultural diversity effectively:

> More than 46 percent of the nearly three million-strong population is foreign-born, and their reception game is so strong that they refer to immigrants as "newcomers". This bear hug of a welcome is central to what makes this city what it is: a true meeting ground of different cultures, cuisines, and faiths, a pluralist paradise up north. It's a city with a Little India, Chinatown, Greektown, Koreatown, Portugal Village, *two* Little Italys, and more than 150 spoken languages.
>
> *(emphasis in original; para. 1)*

In 2002, tourism was Ontario's "seventh largest export industry" generating almost CAD20 billion in revenues (McPeak, 2004). The city's thriving tourism industry hit a serious downturn when SARS spread to Toronto. Hotel occupancy rates dropped to 46.6% in April 2003, compared to 68% the previous year. Some conferences were canceled, such as the American Association for Cancer Research's conference with 28,000 delegates (Wall, 2006). Elton John, Billy Joel, and Anthrax, a thrash metal band, canceled their concerts (Heinzl, 2003). Attendance at tourist attractions plummeted by an estimated 40% to 60% while the zoo visitors dropped 35%. The popular *Mamma Mia* musical shut down in the theater district for the summer (Bray, 2003). Tourism declines also negatively affected airlines, local transportation, tour operators, retailers, restaurants, and other tourism-related businesses. Part of the losses could be attributed to a drop in U.S. vacationers who traditionally contribute to one-third of the city's tourism revenue, particularly Americans living in states near Ontario, such as New York, Pennsylvania, Ohio, Michigan, Wisconsin, and Minnesota (Black, 2004).

The entire country faced challenges with a decline in tourism due to SARS; other factors included the war in Iraq starting in March 2003 and lingering terrorism fears from 9/11. According to Statistics Canada (2007), international visits to the entire country declined 33% in May 2003 from the previous year. Visitors from Asia between April and May 2003 declined 32%. In 2003, international visitors (excluding the U.S.) dropped 13.4% over the previous year. Fewer Americans were staying overnight in Canada throughout 2003, with Ontario experiencing the most severe drop with 1.4 million (-17.3%) fewer overnight American visitors, resulting in the province losing over CAD500 million in its economy in 2003 over 2002 (Statistics Canada, 2005).

According to WHO (2015), Canada had the highest number of SARS cases (251) and deaths (43) outside of Asia. In Ontario, the province where Toronto is located, 247 probable cases and 44 deaths (one more than WHO reported) occurred. The average age of death was 71 and many had preexisting illnesses (Infection Prevention and Control Canada, n.d.). Canadians returning from Asia carried SARS to Ontario and British Columbia. WHO also issued travel advisories for the first time during SARS (Health Canada, 2003; WHO, 2003b), with two travel advisories against non-essential travel to Toronto; the first from April 23 to April 30 and again from May 20 to July 2 (Quigley & Lowe, 2020).

Communication and execution

Toronto's Mayor Mel Lastman announced the theme of the new tourism revitalization campaign, "Toronto: You belong Here," on May 7 with his SARS Recovery Task Force and the Economic Development, Culture and Tourism Department (Rendon, 2003). The city of Toronto hired Fleishman-Hillard (now FleishmanHillard), a global public relations and marketing agency, and BBDO, a global advertising agency, both part of the Omnicom Group, to promote its "Toronto: You Belong Here" campaign from July to September 2003 (Daniels, 2003; Van Der Pool, 2003). A news release issued by the Economic Development, Culture and Tourism Division of Toronto (2003a) addressed the slogan: "The campaign slogan reflects Toronto's inclusiveness and diversity in a way that greets the world with open arms. The theme speaks to Torontonians who were born here and those who came from elsewhere" (para. 6). Other agencies also took on specific roles: BBDO's Proximity Canada for direct marketing, GMR Marketing for events, and OMD for pro bono media planning. BBDO created the campaign's slogan as part of the city's integrated campaign (Rendon, 2003).

The campaign's primary objective was to help the tourism industry recover from lost revenue during SARS by increasing local travel. The targeted audiences were primarily Torontonians and people living within a two-hour driving distance of Toronto. The rationale was that many tourists outside of that range probably had made summer vacation plans, and people residing close to or within Toronto were aware of the city functioning normally (Daniels, 2003). The strategies were as follows:

- Persuade Torontonians to become tourists in their own city.
- Encourage Canadians residing within a two-hour drive of Toronto, whether they were commuters working in Toronto or those wanting

a vacation closer to home, to select nearby Toronto for leisure summer travel.
- Build excitement of the variety of summer events, some of which were created by the City of Toronto, and travel discounts of appeal to the local community.

BBDO launched its "Toronto: You Belong Here" creative work to coincide with Mother's Day held on the second Sunday of May (the same in the U.S.). In addition to creating the slogan, the agency designed a logo and began placing advertisements in local print, radio, and television outlets. The Mother Day's television ads featured "Happy Mother's Day" greetings in a few languages, "followed by a voiceover saying: 'No matter how you say it, there's no place like Toronto to celebrate Mother's Day'" (Rendon, 2003, para. 7). BBDO also created television advertisements showcasing Canadian celebrities, including actor Jason Priestly and rock band Barenaked Ladies to encourage local tourism (Daniels, 2003).

Fleishman-Hillard began its initial public relations efforts around Victoria Day, which was named in honor of Queen Victoria to celebrate her birthday, May 24. As a federal Canadian public holiday, it is now celebrated on the last Monday in May. Canadians traditionally celebrate it with outdoor activities and fireworks to welcome the summer season during the three-day weekend, just like many Americans enjoy Memorial Day held the same day. The client and agency staff shared media lists to expand media relations and promoted traditional summer events and newly created events from fireworks and live music and promotional incentives like a weeklong CAD 5 admission to CN Tower, Toronto's tallest building with vistas of the city and Lake Ontario (Calabro & Daniels, 2003).

The City of Toronto employed 20 young people to serve as the "city's ambassadors." They wore uniforms with "Toronto: You Belong Here" logos and drove around the city in branded SUVs while making stops at the main train station, shopping malls, fast food restaurants, and a newspaper's office. The ambassadors distributed a million "Toronto: You Belong Here" packages with information and coupons on summer events. The ambassadors also made appearances at major events while passing out flyers on upcoming events. The goal was to encourage Torontonians to attend more than one of the eight popular events (Daniels, 2003).

Fleishman-Hillard also arranged for its six-person account team to provide support to the in-house public relations departments of event planners (Daniels, 2003). Here are a few examples of the 2003 summer events:

- June—The new "Concert for Toronto" featured Canadian musicians, such as Neil Young, Sarah McLachlan, Avril Lavigne, and the

Barenaked Ladies, at the SkyDome (now called Rogers Centre) and Air Canada Centre.
- July—The Rolling Stones headlined the Molson Canadian Toronto Rocks concert (some fans called it "SARStock") in Downsview Park. Other performers included AC/DC, Justin Timberlake, The Guess Who, and Blue Rodeo (Shier, 2020).
- August—Toronto Caribana (now called the Toronto Caribbean Carnival), a popular annual festival celebrating Caribbean traditions, held at Exhibition Place with a parade along Lakeshore Boulevard.

Building on the strengths of the "Toronto: You Belong Here" campaign, particularly for Victoria Day and Mother's Day, Toronto Mayor Lastman announced an advertising and public relations campaign to help revitalize Chinese businesses post-SARS by promoting Chinese festivals, shops, and restaurants in Toronto's Chinatowns. In a news release, Mayor Lastman stated, "This campaign will bring Torontonians and tourists back to where they belong—our Chinese businesses" (Economic Development, Culture and Tourism Division of Toronto, 2003b, para. 2). Toronto's population is approximately 9% Chinese (Lindsay, 2001).

Results

Each of the post-SARS tourism campaigns for the City of Toronto and other Canadian organizations was focused on specific target audiences, yet some promotional activities overlapped and complemented each campaign. This case study analyzed The "Toronto: You Belong Here" campaign overseen by the City of Toronto that catered to reaching the local community. The Ontario Marketing Partnership hired FCB Toronto to create its "It's Time for a Little T.O." travel packages by working "with Toronto tourism stakeholders to build a series of imaginative, price-point-driven packages highlighting several of Toronto's signature attractions and experiences" (Shier, 2020, para. 4). Over 450,000 packages were sold, with the intention of appealing to the rest of Ontario and throughout Canada (Quigley & Lowe, 2020). The Toront03 Alliance, a newly formed nonprofit with funding by banks and government offices, was dedicated to attracting tourists from the U.S., primarily from states near Ontario, with a "Summer in the City" plan that included organizing the Molson Canadian Rocks for Toronto concert among other cultural and sporting initiatives (Black, 2004).

The *Assessment of the Toront03 Alliance's Tourism Recovery Efforts* report from August 2004 highlighted key points from PKF Consulting's *Ontario's Tourism Recovery Program* on the benefits of the collaborative post-SARS tourism recovery efforts (Black, 2004). McPeak (2004) documents the results of an:

> independent analysis of the Tourism Recovery program conducted by PKF consulting, which showed that every dollar invested through the program yielded $11 in tourism industry revenue. Between July 1, 2003 and March 31, 2004 the province invested $62.5 million in tourism recovery initiatives, resulting in an additional 3.6 million visitors to Ontario. These visitors injected an additional $687 million into the economy ($285 million in the GTA, and $402 million in other parts of Ontario) and supported 13,700 direct and indirect jobs.
>
> *(paras. 4–5)*

Events were widely promoted and attended. "Concert for Toronto" sold 70,000 tickets in a few hours (Bray, 2003). Publicity efforts generated over 7.5 million media impressions of Caribana. The Molson Canadian Rocks for Toronto concert drew a crowd of an estimated 500,000 concertgoers of which 42,000 came from the U.S. (Black, 2004). With star cache, this event made over one billion PR impressions and the webcast attracted 250,000 global viewers (Black, 2004). The Molson Indy race attracted over 167,000 people, just a decline of -1% over the previous year (Black, 2004).

Each of the summer events brought in tourism dollars, particularly the Rocks for Toronto concert, for restaurants, retailers, pharmacies, credit cards expenditures, car rentals, and other travel-related services. With many event participants being local, hotels received less of a boost except on the night of the July 30 rock concert when hotels achieved an occupancy rate of 90% (Black, 2004; Quigley & Lowe, 2020). The Canadian Tourism Commission (2003) indicated that Canada's tourism revenues of CAD35.1 billion were generated from Canadians traveling within Canada, indicating a 3.0% rise in domestic travel spending in 2003.

Taxation is a significant indicator of success for the post-SARS campaigns as addressed in a research briefing *Observations from Toronto's Tourism Recovery Post SARS in 2003*: "The federal and provincial governments recouped CAD12–19.5 million in taxes from the extra spending, more than doubling the CAD5 million that the two governments initially invested" (Quigley & Lowe, 2020, p. 6).

Theoretical perspectives

Seeman (2003) in his commentary about news media coverage of SARS in Toronto states "the SARS epidemic will always be more about psychology than epidemiology" (para. 8). Within emerging infectious diseases like

SARS, psychology plays an important role in pandemic management, specifically in "keeping the public calm in order to limit the spread of excessive anxiety" (Taylor, 2022, p. 234).

The quick actions of the Ontario Government and "the strict adherence to precautions—and practice implementing them—was critical to the containment of SARS in Toronto and the restoration of safe conditions" (Low et al., 2004, para. 27). Yet, anxiety about SARS still spread, which impacted the tourism industry.

What is unique about this case study is the amplified level of fear associated with travel and tourism. The number of cases and deaths were lower in Toronto than in other countries and cities. Yet, Bob McKercher (2003), associate head of the School of Hotel and Tourism Management at the Hong Kong Polytechnic University in Hong Kong, attributed the severe downturn in the tourism and hospitality industry to not just SARS, but also to SIP (Sars Induced Panic):

> It is the hysteria surrounding SARS that causes people to behave irrationally in the face of a new disease whose real impact is far less than the fear it provokes ... And its social, economic and emotional impacts are devastating. Tourism is especially hit by SIP.
>
> *(McKercher, p. 18)*

On April 23, the mayor of Toronto urged residents to go about their lives as normal and was quoted as saying: "It's not the disease that's doing the damage; it's public perceptions about SARS that's hurting Toronto's tourism industry, and it's getting worse" (Lewington, 2003, para 10).

What accounts for this phenomenon? The perceptions of risk and the social amplification of risk might be useful in understanding this heightened fear and its impacts on the tourism industry.

Wildavsky and Drake (1990) explore five theoretical approaches to risk perceptions (knowledge, personality, economic, political and cultural) that may explain or predict choices people make based on perception of risk. For the purposes of this case study, the focus will be on the personality theory of risk perception and the amplification effect, whereas the next case study on Hong Kong's response to SARS will explore the knowledge and cultural theories of risk perception.

From a personality perspective, "some individuals love taking risk ... while others are risk averse and seek to avoid as many risks as they can" (Wildavsky & Drake, 1990, p. 42). Individuals who seek risk, accept risk or have a lower risk perception may downplay the risk, may experience less worry, may perceive health behaviors recommendations "as voluntary, controllable, and as affecting people one at a time rather than simultaneously endangering whole populations" (Leppin & Aro, 2009, p. 8), and may experience optimism toward prevention and risks (Brug et al., 2009). Conversely, risk averse individuals may experience dread, worry or concern, perceive "the possibility that oneself might become instrumental in infecting others [which] can evoke anticipations of guilt and blame," and in some with a high risk perception "might evoke feelings of helplessness which could paralyze rather than provoke protective behaviors" (Leppin & Aro, 2009, pp. 9–10). In the tourist industry, people who like to travel embrace risk as a part of excitement whereas some tourists avoid destinations that are perceived as risky which might impact their decision to visit revisit a destination (Hasan et al., 2017).

Leppin & Aro's examination of articles related to risk perception, SARS and Avian Influenza between 2003 and 2007 revealed one important and relevant insight about risk perception and behavior, that has implications for understanding the social amplification of risk: "the value -or severity-component" (p. 23). What this means is that despite the low number of SARS cases and deaths in Toronto, people perceived a higher risk in traveling to the infected area that impacted the tourism industry. As an example of this, Brug et al. (2004) found in their report on Netherland's public perceptions of SARS outside the affected area: "Higher perceptions of risk were associated with more worry and more self-reported precautionary actions, which is in line with predictions from risk perception theory and previous research. Avoiding air travel was the only precautionary action that was mentioned often" (p. 1488).

Social amplification of risk is based on the assumption that hazardous events like SARS interact with various psychological, social, institutional and cultural processes, which can "heighten or attenuate individual and social perceptions of risk and shape risk behavior" (Renn et al., 1992, p. 139). As an example, Stephen Taylor (2022), professor and clinical psychologist at the University of British Columbia, Canada, explains how the labels of diseases matters because:

> naming conventions can lead to misconceptions among the public and can amplify discrimination and stigmatization … Labels of disease outbreaks can also be inadvertently offensive. Calling an outbreak "SARS" might seem innocuous to some people but was offensive to people in Hong Kong, because Hong Kong is known as one of the SARs; that is Special Administrative Regions of China.
>
> The labels given to pandemics convey the degree of threat associated with the pathogen, which in turn influences how the public responds to the disease threat. If the label is a highly dramatic (e.g., "flesh-eating disease"), then there is the risk that some people will become unnecessarily anxious, while other people will dismiss the threat as exaggerated. *(p. 236)*

In mid-April 2003, WHO issued a short-lived travel advisory that included Toronto. A week later, the United Nations (UN) lifted the non-essential travel advisory to Toronto, while WHO added the "lifting of the advisory does not change its status as an 'affected' area ... [as] Canada had 146 cases, 20 of them fatal" (United Nations, 2003, para. 4). This type of social amplification might explain why the number of visitors from Asia to Canada declined 32% between April and May 2003.

Lastly, exposure to media, whether traditional or social, can also amplify the perception of risk as the deluge of information and rumor, known as an infodemic, "amplifies uncertainties, including uncertainties about which news stories or rumors are accurate and which are not" (Taylor, 2022, p. 237). Tew et al. (2008) explain how:

> Inherent in the "tourist in your own city" strategy is the need to increase or at least maintain the marketing budget of an organization and destination. Communication is a key in the fight against bad publicity and negative press is communication.
>
> *(p. 342)*

The tourism industry has a duty to communicate information to guests and tourists, especially around safety and any strategic plans for combating the pandemic, thereby reducing uncertainties associated with travel and favorably influencing tourists' perceptions of risk. Reducing uncertainties and perceptions of risk increases the likelihood that customer satisfaction and confidence in hotels and products will be restored (Tew et al., 2008). As Hasan et al. (2017) found in their literature review of tourist risk perceptions and revisit intentions, "Customer perceptions of risk arising from their experiences with products and services may influence their satisfaction either positively or negatively," and their behavioral intention to revisit a particular travel destination (p. 10).

The "Toronto: You Belong Here" campaign, through a collaborative effort involving stakeholders, industry leaders, and government officials, promoted the city as a viable and safe travel destination by "organizing familiarization trips and site tours; portraying the merits of the city and identifying new markets; and alleviating fears of travelers" (Tew et al., 2008, p. 342).

Key words

BBDO
CAD and USD
FCB Toronto

FleishmanHillard
GMR Marketing
Infection Prevention and Control Canada
Molson
Omnicom Group
Ontario Marketing Partnership
Province

Discussion questions

1 The perception of risk contributed to the amplification of the severity of the SARS outbreak in Toronto. Why do you think this happened? What else might account for the huge impact on the tourism industry, when the numbers of cases and deaths were less elsewhere?
2 If you were in a position "to persuade Torontonians to become tourists in their own city," would you do anything different? If so, what? And, why?
3 What other implications might SARS have had on other industries, besides tourism?

8.3 HONG KONG TOURISM BOARD'S PRE-SARS "TAKE YOUR BREATH AWAY" TOURISM CAMPAIGN REBRANDED TO "GLOBAL TOURISM REVIVAL" DURING SARS

Situational analysis

Located on the south-eastern coast of China on the South China Sea, the region of Hong Kong includes three main sections, Hong Kong Island, Kowloon, and the New Territories. After being under British rule for 156 years, Hong Kong was returned to China in 1997 as a Special Administrative Region of the People's Republic of China under "one country, two systems" (BBC, 2020, para. 16), meaning it rejoined China as one country but observes its own laws and regulations with overall autonomy for 50 years. Its official languages are Chinese (predominately Cantonese) and English (Government of the Hong Kong Special Administrative Region, 2025).

In February 2003, a doctor from China, who earlier had been treating patients with the yet-to-be identified SARS in Guangdong located in the southernmost mainland about 100 miles from Hong Kong, checked into a hotel in Hong Kong and quickly infected other guests, and the flu eventually spread throughout Hong Kong, leading to 1,755 cases of SARS and 299 deaths (Abraham, 2004; WHO, 2015). WHO initially distributed a global alert about SARS in early March and issued a travel alert for only essential travel to Hong Kong and Guangdong in early April. The impact was immediately felt by the travel industry in Hong Kong (McKercher, 2003; Pine & McKercher, 2004):

- Easter travel bookings plummeted more than 80% over the previous year.
- Outbound and inbound tourist arrivals fell approximately 80%. Visitors from the major regional markets of Malaysia, Singapore, and Thailand fell to almost 90%.
- Conventions and business trips were canceled.
- Hotel occupancy rates hovered under 20% while five-star hotels had single-digit occupancy rates. Six or more hotels went up for sale while other hotels had to cut back on costs from having employees take their annual leave or unpaid leave, closing swimming pools and health centers temporarily, and reducing restaurant hours of operation.
- Airline passengers at its international airport dropped almost 80%.
- Airlines serving Hong Kong canceled over 40% of their flights while Cathay Pacific, the flag carrier of Hong Kong, had to cancel 45% of its flights, and Hong Kong Dragon Airlines (Dragonair) experienced a 50% cut in passenger capacity. Some airline staff had to take temporary unpaid leave.

Other impacted tourism sectors included cruise lines, retailers, tourist attractions, and special events such as the International Dragon Boat Races set for June were rescheduled in the fall with a smaller-scale version (Yan, 2003).

The Hong Kong Tourism Board's pre-SARS "Take your breath away" slogan and campaign took on another meaning when SARS began to take the breath away of residents and visitors literally as the respiratory disease expanded from China in late 2002 to Hong Kong in February 2003 (Deans, 2003). The long-running advertising campaign created by Banks Hoggins O'Shea FCB, a London-based creative agency now called FCB London, was designed to show "how a visit to Hong Kong can offer a whirlwind of cultural and culinary diversity" (Hong Kong pulls 'Breath' ad due to outbreak of SARS, 2003, para. 4) before SARS. The tourist bureau was unable to cancel or change the title to "There's no place like Hong Kong" in all scheduled British print ads since a few magazines were under production (Deans, 2003). The Hong Kong Tourism Board (HKTB) had to figure out other solutions to rebrand and communicate safety measures for travelers. The HKTB (2003) describes its responsibilities and mission:

> The primary responsibilities of the HKTB are to market and promote Hong Kong as a destination worldwide, as well as to take initiatives to enhance visitors' experience once they arrive. This includes making recommendations to the Hong Kong Special Administrative Region (SAR) Government and other relevant bodies on the range and quality of visitor facilities. The HKTB's mission is to maximise the social and

economic contribution that tourism makes to the community of Hong Kong, and to consolidate Hong Kong's position as a unique, world class and most desired destination.

(p. 2)

Communication and execution

The Pacific Asia Travel Association (PATA) published a case study summarizing Hong Kong's recovery from SARS. In April 2003, Hong Kong's government launched a USD 1.5 billion package for economic relief and recovery from SARS in three strategic phases:

- The **Response** phase aimed to keep audiences updated—the local residents and businesses along with potential international visitors. WHO officials were invited to inspect a variety of venues to validate changing the travel advisory in the second recovery phase.
- The **Reassurance** phase occurred when WHO's travel advisory took Hong Kong off its travel advisory, thereby enabling public health communicators to convey reassuring messages about the return to normalcy postSARS and the safety of hotels and tourist attractions, which had imposed more rigorous standards for cleanliness and health.
- The **Recovery** phase required collaboration with tourism organizations. In June 2003, HKTB debuted its "Global Tourism Revival" campaign while the Hong Kong Hotel Association unveiled its "Be Our Guest" promotion to increase hotel occupancy rates (PATA, 2020). HKTB hired Omnicom's Foote, Cone & Belding (now called FCB) for advertising (Van Der Pool, 2003) and contracted WPP Group's Burson-Marsteller (now called Burson) for a tourism revival public relations campaign without undergoing the traditional request for proposal process with multiple competing agencies. Burson had been representing the Hong Kong government for a few years and was awarded the Hong Kong Economic and Trade Office account the previous month (Quenqua, 2003). The primary goal was to be prepared when WHO announced Hong Kong's containment of SARS on July 5, 2003. CDC also removed its travel alert for Hong Kong later in July 2003 (CDC, 2013).

Here are highlights of the major tactics undertaken by the synchronized collaboration of organizations and creative agencies with consistent messaging on how safe it is to visit Hong Kong (PATA, 2020).

- A global "blitz" of advertisements targeted business and leisure travelers.
- Hotel members of the Hong Kong Hotel Association provided discounts for standard rooms up to 50% off regular room rates at 77 hotels.

- HKTB conducted familiarization trips for over 600 journalists and 2,000 travel industry representatives from 17 identified markets worldwide.
- Cathay Pacific and Dragonair sponsored 28,000 complimentary trips to Hong Kong.

Results

With tourism recovery being a major goal of the collaborative communication efforts, the results indicated vast improvements in tourist arrivals, hotel occupancy rates, and airline capacity post-SARS 2003:

- Visitor arrivals were 15.54 million in 2003, despite the 2.34 million loss in arrivals from April to July. In fact, Hong Kong arrivals broke records in August, October, and December. Comparing 2003 to the record-setting 2002 tourist arrivals, annual tourist arrivals dropped only 6.2% (HKTB, 2004).
- Hotel occupancy rates rose from a low of 17% during May to a high of 93% in November (PATA, 2020).
- Airline capacity began to improve a month after WHO declared Hong Kong free of SARS. Cathay Pacific, for example, expected to return to 90% capacity in August and back to a regular, full schedule in late September (Pine & McKercher, 2004).

Theoretical perspectives

In the previous case study, the perception of risk was discussed in reference to the impact SARS had on the tourism industry in Toronto, Canada. Perceptions of risk may explain the impact to the travel industry in Hong Kong, as the "panic caused by SARS had an enormous *economic* impact ... because of health fears ... The global travel, tourism and related industries in particular faced a significant downturn in income" (Brug et al., 2009, p. 4).

Wildavsky and Drake (1990) explored five theoretical approaches to risk perceptions—knowledge, personality, economic, political, and cultural. For the purposes of this case study, the focus will be on knowledge and cultural theoretical approaches to risk perception. From a knowledge perspective, people perceive risky "technologies (and other things)," like pandemics and epidemics, "to be dangerous because they *know* them to be dangerous" (emphasis in original, p. 42).

Lau et al. (2005) stated that roughly 20% of SARS cases and 30% of SARS deaths occurred in Hong Kong. The World Health Organization issued a travel advisory warning individuals against traveling to Hong

Kong for almost two months in 2003, as population mobility increased the "potential for bi-directional disease transmission; the virus may be imported from or exported to the passenger's home country" (Lau et al., 2004, p. 728).

Other important measures of knowledge included the awareness of how SARS was spread "through droplets, fomites, and sewage systems; by eating wild animal meat; or by rats, cockroaches, or pets, while 49.2% of respondents believed that SARS is transmittable through aerosols" (Lau et al., 2005, p. 418) and awareness of preventive measures, as a majority of respondents "perceived that mask use, frequent hand washing, and disinfection of living quarters are efficacious means of SARS prevention" (p. 422).

Risk perception associated with travel to SARS-affected areas is important especially when managing pandemics and is "largely dependent on precautionary behavior of the population … For people to voluntarily engage in precautionary actions, they first of all need to be aware of the risk" (Brug et al., 2009, p. 4); yet perceptions can be biased in potentially optimistic and pessimistic ways (Brug et al., 2009; de Zwart et al., 2009).

All of the knowledge of risks associated with SARS further shaped optimistic perceptions of risk and precautionary behaviors associated with traveling. Over 75% of respondents in Lau et al.'s (2005) survey "would make a health declaration to customs, use a mask on a flight, or see a doctor when traveling overseas" (p. 418). Additionally, respondents revealed a potentially pessimistic perception of risk as "More than 70% of respondents would avoid visiting hospitals or mainland China to avoid contracting SARS" (p. 417). In another study that surveyed Hong Kong Chinese returning to Hong Kong via air travel, Lau et al. (2004) found 75% of respondents "who perceived SARS to be likely/very likely to be fatal" "wore a mask all the time or most of the time during the flight" and had a perceived "high/very high risk of in-flight SARS transmission" (p. 729). These perceptions of risk reveal a psychological factor in pandemics. "When people feel threatened about becoming infected with some pathogen, they tend to avoid or stigmatize out groups" (Taylor, 2022, p. 235).

At the same time, these perceptions of risks may also explain the effectiveness of HKTB's campaign. Perceptions of risk from a cultural perspective view "individuals as active organizers of their own perceptions … [who] choose what to fear (and how much to fear it), in order to support their way of life" (Wildavsky & Drake, 1990, p. 43) and to maintain certain social relationships, whether hierarchal, egalitarian (collectivist) or individualistic. In some collectivist Asian cultures like Hong Kong, "'social risk perceptions' are even stronger in the collectivist societies of Asia than in the more individualist cultures of the West. Factoring in such processes of perceiving and reacting to collective threat is unquestionably an essential element of pandemic influenza preparedness" (Leppin & Aro, 2009, p. 10). Lau et al. relied on self-reports (2005) in their study on SARS-related perceptions in Hong Kong discovered that a high percentage of survey "respondents felt helpless, horrified, and apprehensive because of SARS or worried that they or family members would contract the virus" (p. 420).

The effectiveness of control measures to mitigate the spread of the virus, to reduce mass hysteria, and to ensure that society as a whole is protected "depends fundamentally on the public's willingness to cooperate" (Leppin & Aro, 2009, p. 7) and confidence and trust in institutions to restore normalcy and keep the pandemic from resurging (Lau et al., 2005). Within the reassurance phase of the recovery efforts, when Hong Kong was taken off WHO's travel advisory, public health communicators were able to convey reassuring messages about the return to normalcy post-SARS and the safety of hotels and tourist attractions, which had imposed more rigorous standards for cleanliness and health. With tourism recovery being a major goal of the collaborative communication efforts, the results indicated vast improvements in tourist arrivals, hotel occupancy rates, and airline capacity post-SARS.

Key words

Burson
CDC
Guangdong
Hong Kong Hotel Association
Hong Kong Tourism Board
One Country, Two Systems
Response, Reassurance, Recovery
SARS
Travel Advisories
Special Administrative Region of the People's Republic of China
WHO

Discussion questions

1 Discuss similarities and differences between Hong Kong's approach to tourism recovery to Toronto's approach.
2 How would you create a localized tourism campaign for your community?
3 When traveling, do you consult travel advisories to determine if the location is safe?

8.4 SAUDI ARABIA'S MINISTRY OF HEALTH's "WE CAN STOP IT" CAMPAIGN WARNS PUBLIC TO AVOID CAMELS AS HOSTS OF MERS

Situational analysis

The Kingdom of Saudi Arabia (KSA) is the second largest Arab country in the Middle East, with an estimated population of 35 million (Alhassan & AlDossary, 2021; General Authority for Statistics, 2024). The form of government is monarchy, and King Salman bin Abdulaziz Al Saud has served as king since 2015 and appointed his son, Crown Prince Mohammed bin Salman, as prime minister in 2022 (Ochsenwald & Philby, 2024). The Ministry of Health (MOH) provides approximately 60% of health care services, whereas government agencies or private facilities cover the rest (Alhassan & AlDossary, 2021).

The center of the MERS (Middle East Respiratory Syndrome) epidemic was KSA, experiencing 2,204 cases and 860 deaths, a high case fatality ratio of 39% (WHO, 2024). The disease was first reported at the end of September 2012 by Dr. Al Mohammed Zaki, an Egyptian virologist, after a 60-year-old man from Bisha, a small city near the Saudi port of Jeddah died from a mysterious virus (Gorney, 2014; Naeem, 2013). Because the respiratory virus was similar in nature to SARS, MERS was not officially named and identified until May 2013 (Enserink, 2013).

The World Health Organization Eastern Mediterranean Region (WHOEMR) issued an official statement about three main epidemiological patterns that MERS exhibited and potential sources, and stated, "At present, we do not know the source or how these people became infected" (2013, para. 5). It first appeared that transmission occurred person-to-person but only in specific places—families in which one member was sick or within a health care facility in which a patient or health care worker was in contact with someone with the virus. However, "scientists suspected that the virus might be transmitted from bats" (Al-Mohrej et al., 2016, p. 260).

Research on the zoonotic origin of the MERS virus ensued. Unlike SARS, the "reservoir—as scientists call the living being that hosts the virus until it makes the jump into humans" (Gorney, 2014, para. 15) did not appear to be bats. After testing samples from camels thousands of miles away from one another, health researchers found that camels had developed antibodies for a form of MERS, dating all the way back to samples from 1992; meaning, camels not only had transmitted the virus to humans but the virus had been carried by camels for nearly 20 years until its prevalence in humans in 2012 (Gorney, 2014; Willman et al., 2019). This finding created multiple complications related to the deep religious and cultural ties to camels in Saudi Arabia. Camels carry many symbolic meanings within

Arab culture. For example, camel's milk is believed to cure diseases. Camels can even be passed down from generation to generation as heirlooms or as household pets (Zacharias, 2014)

In addition to these ingrained beliefs, MOH officials had to manage poor access to healthcare professionals (Barry et al., 2020); hospital breaches in infection prevention and control measures (Westall, 2014); poor communication between hospitals, government departments and labs, and a lack of initial preparedness for an outbreak (Alsulaiman & Renter, 2018); poor facilities for quarantine, the firing of a Minister of Health, and the coming of the annual pilgrimage to Mecca during Hajj. Muslims are encouraged to make the trip to Mecca once in their life, bringing in over 1.4 million pilgrims in 2013 (Gorney, 2014).

Ministry of Health's "We Can Stop It" campaign

In 2014, MOH developed a campaign with the slogan "We Can Stop It," to inform the public and raise awareness of "protective measures to prevent the transmission of the virus," as Saudi communities lacked awareness of available options for preventing the spread of MERS (Jradi, 2016, p. 12). The timing of this campaign was crucial to reducing the spread of this deadly contagion; however, significant challenges presented themselves when camels proved to be the viral reservoir of the contagion. Avoidance of camels clashed with widespread religious and cultural beliefs in the purity and healing attributes of the dromedary camels, resulting in backlash from camel owners and farmers in a country with 2 million camels (World Population Review, 2025), where the camel is a traditional part of life, if not one's livelihood or beloved pet. See Figure 8.1 of a man with camels at a cultural festival near Riyadh.

Owners of beautiful camels can show off their camels and their talents at events like the annual King Abdulaziz Camel Festival, which is "aimed to elevate camels as a cornerstone of Saudi Arabia's rich heritage and as a source of both local and global pride and interest" (Saudi Press Agency, 2025, para 1). Some camel owners protested through "a kind of unorganized campaign against the government's warning" (Alhames, 2014, para. 2) called "Kiss Your Camel" with images showing selfies of people—without wearing masks or gloves—smooching their camels on social media.

Research and target audiences

As research around the virus was conducted, the most susceptible to serious illness were immunocompromised people, the elderly, pregnant women, and young children. Additional research showed that the number of people an infected person can in turn infect—the basic reproduction number—was relatively low, with most transmission coming from contact

FIGURE 8.1 A man with his camels at the Janadriyah Festival near Riyadh, Saudi Arabia, in 2018. Shutterstock.

with the virus reservoir, dromedary camels (Willman et al., 2019). This determined the target audience for the campaign—all members of the public, particularly in those spaces with high population density, those working with camels, and any immunocompromised individuals to minimize harm from the virus as best as possible.

Objectives, strategies, key messages, and tactics

Major strategies of this campaign were to keep the public informed with updates on the status of the disease and educate people on how the disease is transmitted and what preventive measures to take through an integrated plan across multimedia platforms, and in cooperation with WHO, CDC, international specialist medical centers, and other government sectors (MOH, 2015b).

In 2014, the Saudi government created a rapid response team (RRT) to manage the spread and treatment of the virus in medical facilities as well as to establish clear guidelines around transmission. It rolled out a public awareness campaign with goals "to empower the public with crucial up to date information required to play their part in combating the virus" (MOH, 2014a, para. 1).

The campaign slogan, "We Can Stop It," was used to further empower the public, help with awareness, and ease public concerns. Messages were spread on a variety of platforms and adapted to the public's response (MOH, 2014a):

- Exercise good hygiene, wash hands often, and avoid touching one's face with unwashed hands.
- Stay away from camels, avoid raw camel meat including liver and unpasteurized camel milk, especially during hajj, the annual pilgrimage to mecca (MOH, 2014b).

Tactics used by MOH included a multimedia approach to distributing information about the virus. With the announcement of the 2014 campaign, MOH launched an official website as a source for additional information included in all official communications, material for consumption by the public, and a toll-free number to address questions and inquiries.

Other media used by the MOH to spread awareness and information included television and radio advertisements, public posters, 35,000 pamphlets and brochures distributed to more than 12,000 individuals in Riyadh's malls and shopping centers (MOH, 2015c), social media platforms like Twitter (now known as X), and MOH's YouTube account, which published an informational video (MOH, 2015a) instructing its viewers to fully cook camel meat, to boil camel milk if not pasteurized, and to avoid any close contact with camels (MOH, 2015a).

Results

WHO demonstrated the slow decline in MERS cases following the bulk of campaigning against the virus in 2014, and between 2015 and 2016, infection and fatality rates sharply declined (WHO, 2022). The World Health Organization-Eastern Mediterranean issued a press release praising the Joint Kingdom of Saudi Arabia/WHO mission for its handling of the outbreak, concluding "that the country has done an excellent job in investigating and controlling the outbreaks" (WHOERM, 2013, para. 13). Several steps were taken yielding these results:

- Infection control measures were implemented thereby reducing hospital outbreaks.
- Increased surveillance for MERS cases and reporting to WHO.
- Investigations identified the source of infection and its transmission and risk factors

Hoda Jradi (2016), professor of epidemiology and program director for the Department of Community and Environmental Health at King Saud Bin

Abdulaziz University in Saudi Arabia, surveyed Saudis, mostly residents of the capital Riyadh, about their preferred sources and media platforms to access information about MERS. The results revealed that the preferred source of information delivered via the health promotion campaign were physicians (46%), other health care providers (32%), MOH (29%), and family and friends (20%). In reference to media channels, "an internet campaign was the most endorsed (a special website for MERS-CoV; selected by 40.4% of participants), followed by hospital and clinic programs (32.5%), local television (29.5%) and SMS (i.e. mobile phone; 26.4%)" (p. 19).

Another study conducted with university students revealed that 23% of respondents received information from MOH while roughly 20% used social networks like WhatsApp and Facebook, while the rest accessed information on WHO and MOH's websites (Al-Rabiaah et al., 2020). Aside from these platforms, YouTube and Twitter were additional sources of information

Al-Mohrej et al. (2016) conducted another study after the campaign to directly measure awareness of MERS, its transmission, and threats to the general public, demonstrating that 97% of participants were aware of MERS, 72% knew coughing and sneezing could spread the infection, and 62% knew there was no cure. However, only 47% knew that camels and bats were primary sources of the virus, almost half of the participants avoided crowded spaces, and 11% wore masks in public spaces.

Theoretical perspectives

A combination of theoretical perspectives is potentially useful in understanding the contexts surrounding the campaign and resistance to it. Chaos Theory, which originated out of mathematics, has been used to understand how complex systems, like public health care, behave especially in relation to crises (Sellnow & Seeger, 2021) and pandemics (Calistri et al., 2024). Chaos Theory provides insight into the unpredictability of a crisis or pandemic. An important concept is the butterfly effect in which small changes have a potentially larger impact on the system (Sellnow & Seeger, 2021). When applied to the epidemiology of how a disease spreads, the small changes might be the initial cases, location of onset, timing, social behavior, population density, and mobility of the population (Calistri et al., 2024). In the case of MERS, one significant butterfly effect was the difference in origin which impacted MOH's efforts to contain and prevent the virus from spreading, especially given the zoonotic nature of MERS and its impact on Saudis health beliefs and protective actions toward camels.

The Health Belief Model (HBM), originally developed in the 1950s by U.S. Public Health Service psychologists, is one of several information-processing and cognitive theories useful in explaining health behaviors as a function of individual perceptions, attitudes, and beliefs about risks (Turner et al., 2021). Psychologically based in four dimensions of perceived susceptibility, severity, benefits and barriers to risk, the model provides insight into "why individuals do not adopt disease strategies and behaviors during health campaigns and refuse to engage in preventative behaviors" (Alsulaiman & Rentner, 2018, p. 33). Alsulaiman & Renter's (2018) study of college students from King Saud University "on the credibility of MOH information and effectiveness" within the "We Can Stop It" campaign found along the four dimensions of HBM these results:

- Perceived susceptibility: Only **one** preventive measure was significantly related to susceptibility. Those who perceived a higher risk of contracting MERS-CoV were more likely to wear a mask and see the benefit of doing so. As part of the campaign, **posters depicted people wearing a mask when visiting sick people, thus indicating that this guideline was being followed** (emphasis added; p. 46)
- Perceived severity: although people **perceive the severity** of contracting MERS-CoV as being great, they have **not been influenced** to get more sleep or exercise, eat a healthier diet, or wear a mask when visiting sick people (emphasis added; p. 47)
- Perceived benefits: Five preventive measures were associated with **benefits** of practicing the behaviors. These were wearing a mask when visiting sick people, staying away from camels, getting enough sleep, getting enough exercise, and covering the mouth or using a tissue when coughing or sneezing. Key campaign messages providing step-by-step guidance through verbal and visual methods may have contributed to these healthy practices (emphasis added; p. 47)
- Barriers to risk: For camel herders, it is not possible to stay away from camels—their livelihood. If people are working long hours at a job and/or tending to family needs, sleep and exercise may suffer. If people do not have access to a tissue, they may cough or sneeze into their hands, which is an unsanitary practice. Decreasing barriers to practice is probably **the greatest challenge this campaign faces**, as many situations, such as being a camel herder or being a working parent, cannot be changed (emphasis added; p. 47).

One specific disease strategy from MOH was advising people to wear masks and gloves when handling camels and to avoid camels. For herders whose livelihoods depend on dromedaries, they may perceive this strategy as a barrier to complying with the MOH's advice.

Another theoretical perspective relevant in this case study is the Protective Action Decision Model (PADM). This framework "integrates the processing of information derived from social and environmental cues with messages that social sources transmit through communication channels to those at risk" (Lindell & Perry, 2012, p. 616). These cues can include mass media messages, peers, friends and family, or authorities.

Decisions are made based on three subprocesses: 1) how the warning message is communicated by channel, 2) how the target audience receives and comprehends the warning message via personal risk assessment, and 3) how individuals respond to cues (Lindell & Perry, 2012) and adopt a protective action decision based on prior experience, cost, time, and barriers (Sellnow & Seeger, 2021). Citizens of Saudi Arabia underwent the PADM process when given warning on the spread of MERS, some to protect themselves and their family members, and others to protect the camels.

Because camels carry many symbolic meanings, this might explain "the reluctance and sensitivity governments face when telling people to steer clear of camels," as individuals defied authoritative warnings, deciding to protect camels (Zacharias, 2014, para. 5). This model may also explain why individuals decided to risk engagement with camels by kissing them amid MOH'S campaign to stop the spread of MERS (Alhames, 2014; BBC, 2014; Taylor, 2014; Ynetnews, 2014).

Key words

Chaos Theory
Dromedary
Hajj
Health Belief Model
Kingdom of Saudi Arabia
Mecca
Protective Action Decision Model
MERS
WhatsApp
WHO-Eastern Mediterranean Region
Zoonotic

Discussion questions

1 How did public response and reaction to transmission guidelines differ from public responses to the COVID-19 pandemic based on your own lived experiences?
2 Think about the place that camels occupy in the culture in Saudi Arabia. What would be a similar cultural equivalent in terms of animals for

you? What would the public response be if it turned out the animal was detrimental to your health?

3 Imagine you were running a privately run organization in KSA during the MERS outbreak, how would you change operations to accommodate for the infection?

Note: The authors edited, modified, and expanded this case study on MERS from a report written by Riley Maynard, Class of 2025, as a final project for the crisis communication course. Riley was an undergraduate student in the Communication Strategy and Design program within the Roy H. Park School of Communications at Ithaca College in New York.

References

Abraham, T. (2004). *Twenty-first century plague: The story of SARS* (1st ed.). John Hopkins University Press.

Alhames, R. (2014, May 21). Why are Saudis kissing their camels? *Global Voices*. https://globalvoices.org/2014/05/21/why-are-saudis-kissing-their-camels/

Alhassan, F. M., & AlDossary, S. A. (2021). The Saudi Ministry of Health's Twitter communication strategies and public engagement during the COVID-19 pandemic: Content analysis study. *JMIR Public Health and Surveillance*, *7*(7), 1–14. https://publichealth.jmir.org/2021/7/e27942

Al-Mohrej, O. A., Al-Shirian, S. D., Al-Otaibi, S. K., Tamim, H. M., Masuadi, E. M., & Fakhoury, H. M. (2016). Is the Saudi public aware of Middle East respiratory syndrome? *Journal of Infection and Public Health*, *9*(3), 259–266. https://doi.org/10.1016/j.jiph.2015.10.003

Al-Rabiaah, A., Temsah, M. H., Al-Eyadhy, A. A., Hasan, G. M., Al-Zamil, F., Al-Subaie, S., Alsohime, F., Jamal, A., Alhaboob, A., Al-Saadi, B., & Somily, A. M. (2020). Middle East Respiratory Syndrome-Corona Virus (MERS-CoV) associated stress among medical students at a university teaching hospital in Saudi Arabia. *Journal of Infection and Public Health*, *13*(5), 687–691. https://doi.org/10.1016/j.jiph.2020.01.005

Alsulaiman, S. A., & Rentner, T. L. (2018). The health belief model and preventative measures: A study of the Ministry of Health campaign on coronavirus in Saudi Arabia. *Journal of International Crisis and Risk Communication Research*, *1*(1), 27–56. https://doi.org/10.70135/jicrcr.v1i1.1

Arguin, P. M., Navin, A. W., Steele, S. F., Weld, L. H., & Kozarsky, P. E. (2004, February). Health communication during SARS. *Emerging Infectious Diseases*, *10*(2), 377–380. DOI: 10.3201/eid1002.030812

Barry, M., Amri, M. A., & Memish, Z. A. (2020). COVID-19 in the shadows of MERS- CoV in the Kingdom of Saudi Arabia. *Journal of Epidemiology and Global Health*, *10*(1), 1–3. https://doi.org/10.2991/jegh.k.200218.003

BBC. (2014, May 13). *Saudi Arabia: Farmers flout Mers warning by kissing camels*. https://www.bbc.com/news/blogs-news-from-elsewhere-27393045

BBC. (2020, June 4). *Hong Kong and the UK: What's the history between the two?* https://www.bbc.co.uk/newsround/52907269

bin Saud, B. (2024, January 8). Camels: A repository of Saudi Arabian history. *Arab News*. https://www.arabnews.com/node/2437986/camels-repository-saudi-arabian-history

Black, J. (2004, August). *Assessment of the Toront03 Alliance's Tourism Recovery Efforts*. https://civicaction.ca/app/uploads/2021/03/T03Assessment.pdf
Bray, D. (2003)., July 28 to August 4) Marketing after SARS. *Marketing Magazine*, *108*(27), 15. https://www.proquest.com/docview/227171187?sourcetype=Trade%20Journals
Brug, J., Aro, A. R., & Richardus, J. H. (2009). Risk perceptions and behaviors: Towards pandemic control of emerging infectious diseases. *International Journal of Behavioral Medicine*, *16*, 3–6. DOI 10.1007/s12529-008-9000-x
Brug, J., Oenema, A., de Zwart, O., Richardus, J. H., & Bishop, G. D. (2004). SARS risk perception, knowledge, precautions and information sources, the Netherlands. *Emerging Infectious Diseases*, *10*(8), 1486–1488.
Calabro, S., & Daniels, C. (2003, May 19). Toronto Tells outside world City. *PRWeek*, *6*(20), 2.
Calistri, A., Roggero, P. F., & Palú, G. (2024). Chaos theory in the understanding of COVID-19 pandemic dynamics. *Gene*, *912*, 148334. https://doi.org/10.1016/j.gene.2024.148334
Canadian Tourism Commission. (n.d.) *2003 Annual Report*. https://publications.gc.ca/collections/Collection/Iu82-2003E.pdf
CDC. (n.d.). *Common human coronaviruses*. https://www.cdc.gov/coronavirus/downloads/Common-HCoV-fact-sheet-508.pdf
CDC. (2003, December 12). Revised U.S. surveillance case definition for Severe Acute Respiratory Syndrome (SARS) and update on SARS Cases—United States and worldwide, December 2003. *Morbidity and Mortality Weekly Report*, *52*(49), 1202–1206. https://www.cdc.gov/mmwr/preview/mmwrhtml/mm5249a2.htm
CDC. (2013, April 26). *CDC SARS response timeline*. https://archive.cdc.gov/#/details?url=https://www.cdc.gov/about/history/sars/timeline.htm
CDC. (2024, February 12). *About CDC*. https://www.cdc.gov/about/cdc/index.html
CDC Office of Readiness and Response. (2014, May 2-June 12). *Middle East Respiratory Syndrome Coronavirus*. https://www.cdc.gov/orr/responses/middle-east-respiratory-syndrome.html
CEPI. (n.d.). *Middle East Respiratory Syndrome*. https://cepi.net/MERS
Ceylan, R. F., & Ozkan, B. (2020, June 30). The economic effects of epidemics: From SARS and MERS to COVID-19. *Research Journal in Advanced Humanities*, *1*(2), 21–29. https://doi.org/10.58256/rjah.v1i2.132
Conde Nast Traveler. (n.d.). *Toronto travel guide*. https://www.cntraveler.com/destinations/toronto
Daniels, C. (2003, September 1). Toronto looks into tourism recovery after SARS scares. *PRWeek*, *6*, 19.
Deans, J. (2003, April 9). Hong Kong in hot flush over ad blunder. *The Guardian*. https://www.theguardian.com/media/2003/apr/09/pressandpublishing.marketingandpr
de Zwart, O., Veldhuijzen, I. K., Elam, G., Aro, A. R., Abraham, T., Bishop, G. D., Voeten, H. A. C. M., Richardus, J. H. & Brug, J. (2009). Perceived threat, risk perception, and efficacy beliefs related to SARS and other (emerging) infectious diseases: Results of an international survey. *International Journal of Behavioral Medicine*, 16, 30–40. https://doi.org/10.1007/s12529-008-9008-2
Economic Development, Culture and Tourism Division of Toronto. (2003a, May 9). Mayor launches "Toronto: You Belong Here" campaign in time for Mother's Day. *Canada NewsWire*. https://www.proquest.com/docview/455239784?accountid=11644&sourcetype=Wire%20Feeds
Economic Development, Culture and Tourism Division of Toronto. (2003b, May 21). Mayor Lastman launches City's Chinese business recovery campaign. *Canada NewsWire*. https://www.proquest.com/wire-feeds/mayor-lastman-launches-citys-chinese-business/docview/455728311/se-2?accountid=11644

Enserink, M. (2013, May 8). International Group settles on name for new coronavirus. *Science*. https://www.science.org/content/article/international-group-settles-name-new-coronavirus

General Authority for Statistics. (2024). Total Kingdom population exceeds 35 million by mid- 2024. *Population Estimates Publication 2024*. https://www.stats.gov.sa/documents/20117/2435273/Population+Estimates+Statistics+2024+EN.pdf/9b71e303-5fd9-19cb-9913-850a9d521639?t=1738859947691

Global Policy Forum. (n.d.). *Internet users 1995-2008*. https://archive.globalpolicy.org/component/content/article/109-tables-and-charts/27519-internet-users.html

Gorney, C. (2014, May 13). The camels and the contagion: Inside the international hunt for the source of MERS. *National Geographic*. https://www.nationalgeographic.com/science/article/140513-mers-saudi-camels-health-contagion-spillover-bats-disease

Government of the Hong Kong Special Administrative Region. (2025, July). *Hong Kong: The facts*. https://www.gov.hk/en/about/abouthk/facts.htm

Hasan, M. K., Ismail, A. R., & Islam, M. F. (2017). Tourist risk perceptions and revisit intention: A critical review of literature. *Cogent Business & Management Journal (Online)*, *4*(1), 1–21. DOI: 10.1080/23311975.2017.1412874

Health Canada. (2003, September 24). *Learning from SARS: Renewal of public health in Canada* [Report] National Advisory Committee on SARS and Public Health. https://publications.gc.ca/site/eng/9.686722/publication.html

Heinzl, M. (2003, May 29). SARS derails tourism in Toronto—Ontario Government halts U.S. marketing campaign due to the latest outbreak. *Wall Street Journal*, (Eastern edition), p. D3.

HKTB. (2003). *HKTB Annual Report 2002-2003*. https://www.discoverhongkong.com/content/dam/dhk/intl/corporate/about-hktb/annual-report/02-03pdf/2002-2003-02.pdf

HKTB. (2004). Chairman's message. *HKTB Annual Report 2003/2004*. https://www.discoverhongkong.com/content/dam/dhk/intl/corporate/about-hktb/annual-report/03-04pdf/2003-2004-02.pdf

Hong Kong pulls 'Breath' ad due to outbreak of SARS. (2003, April 10). *Campaign*. https://www.campaignlive.com/article/hong-kong-pulls-breath-ad-due-outbreaksars/176832

Hutchinson, A. (2019, July 23). The history of social media. [Infographic]. *Social Media Today*. https://www.socialmediatoday.com/news/the-history-of-social-media-infographic-2/559273/

Infection Prevention and Control Canada. (n.d.). *SARS-CoV*. https://ipac-canada.org/resource-centre/infectious-disease-resources/coronavirus-covid-19/sars-cov/

Joo, H., Maskery, B. A., Berro, A. D., Rotz, L. D., Lee, Y. K., & Brown, C. M. (2019). Economic impact of the 2015 MERS outbreak on the Republic of Korea's tourism-related industries. *Health Security*, *17*(2), 100–108. https://doi.org/10.1089/hs.2018.0115

Jradi, H. (2016). Identification of information types and sources by the public for promoting awareness of Middle East respiratory syndrome coronavirus in Saudi Arabia. *Health Education Research*, *31*(1), 12–23. https://doi.org/10.1093/her/cyv061

Karan, K., Lee, A., & Pong, E. Y. L. (2007, November). Emerging victorious against an outbreak: Integrated communication management of SARS in Singapore media coverage and impact of the SARS campaign in moving a nation to be socially responsible. *Journal of Creative Communications*, *2*(3), 383–403. https://doi.org/10.1177/097325860700200307

Keogh-Brown, M. R., & Smith, R. D. (2008, October). The economic impact of SARS: How does the reality match the predictions? *Health Policy*, *88*(1): 110–120. DOI: 10.1016/j.healthpol.2008.03.003

Lau, J. T. F., Yang, X., Pang, E., Tsui, H. Y., Wong, E., & Wing, Y. K. (2005). SARS-related perceptions in Hong Kong. *Emerging Infectious Diseases*, *11*(3), 417–424.

Lau, J. T. F., Yang, X., Tsui, H., Pang, E., & Kim, J. H. (2004). SARS preventive and risk behaviours of Hong Kong air travellers. *Epidemiology & Infection*, *132*, 727–736. DOI: 10.1017/S0950268804002225

Leppin, A., & Aro, A. R. (2009). Risk perceptions related to SARS and avian influenza: Theoretical foundations of current empirical research. *International Journal of Behavioral Medicine*, *16*, 7–29. DOI 10.1007/s12529-008-9002-8

Lewington, J. (2003, April 25). Blitz aims to calm fears of SARS, get tourists back. *The Globe and Mail*. https://www.theglobeandmail.com/news/national/blitz-aims-to-calm-fears-of-sars-get-tourists-back/article25283177/

Lindell, M. K., & Perry, R. W. (2012). The protective action decision model: Theoretical modifications and additional evidence. *Risk Analysis*, *32*(4), 616–632. DOI: 10.1111/j.1539-6924.2011.01647.x

Lindsay, C. (2001). Profiles of ethnic communities in Canada: The Chinese community. *Statistics Canada*. [Social and Aboriginal Statistics Division Catalogue no. 89-621-XIE] https://www150.statcan.gc.ca/n1/en/pub/89-621-x/89-621-x2006001-eng.pdf?st=5eVzM1ki

Low, D. E. (2004). Sars: Lessons from Toronto. In: *Institute of medicine (US) forum on microbial threats*; S. Knobler, A. Mahmoud, & S. Lemon, et al., (eds.). *Learning from SARS: Preparing for the next disease outbreak: Workshop summary*. Washington (DC): National Academies Press (US). https://www.ncbi.nlm.nih.gov/books/NBK92467/

McKercher, B. (2003). SIP (Sars Induced Panic), a greater threat to tourism than Sars (Severe Acute Respiratory Syndrome). *e-Review of Tourism Research (eRTR)*, *1*(1), 17-18. https://ertr.tamu.edu/files/2012/09/132_c-1-7.pdf

McPeak, J. (2004, June 22). McGuinty government launches new Ontario Tourism Strategy. *Canada NewsWire*. https://www.proquest.com/wire-feeds/mcguinty-government-launches-new-ontario-tourism/docview/455653680/se-2

MOH. (2014a, May 7). *Ministry of health rolls out public awareness campaign to combat MERS corona* virus. https://www.moh.gov.sa/en/Ministry/MediaCenter/News/Pages/News-2014-05-07-003.aspx

MOH. (2014b, September 13). *Saudi Health Ministry urges public to take proper precautions around camels*. https://www.moh.gov.sa/en/Ministry/MediaCenter/News/Pages/News-2014-09-13-001.aspx

MOH. (2015a, February 12). *Important guidelines outline how to handle camels to avoid infection of #Corona Virus* [YouTube video]. https://www.youtube.com/watch?v=oX3He0bUZcY

MOH. (2015b, March 4). *MOH continues its health awareness campaign on MERS-CoV under the theme: "We Can Stop It."* https://www.moh.gov.sa/en/Ministry/MediaCenter/News/Pages/News-2015-03-04-002.aspx

MOH. (2015c, March 30). *40,000 MERS-CoV awareness brochures distributed to the public in Riyadh's shopping centers*. https://www.moh.gov.sa/en/Ministry/MediaCenter/News/Pages/News-2015-03-30-002.aspx

Naeem, Z. (2013, November). Editorial—Middle East Respiratory Syndrome (MERS)—An update. *International Journal of Health Sciences*, *7*(3), V–VI. https://doi.org/10.12816/0006053

Ochsenwald, W. J., & Philby, H. S. J. B. (2024, July 13). Saudi Arabia. *Encyclopedia Britannica*. https://www.britannica.com/place/Saudi-Arabia

PATA. (2020). *Case study: Hong Kong's recovery from SARS*. https://src.pata.org/wp-content/uploads/Case-Study-Hong-Kongs-Recovery-from-SARS.pdf

Pine, R., & McKercher, B. (2004). Research in brief: The impact of SARS on Hong Kong's tourism industry. *International Journal of Contemporary Hospitality Management*, *16*(2), 139–143. https://doi.org/10.1108/09596110410520034

Quenqua, D. (2003, May 19). Burson to aid Hong Kong in recovery from SARS fallout. *PR Week* [US], p. 1.

Quigley, K., & Lowe, K. (2020, June) Observations from Toronto's Tourism Recovery Post SARS in 2003. *MacEachen Institute for Public Policy and Governance at Dalhousie University*. https://cdn.dal.ca/content/dam/dalhousie/pdf/dept/maceachen-institute/Briefing%20Note_SARS%20and%20COVID19_June5.pdf

Rendon, P. M. (2003, May 19). BBDO kicks off Toronto SARS effort. *Marketing Magazine*, *108*(19), 3.

Renn, O., Burns, W. J., Kasperson, J. X., Kasperson, R. E., & Slovic, P. (1992). The social amplification of risk: Theoretical foundations and empirical applications. *Journal of Social Issues*, *48*(4), 137–160.

Rothkopf, D. J. (2003, May 11). When the buzz bites back: [FINAL Edition]. *The Washington Post*. https://www.proquest.com/newspapers/when-buzz-bites-back/docview/409459437/se-2

Saudi Press Agency. (2025, January 2). *Cultural activities of King Abdulaziz Camel Festival conclude with over 320 competitive rounds*. https://www.spa.gov.sa/en/N2236819

Seeman, N. (2003, April 25). Toronto under SARS: A media fever. *Fraser Institute*. https://www.fraserinstitute.org/commentary/toronto-under-sars-media-fever

Sellnow, T. L., & Seeger, M. W. (2021). *Theorizing crisis communication*. John Wiley & Sons.

Shier, P. (2020).The lessons SARS offers on how to rebound from a crisis. *Strategy*. https://strategyonline.ca/2020/03/31/the-lessons-sars-offers-on-how-to-rebound-from-a-crisis/

Statista. (2024). *Percentage of population using the internet in the United States from 2000 to 2024*. https://www.statista.com/statistics/209117/us-internet-penetration/

Statistics Canada. (2005). *International Travel 2003 Catalogue no. 66-201-XIE*. https://publications.gc.ca/Collection-R/Statcan/66-201-XIE/0000366-201-XIE.pdf

Statistics Canada. (2007, July 9). *2003: A bad year for tourism*. https://www150.statcan.gc.ca/n1/pub/11-402-x/2007/4007/ceb4007_002-eng.htm

Taylor, A. (2014, May 16). *The scary reason Saudi farmers are kissing camels*. WP Company LLC d/b/a *The Washington Post*. https://www.washingtonpost.com/news/worldviews/wp/2014/05/16/the-scary-reason-saudi-farmers-are-kissing-camels/?=undefined

Taylor, S. (2022). The psychology of pandemics: Lesson learned for the future. *Canadian Psychology*, *63*(2), 233–246. https://doi.org/10.1037/cap0000303

Tew, P. J., Lu, Z., Tolomiczenko, G., & Gellatly, J. (2008). SARS: Lessons in strategic planning for hoteliers and destination marketers. *International Journal of Contemporary Hospitality Management*, *20*(3), 332–346. DOI 10.1108/09596110810866145

Turner, M. M., Jang, Y., & Turner, S. (2021). Information-processing and cognitive theories. In T.L. Thompson & P. J. Schulz, (eds.). *Health communication theory*, (1st ed.), (pp. 135–156). John Wiley & Sons, Inc.

United Nations. (2003, April 30). *UN health agency removes SARS travel advisory for Toronto*. https://news.un.org/en/story/2003/04/66222

Van Der Pool, L. (2003, May 19.) Cities tap shops to aid post-SARS recovery. *ADWEEK*, *44*(20), 20. https://www.adweek.com/brand-marketing/cities-tap-shops-aid-post-sars-recovery-64207/

Wall, G. (2006). Recovering from SARS: The case of Toronto tourism. *Tourism, Security and Safety*, 143–152. https://doi.org/10.1016/B978-0-7506-7898-8.50014-X
Westall, S. (2014, May 11). Saudi Arabia warns of MERS risk from camels as cases rise. *Reuters*. https://www.reuters.com/article/health-saudi-camels-idINL6N0NX08N20140511/
WHO. (n.d.a). *Severe Acute Respiratory Syndrome (SARS) overview*. https://www.who.int/health-topics/severe-acute-respiratory-syndrome#tab=tab_1
WHO. (n.d.b). *Severe Acute Respiratory Syndrome (SARS) treatment*. https://www.who.int/health-topics/severe-acute-respiratory-syndrome#tab=tab_3
WHO. (2003a, July 3). *SARS outbreak contained worldwide*. [News release]. https://www.who.int/news/item/05-07-2003-sars-outbreak-contained-worldwide
WHO. (2003b, March 15). *World Health Organization issues emergency travel advisory*. [Departmental update]. https://www.who.int/news/item/15-03-2003-world-health-organization-issues-emergency-travel-advisory
WHO. (2015, July 24). *Summary of probable SARS cases with onset of illness from 1 November 2002 to 31 July 2003*. [Meeting report]. https://www.who.int/publications/m/item/summary-of-probable-sars-cases-with-onset-of-illness-from-1-november-2002-to-31-july-2003
WHO. (2022, August 5). *Middle East respiratory syndrome coronavirus (MERS-CoV)*. https://www.who.int/news-room/fact-sheets/detail/middle-east-respiratory-syndrome-coronavirus-(mers-cov)
WHO. (2024, May 8). *Middle East respiratory syndrome coronavirus –Saudi Arabia*. https://www.who.int/emergencies/disease-outbreak-news/item/2024-DON516
WHO Eastern Mediterranean Region. (2013). *Middle East respiratory syndrome coronavirus: Joint Kingdom of Saudi Arabia/WHO mission*. [Press archive]. https://www.emro.who.int/press-releases/2013/corona-virus-who-saudi-arabia-mission.html
WHO Eastern Mediterranean Region. (2025, July 6). *MERS situation update*. https://applications.emro.who.int/docs/WHOEMCSR832E-eng.pdf?ua=1
WHO Regional Office for the Eastern Mediterranean. (2018, December). *MERS situation update*. https://www.emro.who.int/pandemic-epidemic-diseases/mers-cov/mers-situation-update-december-2018.html
Wildavsky, A., & Drake, K. (1990). Theories of risk perception: Who fears what and why? *Daedalus*, *119*(4), 41–60. https://www.jstor.org/stable/20025337
Willman, M., Kobasa, D., & Kindrachuk, J. (2019). A comparative analysis of factors influencing two outbreaks of Middle Eastern Respiratory Syndrome (MERS) in Saudi Arabia and South Korea. *Viruses*, *11*(12), 1119. https://doi.org/10.3390/v111211192015
World Population Review. (2025). *Camel population by country 2025*. https://worldpopulationreview.com/country-rankings/camel-population-by-country
Wyman, O. (2020, January 31). Why coronavirus may pose more risks to aviation than SARS did. *Forbes*. https://www.forbes.com/sites/oliverwyman/2020/01/31/why-the-wuhan-coronavirus-may-pose-more-risks-to-aviation-than-sars-did/
Yan, L. (2003, April 23). International dragon boat races cancelled over Sars fears. *South China Morning Post* (Hong Kong), p. 1. https://www.scmp.com/article/413290/international-dragon-boat-races-cancelled-over-sars-fears
Ynetnews. (2014, May 14). *Saudi's fight back against MERS warning by kissing their camels on film*. https://www.ynetnews.com/articles/0,7340,L-4519744,00.html
Zacharias, A. (2014, May 20). Kissing camels in response to mers [sic]. *The National*. https://www.thenationalnews.com/arts/kissing-camels-in-response-to-mers-1.241120

9

CASE STUDIES ON THE A(H1N1) "SWINE FLU" PANDEMIC, 2009

9.1 INTRODUCTION: A(H1N1) PANDEMIC IN CONTEXT

As the first pandemic in the 21st century, the newly discovered (H1N1) pdm09 influenza strain was also called the 2009 H1N1 or the A(H1N1) influenza, or more colloquially as "swine flu," with gene segments originating from pigs, humans, and birds. The World Health Organization (WHO) declared a phase-5 pandemic alert (considerable pandemic risk) in April 2009 after cases were reported in Mexico and the U.S. and later elevated to a phase-6 alert (pandemic with high transmission) in June 2009 due to its rapid spread throughout 70 countries. The pandemic eventually affected a total of 135 countries and territories (Baldo et al., 2016).

The CDC projected that between 151,700 to 575,400 people died globally from the A(H1N1) influenza; in the U.S. alone, the CDC estimated 274,304 people were hospitalized, and 12,469 people died (CDC, 2019). WHO declared the end of the 2009 H1N1 pandemic in August 2010 (WHO, 2010).

A few well-known people survived this pandemic, including Dr. Sanjay Gupta, American neurosurgeon and CNN medical reporter; Marilyn Manson, American rock musician; and Rupert Grint, British actor of *Harry Potter* fame known as Ron Weasley (Desmon, 2009).

Unlike typical seasonal influenzas, the A(H1N1) influenza was contagious year-round, and people under 65 were more likely to become infected. On a global scale from April 2009 to April 2010, people 65 and under comprised 80% of deaths from the (A)H1N1, whereas 70% to 90% of people 65 years old and older died from seasonal influenza epidemics. Younger people perished more than the older population since older

DOI: 10.4324/9781003434382-9

people had been exposed to earlier H1N1 influenzas and built up antibodies to combat the latest strain (CDC, 2019).

Transmission and symptoms

The pandemic spread human-to-human transmission via droplets from infected people sneezing or coughing near healthy people and when uninfected people touched their mouth or nose after touching an infected surface. Although rare, this influenza also can be transmitted from pigs to people. For example, healthy people can be infected by being scratched or bitten by a pig or by consuming food or water without washing their hands after touching pigs. Conversely, infected people can contaminate pigs with the virus. Potential locations for infection included barns and livestock fairs with pigs (Frenck, 2023).

Misinformation circulated on how people could catch the A(H1N1) influenza by eating pork and pork products, such as bacon and sausage. Consuming pork and handling raw pork does not spread the virus. The Food and Agriculture Organization of the United Nations (FAO) issued a news release explaining that the virus is not foodborne with a quote from an FAO chief veterinary officer: "There is no evidence of a threat to the food chain; at this stage it is a human crisis and not an animal crisis, but we have to be alerted and prepared" (FAO, 2009, para. 4).

Flu-like symptoms along with frequent coughing jags and upset stomachs were commonly experienced by people who contracted this influenza. People with higher risks included pregnant women, obese people with a body mass index of 35 kg/m2 (Obesity Class II) and above, and those with preexisting chronic illnesses of the respiratory system, liver, diabetes type 1 and 2, among others. People with severe cases died primarily from respiratory complications and shock (Jilani et al., 2024).

Prevention and treatment

Common daily preventive methods included washing one's hand frequently for 20 seconds, drinking fluids regularly, maintaining a healthy diet, and eschewing crowds and large gatherings of people. Healthy people also were advised to stay away from infected people and to avoid touching surfaces that could be potentially infected and using their hands to touch their face before handwashing or using disinfectant wipes or hand sanitizers regularly. Infected people were told to stay home until they recovered and to seek medical care if needed (ECDC, 2009).

At that time, seasonal flu vaccines did not protect against the A(H1N1) influenza. An effective vaccine was not available until November 2009 after the second wave had peaked (CDC, 2019). Today, this influenza virus is prevented by annual flu shots that include this strain, among others.

Transmission and treatment for pigs

For pigs, H1N1 swine viruses cause a respiratory disease in which swine herds can become ill but few pig deaths occur. The flu is spread airborne when infected pigs spread droplets by coughing or sneezing in proximity to healthy pigs, when pigs touch contaminated objects or are up close to infected humans. Flu vaccines are on the market to reduce infection in pigs (CDC, 2024a).

Widely used communication tools

Although this influenza was the first global flu pandemic since the 1960s, it also was the first one in which communicators were able to employ fully the internet and social media platforms to reach the public.

Hosted by the Wikimedia Foundation (n.d.), Wikipedia launched in 2001 as "the free online encyclopedia, created, edited, and verified by volunteers around the world" (para. 1).The online world expanded after Google's debut in 1998 when a variety of social media platforms became available: LinkedIn in 2002, MySpace in 2003, Facebook in 2004, Reddit in 2005, Twitter (now called X) in 2006, Tumblr in 2007, and Weibo (in China) in 2009. Visual imagery sharing transformed with Flickr in 2003 and YouTube in 2005. Blogging become easier with the introduction of LiveJournal in 1999 and WordPress in 2003 (McFadden, 2025).

In 2009, almost 50% of U.S. households (U.S. Energy Information Administration, 2011) and 35% of households worldwide had a computer at home (ITU, 2021) and 71% of individuals in the U.S. used the internet (DataReportal, We are Social & Meltwater, 2025) while 26% of individuals worldwide accessed the internet (ITU, 2024).

Mobile technology also was becoming mainstream: 84% of adults in the U.S. owned cellphones in 2009 (Pew Research Center, 2024). The iPhone 2G debuted in 2007 and revolutionized mobile phone technology. As Apple's co-founder Steve Jobs explained during the iPhone launch at Mac World Expo in San Francisco to an audience of 45,000:

> 1984 – we introduced the Macintosh. It didn't just change Apple. It changed the whole computer industry.
>
> In 2001, we introduced the first iPod. And it didn't just change the way we all listen to music, it changed the entire music industry.
>
> Well, today we're introducing three revolutionary products of this class. The first one is a **widescreen iPod with touch controls**. The second is a

> **revolutionary mobile phone.** And the third is a **breakthrough internet communications device** ... These are not separate devices, this is one device, and we are calling it iPhone. Today, Apple is going to reinvent the phone, and here it is.
>
> *(emphasis in original; Jobs, 2020, paras. 3–5)*

The first android Samsung smartphone, the Galaxy GT-I7500, made its debut later during the same year as the iPhone (Samsung Wiki, n.d.). Samsung and Apple have continued to dominate the smartphone market share since then (IDC, 2024).

Impact

WHO, CDC, other government agencies, and the media referred to the new influenza as "swine flu" initially, resulting in public fear of pork products, country bans of pork, and a slump in pork sales. The pork industry was invested in reaching the public and health officials with safety messages on consuming pork as covered in case study 9.2.

This situation led to WHO developing new best practices for nomenclature of human infectious diseases in 2015. Previous pandemics were named after specific countries or regions (Asian flu, Hong Kong flu, Middle East Respiratory Syndrome), after a person's name (Creutzfeldt-Jakob disease), animals (swine flu, monkey pox), industries or occupations (Legionnaires disease), among other terms. WHO (2015) stated its goal: "to minimize unnecessary negative impact of disease names on trade, travel, tourism, or animal welfare, and avoid causing offence to any cultural, social, national, regional, professional or ethnic groups" (para. 1).

A second impact was how CDC and the Association of State and Territorial Health Officials (ASTHO) changed the way people could receive vaccinations nationwide and in the District of Columbia and Puerto Rico in 2009. The CDC 2009 H1N1 Vaccine Pharmacy Initiative offered the A(H1N1) vaccine to participating pharmacies, thereby making it easier and faster for the public to get vaccines at their local pharmacies instead of making appointments with their doctors (Koonin et al., 2011). Case study 9.3 reviews this initiative that required pharmacies to become certified to offer vaccines to the public.

9.2 "PORK IS SAFE" CAMPAIGN: U.S. PORK INDUSTRY FIGHTS SWINE FLU MISNOMER AND MISINFORMATION ABOUT PORK CONSUMPTION

Situation analysis

In 2009, when the world was hit with a new strain of the influenza—A(H1N1)—pigs and people were not the only stakeholders affected.

The U.S. pork industry is supported by two major industry trade groups: the Iowa-based National Pork Board (NBP) and National Pork Producers Council (NPPC) with offices in Iowa and Washington, D.C. The Promotion, Research, and Consumer Information Act of 1985 authorized the creation of the NBP, which also oversees the Pork Checkoff program with funding from pork producers and importers who pay a "mandatory assessment of $0.35 of $100 market value (effective January 1, 2023) of all pigs sold in the United States, as well as an equivalent amount on imported pigs, pork, and pork products" (USDA, n.d., para. 1).

The program undertakes the following activities for national pork producers and importers (Pork Checkoff, 2025a):

- **Promotional activities** to expand sales of pork products nationwide and net exports abroad. Target audiences include consumers, retail outlets, and food services.
- **Research** on pork-related topics, such as responsible pork production and human nutrition.
- **Producer education** to keep the industry updated and competitive on the latest technologies and intelligence through seminars, videos, and other instructional content for pork producers.
- **Consumer education** to reach journalists, chefs, and food influencers about the pork industry. Messages on the dietary benefits of pork are also shared with dieticians, teachers, and various health professionals.

The Pork Checkoff program is unable to allocate funds for lobbying or influencing government policies, whereas NPPC serves as the lobbying group for the U.S. pork industry. Its mission statement reads as follows: "We advocate for the social, environmental and economic sustainability of U.S. pork producers and their partners by fighting for reasonable public policy, advancing our freedom to operate and expanding access to global markets" (NPPC, 2025, para. 3).

The Pork Checkoff program has created a few branding initiatives. It created the 100% Real Pork brand message to differentiate pork from other food alternatives and to create an "identity for the pork industry from farm to fork" (Pork Checkoff, 2025b, para. 3) by conveying the authenticity of pork, producers, and farms. "The Other White Meat®" tagline and campaign began in 1987 and focused on positioning pork as a tasty and lean protein for any meal of the day to dispel pork's image as a fatty meat (Pork Checkoff, 2025c). See Figure 9.1 of a "Pork: The Other White Meat" ad.

FIGURE 9.1 Full-page ad from *Life Magazine*, November 1997, of "Pork: The Other White Meat." Patti McConville/Alamy Stock Photo.

With the A(H1N1) influenza being called the swine flu, the U.S pork industry, the world's largest exporter of pork, contended with a severe drop in domestic sales and 27 nations temporarily banning pork imports, resulting in an estimated loss of USD 1.1 billion from April to October 2009 (ABC News, 2009).

Communication programming and execution

In April 2009, NBP hired a few agencies from the Interpublic Group, which is a publicly held company (NYSE: IPG) with agencies worldwide, specializing in public relations, public affairs, market research, and multicultural marketing. The following four agencies were retained to help with the NBP crisis communication (PRovoke Media, 2010):

- Weber Shandwick calls itself "the earned-first global communications agency" (Weber Shandwick, 2023, para. 1), based in New York City with offices on six continents.
- Powell Tate, based in Washington, D.C., is a public affairs agency.
- The AXIS Agency, based in Burbank, California, specializes in multicultural communications.
- KRC Research, based in Washington, D.C., conducts public opinion quantitative and qualitative market research worldwide.

The agencies' primary objective was to protect the pork industry from misinformation and slumping sales of pork products due to the influenza. They quickly assembled a crisis management team to reach U.S. consumers of pork products with important strategic messages:

- A(H1N1) is not spread by eating and handling pork and pork-related products.
- Pork and pork-related products are safe to consume during the influenza.

Research was an important initial step. In partnership with KRC Research, Weber Shandwick undertook a series of telephone surveys over six weeks from late April to early June to track consumers and their sentiments regarding pork safety. The first surveys of 750 consumers were conducted with the purpose of benchmarking, understanding consumers' knowledge of the influenza and pork consumption, and determining the best target audiences. The findings showed that 88% of respondents who bought pork over the previous two months believed that pork was safe to consume, and 19% were aware of the flu and questioned pork safety, so they were unlikely to buy pork products (Provoke Media, 2010). The surveys also revealed that Latinos were more concerned about pork safety than the general population. This finding led to conducting a supplemental survey by polling 150 Spanish-speakers. Overall, the surveys provided guidance on target audiences, relatable messaging and responses to consumers, and evaluating the campaign's effectiveness in communicating safety of pork consumption and handling (PRovoke Media, 2010).

Based on the survey findings, the agencies quickly tweaked their consumer messaging since the research revealed confusion about pork:

- **Consumers can safely consume pork and handle raw pork products.** Previously, pork industry and government spokespeople emphasized pork must be cooked to 145° F, which should be checked by using a thermometer for an accurate internal temperature but amended the temperature to 160° F to include a 3-minute rest time (USDA, 2011). Research showed this advice could lead to consumers thinking the influenza was foodborne and possibly contained in raw pork. The surveys indicated that consumers had more concerns about handling raw pork than consuming pork (PRovoke Media, 2010).
- **The H1N1 virus is a respiratory illness, not a foodborne illness.** Earlier, spokespersons conveyed that U.S. swine herds were not infected with A(H1N1) and U.S. pork products was safe to eat. Research findings suggested that consumers could misinterpret this information and believe the virus was foodborne instead of airborne.

The agency undertook the following tactics:

- Provided an analysis of print, broadcast, digital, and social media by monitoring coverage three times daily on weekdays and twice daily on weekends over the first few weeks. TweetDeck was used for tracking Twitter content.
- Set up a Twitter handle, @FactsAboutPork, monitored tweets, and corrected misinformation as needed.
- Developed a FactsAboutPork microsite that was promoted with online search ads and display ads.
- Contacted leading food and health bloggers to share messages.
- Educated traditional and social media on a real-time basis about the facts and corrected misinformation.
- Pinpointed a veterinarian with professional experience at a CDC-funded influenza center, a registered dietician and a mother of three children, and a Spanish-speaking medical doctor for addressing Latino communities. They were media trained and participated in a nationwide satellite and radio media tour as NPB spokespeople to address the facts. Axis Agency managed outreach with Latino media.
- Distributed news releases and B-roll packages, as well as online video and audio soundbites.
- Prepared NPB and NPPC to ask U.S. government public health agencies and WHO "to use the scientific name H1N1 not 'swine flu,' given the fact that the virus contained human, avian, and swine genes" (PRovoke Media, 2010, para. 17).

Results

The following lists the agencies' accomplishments to help the pork industry (PRovoke Media, 2010):

- Focused on eliminating usage of swine flu. WHO and U.S. health agencies starting using H1N1 flu or A(H1N1) instead of "swine flu" after being approached by NPB and NPPC. A journalist summed up the problem: "The villain isn't the virus itself, actually, but the name by which it commonly goes: swine flu" (Haga, 2009, para. 2). In fact, WHO later changed the nomenclature of all human infectious diseases named after an industry, location, and other terms as covered in this chapter's overview section.
- Generated almost 600 million consumer impressions on the NBP and from interviews with its spokespeople about pork safety and handling.
- "Decreased the number of pork consumers who said they were less likely to eat pork by 11 percentage points or 58% over a 6-week period beginning April 29 and ending June 4" (PRovoke Media, 2010, para. 20)
- Improved the percentage from 6% to 7% over a six-week period of pork consumers who believed consuming pork was safe.
- Contacted Reuters to correct a story containing misinformation using this title, "WHO casts wary eye on meat, blood of H1N1-infected pigs," which was found by steadily monitoring TweetDeck (Reuters, 2009a, para. 1). The updated story's new headline became "WHO says no infection risks from eating pork" (Reuters, 2009b, para. 1).
- Increased fresh pork sales by 6.3% over the same period in 2010, a year after A(H1N1) occurred and led to a slump in pork sales.

Weber Shandwick, Powell Tate, and NPB received an Honorable Mention for its "Protecting Pork Sales During H1N1" campaign from PRNEWS' 2010 Platinum PR Awards in crisis management (PRNews, 2010).

Theoretical framework

For this particular case study, the Situational Crisis Communication Theory (SCCT) provides a framework for understanding how organizations can protect reputations during a crisis (Coombs, 2007). Briefly, this theoretical framework identifies reputational threats to an organization, the attributions associated with these threats, and how organizations choose crisis response strategies to protect an organization's reputation.

Beginning with reputation, an organization's reputation is generally conceptualized as an asset the organization, its identity and brand have and how stakeholders perceive the organization and its ability to meet their expectations and needs (Coombs, 2007). Reputation also refers to "what an organization does. What it produces and how it behaves" (Langham, 2019, p. 18).

Stakeholders form favorable or unfavorable perceptions as they interact with the organization, read news reports, and receive indirect information from social media or word of mouth (Coombs, 2007). It is important to keep in mind that within the time period A(H1N1) occurred, "organizations were just beginning to develop formal policies for how to use social media ... without formal policies to guide social media responses, communicators might have been restricted in their ability to create unique frames and messages," and defaulted to traditional media outlets (Liu & Kim, 2011, p. 241). Regardless of the medium, positive reputations can buffer or shield an organization during a crisis whereas negative reputations threaten to damage the organization and impact crisis response strategies.

Greyser (2009) studied major organizational crises to ascertain any threats to the meaning of a brand and its marketplace favorability during a crisis. Threats to a brand have the potential to damage reputation, depending on how an organization responds, especially during pandemics (Nuortimo et al., 2024). Sources of reputational trouble can include product failure and tampering, corporate social irresponsibility and misbehaviors, loss of sales and public support, and failure to adapt (Greyser, 2009). Other sources of reputational trouble, especially with the advent of social media, include misinformation, disinformation, fake news, rumors, confusion, and inconsistent messaging, and how the diffusion of this type of information may impact policies related to lessening the spread of the virus and safety measures (Prandi & Primero, 2020).

A(H1N1) represented a serious reputational threat to pork farmers, distributors, consumers, and the food supply chain (Wenig, 2011). The CDC and WHO also faced a reputation threat as they tried to combat misinformation regarding the safety of pork, especially given bans of pork products and restrictions (Congressional Research Service, 2010; Lucivero, n.d.). As an example, Wenig (2011) researched "consumer preferences, knowledge of and attitudes toward pork products and producers, and how crisis management issues affect the larger industry" (p. 11) in Ohio. Participants were asked about "their perception of the industry and pork purchasing habits changing with the threat of H1N1, and whether or not they thought they could get H1N1 from eating pork" (p. 40). The results revealed that participants believed the swine flu was a threat and had a negative impact on the industry, but that nearly all participants believed the pork was safe to eat.

Other reputational threats emerged through confusion over the name and nature of the H1N1 influenza. Regarding the nomenclature, Vigsø (2010) acknowledged how the name was referred to as the: Mexican flu > Swine Flu > New Flu > Novel Flu > New/Novel Flu and A(H1N1). Not only was there a lack of clarity on the name, but there was also a lack of agreement as to how the virus would behave, based on previous experiences with the 1918–1919 influenza, Asian flu, and SARS all of which originated in Europe and Asia (Nerlich & Koteyko, 2011). The fact that the A(H1N1) strain of influenza was traced to pigs, not birds, out of Mexico and that it jumped the barrier between animals and humans perplexed scientists and government agencies (Nelson, 2022), and generated uncertainty about the "rate of transmission, the best means of containment, treatment and so on" (Nerlich & Koteyko, 2011, p. 710).

Equally as perplexing was the declaration from WHO and CDC as to levels of the outbreak from four to five to six and news headlines of alarming levels and mild cases of the outbreak. Such news stories lead to speculations about "the dangers of 'under' or 'over' reporting as well as on the possibility that the outbreak may have been hyped up and by whom (governments, pharmaceutical companies or media, especially the internet itself" (Nerlich & Koteyko, 2011, p. 711).

These reputational threats and uncertainties produced psychological and physical stress for stakeholders, generated information gaps that needed to be addressed with corrective actions to ensure consumer safety, and engendered the formation of weak, minimal or strong attributions of responsibility to situational factors or level of control (Coombs, 2007).

Returning back to SCCT, Coombs (2007) recommends several crisis response strategies that align with the different levels of attributed responsibility. The one most relevant to this case study is based on adjusting information and rebuilding the organization's reputation. The reputational threats described above and stakeholders concerns related to eating pork were functions of situational factors. NBP was minimally responsible for creating the crisis but needed to reduce the psychological and physical impacts to stakeholders.

In the context of reputation management and public relations, both aim to shape public opinions of an organization during a crisis. Dora (2024) explains the subtle difference in approach between the two. PR is concerned with improving image and visibility and building media relationships. As evident from the campaign, Weber Shandwick and the other agencies distributed news releases and B-roll packages, as well as online video and audio soundbites in order to improve image of the NBP.

Reputation management encompasses enhancing the perception of an organization online by culling customer feedback, identifying threats to the organization, and managing a crisis (Rodsevich, 2024). As Coombs (2007) articulates:

> The first priority in any crisis is to protect stakeholders from harm, **not to protect the reputation** (emphasis added). Instructing information tells stakeholders what they must do to protect themselves from the *physical* threat of a crisis. Examples would be telling consumers not to eat contaminated foods ...
>
> *(p. 165)*

This strategy was integrated into the public relations campaign as consumers were surveyed. Based on feedback, messages about the safety of pork and the nature of the virus were tweaked to lessen confusion and increase confidence in buying pork products and cooking products safely. Additionally, NPB embraced social media to respond to the A(H1N1) than other organizations during the same time (Liu & Kim, 2011). Overall, the campaign was a success and the SCCT was a valuable framework for understanding how organizational reputations can be protected.

Key words

A(H1N1)
Axis Agency
Earned-first Agency
Foodborne
National Pork Board (NBP)
National Pork Producers Council (NPPC)
Lobbying
Platinum PR Awards
Pork Checkoff Program
TweetDeck (now called X Pro)
Weber Shandwick

Discussion questions

1 If you were a member of the National Pork Board and in a position to respond to the A(H1N1) health crisis, what would you do differently, if anything?
2 This case study happened at a time when social media was just beginning to be used as a communication platform for organizations. How has the use of social media changed since 2009?
3 What lessons can be learned from this case study about how to response to a health crisis?

9.3 AMERICAN PHARMACIES ALLOWED TO GIVE VACCINES IN ALL 50 STATES: INDUSTRY INITIATIVE PROMOTES CERTIFICATION AND COMMUNICATION TOOLS FOR PHARMACISTS

Situation analysis

Amid the A(H1N1) flu outbreak in 2009, all pharmacists in the U.S., Washington, D.C., and Puerto Rico were allowed to administer vaccines for the first time. Pharmacies typically offer customers wanting to get vaccinated more convenient locations, daily hours, and longer hours than local hospitals and health clinics. Other benefits for customers at most pharmacies include the ability to walk in without having to make an appointment (with some exceptions), without waiting a long time, and without paying a visit fee, all of which increases the likelihood of getting vaccinated (Bach & Goad, 2015).

Proximity of pharmacies to the U.S. population is a significant convenience factor: an estimated 90% of Americans reside within 5 miles of a pharmacy—48.1% within 1 mile, 73.1% within 2 miles, 88.9% within 5 miles, and 96.5% within 10 miles. Not surprisingly, large urban areas have the closest proximity of pharmacies while rural areas the least (Berenbrok et al., 2022). A study on the accessibility of pharmacies and pharmacists as health care providers discovered that patients go to their pharmacies nearly twice as often as they visit their physicians or other qualified health care professionals (Valliant et al., 2022).

Based in Washington, D.C., the American Pharmacists Association (APhA, 2025a) plays a vital role in the pharmacy industry and provides vaccine certifications. It describes itself as a leader in the pharmacy profession:

> by supporting pharmacists, student pharmacists, and pharmacy technicians in their role optimizing medication use and patient health outcomes and ensuring patients have access to pharmacists' care. We do this through our strong and effective advocacy, top notch education, practice tools, and resources, dissemination of evidence, and opportunities for members to engage and learn from each other. APhA is the pharmacy voice at the table in developing national guidelines, policies, and best practices that advance the profession and patient care.
>
> *(para. 2)*

APhA pharmacy-based immunization delivery certificate

The Accreditation Council for Pharmacy Education certifies APhA to offer its Pharmacy-Based Immunization Delivery certificate training program and maintains license agreements for APhA training programs to be hosted by other pharmacy associations, higher-education institutions, and pharmacy chains. The program was designed in compliance with the CDC's national standards for educating pharmacists in practice-based immunization (APhA, 2025b). APhA describes the benefits of certification: "The purpose of this certificate training program is to prepare pharmacists with comprehensive knowledge, skills, and resources necessary to provide immunization services to patients across the life span" (APhA, 2025b, para. 2).

Pharmacists and pharmacy students must complete the training program in any state for 20 credit hours of continuing education—a 12-hour interactive eLearning self-study with modules, assessments, and a video, and an 8-hour live seminar and assessment. After receiving a passing grade (70% or higher) on the self-study and final assessments, they can obtain a certification recognized in the state of their practice (APhA, 2025b). Although all states, Washington, D.C. and Puerto Rico permit pharmacists to provide vaccines, the requirements vary in numerous states, particularly who has the authorization to prescribe vaccines, and what age groups can be vaccinated and with which specific vaccines, among other possible restrictions (National Alliance of State Pharmacy Associations, 2024).

Organizations promoting vaccines

Health departments in all states, Washington, D.C., and Puerto Rico promote vaccines within their geographic locations. The Association of State and Territorial Health Officials (ASTHO) is a nonprofit focused on supporting state and territorial public health officials and senior-level health department executives. ASTHO's membership is comprised of chief health officials from each state, Washington, D.C., five U.S. territories (American Samoa, Guam, Northern Mariana Islands, Puerto Rico, and U.S. Virgin Islands), and three Freely Associated States—the Federated States of Micronesia, the Republic of Palau, and the Marshall Islands (U.S. Department of the Interior, 2019). ASTHO's (2025a) mission is: "To support, equip, and advocate for state and territorial health officials in their work of advancing the public's health and well-being" (para.4).

As a major part of the U.S. Department of Health and Human Services, CDC maintains a comprehensive website with extensive information on vaccines. CDC is responsible for setting immunizations schedules for children and adults; the process is based on feedback from the federal-level Advisory Committee on Immunization Practices that examines vaccine usage of American civilians (CDC, 2024b).

Another important player in promoting vaccines is the pharmacy itself, whether retail, regional, independent, or mail order/online. Retail chains, such as CVS and Walgreens, are the largest type of pharmacies, a third of all locations (n=21,000). A few retail chains have been evaluating ways to be more cost-effective, including closures, after acquiring numerous pharmacies. Regional pharmacies at supermarkets and consumer goods retailers account for about 30% of all pharmacies (n=16,500 locations). Independent pharmacies (n=19,500 locations) have declined by almost 50% since 1980 due to large-scale acquisitions. Mail-order and online pharmacies, which focus on prescriptions, account for approximately 500 locations (McKinsey & Company, 2023).

Communication and execution

The objective of the collective interests of APhA, ASTHO, CDC, and pharmacies is to increase the number of people receiving vaccinations. Their strategies vary based on their constituents. APhA informs and encourages pharmacists and student pharmacists to become certified. ASTHO collaborates with state and territorial health officials to promote vaccinations of their local residents. CDC keeps the public updated on various vaccines throughout the year and provides health officials with updated vaccine schedules and vaccine information. Pharmacists aim to be positioned as vaccine experts to provide immunizations and to address vaccine hesitancy and any concerns of their customers.

APhA business-to-business communication

APhA (2025a) promotes its certifications on its website that can be accessed without being a member. Pharmacy-Based Immunization Delivery certificate training program provides details on learning objectives and module details, how to obtain a certificate of completion, accreditation information, and technology requirements. The site includes links to APhA's hosts for information on certification pricing. Other useful tools for pharmacists include free downloadable Get Ready preparedness infographics, which include various health and safety topics, including the measles and flu vaccines. APhA acknowledges the accomplishments of pharmacists and pharmacies for helping to improve their community's vaccination rates with its Immunization Champion Awards (APhA, 2025c). The organization also hosts an annual conference, seminars, and other events, such as a Summer Leadership Institute.

One of the ancillary self-study modules for the immunization certificate is titled "Marketing an Immunization Program." Its learning objectives after completion of the module are to outline strategies to promote vaccination services in various media platforms, to identify free print and online materials for promotional purposes, and to understand how pharmacists can maintain strong relationships within their community to build awareness of their vaccination services (APhA, 2025a).

Public health collaboration

ASTHO collaborates with health organizations to provide effective strategies to communicate with the public and coordinate resources between pharmacies, public health organizations, and health care providers during emergencies, pandemics such as the A(H1N1), and seasonal influenza (ASTHO, 2025b).

With funding from CDC, ASTHO (2014) published a report, *Addressing communication challenges during an infectious disease emergency response: State experiences from the H1N1 pandemic*, that examines challenges faced by state health agencies during the A(H1N1) pandemic. The findings attribute communication overload as the major problem with quickly and rapidly changing data and recommendations from federal, state, and local public health offices. The report also addresses what communication tactics, processes, and shared resources could be improved during a future health crisis, such as consistent messaging and communications with internal and external stakeholders.

The communication channels employed during the pandemic included public health publications (local, state, and federal), websites, fax blasts, billboards, media coverage, and radio and television PSAs, among other tools during 2009. ASHTO's (2014) report offered suggestions for improvements for future campaigns; a few recommendations were outlined as follows:

- Be consistent in wording (such as terms related to the pandemic) and avoid conflicting messaging in all media used among health agencies on all levels. The goal would be for all agencies to share media materials efficiently.
- Utilize websites overseen by state health agencies fully by providing up-to-date prevention and guidance information, posting all news releases, and setting up tabs for various audiences (public, healthcare providers, media schools, etc.), which would allow local health agencies to link other websites as a resource hub of current information. Accurate and consistent information gains the public's trust.
- Be active on new social media platforms to reach the public with current information and to track sentiment and misinformation. State health agencies would benefit by setting up social media guidelines and policies, as well as templates and suggested hashtags, which also could be used by local agencies.
- Establish relationships with print and broadcast media within the agency's state or local community on a steady basis, so relationships are in place before a health emergency occurs.
- Prepare vaccination campaigns with unified messaging on health prevention and vaccine safety availability as early as possible. Federal public health offices can supply information to all levels to increase the public's interest and motivation to become vaccinated.

- Consider a national advertising campaign by the CDC to complement statewide and local advertising efforts. Other suggestions regarding CDC were to offer more flexibility with CDC funding for public communication campaigns and to create templates for promotional materials for local agencies to adapt to their communities. State and local agencies were encouraged to use CDC's social media web page and toolkit for developing a state and local presence on social media.

Pharmacies

The National Alliance of State Pharmacy Associations (NASPA) (2024) recommends that pharmacists organize their promotional activities for vaccines by season: year-round, back to school (May to September), travel (April to July; November to December), and influenza season (September to February). For lower cost promotions, pharmacies use readily available tools, such as on-hold phone messages, prescription labels, front window signs, in-store signage, websites, and social media, stating which vaccines are offered and when they are available (National Community Pharmacists Association, 2021). Other affordable options include hiring college students in communication fields as interns or as part of a class assignment. Developing a dialogue with customers is essential in sharing knowledge about vaccines, checking if they are up to date on scheduling, and answering any questions they may have.

Larger chain pharmacies traditionally have greater resources and can afford paid media including print, television, and online ads, and other creative solution to promote vaccines. For example, CVS offered its pharmacy staff incentives—bonuses, raffles for pizza parties and taco meals, or a day off at beach—when they surpassed immunizations targets (Williams, 2025). Earlier in 2021 when COVID-19 vaccinations were waning, CVS offered its customers (18 and older) incentives through a six-week summer sweepstakes to join after receiving a vaccination or certifying registration for one at a CVS pharmacy. Prizes include money (USD 500 or USD 5,000 for a family reunion), a trip to the Super Bowl, weeklong cruises, and USD 100 dates sponsored by a dating app (Pietsch, 2021). CVS's website posts its Immunization Media Assets with ads and imagery on its Media Library section.

As part of the COVID Collaborative, CVS Health, Walgreens, and Walmart created several PSAs on pharmacy vaccinations, with the advertising expertise of the Ad Council and public health expertise of CDC and the National Institutes of Health (Ad Council, 2021). The Ad Council's news release explains the purposes: "The content serves a dual-purpose—educating consumers directly, while also serving as a resource to help pharmacists nationwide prepare to answer questions from their own patients" (para. 5). The PSAs display pharmacists as vaccine experts answering frequently asked question about the COVID-19 vaccine.

Results

The shared goal of the organizations was to increase vaccinations—and it was achieved, despite distribution challenges and an insufficient tracking system (Institute of Medicine, 2010). Many readers may recall where they received their flu shots or COVID-19 vaccines, and many were most likely administered at pharmacies. Here are a few numbers to look at in reference to the impact that resulted from collaborations between the pharmaceutical industry, pharmacies, and government agencies, that extend beyond 2009 and the A(H1N1) pandemic:

- As part of the CDC 2009 H1N1 to Vaccine Pharmacy Initiative, the CDC directly distributed almost 5.5 million doses of the 2009 H1N1to participating pharmacy chains—10,700 retail stores nationwide (Koonin et al., 2011).
- Over 60 million individuals were vaccinated within the first three months (Institute of Medicine, 2010).
- Influenza vaccinations, which now include the A(H1N1) strain, increased at pharmacies from 3.2 million in 2007 to 20.9 million in 2013 (McConeghy & Wing, 2016).
- During the flu season, 60% to 70% of vaccines were administered at pharmacies, and flu vaccine claims for pharmacies increased 30–40% between 2018/2019 and 2022 (IQVIA Institute, 2023).
- Vaccine trends overall indicate no differences regardless of gender, race, and income. Hispanic and Asian American populations use pharmacies for vaccines more frequently than other racial/ethnic categories (IQVIA Institute, 2023).
- More than 90% of COVID-19 vaccinations were provided through pharmacies or medical centers (excluding temporary locations, government public health sites, and sites where a claim would not be generated) (IQVIA Institute, 2023).

Although studies have shown a rise in pharmacy vaccines, new numbers reflect a current rise in vaccine hesitancy. A KFF Poll (2025) discovered that trust in childhood vaccines and the school requirements is eroding:

- About 82% of parents with children under 18 state that they keep up with vaccines for their children, a decline of 8% from 2023.
- About 17% delay or skip shots for their children, a rise of 10% from 2023.
- About 26% of Republican parents skip or delay their children's vaccine, a rise of 13% in 2023.

This insight is important as pharmacists during the 2009 pandemic were "trusted members of the community" (ASTHO, 2009, p. 4). The success of the vaccination campaign and the subsequent behavior change to get vaccinated within pharmacies would not have happened without the public's confidence and trust in pharmacies and pharmacists to provide vaccines.

Theoretical framework

Trust is an important factor during health crises, epidemics and pandemics (Seeger & Seeger, 2023). In times of uncertainty, it becomes difficult to know who or what organizations to trust in providing information about risks, safety, vaccinations, prevention, and other health behaviors (Larson & Heymann, 2010). Building trust with stakeholders, clients, other organizations and community members *before* a pandemic hits is essential for ensuring that individuals get and heed important safety messages. When trust is not established or when messages are unclear or inconsistent, distrust develops and breeds a lack of confidence in the source, confusion, and hesitancy to accept or comply with recommendations, which prevents individuals from receiving life-saving measures like vaccines (Siegrist & Zingg, 2013).

The challenge with understanding trust and how to operationalize it, especially during pandemics, is that there is no generally accepted theory (Quinn et al., 2013). However, some general agreed-upon theoretical and communication-based concepts can be applied to this case study: clarity, compassion, competence, confidence, and credibility.

In the midst of a pandemic, the population "lacks understandable, dependable, and timely information about the outbreak. Social and institutional trust that provides legitimacy to policymakers' actions might be undermined because of lack of reliable and truth information" (Mesch & Schwirian, 2015, p. 1161). Therefore, clearly communicating information is necessary. *Clarity* refers to the quality of information disseminated and whether the messages created for intended audiences are clearly communicated, easily understood, digested, timely, and transparent "describing what is known or unknown, and providing concrete recommendations for behavior" (Quinn et al., 2013, p. 97). Clarity of information is essential for individuals to make choices and for building trusting relationships (Larson & Heymann, 2010), especially with spokespersons and other health officials like pharmacists. Mullen (2009) acknowledged the efforts of pharmacists in undertaking the vaccination campaign, reminding them why clear communication to pharmacy patrons is necessary:

> Your patients or their parents may be confused, particularly as recommendations for community mitigation efforts (such as school closures)

> change with the evolving situation … By sorting through the hype and misinformation that can abound in times of apparent uncertainty, you can be a trusted health resource for your patients.
>
> *(p. 723)*

Compassion can be defined as the care and concern exhibited for customers and stakeholders (Quinn et al., 2013) and how well an organization or government has listened to their needs and vaccine concerns, answered questions, and corrected any misinformation (Shen & Tan, 2022). This quality has also been referred to as fiduciary responsibility in which individuals, organizations and governments are acting on behalf of and in the best interests of society during a pandemic (Freimuth et al., 2014; Mesch & Schwirian, 2015; Quinn et al., 2013). The roles and responsibilities of pharmacies and pharmacists shifted during this pandemic. They became health care providers for services and products and deliverers of information, interventions, and prevention services like vaccinations, through a care model—ASPIRE—that recommends responding to questions, actively listening, empathizing and understanding concerns (Shen & Tan, 2022).

The concept of *confidence* has dual connotations in this case study; confidence or trust in "the federal government's ability to respond effectively to an outbreak of swine flu" (Mesch & Schwirian, 2015, p. 1161) and vaccine confidence "defined as trust in the vaccine itself, in providers who administer vaccines, and in the process that leads to vaccine licensure and the recommended vaccination schedule" (Shen & Tan, 2022, p. 306). *Competence* and *credibility*, the last two Cs, are similar to confidence but differ in subtle ways. Competence has to do with the skills and abilities of health officials and organizations to manage the pandemic and the extent to which the actions of government in response to swine flu are in the best interests of protecting society (Freimuth et al., 2014). Credibility is perceived by others and granted when spokespersons are trustworthy role models and experts (Quinn et al., 2013; Shen & Tan, 2022). Confidence, competency, and credibility are all interrelated, as explained by Shen and Tan (2022):

> Building confidence requires a collective effort from all healthcare providers who engage with patients and communities. Pharmacists' confidence in these areas and their ability to communicate effectively to the community is a key factor to building vaccine confidence. Pharmacists are … key actors involved in establishing, maintaining, and building confidence in vaccines because their credibility (expertise, trustworthiness, caring) can influence whether individuals accept health advice
>
> *(p. 306)*

The collaboration between APhA, ASTHO, CDC, and pharmacies to increase vaccinations was successful in part due to the trust instilled in the industry, government, and organizations. APhA's training prepared both pharmacists and pharmacies to maintain strong relationships within their community to build awareness of their vaccination services. ASHTO and CDC collaborated to ensure consistent messaging and communications with internal and external stakeholders. Pharmacists and pharmacies tapped into their core competencies—"counseling patients, accurate dispensing of medication, vaccine administration, and electronic documentation and reporting" (Mullen, 2009, p. 722) and met the needs of their local communities by answering the call, "offering convenience, accessibility, extended hours of operation, and health professionals who [were knowledgeable and] are licensed to vaccinate" (Shen & Tan, 2022, p. 305).

Key words

Ad Council
Advisory Committee on Immunization Practices
American Pharmacists Association
Association of State and Territorial Health Officials
Pharmacy-Based Immunization Delivery Certificate

Discussion questions

1 Where do you prefer to get your vaccinations—at a doctor's office, medical facility/clinic, or the pharmacy? Provide reasons for your choice.
2 What do you think contributed to the rise in public confidence and trust in pharmacists?
3 What other communication methods could pharmacists use to promote vaccines to their customers?

References

ABC News. (2009, October 15). *Pork industry still reeling from swine flu*. https://abcnews.go.com/Business/pork-industry-reeling-swine-flu/story?id=8840004
Ad Council. (2021, March 19). *CVS Health, Walgreens and Walmart join together with the Ad Council and COVID Collaborative to educate Americans about the COVID-19 vaccines*. [News release]. https://www.adcouncil.org/press-releases/cvs-health-walgreens-and-walmart-join-together-with-the-ad-council-and-covid-collaborative-to-educate-americans-about-the-covid-19-vaccines
APhA. (2025a). *About APhA*. https://www.pharmacist.com/who-we-are
APhA. (2025b). *Pharmacy-Based Immunization Delivery*. https://www.pharmacist.com/Education/Certificate-Training-Programs/Immunization
APhA. (2025c, February 20). *APhA announces 2025 Immunization Champion Award winners*. [News release]. https://www.pharmacist.com/APhA-Press-Releases/apha-announces-2025-immunization-champion-award-winners

ASHTO. (2009, September 16). *Operational framework for partnering with pharmacies for administration of 2009 H1N1 vaccine*. https://eziz.org/PDF/ASHTOH1N1Pharmacies.pdf

ASTHO. (2014). *Addressing communication challenges during an infectious disease emergency response: State experiences from the H1N1 pandemic*. https://stacks.cdc.gov/view/cdc/140843

ASTHO. (2025a). *About us*. https://www.astho.org/about/

ASTHO. (2025b). *Influenza*. https://www.astho.org/topic/infectious-disease/influenza/

Bach, A. T., & Goad, J. A. (2015). The role of community pharmacy-based vaccination in the USA: Current practice and future directions. *Integrated Pharmacy Research & Practice*, *4*, 67–77. https://doi.org/10.2147/IPRP.S63822

Baldo, V., Bertoncello, C., Cocchio, S., Fonzo, M., Pillon, P., Buja, A., & Baldovin, T. (2016). The new pandemic influenza A/(H1N1)pdm09 virus: is it really "new"? *Journal of Preventive Medicine and Hygiene*, *57*(1), E19–E22.

Berenbrok, L. A., Tang, S., Gabriel, N., Guo, J., Sharareh, N., Patel, N., Dickson, S., & Hernandez, I. (2022). Access to community pharmacies: A nationwide geographic information systems cross-sectional analysis. *Journal of the American Pharmacists Association*, *62*(6),1816–1822. DOI: 10.1016/j.japh.2022.07.003

CDC. (2019, June 11). *2009 H1N1 Pandemic (H1N1pdm09 virus)*. [CDC Archives]. https://archive.cdc.gov/www_cdc_gov/flu/pandemic-resources/2009-h1n1-pandemic.html

CDC. (2024a, March 22). *About Influenza in Swine (Pigs)*. https://www.cdc.gov/swine-flu/about/influenza-in-swine.html

CDC. (2024b, December 16). *General committee-related information*. https://www.cdc.gov/acip/about/index.html

Congressional Research Service. (2010, January 12). *Potential farm sector effects of 2009 H1N1 "Swine Flu": Questions and answers*. (CRS Report No. R40575). https://crsreports.congress.gov/

Coombs, W. T. (2007). Protecting organization reputations during a crisis: The development and application of Situational Crisis Communication Theory. *Corporate Reputation Review*, *10*(3), 163–176. DOI: 10.1057/palgrave.crr.1550049

DataReportal, We Are Social, & Meltwater. (2025, February). Percentage of population using the internet in the United States from 2000 to 2025. [Graph]. In *Statista*. https://www.statista.com/statistics/209117/us-internet-penetration/

Desmon, S. (2009, Sept. 24). Even celebs get swine flu. *Baltimore Sun*. https://www.baltimoresun.com/2009/09/24/even-celebs-get-swine-flu/

Dora, Z. (2024, May 17). *Reputation PR: Effective strategies & management tips (w/examples)*. https://prowly.com/magazine/reputation-pr/

ECDC. (2009, October 8). *Questions and answers on the pandemic (H1N1) 2009*. https://www.ecdc.europa.eu/en/seasonal-influenza/2009-influenza-h1n1-faq

Food and Agricultural Organization of the United Nations. (2009, April 27). *FAO acts over H1N1 human crisis*. https://www.fao.org/newsroom/detail/FAO-acts-over-H1N1-human-crisis/en

Freimuth, V. S., Musa, D., Hilyard, K., Quinn, S. C., & Kim, K. (2014). Trust during the early stages of the 2009 H1N1 pandemic. *Journal of Health Communication*, *19*, 321–339. DOI: 10.1080/10810730.2013.811323

Frenck, R. W. Jr. (2023, August 4). *Swine flu: Facts for families*. https://www.healthychildren.org/English/health-issues/conditions/flu/Pages/swine-flu-facts-for-families.aspx

Greyser, S. A. (2009). Corporate brand reputation and brand crisis management. *Management Decision*,*47*(4), 590–602. DOI: 10.1108/00251740910959431

Haga, C. (2009, September 25). H1N1 flu scare hits pork industry. *Grand Forks Herald*, *A1*. https://www.proquest.com/newspapers/h1n1-flu-scare-hits-pork-industry/docview/376047293/se-2

IDC. (2024, April 15). *Worldwide smartphone market up 7.8% in the first quarter of 2024 as Samsung moves back into the top position, according to IDC Tracker* [News release]. https://www.idc.com/getdoc.jsp?containerId=prUS52032524

Institute of Medicine (US). (2010). *The 2009 H1N1 influenza vaccination campaign: Summary of a workshop series.* [Forum on medical and public health preparedness for catastrophic events—Vaccine distribution]. National Academies Press. https://www.ncbi.nlm.nih.gov/books/NBK54182/

IQVIA Institute. (2023, January 13). *Trends in Vaccine Administration in the United States.* https://www.iqvia.com/insights/the-iqvia-institute/reports-and-publications/reports/trends-in-vaccine-administration-in-the-united-states

ITU. (2021, November 26). Share of households with a computer at home worldwide from 2005 to 2019. [Graph]. In *Statista.* https://www.statista.com/statistics/748551/worldwidehouseholds-with-computer/

ITU. (2024). *Individuals using the internet * (in billions).* [Graph]. https://www.itu.int/en/ITU-D/Statistics/Pages/stat/default.aspx

Jilani, T. N., Jamil, R. T., Nguyen, A. D., & Siddiqui, A. H. (2024). *H1N1 influenza. StatPearls Publishing.* https://www.ncbi.nlm.nih.gov/books/NBK513241/

Jobs, S. (2020). Transcript: Steve Jobs-Apple CEO. [Full transcript]. *Singju Post.* https://singjupost.com/wp-content/uploads/2014/07/Steve-Jobs-iPhone-2007-Presentation-Full-Transcript.pdf

KFF Poll. (2025, January 28). *Trust in public health agencies and vaccines falls amid republican skepticism.* [News release]. https://www.kff.org/health-information-trust/press-release/poll-trust-in-public-health-agencies-and-vaccines-falls-amid-republican-skepticism/

Koonin, L. M., Beauvais, D. R., Shimabukuro, T., Wortley, P. M., Palmier, J. B., Stanley, T. R., Theofilos, J., & Merlin, T. L. (2011). CDC's 2009 H1N1 vaccine pharmacy initiative in the United States: Implications for future public health and pharmacy collaborations for emergency response. *Disaster Medicine and Public Health Preparedness*, *5*(4), 253–255. https://doi.org/10.1001/dmp.2011.83

Langham, T. (2019). *Reputation management: The future of corporate communications and public relations.* Emerald Publishing Limited.

Larson, H. J., & Heymann, D. L. (2010, January 20). Public health response to influenza A (H1N1) as an opportunity to build public trust. *Journal of the American Medical Association*, *303*(3), 271–272.

Liu, B. F., & Kim, S. (2011). How organizations framed the 2009 H1N1 pandemic via social and traditional media: Implications for U.S. health communicators. *Public Relations Review*, *37*, 233–244. DOI:10.1016/j.pubrev.2011.03.005

Lucivero, M. (n.d.). *Swine flu scare causes some countries to ban pork products.* https://fpa.org/swine-flu-scares-causes-some-countries-to-ban-pork-imports/

McConeghy, K. W., & Wing, C. (2016, June 24). A national examination of pharmacy-based immunization statutes and their association with influenza vaccinations and preventive health. *Vaccine*, *34*(30), 3463–3468. https://doi.org/10.1016/j.vaccine.2016.04.076

McFadden, C. (2025, May 15). The long and short chronological history of social media. *Interesting Engineering.* https://interestingengineering.com/lists/a-chronological-history-of-social-media

McKinsey & Company. (2023, March). *Meeting changing consumer needs: The US retail pharmacy of the future.* [Healthcare Practice report]. https://www.mckinsey.com/industries/healthcare/our-insights/meeting-changing-consumer-needs-the-us-retail-pharmacy-of-the-future#/

Mesch, G. S., & Schwirian, K. P. (2015). Social and political determinants of vaccine hesitancy: Lessons learned from the H1N1 pandemic of 2099-2010. *American Journal of Infection Control*, *43*, 1161–1165. http://dx.doi.org/10.1016/j.ajic.2015.06.031

Mullen, E. (2009, November/December). Pandemic H1N1 influenza virus: Academy perspectives on pharmacy's critical role in treatment, prevention. *Journal of the American Pharmacists Association*, 49(6), 722–723. DOI: 10.1331/JAPhA.2009.09539

NASPA. (2024, September 3). *Pharmacist and pharmacy technician vaccination authority*. https://naspa.us/blog/resource/2024-pharmacist-immunization-authority/

National Community Pharmacists Association. (2021). *A guide to implementing vaccine services in community pharmacy*. https://ncpa.org/sites/default/files/2021-09/2021_NCPAPfizerVaccinationBooklet_Final.pdf

National Pork Producers Council. (2025). *About NPPC*. https://nppc.org/about-nppc/

Nelson, M. (2022, January). The hunt for a pandemic's origins. The Scientist Digest, 1. https://www.the-scientist.com/the-hunt-for-a-pandemic-s-origins-69502

Nerlich, B., & Koteyko, N. (2012). Crying wolf? Biosecurity and metacommunication in the context of the 2009 swine flu pandemic. *Health & Place*, *18*, 710–717. DOI:10.1016/j.healthplace.2011.02.008

Nuortimo, K., Harkonen, J., & Breznik, K. (2024, October). Exploring corporate reputation and crisis communication. *Journal of Marketing Analytics*. https://doi.org/10.1057/s41270-024-00353-8

Pew Research Center. (2024, January 31). *Mobile fact sheet*. https://www.pewresearch.org/internet/fact-sheet/mobile/

Pietsch, B. (2021, May 27). As U.S. vaccinations slump, CVS offers cruises, money and a Super Bowl trip to get a shot. *New York Times*. https://www.nytimes.com/2021/05/27/world/cvs-coronavirus-vaccines.html

Pork Checkoff. (2025a). *About Pork Checkoff*. https://porkcheckoff.org/about/

Pork Checkoff. (2025b). *100% Real Pork*. https://porkcheckoff.org/pork-branding/pork-brands/real-pork/

Pork Checkoff. (2025c). *The Other White Meat®*. https://porkcheckoff.org/pork-branding/pork-brands/the-other-white-meat-brand/

Prandi, L., & Primiero, G. (2020). Effects of misinformation diffusion during a pandemic. *Applied Science Network*, *5*(82), 1–20. https://doi.org/10.1007/s41109-020-00327-6

PRovoke Media. (2010, February 3). *Protecting pork sales during the "swine flu" pandemic*. [Holmes Report]. https://www.provokemedia.com/latest/article/protecting-pork-sales-during-the-swine-flu-pandemic

Quinn, S. C., Parmer, J., Freimuth, V. S., Hilyard, K. M., Musa, D., & Kim, K. H. (2013). Exploring communication, trust in government, and vaccination intention later in the 2009 H1N1 pandemic: Results of a national survey. *Biosecurity and Bioterrorism: Biodefense Strategy, Practice and Science*, *11*(2), 96–106. DOI: 10.1089/bsp.2012.0048

Reuters. (2009a, May 6). *WHO casts wary eye on meat, blood of H1N1-infected pigs*. https://www.reuters.com/article/economy/who-casts-wary-eye-on-meat-blood-of-h1n1-infected-pigs-idUSHKG219102/

Reuters. (2009b, May 7). *WHO says no to infection risks from eating pork*. https://www.reuters.com/article/business/healthcare-pharmaceuticals/who-says-no-infection-risks-from-eating-pork-idUSTRE5464VD/

Rodsevich, M. (2024, October 4). *Reputation management PR: The insider's guide*. https://prlab.co/blog/reputation-management-pr-guide/

Samsung Wiki. (n.d.). *Samsung Galaxy GT-I7500*. https://samsung.fandom.com/wiki/Samsung_Galaxy_GT-I7500

Seeger, M. W., & Seeger, H. S. (2023). Pandemic communication: CDC and WHO approaches to emergency risk communication and emerging infectious disease crises. In s. M. Croucher & A. Diers-Lawson, *Pandemic communication*, (pp. 59–78). Routledge. DOI:10.4324/9781003214496-4

Shen, A. K., & Tan, A. S. L. (2022). Trust, influence and community: Why pharmacists and pharmacies are central for addressing vaccine hesitancy. *Journal of the American Pharmacists Association*, 62, 305–308. https://doi.org/10.1016/j.japh.2021.10.001

Siegrist, M., & Zingg, A. (2013). The role of public trust during pandemics. *European Psychologist*, *19*(1), 23–32. DOI: 10.1027/1016-9040/a000169

U.S. Department of the Interior. (2019, July 23). *Freely Associated States*. https://www.doi.gov/ocl/freely-associated-states

U.S. Energy Information Administration. (2011, March 28). Distribution of U.S. households with computers in 2009, by number of computers per household *(in millions) [Graph]. In *Statista*. https://www.statista.com/statistics/187606/average-number-of-computers-per-household-in-the-united-states/

USDA. (n.d.). *National Pork Board*. https://www.ams.usda.gov/rules-regulations/research-promotion/pork

USDA. (2011, May 25). *Cooking meat? Check the new recommended temperatures*. https://www.usda.gov/about-usda/news/blog/cooking-meat-check-new-recommended-temperatures

Valliant, S. N., Burbage, S. C., Pathak, S., & Urick, B. Y. (2022, January). Pharmacists as accessible health care providers: Quantifying the opportunity. *Journal of Managed Care & Specialty Pharmacy*, *28*(1), 85–90. https://doi.org/10.18553/jmcp.2022.28.1.85

Weber Shandwick. (2023). *About*. [LinkedIn profile]. https://www.linkedin.com/company/weber-shandwick/

Wenig, S. N. (2011). *Perceptions of the pork industry and agriculture practices related to agricultural crisis communication and media use*. [Master's thesis, Ohio State University]. OhioLINK Electronic Theses and Dissertations Center. http://rave.ohiolink.edu/etdc/view?acc_num=osu1298482572

WHO. (2010, August 10). *H1N1 in post-pandemic period: Director-General's opening statement at virtual press conference*. https://www.who.int/news/item/10-08-2010-h1n1-in-post-pandemic-period

WHO. (2015, May 15). *World Health Organization best practices for the naming of new human infectious diseases*. https://www.who.int/publications/i/item/WHO-HSE-FOS-15.1

Wikimedia Foundation. (n.d.). *Home page*. https://wikimediafoundation.org/

Williams, A. (2025, May 21). CVS staff get perks like beach days and donuts for hitting vaccine goals. *Live Now Fox*. https://www.livenowfox.com/news/cvs-vaccine-incentives

10

CASE STUDIES ON THE COVID-19 (CORONAVIRUS DISEASE) PANDEMIC, 2019 TO PRESENT

10.1 INTRODUCTION: COVID-19 IN CONTEXT

Unlike most of the other case studies in this book, readers of the COVID-19 pandemic generation have firsthand familiarity with this public health crisis. However, they may be unaware of the worldwide impact and other complexities, as well as the variety of communication campaigns in the U.S. and abroad. The coronavirus disease, widely referred to as COVID-19, has been the most severe pandemic since the 1918–1919 influenza. Since the discovery of COVID-19 in Wuhan, China, in December 2019 to August 2024, approximately 776 million cases worldwide have been reported (WHO, 2024a) and almost 7.1 million people have died (WHO, 2024b) while 67% of the global population has been vaccinated with the complete primary series and 32% with one booster (WHO, 2023a). In May 2023, WHO declared that COVID-19 was no longer a global public health emergency (WHO, 2023b). Since many countries have stopped reporting COVID data, WHO (n.d.) continues to monitor the virus worldwide and maintains a dashboard with data updated weekly on a global and regional basis on cases, deaths, and vaccinations. CDC (n.d.) provides current data and trends on COVID-19 in the U.S. that is updated weekdays.

Readers also may have firsthand experience with COVID-19 by catching the virus, knowing others who have been infected, or hearing stories of survivorship. COVID-19 celebrity survivors include actors and entertainers Antonio Banderas, Hugh Grant, Tom Hanks, Neil Patrick Harris, Alyssa Milano, Dwayne "The Rock" Johnson, Khloé Kardashian, and Tony Shalhoub; TV show personalities Ellen DeGeneres and Sharon

DOI: 10.4324/9781003434382-10

Osbourne; musician Sir Elton John; soccer player Cristiano Ronaldo; royals King Charles III and Prince William of the U.K.; and politicians Boris Johnson, former U.K. prime minister, Donald Trump, 45th and 47th U.S. president, and his wife, Melania Trump (Hollimon, 2022).

Influential and accomplished people in the arts and other areas lost their lives to COVID-19, such as chef Floyd Cardoz; actors Cloris Leachman and Dawn Wells; magician Roy Horn of Siegfried & Roy; musicians Trini Lopez, Ellis Marsalis, Jr., Meat Loaf, Mike Longo, Phil Spector, and Adam Schlesinger; politician General Colin Powell; baseball pitcher Tom Seaver; disc jockey Kay Slay; and fashion designer Kenzo Takada (Sánchez, 2022).

Transmission and symptoms

COVID-19 is highly contagious. Infected people can spread the virus through oral or nasal droplets by sneezing, coughing, or talking within six feet of healthy individuals who can inhale the droplets. In addition, healthy people can contract the virus by touching surfaces or objects infected by ill people and then touch their faces before they wash their hands. The contamination period lasts a few hours to a few days (CDC, 2020).

Most people feel flu-like symptoms within five to six days after being infected. Symptoms usually last one day to two weeks. Other symptoms may include fatigue, headaches, dizziness, chest pain, and persistent coughs, as well as a loss of appetite, and sense of touch and smell. Those with preexisting health conditions, such as HIV, diabetes, cancer, and chronic heart and respiratory issues, and people taking prescribed immunosuppressive medications face higher risks and may need to be hospitalized (WHO, 2023c). Severe cases can result in "respiratory failure, sepsis, thromboembolism (blood clots), and multiorgan failure, including injury of the heart, liver or kidneys, and death" (WHO, 2023c, para. 13). Some individuals who contract COVID-19 may experience long-term symptoms called post COVID-19 condition or long COVID that cause tiredness, breathing problems, and cognitive impairment (WHO, 2023c).

Prevention and treatment

When COVID-19 was rapidly spreading around the globe, the U.S. and other countries went into lockdown, except South Korea as covered in Case Study 10.3. Public health officials provided updates and many mandated closures. Educational classroom instruction of all levels went from in-person to online for students in households with computers or smartphones. Business offices temporarily shut down while staff telecommuted. Restaurants and stores provided delivery services or shut down temporarily. Cultural institutions like theaters and museums closed for months, as explored in Case Study 10.2. Essential services such as pharmacies, hospitals, medical clinics, and grocery stores remained operational while requiring that people wear masks and follow social distancing. The tourism industry tanked as people stayed home while being afraid of potentially contagious environments on airplanes or cruise ships.

In addition to wearing masks and maintaining a distance of six feet from others, people followed other preventive measures to avoid catching the virus or spreading it to others; for example, washing one's hands for 20 seconds or using hand sanitizers; cleaning frequently touched surfaces regularly; discarding tissues after coughing or sneezing; and avoiding sitting next to people and going to places with large crowds (i.e., superspreader events). Infected people isolated themselves in a safe location until they became well; people who had been in close encounters with COVID-infected individuals also isolated themselves until they received the test results (CDC, 2020).

Getting tested for COVID-19 is an important first step. During the height of the pandemic, emergency testing facilities were set up at parking lots, shopping malls, and other accessible places for the public. Pharmacies and health clinics offered COVID-19 testing in person and self-administered at-home testing kits. COVID-19 vaccines provide strong protection against serious illness, hospitalization, and death (CDC, 2024a). As vaccines and subsequent boosters were becoming available, people were able to experience a greater sense of normalcy with places reopening and fear of dying from COVID-19 subsided. Many locations still required people to wear masks and keep their distance from others. Some institutions required students and employees to be vaccinated, resulting in backlash from antivaxxers. Although vaccines can help prevent severe illness, hospitalization, and death, they cannot stop the recurrence of COVID-19 after infection. In addition, infected people, whether vaccinated or unvaccinated, can still spread the virus to healthy people.

Widely used communication tools and issues

The COVID-19 pandemic became an infodemic with public health organizations combatting misinformation. As social media companies struggled to deal with misleading information about COVID-19 and other issues, people turned to social media for news, with Facebook being the primary source, followed by YouTube and Twitter (Shearer & Mitchell, 2021). Myths emerged about how COVID-19 spread in water while swimming; side effects of alcohol-based hand sanitizers; glove wearing instead of hand sanitizing; vitamins as preventive methods; and mask wearing causing CO2 intoxication or deficient oxygen, among others (WHO, 2022a).

The most dangerous myth—using cleaning disinfectants to prevent or cure COVID-19—was suggested by the U.S. president. At a White House briefing in 2020, President Trump implied that ingesting a disinfectant may prevent COVID-19. Although he did not suggest a brand name, Lysol quickly issued a statement about the dangers of internal consumption of its product (Clark, 2020). The next day, Trump claimed his remarks on disinfectants were "sarcasm" (Timm, 2020).

Vaccination disinformation also contributed to the infodemic. Claims spread that the COVID-19 vaccines cause infertility, contain microchips to make people magnetic and trackable, and alter people's DNA, as well as its ingredients contain metals and aborted fetal cells (CDC, 2024b). KFF, a public health research nonprofit formerly known as the Kaiser Family Foundation, found that 67% of unvaccinated adults held strong beliefs about one of the vaccine myths, with 36% believing that getting the COVID-19 vaccine itself causes the virus (Altman, 2021).

The Biden White House administration encouraged Facebook and social media sites to take down disinformation about COVID-19 vaccinations in 2021. Surgeon General Dr. Vivek Murthy issued his first official advisory on misleading tech and social media content and stated at a White House press briefing: "Modern technology companies have enabled misinformation to poison our information environment, with little accountability to their users" (Stolberg & Alba, 2021, para.7). President Biden responded to reporters asking about social media COVID-19 disinformation: "Look, the only pandemic we have is among the unvaccinated" (Miller, 2021, para. 4), when mostly all deaths were among the unvaccinated at a time when the vaccine supply in the U.S. was abundant (Johnson & Stobbe, 2021).

Almost 68% of the global population was connected online in 2024, with the greatest regional internet penetration in Canada (94%), U.S. (93.1%), and Europe (91.2%), and a number of individual countries in the Arabian Peninsula and Europe were at or close to 100% penetration (World Population Review, 2025).

Although slightly more than half of U.S. adults sought out news on social media, viewership of TV news increased or remained stable due to significant news in 2020—the COVID-19 pandemic, the presidential race and election, and large-scale social justice protests. Fox News, MSNBC, and CNN received more viewers than network news (ABC, CBS, and NBC) experienced during major events, a collective 46% rise in day audiences and 51% during primetime over the previous year (Potter, 2020).

U.S. daily newspapers' circulation in 2020 continued to drop, with a 6% decrease in weekday print and digital circulations over the previous year (Barthel, 2021). Consumer magazines grew with 7,416 print editions, up from their previous peak in 2012 with 7,390 magazines in circulation since 2002 (MPA, 2021). Public service announcements to educate the public about the pandemic about preventive measures and vaccinations were widely used worldwide. Case study 10.4 shows a variety of creative video PSAs from Peru, Mexico, and Vietnam.

Artificial intelligence (AI) made its debut in November 2022, three years after COVID-19 began, with its ChatGPT demo that brought in in over one million users in five days (Marr, 2023).

Impact

As of 2025, the COVID-19 pandemic has subsided but is not yet over. The director-general of WHO declared in May 2023: "It is therefore with great hope that I declare COVID-19 over as a global health emergency. However, that does not mean COVID-19 is over as a global health threat" (WHO, 2023d, paras. 17–18).

The pandemic's impact has been far-reaching and lingering, affecting the economy, education, mental health, and other areas. Racial discrimination and hate crimes increased in parts of the world, primarily affecting Asians after COVID-19 spread from China. United Nations Secretary-General António Guterres pled to end hate speech and summed up the situation in a statement (United Nations, 2020):

> COVID-19 does not care who we are, where we live, what we believe or about any other distinction. We need every ounce of solidarity to tackle it together. Yet the pandemic continues to unleash a tsunami of hate and xenophobia, scapegoating and scare-mongering.
>
> *(para. 2)*

End Violence and Racism Against ESEA Communities (EVR), a London-based advocacy organization now called the Sesame Organisation, reported a 300% rise in hate crimes and discriminatory racial incidents against East and Southeast Asian communities in the U.K. during the first quarter of 2020 in comparison to the previous year (U.K. Parliament Committees, 2021). The Center for the Study of Hate & Extremism at California State University, San Bernardino, determined that anti-Asian hate crimes rose 164% in first quarter 2021 based on reported incidents in 16 of the largest cities and counties in the U.S. over the same time last year (Levin, 2021).

A director of the International Monetary Fund described the economic impact within the first year of COVID-19: "This makes the Great Lockdown the worst recession since the Great Depression, and far worse than the Global Financial Crisis" (Gopinath, 2020, para. 3). Readers may recall the impact the pandemic had on themselves, friends, family, and relatives during a time of layoffs, bankruptcies, and closures, as well as the impact on businesses, particularly airlines, hotels, resorts, restaurants, and cruise lines tanking with an abrupt loss of business. As one of the major global industries, travel and tourism amounted to 10% of the global GDP with over 320 million jobs before the pandemic. Tourist arrivals worldwide during the first half of 2020 declined by over 65%, severely impacting the overall industry and particularly tourism-dependent economies such as the Caribbean islands (Behsudi, 2020).

Many educational institutions—nursery schools, elementary and high schools, colleges, and universities—were closed or partially open, or switched to TV, radio, or online courses in many parts of the world. Students returning to school experienced slow transitions with hybrid learning, preventive measures such as social distancing, vaccination and quarantine requirements, and cancellation of extracurriculars, large-scale events, and study abroad programs. McKinsey & Company, a global management consultancy, estimated that educational disruptions during the pandemic could result in yearly losses of USD 1.6 trillion globally by 2040 (Bryant et al., 2022).

WHO (2022b) estimated that the pandemic caused a 25% rise in mental health issues, primarily anxiety and depression, around the globe. The reasons were numerous—loneliness and social isolation for people of all ages, fear of contagion, loss of loved ones, strained relationships with families and colleagues, and financial losses and limited job opportunities, among others.

Health inequities increased during the pandemic due to financial losses, health care access, and other reasons. Case study 10.5 shows how Australia and New Zealand created culturally appropriate campaigns to reach its Indigenous populations, with many residing in remote areas.

10.2 ENGAGING PEOPLE WITH ART: "GETTY MUSEUM CHALLENGE" SPARKS CREATIVITY DURING PANDEMIC LOCKDOWN

Situation analysis

Lockdown during COVID-19 impacted cultural institutions worldwide from museums and galleries to historic monuments and UNESCO heritage sites. Museums were particularly hard hit, with about 90% (85,000 museums worldwide) closing their doors temporarily for the public health safety of their visitors and employees (UNESCO, 2020). Closures resulted in financial losses due to a steep drop in tourism, museum admission fees and gift shop purchases, and a decline in public and donor funding. UNESCO noted the location of museums is unevenly distributed worldwide, with 65% of museums in North America and Western Europe. Museums with digitalized imagery of their collections and a strong online and social presence were at an enormous advantage unlike museums in Africa and Small Island Developing States (Cuba, Haiti, and Mauritius, for example) that comprise 5% of museums with online content (UNESCO, 2020). The International Council of Museums (2021) reported that "the Covid-19 crisis has changed museums' perception of the digital world forever, highlighting existing issues and accelerating changes that were already underway" (p. 17).

UNESCO (2020) also reported how staff at some museums became resilient and embraced creativity during lockdown to reach their audiences via their websites and social media. The "Getty Museum Challenge" in Los Angeles encouraged public participation with the museum's art collections online, which drew extensive traditional media exposure. Other museums developed challenges, games, and engagement activities for adults and children during lockdown.

Unlike many museums which may be supported by state or governmental funds (Khlystova et al., 2022), the Getty Museum in Los Angeles is fortunate that the J. Paul Getty Trust—a large and wealthy arts organization—funds its operations by offering free admission, numerous public programs, and grants to Los Angeles students, among other initiatives (Influence Watch, 2024). Getty Trust leadership also vouched to pay salaries and benefits of hourly and salaried employees during the pandemic (without stating a specific time limit). To help the local art community, Getty Trust set up a USD 10 million COVID-19 relief fund to provide support to small, mid-sized nonprofit museums and visual arts organizations in Los Angeles (Getty, 2020).

The Getty describes its mission as "a leading global arts organization committed to exhibiting, conserving, and understanding the world's artistic and cultural heritage" (Getty, n.d.a., para. 1). Named after J. Paul Getty (1892–1976), an art collector, oil industrialist, and philanthropist, who set up the J. Paul Getty Trust in 1953, the Getty is considered "one of the world's largest cultural and philanthropic institutions dedicated to the visual arts" (Getty, n.d.b., para. 1). The first Getty Museum was a part of Mr. Getty's Pacific Palisades home on the Malibu coast that displayed his art collection, which expanded and later required construction of a larger museum called the Getty Villa on the same 64-acre estate. Getty Villa, a re-creation of ancient Roman villas, opened to the public in 1974.

After Mr. Getty's death in 1976, the Getty Trust continued to fulfill Mr. Getty's vision "to establish an institution that served all facets of the art world, including research, display, conservation, publishing, grants, and education" (Getty, n.d.b., para. 3). An important development was the Getty Center built on a 110-acre hilltop on the Santa Monica Mountains in Los Angeles. Opened to the public in 1997, the Center contains the Getty Museum, along with a library, research institutions, foundation, and conservation institute. Today, the Getty continues to operate two museums: Getty Museum in Los Angeles, displaying Medieval to contemporary art, as part of the Getty Center; and Getty Villa Museum in Pacific Palisades, focusing on Greek and Roman art and culture (Getty, n.d.c).

Communication programming and execution

The Getty Museum's campaign had two objectives: 1) connect its extensive art collections and digital presence with people in an entertaining and positive way during the initial disruptions of life during the pandemic and 2) build awareness of its rebranded social media platforms and its digital library of artwork (Shorty Awards, 2021). The "Getty Museum Challenge" was created to encourage people to re-create works of art from its database using found items from their homes. The timing was important as the campaign began in late March 2020, a few weeks after Los Angeles' lockdown began when people were adjusting to remote employment and education amid shutdowns of stores, restaurants, cultural attractions, and public events.

Getty's staff was inspired by the Netherland's "Tussen Kunst & Quarantaine" ("Between Art and Quarantine") stay-at-home re-creation challenge on its Instagram account, but staff developed their own challenge by encouraging anyone to access Getty's Open Content Program with a digitalized collection of over 160,000 high-resolution images of works of art for free use (Getty, n.d.d.). The campaign's primary objectives were to bolster interaction creatively with its museum-goers and other art enthusiasts during the pandemic and to build awareness of its newly rebranded social media platforms and Open Content Program (Shorty Awards, 2021).

Getty's entry submission to the Shorty Awards (2021) for best hashtag provided background on the rationale for re-creations and the benefits as a learning experience for participants:

> Re-creating art is a long, venerable, and delightfully wacky tradition, from the tableau vivant to the museum selfie, and over the years many museums have encouraged their visitors to join in. There's a long tradition of artists, arts educators, and museums encouraging people to do this. It's a great exercise to really look closely at an artwork, to see the colors, forms, and composition needed to re-create it.
>
> *(para. 6)*

By using Instagram, Facebook, and Twitter (before Musk's acquisition) with the hashtag #gettymuseumchallenge, Getty reached various demographics and encouraged individuals, couples, and families to enter the challenge by sharing their re-creations (Shorty Awards, 2021).

While the campaign was underway, Getty's staff maintained the official Getty social media sites by liking and responding to entries, particularly in the initial stages, while saving, sharing, and reposting submissions. The staff developed a Facebook album and posted round-ups of re-creations on Instagram and Facebook. Rules remained flexible to capture as many entries as possible. The team accepted re-creations that used more than three household items than originally requested, non-Getty artwork, and Facebook Inbox submissions. Staff then uploaded re-creations to its Facebook account for followers to like and respond to entries. As more submissions were received, staff wrote a blog on the "viral phenomenon" (Shorty Awards, 2021, para. 15) across Getty's owned social media, electronic newsletters and RSS feeds. Media relations staff pitched stories to traditional media while maintaining news bureau operations for media requests.

To continue the lifespan of the Getty Museum Challenge, Getty Publications (2020) curated the submissions and published a 144-page paperback, *Off the walls: Inspired re-creations of iconic artworks*, (also e-book) highlighting a wide assortment of re-creations next to the original artwork. Getty Publications donated profits from the book to charities supporting the arts and artists (Getty Museum, 2020).

Results

The Getty Museum Challenge achieved its objectives to entertain and educate people about its extensive digital library and to create an online community of art lovers engaging in its digital art collection on its social media sites during the lockdown phase of the pandemic. The Getty Museum concluded that over 100,000 people shared their art re-creations while the museum gained social media followers, received peer-reviewed kudos, generated media coverage worldwide, and curated a new book on the user-generated imagery. The museum gained a 207% increase in new followers (120,000) on Instagram and a 366% rise on Facebook with 18,000 new followers over the first two months (Shorty Awards, 2021). Its most followed social media platform was Twitter with more than 1.3 million followers, Instagram was second (530,000), and third was Facebook (361,000) (Romero, 2020).

Reactive and proactive media relations resulted in 300 stories about the challenge in the U.S. and across the globe in Canada, Central and South America, the Middle East, Asia, and Asia/Pacific. Media coverage spanned leading local, regional, national, and international digital, print, and broadcast outlets. A few examples include CNN, BBC News,

CBS Evening News, PBS Newshour, Today Show, ABC News Live Prime, The New York Times, Washington Post, USA Today, The Guardian, The Economist, and *PRWeek* (Shorty Awards, 2021).

The following excerpts from journalists on the Getty Museum Challenge illustrate the creative energy and positive image of the digital campaign:

- *Smithsonian Magazine*—"After days of being cooped up inside, members of the public proved more than willing to accept the challenge, responding with personalized remakes of pieces by the likes of Paul Cézanne, Rembrandt van Rijn, Johannes Vermeer, Salvador Dalí and Pablo Picasso. Some stay-at-home artists pulled from their stashes of coronavirus supplies (rolls of toilet paper and coffee filters, for instance), while others enlisted the help of their pets, children's toys and even that morning's breakfast toast to remake the perfect portrait." (Nalewicki, 2020, para. 3).
- *USA Today*—"We can't admire paintings on the walls of museums these days, but that doesn't mean art appreciation is off limits. On the contrary, Los Angeles' Getty Museum has presented a social media activity that encourages those stuck inside to connect with historical artwork." (Mallenbaum, 2020, para. 1).

In addition, the Getty Museum Challenge won the Technique award by *PRWeek USA*, one of the leading public relations trade publications, in the social media category for best campaigns (PRWeek, 2021) and was a finalist in the Shorty Awards (2021), which acknowledges talent in digital content for best hashtag.

Timothy Potts (2020), the museum's director, reflected on the process of coping with the closure of the museum with questions and comments based on the pandemic and the museum world:

> The social aspect of the museum experience—bringing communities together to engage with art, inspiring and educating the public, transforming lives through the lens of culture—how does that fundamental role of the art museum adjust to the legacy of this crisis? Writing now, in the midst of events, it is hard to imagine a return to a 'pre-corona normal;' is that possible or even desirable? It is best that we begin to attend to its lessons now, so that we are better prepared for whatever the future brings.
>
> *(p. 220)*

His observations reveal important theoretical perspectives that are relevant to understanding the phases of a health crisis or pandemic and how creative organizations like a museum became resilient by making flexible and adaptive decisions.

Theoretical perspectives

The Institute for Public Relations (2007) published a white paper that divided the management of crises into three distinct phases: 1) pre-crisis, 2) during the crisis when organizations respond, and 3) post-crisis. Other crisis communication scholars theorized additional phase and stage models for how crises evolve (George, 2012; Sellnow & Seeger, 2021) that include similar concepts like detection of prodromes or risk, prevention, crisis development, containment, crisis outcomes, and organizational learning. Similarly, Migus et al. (2020) outline four phases of the COVID-19 pandemic: 1) slow the spread of the disease; 2) lift confinement and social distancing measures prudently; 3) establish immunity protections; and 4) learn from the pandemic and prepare for the next one.

Within each phase are communication decisions that need to be made to protect an organization and its stakeholders; for example, the Protective Action Decision Model (PADM) which "integrates the processing of information derived from social and environmental cues with messages that social sources transmit through communication channels to those at risk," eliciting a behavioral response to the threat (Lindell & Perry, 2012, p. 616).

Weeks before the pandemic broke in the U.S. in March 2020, the museum had already been monitoring environmental cues and processing what was happening in Asia and Europe by anticipating the decisions it was going to make regarding the health and safety of staff and visitors. The Getty decided to "curtail business travel ... and impose a two-week self-quarantine on any staff who had recently been on an airplane. When ... the inevitability of a shutdown, became clear, we were thus able to respond with dispatch" (Potts, 2020, para. 1). This is parallel with COVID-19 phase one of slowing the spread of the disease and decisions made to close schools and gathering spaces (Migus et al., 2020).

Phase two identified by Migus et al. (2020) was partial deconfinement in which decisions were made to socially distance, limit large public gatherings, wear masks, and other non-pharmaceutical interventions. The Getty Museum closed its sites to the public, cancelled planned public programing through the end of May, and initiated remote work for non-essential staff (Potts, 2020). As the museum's director recalls, these decisions were made with "an entirely atypical rapidity and revisited daily as current information became available. Managers had a single day to discuss with their staff the process for gathering the necessary materials and equipment from their workspaces before heading home" (Potts, 2020, para. 2).

The Getty Museum also responded with a protective action by mobilizing equipment and technology, providing access to information on Getty's servers, and offering training resources for its remote staff. For its stakeholders and customers, Getty created an audience-first digital strategy, emphasizing "initiatives that were participatory or created 'conversations,' with the goal of publishing content that was uplifting, inspirational, and focused on creating community through art" (Potts, 2020, para. 5). The Getty Museum Challenge campaign encouraged individuals to respond to the social and environmental cues within their homes to re-create art. This campaign resulted in "an adaptive and resilient response to the pandemic" (Elisondo, 2022, p. 60) on the part of the museum and allowed patrons and visitors to adapt to the new normal by modifying their behavior through improvising (Khlystova et al., 2022).

As phase three of COVID-19 was implemented and individuals were vaccinated, the immediate threat of the pandemic had abated. Organizations entered phase four as they began thinking about what happened and how to learn from the pandemic. A learning organization is "characterized by open communications … recognition for learning … rewards for learning" and for the ability to "develop and retain organizational sustainability" (Vainauskienė & Vaitkienė, 2022, p. 333). The Getty museum's director Tim Potts (2020) candidly shared what was learned about the organization's internal and external vulnerabilities:

> We have already begun to think ahead … working through a set of scenarios predicated on different assumptions … [which] sparked a lively discussion among our colleagues, demanding that we look hard at our operational and programing priorities … make any necessary adjustments as we anticipate an uncertain year or two ahead … We have had clear guidance and communication from [Getty] Trust leadership … and a capable and dedicated staff that we have been able to support during these difficult times.
>
> *(p. 219)*

Key words

Getty Museum
Getty Museum Challenge
Getty Trust Leadership
J. Paul Getty
Shorty Awards
Protective Action Decision Model
UNESCO

Discussion questions

1 What work of art would you re-create if you participated in the Getty's challenge? What items found at home would you use in the process?
2 What role does creativity potentially play in crisis communication efforts?
3 Are there other theoretical perspectives that could be used in analyzing this case study?

Note: The authors edited, modified, and expanded the Getty Museum case study from a report written by Rowan Mellin, Class of 2026, as a final project for the crisis communication course. Mellin is an undergraduate student in the Communication Strategy and Design program in the Roy H. Park School of Communications at Ithaca College in New York.

10.3 SOUTH KOREAN COVID-19 HEALTH CAMPAIGN RESONATES WITH THE PUBLIC: "TRUST" CAMPAIGN INSTILLS SOLIDARITY AMONG CITIZENS

Situation analysis

South Korea (officially the Republic of Korea) is located south of North Korea (Democratic People's Republic of Korea) on the Korean Peninsula in East Asia with maritime borders of the Sea of Japan (East Sea) and the Yellow Sea. South Korea operates as a democratic government unlike the neighboring North Korean communist government. Korean is the official language, and English is widely taught as a second language in schools. Its total population is 51.4 million (Population Reference Bureau, 2023) with a largely homogeneous society (World Factbook, 2025a). The internet and social media are widely used in South Korea, with 97.42% internet penetration, ranking ninth highest in the world in 2023 (World Population Review, 2025), and 93.4% of the population using social media (Kemp, 2020). South Korea's population ethnicity estimates were 96.3% Korean and 3.7% foreign born in 2023 (Cultural Atlas, 2025).

The government of South Korea learned about its strengths and weaknesses in dealing with a public health crisis during the MERS outbreak in 2015. MERS arrived in the country by one infected traveler from the Arabian Peninsula, which eventually resulted in 185 laboratory-confirmed cases and 38 fatalities, becoming the largest known MERS outbreak outside the Arabian Peninsula (CEPI, 2024). South Korea set up a quarantine and isolation system for infected people, closed schools, canceled public events, and shared information with the public and other health groups. The lessons learned were to create a tracking system of travelers, strengthen the health care system, amend the Infectious Disease Act, establish bioethics, and adhere to WHO's guidelines, among others (Park, 2019).

After MERS, South Korea's government adopted institutional and legal changes. The Korea Centers for Disease Control and Prevention (now KCDA) gained more authority and autonomy in controlling infectious diseases. The government amended laws to "promote public-private medical partnerships, authorize emergency use of testing kits and treatments, and enable health authorities to collect data needed for contact-tracing of infected individuals" (Government of the Republic of Korea, 2020, p. 26).

The country's first confirmed case of COVID-19 occurred in Daegu, its third largest city, in late January in 2020, and quickly grew to 909 countrywide 40 days later, becoming the second most infected country after China. South Korea quickly undertook the following initiatives (Cha & Kim, 2020; Choi & Kim, 2024; de Groot, 2022; Kang et al., 2020; Oh, 2020; Vergonia, 2020):

- Raised its national alert level to yellow after the first confirmed case, orange after the first four confirmed cases, and red, the highest alert, after the numbers rose. Collaborated with the public and private sector nationwide to arrange for test kits to be ready within two weeks, faster than any other country, and exported test kits.
- Produced medical masks for citizens and export; also fined people KRW 100,000 (USD 73) for noncompliance when masks were required indoors and outdoors in public areas. When the country faced a high demand for masks and limited inventory, the government wanted to avoid mask-buying panic and set up a five-day rotation system for masks to be available on specific days based on year of birth when people could buy two masks every week from pharmacies for a low price.
- Set up drive-through testing locations with 12- to 24-hour test results, allowing public health authorities to identify infected patients quickly.
- Undertook contact tracing to identify people who have been in contact with infected people for testing.
- Treated infected people quickly with appropriate medical resources; some patients were placed in medical centers for isolation and others practiced self-quarantines at home.
- Advised people to postpone or cancel all non-urgent international travel.
- Increased border control and set up more stringent screening of inbound air travelers.
- Used GPS-based mobile applications and contact mapping through data from responses to patient questionnaires; data tracked locations of infected people and credit card usage. App also notified ill people when hospital beds were available.

- Vaccinated high-risk populations at first when only a limited number of vaccines were available; afterward, set up a pre-vaccine registration system.
- Kept the public updated frequently about public resources and safety.

Communication and execution

On January 30, 2020, Korea began COVID-19 communications when just five cases were confirmed (Friedman, 2022). The primary goals were to curtail the spread of COVID-19 by testing people quickly, tracking others who may have been infected, treating infected people, and protecting people from contacting COVID-19 through preventive measures and vaccinations. The major communication strategies were to provide consistent and accurate information in real time to the public using multiple media platforms and to gain the public's trust and encourage solidarity in following all preventive precautions (Government of the Republic of Korea, 2020).

The slogan of South Korea's public relations campaign, "TRUST" was an acronym for two interrelated pillars of the government's responses:

> "**T**ransparency, **R**obust screening and quarantine, **U**nique but universally applicable testing, **S**trict control, and **T**reatment" and calls for solidarity and cooperation of the international community based on the principles of "**T**ransparency, **R**esponsibility, **U**nited Action, **S**cience and Speed, and **T**ogether in Solidarity."
>
> *(emphasis in original; Government of the Republic of Korea, 2020, p. 136)*

Communication tactics included the following activities (Kang et al., 2020; Ahren, 2020; Friedman, 2022):

- News briefings—Conducted daily or twice-daily news briefings in English, which made it easier for international media to produce stories.
- Website resources—Updated site frequently with government data on mask inventories and number of cases and fatalities, as well as other pandemic information.
- A self-diagnosis, user-friendly mobile app—Set up an app to enable people to monitor their health and find available information on health clinics and hospital beds, and next steps for protection and prevention, along with an emergency alert.
- Social media—Created and updated content on Twitter and Instagram.
- A 24-hour COVID-19 hotline—Activated for the public's convenience to answer questions.
- Subway station alerts—Used, as necessary.

- News releases and infographics—Provided preventive precautions such as washing hands frequently, maintaining social distance, and wearing masks.
- Educational brochures—Created 15 versions on health and safety topics, such as how to wear a mask properly.

Results

With the campaign's primary goal to help subside the spread of COVID-19, the percentages reflect South Korea's success. In March 2020, fewer than eight cases in any day were reported, thereby dropping the fatality rate to 1.3% (Choi & Kim, 2024; Key, 2020). Eventually, South Korea's mortality rate dropped further to 0.07%, lower than the worldwide average of 0.09%, and Korea's case fatality rate was 0.1%, lower than the global average of 0.91%. (Choi & Kim, 2024). Mortality rate stands for the number of deaths due to a disease divided by the total population. The case fatality rate measures the percentage of people who died from a particular disease compared to the total number of people who were officially diagnosed with the disease during a specific time. South Korea's fully vaccinated rate of its population was 86%, a higher COVID-19 vaccination rate than the global average of 67% (Holder, 2023)

South Korea faced fewer economic challenges since the country did not institute a countrywide lockdown. Some schools and venues in certain locations were closed temporarily. The campaign messages of compassion and solidarity infused "a near-wartime sense of common purpose" (Key, 2020, p. 5). See Figure 10.1 of how a restaurant in Seoul conveyed preventive measures.

Comments from journalists and scholars conveyed positive sentiment about South Korea's communications and precautionary procedures:

- "At its core PR [Public Relations] is about relating information to the public. Few governments are doing that better than South Korea as it battles coronavirus" (Ahren, 2020, para. 1)
- "As South Korea demonstrated, transparency, communication, and collaboration are the key weapons in this fight against the invisible, mysterious, and debilitating novel coronavirus" (Oh, para. 25).
- "The Korean approach has been reasonably consistent and coherent thanks to a commitment by the government to communicate openly with the public and to follow the advice of health professionals. This has engendered a strong sense of national unity and purpose" (Hundt, 2021).

The reasons for South Korea's success are based on several factors (Kim et al., n.d.). South Korea is like an island instead of a peninsula; its only border is North Korea with its Korean Demilitarized Zone (KDZ) that

FIGURE 10.1 Photograph of Seoul, South Korea, from November 2020 shows tables and chairs with large stuffed toy bears and hand sanitizers to promote social distancing and sanitary precautions against COVID-19. Simon Shin/SOPA Images/ZUMA wire/Alamy Live News.

has separated the two countries since the end of the Korean War. The only way to reach South Korea is by air or sea, where airports and ports can be monitored. Most South Koreans (81%) live in urban areas (World Bank Group, 2024), and most potential super-spreader events took place at a few venues, such as megachurches, large religious observances, and hobby sports group meetings, thereby making contact tracing easier than settings in smaller clusters. Pew Research Center (Poushter et al., 2024) reported that 99% of South Koreans adults are online and 98% own smartphones, both ranking among the highest in the world. According to Kim, et al. (n.d.), "Culturally and legally, South Korea is more tolerant of personal data-sharing" (para. 53), making it easier for the government to track data.

Theoretical framework

PRECEDE-PROCEED

The National Cancer Institute (n.d.), in collaboration with the U.S. Department of Health and Human Services, Public Health Service, and National Institute of Health, created a planners guide *Making health communication programs work*. This guide provides a practical structure and various theoretical models to plan and implement health communication efforts. The focus is on the role that communication—messages, channels, and audience—plays in preventing and controlling diseases.

One theoretical framework within the guide, PRECEDE-PROCEED, stands out as a relevant perspective from which to understand South Korea's "TRUST" campaign. Created by Dr. Lawrence W. Green (2023), professor emeritus, Department of Epidemiology and Biostatistics, School of Medicine at the University of California at San Francisco, the model demands:

- "Active engagement of the community to be served.
- Systematic collection and analysis of diagnostic data starting with ultimate values of their health-related quality of life and social conditions causing or resulting from their health condition.
- Continuation of working backward in the causal chain of determinants of health to find the most important and changeable ones at each level of causation.
- Design interventions that would achieve the changes required at each level, setting quantitative objectives for the practice-based evidence to ensure their achievement.
- Evaluation of the achievement of objectives" (para. 19).

PRECEDE begins the process of planning through an examination of an individual's or community's predisposition (attitudes, values, beliefs) to change, any obstacles to change, and "positive or negative effects of adopting the behavior (including social support) that influence continuing the behavior" (National Cancer Institute, n.d., p. 219).

From here, planners PROCEED in diagnosing "**P**olicy, **R**egulatory, and **O**rganizational **C**onstructs in **E**ducational and **E**nvironmental **D**evelopment" factors that will help with the implementation and execution of a program "for health development, promotion, or protection in the specific communities or settings where they would be applied" (emphasis added; Green, 2023, para. 14).

Application to South Korea

The Ministry of Foreign Affairs for the Government of the Republic of Korea (2020) created the slogan referring to **T**ransparency in data from testing and diagnostic procedures, **R**obust screening and self- quarantine methods, **U**nique drive-through testing sites and mobile apps to track movement of infected individuals, **S**trict control of the flow of people from "exiting Korea" (p. 5) and **T**reatment of confirmed patients "free of charge for both Koreans and foreign nationals" (p. 6). The TRUST slogan "captures the principles of digital technology and ideas of effective government with civic partnership behind" the campaign's response strategies (Kim & Kim, 2020, p. 539).

What makes this case study interesting is that "despite its successful achievements," the Korean model, "can neither be exported nor imitated by the Global South, since it is uniquely home-grown within Korea's specific contexts and domestic multi-stakeholders involved in mixed accountability" (Kim & Kim, 2020, p. 533). The model refers to the "K-Quarantine" scheme that undergirds the "TRUST" campaign and reveals PRECEDE-ing factors that contributed to South Korea's ability to PROCEED with the "TRUST" campaign.

PRECEDE-ing factors include:

- A whole-of-society approach in which civil society, public and private sectors, and formal and information institutions form partnerships "in the pursuit of common solutions to complex problems" (Kjellén & Wong, 2023, p. 173). This approach relies on trust, participation from community members, an integrated campaign based on stakeholder concerns, and "Good governance, where the 'good' includes qualities like transparency, accountability, professionalism and … where 'governance' implies a recognition that it is not only governance but society as whole that makes development happen" (Kjellén & Wong, 2023, p. 173).
- A state-society synergy whereby civic engagement is paired with adaptive and ambidextrous governance (Kim & Kim, 2020), which requires delicately balancing public's fears (prior experience with pandemics, the increasing number of cases, affecting others, etc.) of the disease with government authority to enact prevention measures, in a way that is not coercive and that engenders trust. The Korea Disease Control and Prevention Agency (KDCA) "was given independent authority to set and execute policies related to infectious disease, and have control over budgetary, personnel and organizational matters" (Government of the Republic of Korea, 2020, p. 27) while citizens were expected to comply with government guidelines to protect the society as a whole.
- Digital technologies and infrastructure: social media was a new and faster means of delivering accurate information to the public (Okuhara et al., 2024).
- Lessons learned by the South Korean government from previous pandemics (Kim & Kim, 2020; You, 2020) to improve procedures for managing infectious diseases and clarifying the authority of the government.

These factors were necessary for South Korea's ability to PROCEED with the "TRUST" campaign. Beginning with policies and regulations, "South Korea changed existing policies to address past mistakes … and was prepared to respond to the unprecedented threat" (You, 2020, p. 805); for example, policies and regulations associated with screening, social distancing, traveling, and transparency of information related to an individual's health statue and the government's behavioral recommendations (masks, washing hands) and pandemic management procedures (press briefings, updates). There were five phases of social distancing adjusted daily on the basis of patterns of transmission and the data provided by community members.

To curtail the spread of the virus, the "K-Quarantine" approach was developed. The approach focused on three Ts of testing, tracing and treatment which relied on the public sharing health information by using GPS enabled "mobile applications for tracking self-isolation" and self-check apps for diagnosing symptoms (Kim & Kim, 2020, p. 537). Based on where people were located and what symptoms they were exhibiting, the government was able to mobilize resources to quickly distribute PPEs, rapidly activate national response protocols [lockdowns, travel alerts, vaccines, etc.], and scale up measures for reducing transmission (Kim & Kim, 2020). This allowed for the curve of cases to flatten in a short period of time.

"Although there exist doubts whether South Korea's contract tracing oversteps the boundary of privacy breach," the government efforts contributed to the early reduction of cases (Kim & Kim, 2020, p. 536) and allowed for the government to adapt based on feedback. Korea's approach is a "model to emulate" (You, 2020, p. 801) and shows how "government PR is done" (Ahren, 2020, para. 1).

Key words

Adaptive and Ambidextrous Governance
Case Fatality Rate
Democratic People's Republic of Korea
Korean Disease Control and Prevention Agency
Mortality rate
PRECEDE-PROCEED model
Republic of Korea
State-society Synergy
TRUST

Discussion questions

1 What challenges would the U.S. government encounter if the country were to use all of South Korea's procedures, including data tracking, to combat the spread of COVID-19?
2 If you were handling the public relations campaign for South Korea, what changes would you make if any? Please explain.

10.4 CREATIVE STORYTELLING ON PREVENTIVE CARE: MEXICO'S COVID-19 "SUSANA DISTANCIA AND HEALTH SQUAD," PERU'S "DON'T JOIN ME YET," AND VIETNAM'S "JEALOUS CORONAVIRUS"

Situation analysis

How can public service announcements (PSAs) grab the attention of the local population with compelling preventive healthcare messages? The authors selected PSAs from three countries—Mexico, Peru, and Vietnam—since each one used creative storytelling to reach its publics during COVID-19.

As the furthest north Latin America country, Mexico borders the U.S. (north) and Belize and Guatemala (south) while its maritime borders include the North Pacific Ocean, the Caribbean Sea, and the Gulf of America. Its government type is a federal presidential republic with most of the population speaking Spanish followed by Indigenous languages, such as Mayan and Nahuatl (World Factbook, 2025b). Located in Western South America on the South Pacific Ocean, Peru shares borders with Ecuador (northwest), Colombia (northeast), Brazil (east), Boliva (southeast), and Chile (south). The government operates as a presidential republic with three official languages, Spanish, Quechua, and Aymara (World Factbook, 2025c). Situated on the Indochina peninsula in Southeast Asia, Vietnam neighbors three countries, China (north), Laos (northwest), Cambodia (southwest), and has maritime boundaries with the Gulf of Thailand, Gulf of Tonkin, and South China Sea. Its government type is a communist party-led state with Vietnamese as the official language (World Factbook, 2025d).

Each country has higher internet penetration than the global average of 68% in 2024: Mexico at 81.18%, Vietnam at 84%, and Peru at 71.11% (World Bank Group, n. d.). Each country was impacted by the COVID-19 pandemic. Table 10.1 shows the total population (Population Reference Bureau, 2023) and number of confirmed cases and deaths. According to the JohnHopkins University & Medicine Coronavirus Resource Center, Peru had the highest COVID-19 per capita death rate in

TABLE 10.1 Number of confirmed cases and deaths. Source: John Hopkins University & Medicine Coronavirus Resource Center (data collected until March 10, 2023).

Country	*Total Population*	*COVID-19 Confirmed Cases*	*COVID-19 Deaths*
Mexico	131 million	7,483,444	333,188
Peru	33.8 million	4,487,553	219,539
Vietnam	98.9 million	11,526,994	43,186

the world at 4.9% (2023a) while Mexico was the second highest at 4.5% (2023b). Vietnam's per capita death rate at 0.4% was lower than the rates of both the U.S. and Canada (2023c). The number of confirmed cases and COVID-19 deaths is depicted in Table 10.1.

Communication campaigns

Cartoon cast of health squad heroines battle COVID virtually

Between February and April 2020, Mexico had over 19,000 confirmed cases of COVID-19 and 1,859 deaths while the country conducted 0.69 diagnostic tests for every 1,000 residents. In late March, Mexico started to restrict large-scale events (Suárez et al., 2020). The concept of social distancing seemed daunting in a culture where the "saludo" is the standard greeting, usually starting with a firm handshake along with a smile and eye contact, then a warm hug and a pat on the back, followed by a peck on the right cheek (Kalman, 2020).

Marketers in Mexico have been branding superheroes and characters with humor and personality that result in content shared by memes and Twitter (before renamed X) trends, which have been popular communication tools in reaching Mexico's population (Bartra et al., 2022). For example, a character of an older doctor with a bushy mustache and a cheerful smile wearing a doctor's white uniform called "Dr. Simi" serves as the mascot for the second-largest pharmacy chain in Mexico. People in Dr. Simi costumes dance in front of the stores while Dr. Simi stuffed dolls have made stage appearances outside of the country at concerts by Taylor Swift, Adele, and others (MND Staff, 2025).

"Susana Distancia" was launched as the superhero cartoon character featured in videos, social media, and other media platforms. Her name is a pun on "Su" (your), "sana" (healthy), and "Distancia" (distance) to keeping "Your Healthy Distance" (Bartra et al., 2022). The superhero is depicted as a young woman with long dark hair clad in yellow tights, blue shorts, and pink boots, along with a pullover and headband (both with SD initials in a circle). She appears as a comic book character with a blend of lucha libre, Mexico's professional masked wrestlers (Bartra et al., 2022). Social distancing is her superpower while she is protected by a transparent orb where she can stretch her arms out without touching the width of each side. Her mission was to encourage people to create their own protective bubbles by keeping a safe distance of 6 feet away from others. She also told viewers and readers to listen to the government's health guidelines and to ignore rumors.

In March 2020, Susana Distancia came to life on social media, predominately Twitter, with the hashtag #susanadistancia, to share advice on preventive measures to stop the spread of COVID-19 and to make the most of self-quarantining at home (Puttkamer, 2020). Memes quickly showed up. Critical ones included images of government officials disobeying the social distancing rules, with captions such as, "Is this a healthy distance?" Other playful memes redesigned Susana with Photoshop and made fun of the superhero and her bubble. Fan art later depicted Susana in battle with another popular character, Catalina la Catrina, a figure in *Día de Los Muertos*, a Canal 5 television network production, and redrew her as a sexy, voluptuous figure (Know Your Meme, 2020). The following day, the Ministry of Health Mexico posted a video on Susana Distancia. She quickly became a well-known character, and her social distance stance became a part of people's conversations in person and on social media as her presence spread throughout digital media and traditional print and broadcast media (UCSF Institute for Global Health and Sciences, n.d.; Kalman, 2020).

Following Susana Distancia's success, Mexico's then President Andrés Manuel López Obrador launched the "COVID-19 Health Squad" campaign publicly in March 2020. The four Health Squad cartoon members became the "superheroes" designed to create public awareness of other preventive behaviors to protect Mexicans from COVID-19 infections during each stage of the country's COVID precaution monitoring system from the most severe to normal behavior (Redacción El Universal, 2020).

Health Squad heroines were created (UCSF Institute for Global Health and Sciences, n.d.; Redacción El Universal, 2020) to signify a specific character and color scheme representing one of the four alert levels, along with superhero powers:

- **Refugio** ("Refuge"), depicted as an older woman, symbolized the red tier maximum alert for people to stay at home. Her superpower was maximum care and safety.
- **Prudencia** ("Prudence"), a woman with a disability using a wheelchair, represented the orange high alert to avoid leaving the house unless it is essential. Her superpower was the ability to adjust to precautions.
- **Esperanza** ("Hope") depicted as "muxhe gunaa," which is defined as a third gender originating from the Zapotec community of Oaxaca, Mexico, of "individuals assigned male at birth who identify as women" (Martinez, 2024, para. 5). Esperanza represented the yellow medium alert level with the superpower of caring for others and recommended safety and hygienic measures when outside the house.
- **Aurora** ("Dawn"), depicted as "queer" (LGBTQ) in Spanish, stood for the green tier of no alert, with the superpower of a return to normalcy, but to be prepared that COVID-19 may not be over.

In May 2021, the Ministry of Health introduced another cartoon character, "Armando Vaccuno," a chatbot that offered vaccine information, reminded people of their vaccination appointments, and provided other precautionary safety measures. Amando was available 24/7 and easy to add to a WhatsApp account. The new chatbot was designed to promote vaccinations to pregnant women, educators, and people between the ages of 50 to 59 (Editorial Staff, 2021).

COVID-19 campaign uses deepfake technology

Peru dealt with difficult circumstances during COVID-19—a lack of investment in public healthcare, political instability with short-lived presidencies, inaccurate government reporting on the number of COVID-19 deaths, strict lockdowns ineffective in curbing the virus, and slow vaccine accessibility to the public (Costa et al., 2021). In addition, some Peruvians denied the existence of COVID-19 while others distrusted the government, panicked and overbought basic items resulting in supply shortages, or sought out folk remedies or followed misinformation on social media, such as using ivermectin (a medication traditionally used for infections caused by parasites, such as worms), and other pseudoscientific "miracles" (Lossio, 2023).

"Using influencers is commonplace. But what about enlisting dead influencers to ask you not to join them? How can beloved deceased celebrities offer health advice to the living?," asked executives at the advertising agency, Zavalita Brand Building (2023, para. 1), a creative agency in Lima, Peru. Perú Te Quiero (n.d.), a citizen movement formed in 2020 to help residents throughout all parts of the country cope with mental and physical health challenges, along with support from volunteers, other nonprofits, and corporate donations, hired Zavalita. Perú Te Quiero can be translated as "Peru, I Love You" in a casual affectionate sense.

The "Don't Join Me Yet" COVID-19 campaign was designed to stimulate solidarity among Peruvians and to help them listen to preventive care messages by three famous and beloved Peruvians who passed away long before the pandemic. Zavalita Brand Building produced the PSAs and revived a national hero, a singer, and sports announcer with deepfake technology that enabled re-creations of the deceased blended with videos and sound recordings of actors performing just like the beloved figures whose faces are placed over the actors. Videos were directed by Ricardo Maldonado, director of Cine 70, an audiovisual production company in Lima (Ads of the World, n.d.; Zavalita Brand Building, 2023).

The following celebrities "starred" in PSAs, which were released in January 2021, with uplifting messages for Peruvians to "Don't join me yet" (Ads of the World, n.d.; Zavalita Brand Building, n.d.):

- Miguel María Grau (1834–1879), an illustrious Navy officer and politician, received the distinction of being named the greatest "Peruvian of the Millennium" by citizens in 1999 (Honor, gloria y legado en el Mar Peruano, 2024). Grau's re-creation originated from one 19th-century original photograph. In this PSA, he is shown wearing his uniform and standing proudly while he encourages people to reflect on their values and extols the benefits of unity weaving in naval language. This grainy black-and-white PSA, with movie reel projection sounds and scratchy sound effects, looks as if it were recorded during the early days of filmmaking in the late 1800s. See Figure 10.2.
- Chabuca Granda (1920–1983), a famous singer and composer, who was acclaimed as "the single most important figure in the history of twentieth-century Peruvian music: her most famous ballads ('La Flor de la Canela,' 'Fina Estampa,' 'José Antonio')" are a lyrical celebration of Peru itself, with its Inca heritage and its mixed population of indigenous peoples, mestizos, criollos and Afro-Peruvians" (Allen, n.d., para. 1). Not only her recordings, but also her legacy has survived by influencing other Peruvian musicians using her music. Based on imagery from a television interview from the 1970s, this black-and-white PSA shows

FIGURE 10.2 Perú Te Quiero's "Don't Join Me Yet" COVID-19 campaign with deepfake video still of Miguel María Grau, an illustrious 19th century Navy officer and politician. Advertising agency Zavalita Brand Building with art direction by Pablo Collantes.

FIGURE 10.3 Perú Te Quiero's "Don't Join Me Yet" COVID-19 campaign used deepfake videos of deceased people, including Chabuca Granda, a famous Peruvian singer and composer. Advertising agency Zavalita Brand Building with art direction by Pablo Collantes.

Granda sitting on a stage near a guitarist as she talks about ways to stay alive and for the country to restore its prominence. She concludes with a song on being united to overcome the pandemic. See Figure 10.3.

- Daniel Peredo (1969–2018) was acclaimed as Peru's most famous sports journalist and announcer, who died of a heart attack at 48, months after proclaiming Peru's return to the World Cup after a 36-year hiatus. Soccer fans appreciated his enthusiastic and memorable commentary during the games (Obre, 2018). This full-color PSA shows Peredo standing on the broadcasting tower overlooking Lima's sports stadium as he uses sports terms to encourage people to fight the virus.

Each PSA ended with the hashtag, #PeruTeQuiero, and "te quiero vivo" ("I need you alive"), followed by a montage of the sponsors' logos, and Perú Te Quiero's website, which provided online resources on COVID-19 health precautions and vaccinations. The videos were seen on television, digital content, and on Perú Te Quiero's social networks. They also were discussed on radio and in print media in Peru (Zavalita Brand Building, n.d.).

PSA and TikTok dance challenge go viral worldwide

As part of the Ministry of Health, the Vietnam National Institute of Occupational Safety and Environmental Health (VNNIOSH) applies scientific research and technological findings of occupational safety to create safe and healthy work environments under law provisions (VNNIOSH, 2023). It also establishes cooperative relationships with other scientific and informational exchanges within occupational health and safety. In its newsletter, the acting director general of VNNIOSH (Tho, 2022) stated the following about the impact on COVID-19 on Vietnam:

> The impact of COVID-19 pandemic on development goals in Vietnam from 2020 until now, the COVID-19 pandemic has become complicated, unpredictable and prolonged, seriously affecting all aspects of social life from health and life of all classes of people to production and business activities of enterprises.
>
> *(p. 1)*

VNNIOSH sought to create an uplifting message that would encourage people to apply preventaive measures. The institute commissioned lyricist and musician Khắc Hưng to rewrite a popular Vietnamese song, *Ghen* ("Jealous"), into a video PSA on handwashing and safety measures (Min Official, 2020a). The original *Ghen* music video reached 3.5 million viewers and ranked No. 1 on YouTube's trending list in Vietnam within four days of its release (Dong, 2017). The new version, *Ghen Cô Vy* ("Jealous Coronavirus"), was recorded in February 2020 in Vietnamese with the original Ghen singers from Vietnam, Min and Erik (Min Official, 2020a). In partnership with the United Nations Development Programme (n.d.), VNNIOSH and the Ministry of Health produced an English-language version of *Ghen Cô Vy* that was released in April 2020. The singer Min released both videos on her YouTube channel with 1.2 million subscribers, providing the videos with an instant boost (Wamsley, 2020). Both language versions can be viewed on YouTube.

The animated video, which is just over 3 minutes, depicts an adult couple fighting at home when their television reports on the virus while a big pesky coronavirus—a neon-green circle drawn with spikes on its sides and a yellow crown on its head, and a face with large blinking eyes and a wide black mouth revealing fangs—and his coronavirus "companions" keep coming between the pair until the end when the big coronavirus character is kicked out and the couple reunite happily. During the antics of the coronaviruses, the video shows the couple combatting fake news and trying to stop the virus by washing their hands, avoiding rubbing their mouth and eyes with their hands, maintaining a distance from others, staying away from crowded places, cleaning their house, sharing preventive messages to others, and practicing kindness with the hopes of a return to normalcy. Yang Animation Artist, based in Hanoi, created the animated PSA (Min Official, 2020a).

In addition, VNNIOSH hired Quang Dang, a well-known Vietnamese dancer and choreographer, to create a dance based on the new song. Dang's upbeat "handwashing" dance inspired the "Ghen Cô Vy Challenge" on TikTok, inviting anyone to dance along with the song—and spreading safety precautions to others around the world. The challenge rules were to perform the dance using the six handwashing movements recommended by WHO with the *Ghen Cô Vy* song and share and tag two friends after completion. Apparently, Dang choreographed the handwashing dance in 15 minutes and was quoted in CBS News (O'Kane, 2020):

> 'I think the importance of the song and dance is the RIGHT information that they give to the audience,' the dancer wrote in an email to CBS News. 'And the viral dance will help spread this information to the community. Especially the young people... they tend to not get the right information.'
>
> *(para. 6)*

Results

The World Health Organization published a handbook *WHO strategic communications: framework for effective communications* (2017), which recommends using visual messages because they "make information easier to understand and can reach people of all literacy and education levels" (p. 38). The Peruvian PSA used deepfake technology to fabricate deceased beloved figures. The PSAs from Mexico and Vietnam applied animated cartoon figures to explain how to remain safe during the pandemic. Diamond et al. (2021) examined how to relay medical and scientific information to young people during a pandemic and explained the following about comics:

> Comics are a sequential, narrative art that engages the reader with stories that have emotional impact. They are a highly visual media form that incorporates social-emotional content in storytelling. Whereas many comics tell entirely fictional stories, science comics attempt to weave dramatic stories around scientific information, images, and role models.
>
> *(p. 2)*

Cartoon cast of health squad heroines battle COVID virtually

Mexico's "COVID-19 Health Squad" presence on YouTube continues with an animated series and a variety of news conferences on the topic.

The first Susana Distancia animated PSA was the most successful. The list below includes examples of videos on YouTube and their viewership as of July 13, 2025:

- 5.7 million views of Susana Distancia (animation on precautions) (Secretaría de Salud México, 2020a)
- 223,000 Susana Distancia Niñas, Niños y Adolescentes (animation on precautions for children and adolescents) (Secretaría de Salud México, 2020b)
- 80,000 Susana Distancia ¡No estamos de vacaciones! (animation on vacationing precautions) (Secretaría de Salud México, 2020c)
- 21,952 #SusanaDistancia para salir a comprar (animation on going shopping precautions) (Secretaría de Salud México, 2020d)
- 11,756 #SusanaDistancia (animation on Christmas holiday precautions) (Secretaría de Salud México, 2020e)
- 55,014 Susana Distancia, la heroína durante coronavirus en México (news conference on Susana Distancia) (MILENIO, 2020a)
- 10,483 Susana Distancia vuelve al ataque contra el coronavirus con 'Escuadrón de la salud' (news conference on the Health Squad) (MILENIO, 2020b)

Batraet al. (2022) researched the evolution of Susana's memes from government public health messages to the public's politicized, mainstream, artistic, and erotic manifestations of popular culture and stated:

> ... we argue that Susana Distancia's character embodies popular Mexican cultural narratives through multiple formats that travel fluidly from the governmental sphere to the streets and digital sphere. These narratives challenge the institutional discourses surrounding official health policy and convert the character into a meme that acquires multiple meanings. The massive online and physical circulation of the meme as a cultural unit allows its appropriation and the construction of a popular imaginary. Susana becomes part of everyday life and shows the heterogeneity of popular culture, embodying a festive confrontation against institutions.
>
> *(p. 661)*

On social media, @SusanaDistancia (2020) received the most followers on Twitter (now X) with 50,371 followers; second was Facebook with 22,000 followers (Susana Distancia, n.d.); and Instagram third with 7,366 followers (Susana Distancia, 2025).

COVID-19 deepfake campaign reaches Peruvians

This campaign focused primarily on television PSAs. According to Zavalita Brand Building (2023), the PSAs resulted in a 9 million organic reach, meaning the number of people who view an organization's content without paid promotion, which was 70% positive or neutral sentiment. The agency used advertising equivalency rates on earned media (television placements), estimating the television advertising costs would be approximately USD 640 million. Advertising equivalency rates (also called AVEs) are defined as:

> AVEs are calculated by measuring the column inches (in the case of print), or seconds (in the case of broadcast media) and multiplying these figures by the respective medium's advertising rates (per inch or per second). The resulting number is what it would have cost to place an advertisement of that size in that medium. By assessing all of your media coverage in this way, and aggregating all such calculations, you can assign an overall AVE to your coverage within a certain time period.
>
> *(Jeffries-Fox, 2003, p. 1)*

This quote was part of a report on AVEs by the Institute for Public Relations Commission on PR Measurement and Evaluation in which Jeffries-Fox (2003) recommends using other metrics to evaluate effectiveness of public relations work beyond AVEs, which some organizations still prefer to use.

PSA and TikTok dance challenge go viral worldwide

Vietnam's original PSA, Ghen Cô Vy, in Vietnamese was posted on YouTube in February 2020 and has received over 125.8 million views (Min Official, 2020b) and its English-language version, which premiered in April 2020, has almost 8.4 million views (Min Official, 2020a) while Quang Dang's original handwashing dance on YouTube from April 2020 received over 8.1 million views (Dang, 2020). On TikTok, the #Ghen CôVyChallenge renditions received 20 million views (Wang, 2020). The high viewership can be attributed to exposure in international media outlets and social media.

John Oliver, host of HBO's *Last Week Tonight with John Oliver,* lauded the PSA in an online episode on YouTube: "Vietnam made a song about washing your hands to prevent coronavirus infection and it absolutely slaps. That's a genuine club banger right there!" (LastWeekTonight, 2020). He showed clips of the PSA and Quang Dang's handwashing dance, tried a few dance moves, and talked about the TikTok challenge.

An article in *The Havard Crimson*, Harvard University's student newspaper, stated: "If you're wondering how to make the hours of self-isolation fly past, look no further than 'Ghen Cô Vy.' Watch the video. Sing along. Dance your heart out. And remember to wash your hands" (Nguyen, 2020, para. 10). A writer for *NPR* also commented on the video:

> For sheer danceability, this PSA from Vietnam's Ministry of Health is the early winner. The video features an absurdly catchy beat on the 2017 song "Ghen" by singers Min and Erik. Give it a listen (here with English subtitles) and just try not to groove.
>
> *(Wamsley, 2020, para. 4–5)*

Although the PSAs did not address vaccinations directly, the number of people getting vaccinated indicates a heightened awareness of safety measures. Approximately 67% of the world's population was fully vaccinated with a COVID-19 one-dose or two-dose vaccine. Mexico's population was 65% fully vaccinated, Peru's 88%, and Vietnam's 89% (Holder, 2023).

Theoretical perspectives

Cynthia King, professor of communications at California State University, Fullerton, suggests "if you want to keep an audience's attention, you must do more than inform them. You must entertain them!" (p. 74), especially during a pandemic or health crisis. Storytelling has been increasingly used in public health to disseminate health messages in a format that is more "understandable and engaging" (Paudyal & Ozkosar, 2022, p. 259) and has been used by cultures worldwide in health communication narratives as a tool to grab audience's attention and connect with them on an emotional level (Dudley et al., 2023) with "self-efficacy messaging, fear appeals, and moralizing messaging" (McClaughlin et al., 2023, p. 1). Such messages are instructional and aimed at reducing harm, informing individuals of the consequences of not complying with harm reduction messages, and appealing to social and moral judgments (McClaughlin et al., 2023).

In a media saturated world, the challenge facing public health officials, communities, and governments in using stories is to ensure that the intended audience(s) receives the message(s) rather than "filtering out advertising messages by TiVOing, turning or clicking their attention elsewhere" (King, 2006, p. 74), to social media or other sites of mis/disinformation or fake news. This requires identifying various aspects that can aid in message reception, like demographics and linguistics (McClaughlin et al., 2023), visual designs (Verma et al., 2024), modes of transmission—oral, written, or nonverbal (Dudley et al., 2023), literacy, and cultural characteristics (Lapinski et al., 2025). Knowing this information, however, is not enough. The information must be used to tailor or target messages to the public.

Lapinski et al. (2025) propose a framework "of the process and content features of culturally tailored and culturally targeted messages" (p. 818) in order to theorize "how and why such messages are effective" (p. 808). The CTP/CTC framework is useful in understanding the effectiveness of the COVID-19 campaigns in this case study on the use of storytelling in Mexico, Peru, and Vietnam and in case study 10.5 about the commonwealths of Australia and New Zealand. More specifically, in this case study, the CTC (cultural tailoring content) part of the framework is most relevant, whereas for the commonwealths the CTP (cultural tailoring processes) is more relevant.

CTP/CTC framework

Lapinski et al. (2025) begin with a conceptualization of the terms. **Tailoring** is "the creation of communication interventions or messages (including verbal and non-verbal content, images, sources, etc.) matched or congruent to the needs and preferences of *individuals* based on cultural characteristics" (emphasis in original; p. 808). WHO (2017) recommends in its strategic communications framework that anyone who is communicating information created by WHO should tailor "the relevance of WHO information for target audiences" (p. 27) by customizing messages to be relevant to particular audiences. For instance, "if a target audience has health beliefs and values already consistent with those presented in a message, using statistics can be persuasive. If audience beliefs are counter to WHO recommendations, emotional stories may be more effective" (p. 27), in which case a communicator can use cultural symbols, food, dress and familiar gathering spaces to help audiences relate.

Targeting "involves the design of messages or information" for groups of people like the Māori and Aboriginals who have their own cultural characteristics but live within the commonwealths that share other cultural characteristics. Content of messages include the substance (information, appeal, identity aspects, beliefs, attitudes, and values) and the various elements like design (color, fonts, graphics, characteristic of a culture), language (system, arguments and evidence, style) and structure (call to action). **Cultural-tailoring processes (CTP)** refer to the methods—outreach, consultation, involvement, and participation with communication members—that shape the development of a communication campaign including messages (Lapinski et al., 2025, p. 810)

Cultural tailoring content and Susana Distancia

In order to tailor content (health messages) to a specific culture, it is important to understand how a culture behaves during a health crisis or pandemic. "When attempting to comprehend the spread of COVID-19 in Mexico, we must consider the baseline characteristics of our population" (Ibarrola-Peña et al., 2022, p. 5). Ibarrola-Peña et al. (2022) conducted a cross-sectional study based on surveys of the general public about their use of preventive measures (social distancing, sanitizer, and masks), their confidence in Mexico's health system, and general knowledge of COVID-19. Additionally, the survey requested socio-demographic information such as age, sex, level of education, housing conditions and number of co-habitants, current illnesses or comorbidities, and occupation. The results revealed these characteristics:

- Predominantly female.
- Multiple people live in the same household.
- 25% had elementary education, while 75% had high school education or higher.
- Respondents self-reported breaking social isolation/distancing, for work and essential activities, yet, believed they were maintaining adequate social distancing measures.
- Almost 70% reported their risk for contracting COVID-19 to be low and approximately 85% had never been tested, despite knowing someone who had been diagnosed with the virus; 50% said they used face masks, while 85% used alcohol-based sanitizer. Additionally, over 40% stated they had at least one comorbidity.
- Regarding confidence in Mexico's health system, 65% believed that facilities and equipment were not available and 60% selected not enough supplies from health-care personnel.

The authors conclude:

> it is easy to understand why the COVID-19 fatality rate reached such high levels and why the prevention policies were directed toward isolating the population at risk … In a country where general conditions make a prolonged quarantine unrealistic, the use of preventative measures against the virus becomes the mainstay to control the spread … It is necessary to attack the problems at their roots by starting health education campaigns for the population that will enable people to identify the risk to which they are exposed [and] help them decide to be a part of the strategy to stop the pandemic.
>
> *(pp. 7–8)*

Mexican health authorities "have understood that risk communication and marketing have to be adapted to the local context in order for the message to reach as many people as possible. Susana Distancia fits into that way of communicating beautifully," as this type of approach to COVID-19, using cartoons, is in line with the history of Mexican government's use of "humor as a marketing tool when trying to convey serious messages" (Optidge Internet Marketing Agency, n.d., para 5).

Susana Distancia, hailed as the superheroine of "health and women's empowerment," was conceived by physician Ricardo Cortés, head of the General Directorate of Health Promotion for the Mexican government, to "enforce social distancing measures in a country that, with more than 50 million poor people, cannot afford a mandatory lockdown" (El Universal Editorial Staff, 2020, para. 1–2). Her effectiveness can be attributed to specific culturally tailored content elements, namely graphic design and color.

Using visual imagery is one of the tactics recommended by WHO (2017) to make health care communications understandable and relevant. Using cartoons or comics exert the "greatest influence on the final product" (Verma et al., 2024, p. 119), especially when color is applied. The main character and Health Squad Superheroes were animated in bright vivid colors which added "emphasis" (Lankow, Ritchie & Crooks, 2012, p. 108) and represented the four alert levels associated with COVID-19 cases (Redacción El Universal, 2020). Sutton and Fischer (2021) in their analysis of visual risk messages found that colors (green, yellow and red) can also represent "information of increasing threat" (p. 176). Susana's colors also "bear a strong resemblance to the iconic US-American comic heroine *Wonder Woman*" (Lazo, 2020, para 6), and her persona exhibits "a calm and sweetness that is not at odds with the superhero she should be," stated her creator in an article *El Universal* (El Universal Editorial Staff, 2020, para. 6).

Comics and cartoons are a culturally appropriate method in reaching "people with low literacy or different language skills … characterized by linguistic and cultural diversity and an elevated illiteracy rate" in older people (Lazo, 2020, para. 8) and convey health messages with "immediate visceral understanding in ways that conventional texts cannot" (Green & Myers, 2010, p. 1). Beneath the color schematics of Susana Distancia is the central message of social distancing that aligns with the government's health policy to educate and raise awareness of how to stop the spread of the virus. As Martyr (2020) notes "Susana Distancia is not the only social media health campaign that has proved successful. Vietnam's health authorities released a coronavirus health advice video called Ghen Co Vy that triggered a TikTok dance challenge and has millions of views on YouTube" (para. 8).

Cultural tailoring content and "Jealous coronavirus"

Vietnam was successful in controlling the spread of COVID-19 especially in the early phases, despite geographically bordering China and having open borders for Chinese visitors (Nguyen et al., 2021). One specific strategy used by the Vietnamese government was a public health education campaign on various social media platforms, where "approximately 6 billion text messages were sent to mobile phones" to raise awareness of preventive measures like handwashing. The government collaborated with artists "to reinforce these public health messages, with one handwashing video gaining popularity outside Vietnam" (Nguyen et al., 2021, p. 159). VNNIOSH commissioned Khắc Hung to rewrite a popular song *Ghen* ("Jealous") into a video PSA on handwashing, with millions of followers on YouTube. This PSA was then recorded in Vietnamese and English and morphed into the "Ghen Cô Vy Challenge" on TikTok with Quang Dang's "handwashing" dance.

Verma, Jin, & Liu (2024) claim that video is narrative modality which can be used when communicating important health information. Narratives that emerge from and within local communities showcase how individuals make sense of, represent, and creatively respond through participatory storytelling on social media (Hou, 2023). Although Hou's (2023) study on participatory storytelling was based on an analysis of performative stories within Facebook during COVID-19, four themes about the use of storytelling were evident within the YouTube and TikTok videos. Storytelling is a way to capture disruptions (i.e., hygiene requirements) to normal life; celebrate the mundane within disruptions; reinforce government key messages; and represent "people's creative and resilient efforts in dealing with COVID-19 by acts such as writing songs … [and] making handwashing videos" (p. 10).

Lapinski et al. (2025) identified various design elements to use when culturally tailoring content, two of which are applicable to the YouTube and TikTok videos. The first is a visually tailored message that links cultural characteristics like demographics and group identity in a "video of people who are demographically similar," (i.e. young millennials and Gen Zers in Vietnam), "to the message receiver, wearing clothes that are common in a region, in the process of a doing the behavior recommended in the message" (p. 810). The recommended behavior is the second culturally tailoring content design element, a call "to action in messages … for example, asking recipients to engage in a traditional approach to physical activity such as … dance" (p. 812). Further, Lapinski et al. argue that content elements of tailoring "require an in-depth understanding of potential receiver's cognitions and social interactions related to a particular topic to design messages or information that is congruent to their underlying psychographics" (p. 812)

Nguyen, et al (2020) conducted a study to evaluate preventive behavior and responses of Vietnamese people during COVID-19, using online questionnaires. Preventive behaviors that were measured included social distancing, masks, "cough etiquette, regular handwashing, and using alcohol hand sanitizer" among others (p. 1), all of which were supported by the Vietnamese government. Results revealed "a high degree of adherence [97%] to personal and community preventive behavior among Vietnamese people," especially handwashing (p. 1).

This is not surprising given intrinsic cultural factors, similar to Korea's whole-of-society mentality, that Pham et al. (2020) were instrumental in helping Vietnam contain the initial spread of COVID-19:

- High power distance based in Confucian philosophy, whereby people are more likely to comply with those in positions of power, for example, the government.
- Collectivist orientation toward group versus individual initiatives.
- High uncertainty avoidance relies on "social norms, rules, and procedures to alleviate unpredictability" (Pham et al., 2020, p. 3).
- Face saving and avoidance of embarrassment. "One of the punishments Vietnamese law enforcers used during the COVID-19 social distancing toward those who violated the law was to publish his or her name in media outlets" (Pham et al., 2020, p. 3).
- "'Tai mat la quan chung nhan dan' (aka the government's ears and eyes are people). It means the Government encourages people to report what they think is suspicious or wrong to officers of the law" (Pham et al., 2020, p. 4).

The use of YouTube and TikTok to convey messages regarding handwashing, using culturally tailored design elements, contributed to the Vietnamese government's success in halting the spread of COVID-19. Similarly, within Peru, videos were used to digitally resurrect deceased celebrities.

Cultural tailoring content and "Don't join me yet"

"Faced with a health emergency due to COVID and state inaction, #PerúTeQuiero was born to galvanize the country's solidarity," (Zavalita Brand Building, 2023a, para. 1) at a time when formal pandemic responses lacked solidarity (Villar et al., 2024). Several researchers have examined, documented, and commented on the paradoxical determinants of health that contributed to a high mortality rate, inconsistent government responses, and many official and informal responses to the COVID-19 pandemic in Peru. Understanding these factors are important for establishing the cultural context in which the #PerúTe Quiero advertising campaign and messages are situated.

The collaborative effort from Alvarez-Risco et al. (2020) yielded a perspective piece on insights and strategies of the Peruvian approach to the infodemic of fake news that spread rapidly. The infodemic was "accompanied by reports of racism and discrimination against Chinese nationals … and a surge of unproven and religious" treatments that amplified the low literacy and health literacy rate in Peru. The Peruvian government denied personal commentary, rumors, and hoaxes using social media and "urged people to share only official information [and] … further indicated that those who create and/or share false information … will receive … prison sentences for creating and disseminating fake news" (p. 584).

Battling fake news and low literacy was one challenge for the government. Various social responses were a challenge in Peru, where "scientific ideas around health and disease coexist with religious ideas, conspiracy theories and traditional knowledge," which lead to "denial, panic, search for culprits, search for 'magic remedies,' and in some sectors, mistrust towards the State and science" (Lossio, 2023, p. 1).

Jorge Lossio (2023), senior professor, Department of Humanities/ Pontificia Universidad Católica del Peru, identifies several social and governmental responses that impacted preventive health measures as "213,000 Peruvians died of covid-19" (p. 2), in a period of two years:

- An attitude of indifference toward the emerging pandemic based on the idea that the virus would not reach Peru "Life continued, unchanged" (p. 2)
- Panic buying of essential toiletries and shelf stable non-perishable food items
- Passivity to internal political changes as the then Health Minister was removed from office and replaced, after emphasizing "the importance of social isolation and the government banned public shows with more than 300 people [and] … An order of absolute immobility was given for Sundays. An unprecedented experience in Peruvian history" (p. 3). Additionally, President Martín Vizcarra was removed from office in 2020 and replaced with a new president Manuel Merino, who appointed a new Minister of Health. Merino resigned a few weeks later amid protests and was succeeded by "engineer and academic Franciso Sagasti to the position of president of the Republic. Francisco Sagasti emphasized two aspects: buying vaccines and organizing national elections" (p. 7). Further, two other Health Ministers were appointed and resigned two months later.
- Resistance to quarantine measures as "hundreds of thousands of people had already been seized by the police for disobeying State-imposed

isolation measures" which were enacted for three months, but "extended for two more years" (p. 3). Additionally, many people could not afford to stay at home as they made "a living from daily street vending" (p. 3).
- Blaming and seeking culprits: "Chinese eating habits were blamed for being the root cause of the disease" (p. 3) which "various health specialists (historians, sociologists, health officials, epidemiologists) rejected anti-Chinese racism in various media and questioned the blaming of street vendors as responsible for the failure of State measures" (p. 4).
- Searching for alternative remedies from charlatans, social media, or religious sources as well as Western medicines like ivermectin and chlorine dioxide.

These insights from Lossio (2023) paint a picture different from research conducted by Ivonne Natalia Montes Vega, María Elizabeth Muñoz Castillo, and Felipe Anderson Rios Incio at the Universidad Cesar Vallejo, Trujillo, Perú, with Ángel Emiro Páez Moreno (2022) from the Universidad de Boyacá, Tunja, Columbia.

Vega et al. (2022) analyzed the communication strategies applied by the Peruvian Government during the second wave of COVID-19, specifically "press conferences; 40 communication products from the communication campaigns 'Let's not lower our guard' and 'Put my shoulder' and 200 posts published on Facebook" (p. 288). Additionally, the ministries in Peru addressed the public with messages about quarantine measures through "publicity spots, educational videos, and flyers ... [and] carried out the campaigns 'I stay at home,' 'First my health' and 'The Covid doesn't kill alone. Let's not be an accomplice'" (p. 290). Lastly, various social campaigns, "which execute communication strategies proposed by the government to inform and raise awareness of the problems within the nation ... have placed messages in media that reach large audiences, such as television or radio, or outdoor settings, while other campaigns incorporate new technologies such as digital media" (Vega et al., 2022, p. 290).

It is at the confluence of the infodemic, social and government responses, communication campaigns, and technology that Ricardo Maldonado created the professional campaign that "brought three famous Peruvians back to life" using a deep fake technique and artificial intelligence to transmit "messages of cohesion and 'tips' against COVID, in addition to recruiting thousands of volunteers (citizens and companies) for the cause" (Zavalita Brand Building, 2023, para. 1).

The clear premise of "Peru I Love You--Don't Join Us Yet" is a call to "take care of our lives, expressed in the claim: 'to beat the virus, we must be united, and to be united, we must first be alive'" (Zavalita Brand Building, n.d., para. 2).

Key words

Advertising Equivalency Rates (AVEs)
Deepfake Technology
Memes
Organic Content
Perú Te Quiero (nonprofit)
Public Service Announcements
Susana Distancia
TikTok
Vietnam National Institute of Occupational Safety and Environmental Health (VNNIOSH)

Discussion questions

1 If the U.S. (or your country) were to create a deepfake PSA of distinguished people, who would they be and why?
2 Can you recall a PSA used in your country during the most severe periods of COVID-19? If so, what were the cultural, creative and storytelling elements?
3 Pham et al. (2020) researched cultural factors that helped the government and people of Vietnam overcome COVID-19. The authors compared cultural factors in Vietnam to American cultural factors, proposing this question: "Would Americans agree to lose their privacy freedoms for China-like surveillance if that meant a lower risk of death and infection?" (p. 4). How would you answer this question? What cultural factors should be considered in your answer?
4 The use of deep fake technology has advantages and disadvantages. Discuss what was advantageous about using the technology in the Peru video to impart health messages, and potential disadvantages of the technology within the infodemic of fake news.

10.5 OVERCOMING GAPS IN COVID-19 PUBLIC HEALTH COMMUNICATION: LOCALIZED CAMPAIGNS REACH ABORIGINAL PEOPLE IN AUSTRALIA AND MĀORI COMMUNITIES IN NEW ZEALAND

Situation analysis

Both Australia and New Zealand are part of Oceania, home to over 10,000 islands spanning the Central and South Pacific Ocean, a body of water larger than the world's total landmass of all continents and islands.

Oceania's largest landmass, Australia, is the smallest continent in terms of total land area. Its third largest landmass, New Zealand, is 1,000 miles away from Australia, with two main islands and over 600 small islands belonging to the microcontinent of Zealandia along with Papua New Guinea. According to IUCN (n.d.)—International Union for Conservation of Nature and Natural Resources—the other Oceania islands include Melanesia, Micronesia, and Polynesia, including Hawaii.

Australia and New Zealand are part of the British Commonwealth operating under a federal parliamentary democracy. English is the national de facto language of Australia; the population also speaks an estimated 300 languages, including many Indigenous languages (Macquarie University, n.d.) English is the most widely used language in New Zealand; other official languages are Māori and New Zealand Sign Language, the first country in the world to have sign language as an official language (New Zealand Immigration Concepts, n.d.). Both countries have high internet penetration: Australia at 94.99% and New Zealand at 95.73% (World Population Review, 2025).

First Nations people, meaning the first peoples of Australia before colonization, are referred to as "First Australians" or "Aboriginal people" or "Torres Strait Islander people." An estimated 984,000 Aboriginal and/or Torres Strait Islander peoples, comprising 3.8% of the total Australian population, live in Australia. (The number may be higher since First Nations people may be undercounted in census data). The majority reside in New South Wales, Queensland, and Western Australia (Australian Human Rights Commission, 2025). In New Zealand, the Māori ethnic population was an estimated 922,600, comprising 17.4% of the total population (Stats NZ Tatauranga Aotearoa, 2025). The North Island is home to 90% of the Māori, with 50% living in the Gisborne region located on the island's northeast coast (Wilson, 2015).

The Māori, the Indigenous people of New Zealand, are believed to have arrived in New Zealand from an island or group of Polynesian islands over 1,000 years ago. The Māori share linguistic and cultural similarities of other Polynesian islands, such as Cook Islands, Hawaii, and Tahiti. Tourism New Zealand provides more details (New Zealand Tourism, n.d.):

> Today, Māori are part of an iwi (tribes), a group of people who are descendants of a common ancestor and associated with a certain region or area in New Zealand. Each iwi has their own hapū (sub-tribes). Iwi can trace their entire origins and whakapapa (genealogy) back to certain waka hourua [double-hulled ocean-voyaging canoes]. The seven waka hourua that arrived to Aotearoa were Tainui, Te Arawa, Mātaatua, Kurahaupō, Tokomaru, Aotea and Tākitimu.
>
> *(para. 3)*

Australia experienced 11.4 million confirmed cases and 19,574 deaths due to COVID-19; 87.34% of the total population received at least one vaccine dose (John Hopkins University & Medicine, 2023d). According to the Australian Bureau of Statistics (2023), 274 COVID-19 associated deaths of Aboriginal and Torres Strait Islander people were reported between August 2021 and February 2023 in Australia, and no recorded deaths in 2020 to July 2021. Aboriginal and Torres Strait Islander peoples experienced a mortality rate from COVID-19 that was 1.6 times higher in comparison to non-Indigenous people. In terms of vaccination rates, the percentage of the Aboriginal and Torres Strait Islander population receiving three COVID-19 doses was 53.2% (Poirier et al., 2023).

In New Zealand, COVID-19 caused over 2.23 million cases and 2,550 deaths whereas 89.19% of the population was vaccinated with a minimum of one dose (John Hopkins University & Medicine, 2023e). According to Health New Zealand (2025), the Māori experienced 392,046 COVID-19 cases (14.3% of the total New Zealand population) and 420 deaths. Vaccine rates were high: 88.5% of eligible Māori received two vaccines doses while 95.2% of the entire eligible New Zealand population received two doses (Devine et al., 2022).

Communication campaigns

One Disease: Helping Aboriginal and Torres Strait Islander populations in Australia

The First Nations peoples faced numerous health and socio-economic risks from COVID-19, such as the following:

- Pre-existing chronic diseases, such as "arthritis, asthma, back problems, cancer, chronic obstructive pulmonary disease (COPD), diabetes, heart, stroke and vascular disease, kidney disease, osteoporosis for people aged 2 years and over, mental and behavioural conditions" (Australian Bureau of Statistics, 2024, para. 5).
- Smoking and vaping (29% of people age 15 and over smoked daily) (Australian Bureau of Statistics, 2024).
- Health care inequity since 20% reside in remote locations away from immediate healthcare services (Crooks et al., 2020).
- Food insecurity affected 51% of people living in remote locations (Australia Bureau of Statistics, 2024).
- Disadvantages in housing, education, and employment (Crooks et al., 2020).
- Extended families and groups living in the same crowded household, making quarantining challenging (Crooks et al., 2020).

One Disease, a nonprofit focused on First Nations in Australia originally combatted crusted scabies, a contagious skin rash caused by mites that can be cured by medication, which was widespread in remote Aboriginal communities (One Disease, n.d). Due to COVID-19 lockdowns and travel restrictions, One Disease had to curtail its usual work and redirected some of its funding to a healthcare crowdsourcing campaign on preventive care measures to stop the spread of COVID-19 with videos created by the local communities on preventive measures in Indigenous languages. The nonprofit wanted to explore "a new approach to participatory health promotion" that would benefit the communities to communicate COVID-19 messages but also be applied to future communication efforts about scabies (Glennie et al., 2022, p. 2).

One Disease's goal was to reach Aboriginal and Torres Strait Islander populations, many of whom live in remote areas without nearby medical care, and to communicate COVID-19 preventive health care measures in their languages. The primary strategies were to engage with artists in the local communities to create prevention videos and to identify the most effective medium to share the videos with their target audiences (Glennie et al., 2022).

The nonprofit collaborated with Darwin-based Skinnyfish Music, "a record label…committed to presenting First Nations peoples' music to national and international audience" (Australian Office, n.d., para. 1) on a pro bono basis since the label has experience working with remote Aboriginal and Torres Strait Islander artists. The two crowdsourcing rounds provided an invitation to people or groups in the community who have a background in community projects or within the entertainment industry. Skinnyfish made phone calls and followed cultural protocol in securing local talent to create COVID-19 videos on their cellphones from scripting to designing and producing in local languages (Glennie et al., 2022). Mark Grose, managing director of Skinnyfish, said in an interview with *NME Australia* (Rose, 2020), "Music is not just an entertainment vehicle in remote communities it is part of everyday life it informs, it instructs and it carries cultural weight so it is a perfect vehicle for a COVID campaign" (para. 5).

The guidelines in the creative brief written in an Aboriginal language required the first video submission to cover best practices in handwashing, and the second one needed to focus on social distancing practices of keeping a distance of 1.5 meters (5 feet) from others. The contributors had a 30-second time limit, and they were informed that their videos would be shown as submitted without post-production editing. Submissions were posted on a WhatsApp message to the Skinnyfish director (Glennie et al., 2022).

One Disease staff and public health nurses evaluated the videos to make sure that they covered accurate public health messaging on COVID-19. Contributors of noncompliant videos were able to resubmit their videos based on the evaluators' feedback. Local talent and community figures submitted 19 videos and 18 were accepted. Nine videos covered handwashing, six on social distancing, and three on both topics, spanning six Aboriginal languages, with many incorporating important messages in English. Accepted contributors were paid a day's work (Glennie et al., 2022).

One Disease selected Facebook as the social media platform to share the videos. The reasons were that this social media site is popular within the local communities, and a variety of health services, nonprofits, and Aboriginal Community Controlled Health Organisations have disseminated health-related information on Facebook to the communities. The nonprofit hired a local advertising agency to oversee the video distribution using Facebook ads and applied Australian Bureau of Statistics data for identification of postcodes of residents who speak the languages in the videos. The agency also prioritized ThruPlays to maximize videos played in full (Glennie et al., 2022). Meta (2025), a U.S. multinational corporation and owner of Facebook and other social media platforms, describes ThruPlay:

> ThruPlay is a performance goal and billing option designed for video ads created with the awareness or engagement ad objective in Meta Ads Manager. ThruPlay allows you to optimize and choose to pay only for ads that are played to completion for videos shorter than 15 seconds. For longer videos, ThruPlay optimizes and bills for ads that are played for at least 15 seconds. This optimization is available with auction or reservation campaigns.
>
> *(para. 1)*

Te Ranga Tupua Collective (TRT): Communicating health messages to iwi in New Zealand

As with the Aboriginal and Torres Strait Islander peoples in Australia and Indigenous peoples worldwide, the Māori in New Zealand also contend with chronic health conditions, socioeconomic inequity, and racial discrimination. Socioeconomic data indicates that Māori face greater disadvantages than non-Māori in education, employment, healthcare, and personal income. Māori were also more likely to live in crowded households, smoke or vape, and suffer from psychological distress than non-Māori (Ministry of Health, 2024). This situation meant that the Māori were of high risk to contract COVID-19, and the communities needed to be extra prepared to cope with the spreading pandemic.

The New Zealand government funded NZD 2.8 million for TRT to undertake a 15-week project to reach iwi (Māori tribes) with COVID-19 preventive care information and build healthcare supporting preparation for the pandemic to spread across the Whanganui, Rangitikei, Ruapehu, and South Taranaki regions. Operational expenditures applied to offering COVID response mobile clinics and pop-up clinics managed by experienced iwi health providers; purchasing a van, generators, and personal protective equipment (PPE); setting up a whānau (family group) vax drive-in movie night event; and establishing a community hub to serve as a future vaccination site and to support whānau needs related to COVID-19. Communication initiatives included dedicated Facebook and Instagram sites, and campaigns to promote the mobile and pop-up clinics (Te Ranga Tupua collective secures $2.8m, 2021; Te Puni Kōkiri, 2022).

The target audiences focused on iwi/Māori populations. The primary communication strategies were as follows:

- Apply an "uplifting, positive, and strengths based approach to messaging… an intentional direction from TRT to ensure the well-being of whānau and to lift the spirit of their community" (Boulton et al., 2022, p. 11).
- Share relatable voices within the community—not just from Australian government officials—and to communicate in the Māori language and viewpoints from "tribes, ancestors, elders, Māori youth, Iwi leaders, Māori experts, and Māori community workers" (Devine et al., 2022, p. 12).
- Provide frequent and accurate information on prevention and developments at the Hub and within the communities.
- Collaborate within the communities and share videos and other resources.
- Connect and engage with the community on Facebook and other social media platforms. See Figure 10.4.

The TRT iwi leaders knew that communications needed to be from tribal authorities in iwi communities—not from the New Zealand government authorities—to earn trust. As a fundamental part of the community hub, TRT set up a dedicated communications team to provide frequent updates on health services and preventive measures, including hygiene and available food packs, firewood, and other necessities. A toll-free telephone number was set up for the community to help answer questions regarding available services and support on such topics as rural isolation and health care to financial support and mental health (Boulton et al., 2022). The communications team translated government communiques and other complex technical and academic language into more relatable language and into te reo Māori (the Māori language) and tone. For example, the communications intentionally focused on the concept of whānau, meaning the extended family, family group, or friends in modern context, to convey a sense of connectedness and wellness, particularly during lockdown (Boulton, et al., 2022, Māori Dictionary, 2025).

FIGURE 10.4 Post about mask wearing from Te Oranganui on September 6, 2021. (Whakamau i tō ārai kanohi: Put on your face covering). Courtesy of Te Ranga Tupua Iwi Collective.

Results

One Disease in Australia

The One Disease crowdsourcing campaign reached over 91,000 Facebook users in the Northern Territory plus some users in a part of Western Australia. Here are other results (Glennie et al., 2022):

> Impressions is a Facebook measure of the number of times a video has been displayed. Over the 2 × 3 week distribution periods, a campaign video was displayed to a user 638,294 times. Although it is not possible to disaggregate to individual users, as an indication of frequency of exposure, with a reach of 91,295 individual users, this represents 6.99 impressions per user. ThruPlays of 75,591 represent 0.83 full video views

> per user. In reality, Impression and ThruPlay numbers may be much higher for some users than others, but these aggregate numbers provide an overall indication of exposure.
>
> *(p. 4)*

The most popular handwashing videos showed a local musician singing in English with kids dancing, while the physical distancing video featured an older man in a bank talking in Djambarrpuyngu. An article published in *Rolling Stone* magazine in Australia (Jenke, 2020) stated:

> Having only been uploaded a couple of weeks ago, the campaign is already on track to be one of the most-viewed and most effective of all the public health campaigns launched in the Northern Territory. With the larger campaign featuring messages in five different languages from across the Territory, half of its population have managed to view the campaign via Facebook alone.
>
> *(para. 7)*

TRT in New Zealand

The New Zealand Royal Commission (2024) looked at lessons learned during COVID-19 within iwi and Māori communities. Positive feedback indicated a few key points on how iwi- or community-led responses were more efficient and effective than the government's responses: faster and more relevant engagement with the communities and greater trust in the expertise and leadership of the Māori.

The holistic quality of the TRT communications was applying cultural appropriate messaging within the Māori language, incorporating the cultural values, and sharing the voices of real people within the communities. This quote from McMeeking and Savage (2020) sums up TRT's success during COVID-19: "Māori infection rates from Covid-19 are perhaps the only example in Aotearoa New Zealand's contemporary history where Māori have achieved better social outcomes than non-Māori" (p. 36). The authors argue that the reasons were based on four categories: 1) Cultural adaption reflecting Māori values; 2) social cohesion and information channels with the interconnectedness of the iwi groups and digital platforms reaching people in remote areas; 3) distributive networks providing food packs, iwi-operated mobile and pop-up clinics, and other essential health and human services; and 4) community protection including lawful iwi checkpoints to prevent the pandemic from spreading.

Theoretical framework

Lapinski et al. (2025) explains the differences between tailoring and targeting messages, within a framework that considers culture, process and content elements. The CTP/CTC framework advanced by Lapinski, et al. is useful in understanding the effectiveness of the COVID-19 campaigns. Case study 10.4 explored the **CTC (cultural tailoring content)** part of the framework. In the present case study, the **CTP (cultural tailoring processes)** part of the framework is more relevant.

The United Nations Department of Economic and Social Affairs (2024) created a policy brief *The impact of COVID-19 on Indigenous peoples* to shed light on their experiences during the pandemic. Of note are these threats to the "health and survival of indigenous peoples" (para. 2):

> Higher rates of communicable and non-communicable diseases ... [and] high mortality rates and lower life expectancies ... mal- and under-nutrition, poor access to sanitation, lack of clean water, and inadequate medical services ... stigma and discrimination in health care settings such as stereotyping and a lack of quality in the care provided, thus compromising standards of care and discouraging them from accessing health care, if and when available.
>
> *(para. 2)*

Other impacts were noted with elders and women. Sacha McMeeking (Ngāi Tahu), head of School of Aotahi, the School of Māori and Indigenous Studies at the University of Canterbury, and Catherine Savage (Ngai Tahu), director of an independent research company, lhi Research, noted in their article (2020) that Māori have additional risk factor like diabetes, cardiovascular disease, cancer and chronic respiratory illness. Glennie et al. (2022) also noted in their article how Aboriginal and Torres Strait Islander Australians were hospitalized more frequently and lived in remote areas in overcrowded substandard housing.

Glennie et al. (2022) acknowledge that "Health communication is a critical component of pandemic mitigation, but mainstream prevention messaging often lacks social, cultural and linguistic relevance to vulnerable populations" (p. 1). It is clear from the analysis of the Australian and New Zealand governments' responses in this case study that care was taken to **culturally tailor** the content of messages, by using design elements like native language, "*identity-related content*, content which addresses *deep cultural values*, and other *cognitive, attitudinal and motivational* content" (emphasis in original, p. 12) and technology platforms the Aboriginal and Māori communities had access to.

What is also evident in the campaigns is the use of **cultural tailoring processes**, which refers to "methods used to develop all the elements of a communication campaign/intervention including messages ... which bring the needs and values of communities to the design of messages in various degrees" (Lapinski, et al, 2025, p. 809). More specifically, there are five categories of processes: outreach, consultation, involvement, participatory, and community driven.

In each of these communities, outreach, consultation and community-driven processes were most prevalent. Aboriginal people and Torres Strait Islanders created the preventive videos themselves, in consultation with One Disease and *Skinnyfish*, and used a crowdsourcing funding platform supported by the local community.

Similarly, "By prioritizing equity, self-determination and adopting a holistic approach to well-being, TRT have able to re-frame public health messaging in accordance with our tikanga, customs, and notions of Māori public health" (Devine et al., 2022, p. 6) in a community driven campaign as "members of the comms team were able to leverage their genealogical and kinship connection with the community to quickly develop the trusting relationships required to provide public health information and share data in this intense environment" (Devine et al., 2022, p. 8).

Key words

Aboriginal People
Crowdsourcing
First Nations
Iwi
Māori
One Disease
Te Ranga Tupua Collective
Torres Strait Islanders
ThruPlays

Discussion questions

Thinking of your own community you were a part of during COVID-19, answer these questions:

1 Identify a figure or leader you trusted to provide information. Was this information more or less effective than information from sources like the CDC or the World Health Organization? Why?

2 What social media platforms did you use to get information? Have you used or did you know of Meta's Impressions and ThruPlay?
3 What types of videos did you watch and on which platforms?

References

#Ghen CôVyChallenge. (n.d.). *#ghencovychallenge.* [Page]. TikTok. https://www.tiktok.com/tag/ghencovychallenge?lang=en

Ads of the World. (n.d.) *Perú Te Quiero. Don't join us yet.* https://www.adsoftheworld.com/campaigns/don-t-join-us-yet

Ahren, F. (2020, March 16). In Coronavirus crisis, South Korea shows how government PR is done. *PR News.* https://www.prnewsonline.com/South+Korea-coronavirus-communication

Allen, T. (n.d.). The poet's gun is a rose (El fusil del poeta es una rosa): Chabuca Granda/Notes on this poem. *Modern Poetry in Translation.* https://modernpoetryintranslation.com/poem/the-poets-gun-is-a-rose-el-fusil-del-poeta-es-una-rosa/

Altman, D. (2021, May 26). Persistent vaccine myths. *KFF.* https://www.kff.org/health-misinformation-and-trust/perspective/persistent-vaccine-myths/

Alvarez-Risco, A., Meija, C. R., Delgado-Zegarra, J., Del-Aguila-Arcentales, S., Arce-Esquivel, A. A., Valladares-Garrido, M. J., Rosas del Portal, M., Villegas, L. F., Curioso, W. H., Sekar, M. C., & Yañez, J. A. (2020). Perspective piece—The Peru approach against COVID-19 infodemic: Insights and strategies. *American Journal of Tropical Medicine and Hygiene, 103*(2), 583–586. https://doi.org/10.4269/ajtmh.20-0536

Australian Bureau of Statistics. (2023, March 31). *COVID-19 Mortality in Australia: Deaths registered until 28 February 2023.* https://www.abs.gov.au/articles/covid-19-mortality-australia-deaths-registered-until-28-february-2023

Australian Bureau of Statistics. (2024, November 26). *National Aboriginal and Torres Strait Islander health survey.* https://www.abs.gov.au/statistics/people/aboriginal-and-torres-strait-islander-peoples/national-aboriginal-and-torres-strait-islander-health-survey/latest-release

Australian Human Rights Commission. (2025, July 2). *Statistics about Aboriginal and Torres Strait Islander People.* https://humanrights.gov.au/education/stats-facts/statistics-about-aboriginal-and-torres-strait-islander-people

Australian Office. (n.d.) *Skinnyfish music.* https://australia.org.tw/tpei/Skinnyfish_Music.html

Barthel, M. (2021, June 29). Estimating U.S. newspaper circulation is a challenge—especially for 2020. *Pew Research Center.* https://www.pewresearch.org/decoded/2021/06/29/estimating-u-s-newspaper-circulation-is-a-challenge-especially-for-2020/

Bartra, A. L. M., Caloca-Lafont, E., Ricaurte, P., Paz, E., Elizalde, N. M., Zasso, M., & Loera, L. A. E. (2022). Susana Distancia: Memes and popular culture during the COVID-19 pandemic. *Visual Studies, 38*(3–4), 655–662. https://doi.org/10.1080/1472586X.2022.2059556

Behsudi, A. (2020, December). Wish you were here. *F&D—Finance & Development Magazine.* https://www.imf.org/en/Publications/fandd/issues/2020/12/impact-of-the-pandemic-on-tourism-behsudi

Boulton, A., Devine, T., McMenamin, K., & Walsh-Tapiata, W. (2022). Te Ranga Tupua: An iwi (tribal) response to COVID-19 in Aotearoa New Zealand. *International Journal of Indigenous Health, 17*(1). https://doi.org/10.32799/ijih.v17i1.36718

Bryant, J., et al. (2022, April 4). How COVID-19 caused a global learning crisis. *McKinsey & Company*. https://www.mckinsey.com/industries/education/our-insights/how-covid-19-caused-a-global-learning-crisis
CDC. (n.d.) *COVID data tracker*. https://covid.cdc.gov/covid-data-tracker/#data tracker-home
CDC. (2020, July 6). *Social distancing: Keep a safe distance to slow the spread*. https://stacks.cdc.gov/view/cdc/90522
CDC. (2024a, September 3). *COVID-19: Benefits of getting vaccinated*. https://www.cdc.gov/covid/vaccines/benefits.html
CDC. (2024b, August 30). *Myths & facts about COVID-19 vaccines*. https://archive.cdc.gov/#/details?url=https://www.cdc.gov/covid/vaccines/myths-facts.html
CEPI. (2024). *Middle East Respiratory Syndrome*. https://cepi.net/MERS
Cha, V., & Kim, D. Published March 27, (2020, March 27). A timeline of South Korea's response to COVID-19. *Center for Strategic and International Studies*. https://www.csis.org/analysis/timeline-south-koreas-response-covid-19
Choi, O., & Kim, S. (2024). Comparison of the efficacy of COVID-19 responses in South Korea and the United States. *Global Health Action*, *17*(1), 2370611. https://doi.org/10.1080/16549716.2024.2370611
Clark, D. (2020, April 23). Trump suggests 'injection' of disinfectant to beat coronavirus and 'clean' the lungs. *NBC News*. https://www.nbcnews.com/politics/donald-trump/trump-suggests-injection-disinfectant-beat-coronavirus-clean-lungs-n1191216
Costa, W., Goñi, U., Milhorance, F., Collyns, D., & Jones, S. (2021, June 18). A silent decimation: South America's losing battle against COVID; Strained and underfunded health systems, economics and misinformation have all led to a surge in deaths. (2021, June 18). *The Guardian* [London, England]. https://link-gale-com.ezproxy.ithaca.edu/apps/doc/A665486850/STND?u=nysl_sc_ithaca&sid=bookmark-STND&xid=0a23b4bc
Crooks, K., Casey, D., & Ward, J. S. (2020). First Nations peoples leading the way in COVID-19 pandemic planning, response and management. *Medical Journal of Australia*, *213*(4), 151–152. DOI: 10.5694/mja2.50704
Cultural Atlas. (2025). South Korean culture. *Mosaica*. https://culturalatlas.sbs.com.au/south-korean-culture/south-korean-culture-population-statistics
Dang, Q. [@quangdang]. (2020, April). *HANDWASHING DANCE [ORIGINAL] - "GHEN CO VY."* [Video]. YouTube. https://www.youtube.com/shorts/ctF5aMV05kM
de Groot, K. (2022, October 14). South Korea's response to COVID-19: Lessons for the next pandemic. *Penn Today*. https://penntoday.upenn.edu/news/pwh-chung-sye-kyun-south-koreas-response-covid-19-lessons-next-pandemic
Devine, T., Allport, T., Walsh-Tapiata, W., & Bolton, A. (2022). Equity, public health messaging, and traditional Māori knowledge: The Te Ranga Tupua COVID-19 response. *Journal of Humanistic Psychology*, 1–24. https://doi.org/10.1177/00221678221139013
Diamond, J., Spiegel, A., Hill, T. W., VanWormer, E., gaiashkibos, J., Hall, B., Sutherlen, A., & McQuillan, J. (2021). Developing pandemic comics for youth audiences. *Journal of STEM Outreach*, *4(*2), 1–10. https://doi.org/10.15695/jstem/v4i2.03
Dong, K. (2017, May 27). MV "Ghen" sets a new record in Min and Erik's career [English translation]. *VOV*. https://vov.vn/van-hoa/am-nhac/mv-ghen-xac-lap-ki-luc-moi-trong-su-nghiep-cua-min-va-erik-629235.vov
Dudley, M. Z., Squires, G. K., Petroske, T. M., Dawson, S., & Brewer, J. (2023). The use of narrative in science and health communication: A scoping review. *Patient Education and Counseling*, *112*, 1–18. https://doi.org/10.1016/j.pec.2023.107752

Editorial Staff. (2021, May 14). The 'compa' of 'Susana Distancia' arrives: Health ents the chatbot 'Armando Vaccuno.' [Translated title]. *El Financiero*. https://www.elfinanciero.com.mx/salud/2021/05/14/llega-el-compita-de-susana-distancia-salud-presenta-al-chatbot-armando-vaccuno/

El Universal Editorial Staff. (2020, May 1). Susana Distancia, the heroine of health and women's empowerment. *El Universal*. https://www.eluniversal.com.mx/nacion/susana-distancia-la-heroina-de-la-salud-y-del-empoderamiento-de-la-mujer/

Elisondo, R. (2022). Everyday creativity in pandemic: A systematic review. *Creativity, 9*(2) 55–93. DOI: 10.2478/ctra-2022-0012

Friedman, U. (2022, February 15). The seven habits of COVID-resilient nations. *The Atlantic*. https://www.theatlantic.com/ideas/archive/2022/02/south-korea-resilient-covid-deaths/622085/

George, A. M. (2012). The phases of crisis communication. In A. M. George & C. B. Pratt (Eds.). *Case studies in crisis communication: International perspectives on hits and misses*. (pp. 29–50). Routledge.

Getty. (n.d.a.). *Our mission*. https://www.getty.edu/about/

Getty. (n.d.b.). *History of Getty milestones from 1953–present*. https://www.getty.edu/about/history/

Getty. (n.d.c.). *Getty Villa Museum: Greek and Roman antiquities housed in a re-created Roman country home*. https://www.getty.edu/visit/villa/

Getty. (n.d.d.) *Open content program*. https://www.getty.edu/projects/open-content-program/

Getty. (2020, April 2). *Getty creates $10m LA Arts COVID-19 relief fund for museums and visual arts organizations*. [News release]. https://www.getty.edu/news/getty-creates-10-millionla-arts-covid-19-relief-fund-for-museums-and-visual-arts-organizations/

Getty Museum. (2020). *Getty Museum challenge is now a book, with all profits to charity*. [News release]. https://www.getty.edu/news/getty-announces-new-book-celebrating-creativity-and-joy/

Getty Publications. (2020). *Off the Walls: Inspired re-creations of iconic artworks*. [Book]. https://shop.getty.edu/products/off-the-walls-inspired-re-creations-of-iconic-artworks-978-1606066843

Glennie, M., Dowden, M., Grose, M., Scolyer, M., Superina, A., & Gardner, K. (2022, May 13). Engaging remote Aboriginal communities in COVID-19 public health messaging via crowdsourcing. *Frontiers in Public Health, 10*. DOI: 10.3389/fpubh.2022.866134

Gopinath, G. (2020, April 14). The Great Lockdown: Worst economic downturn since the Great Depression. *IMF Blog*. https://www.imf.org/en/Blogs/Articles/2020/04/14/blog-weo-the-great-lockdown-worst-economic-downturn-since-the-great-depression

Government of the Republic of Korea. (2020, October). *All about Korea's response to COVID- 19*. https://www.mofa.go.kr/viewer/skin/doc.html?fn=20201021031300238.pdf&rs=/viewer/result/202601

Green, L. W. (2023). *The PRECEED-PROCEED Model origins and evolution*. https://www.lgreen.net/precede-proceed

Green, M. J., & Myers, K. R. (2010). Graphic medicine: Use of comics in medical education and patient care. *BMJ, 340*, 1–8. https://www.bmj.com/content/340/bmj.c863

Health New Zealand. (2025, July 3). *COVID-19: Case demographics*. https://www.tewhatuora.govt.nz/for-health-professionals/data-and-statistics/covid-19-data/covid-19-case-demographics

Holder, J. (2023, March 13). Tracking coronavirus vaccinations around the world. *New York Times*. https://www.nytimes.com/interactive/2021/world/covid-vaccinations-tracker.html

Hollimon, N. (2022, November 19). Celebrities with Coronavirus. *WebMD*. https://www.webmd.com/covid/ss/slideshow-celebrities-coronavirus
Honor, gloria y legado en el Mar Peruano. (2024, September 10). *Perú21*. https://peru21.pe/peru/honor-gloria-y-legado-en-el-mar-peruano/
Hou, J. Z. (2023). "Sharing is caring": Participatory storytelling and community building on social media amidst the COVID-19 pandemic. *American Behavioral Scientist*, *69*(12), 1481-1501. https://doi.org/10.1177/00027642231164040
Hundt, D. (2021, December 28). South Korea's developmentalist response to COVID-19. *East Asia Forum*. https://eastasiaforum.org/2021/12/28/south-koreas-developmentalist-response-to-covid-19/
Ibarrola-Peña J.C. et al. (2022, October 11). Preventative measures against the COVID-19 pandemic in Mexico: A cross sectional study. *Frontiers in Public Health*, *10*, 1–10. https://www.frontiersin.org/journals/public-health/articles/10.3389/fpubh.2022.932010/full
Influence Watch. (2024). *Non-profit: The J. Paul Getty Trust*. https://www.influencewatch.org/non-profit/the-j-paul-getty-trust/
Institute for Public Relations. (2007, October 30). *Crisis management and communications*. [White paper]. https://instituteforpr.org/crisis-management-and-communications/
International Council of Museums. (2021, July). *Museums, museum professionals and Covid-19: Third survey*. [Museum report]. https://icom.museum/en/news/museums-and-covid-19-third-icom-report/
IUCN. (n.d.). *About Oceania*. https://iucn.org/our-work/region/oceania
Jeffries-Fox, B. (2003). A discussion of Advertising Value Equivalency (AVE). *The Institute for Public Relations*. https://instituteforpr.org/wp-content/uploads/2003_AVE1.pdf
Jenke, T. (2020, April 29). Indigenous artists go viral with COVID-19 awareness video. *Rolling Stone Australia*. https://au.rollingstone.com/music/music-news/indigenous-artists-viral-covid-19-awareness-video-10342/
John Hopkins University & Medicine. (2023a, March 10). *Peru*. https://coronavirus.jhu.edu/region/peru
John Hopkins University & Medicine. (2023b, March 10). *Mexico*. https://coronavirus.jhu.edu/region/mexico
John Hopkins University & Medicine. (2023c, March 10). *Vietnam*. https://coronavirus.jhu.edu/region/vietnam
John Hopkins University & Medicine. (2023d, March 10). *Australia* https://coronavirus.jhu.edu/region/australia
John Hopkins University & Medicine. (2023e, March 10). *New Zealand*.. https://coronavirus.jhu.edu/region/new-zealand
Johnson, C. K., & Stobbe, M. (2021, June 29). *Nearly all COVID deaths in US are now among unvaccinated. Associated Press*. https://apnews.com/article/coronavirus-pandemic-health-941fcf43d9731c76c16e7354f5d5e187
Kalman, J. (2020, May 14). Signs of the times: Small media during Covid-19 in Mexico City. *Language on the Move*. https://www.languageonthemove.com/signs-of-the-times-small-media-during-covid-19-in-mexico-city/
Kang, J., Jang, Y., Kim, J., Han, S., Lee, K., Kim, M., & Eom, J. (2020). South Korea's responses to stop the COVID-19 pandemic. *American Journal of Infection Control*, *48*(9), 1080–1086. DOI: 10.1016/j.ajic.2020.06.003
Kemp, S. (2020, January 30). Digital 2020: Global digital overview. *DataReportal*. https://datareportal.com/reports/digital-2020-global-digital-overview
Key, M. (2020, April 1). CORONAVIRUS in Asia: Impact on communications & key takeaways [PowerPoint]. *MSL Insights Session*. https://mslgroup.de/wp-content/uploads/2020/04/MSL_Covid_April-1.pdf

Khlystova, O., Kalyuzhnova, Y., & Belitski, M. (2022). The impact of the COVID-19 pandemic on the creative industries: A literature review and future research agenda. *Journal of Business Research, 139*, 1192–1210. https://doi.org/10.1016/j.jbusres.2021.09.062

Kim, J., An, J. A., Oh, S. J., Oh, J., & Lee, J. (n.d.). Emerging COVID-19 success story: South Korea learned the lessons of MERS. *Exemplars in Global Health*. https://www.exemplars.health/emerging-topics/epidemic-preparedness-and-response/covid-19/south-korea

Kim, T., & Kim, B. K. (2020). Enhancing mixed accountability for state-society synergy: South Korea's responses to COVID-19 with ambidexterity governance. *Inter-Asia Cultural Studies, 21*(4), 533–541. https://doi.org/10.1080/14649373.2020.1835094

King, C. M. (2006). Making the case for an entertaining approach to public relations. *Public Relations Review, 32*, 74–76. DOI: 10.1016/j.pubrev.2005.10.011

Kjellén, M., & Wong, C. (2023, December). Governance: A 'whole-of-society' approach. In *The United national world water development report*, (pp. 172–182). United Nations Educational, Scientific and Cultural Organization. https://doi.org/10.18356/9789210026208c021

Know Your Meme. (2020). *Susana Distancia*. https://knowyourmeme.com/memes/susana-distancia

Lankow, J., Ritchie, J., & Crooks, R. (2012). *Infographics: The power of visual storytelling*. John Wiley & Sons, Inc.

Lapinski, M. K., Oetzel, J. G., Park, S., & Willaimson, A. J. (2025). Cultural tailoring and targeting of messages: A systematic literature review. *Health Communication, 40*(5), 808–821. https://doi.org/10.1080/10410236.2024.2369340

LastWeekTonight. (2020, March 2). *Coronavirus: Last Week Tonight with John Oliver (HBO)*. [Video]. YouTube. https://www.youtube.com/watch?v=c09m5f7Gnic&ab_channel=LastWeekTonight

Lazo, C. J. L. (2020, June 30). Mixed messages: COVID-19, a cartoon heroine, and violence against women in Mexico (#WitnessingCorona). [Blog post]. *Medizinethnologie*. https://www.medizinethnologie.net/mixed-messages-mexico-witnessing-corona/

Levin, B. (2021). *Report to the nation: Anti-Asian prejudice & hate crime*. Center for the Study of Hate & Extremism. https://www.csusb.edu/sites/default/files/Report%20to%20the%20Nation%20-%20Anti-Asian%20Hate%202020%20Final%20Draft%20-%20As%20of%20Apr%2BrianLevin030%202021%206%20PM%20corrected.pdf

Lindell, M. K., & Perry, R. W. (2012). The protective action decision model: Theoretical modifications and additional evidence, *Risk Analysis, 32*(4) 616–632. DOI: 10.1111/j.1539-6924.2011.01647.x

Litark. (n.d.). *Off the walls inspired re-creations of iconic artworks with a preface by Sarah Waldorf and Annelisa Stephan*. Getty Publications, Los Angeles. https://litark.com/books/home/422927-sarah-waldorf-off-the-walls-inspired.html

Lossio, J. (2023, August 14). Panic, denial, and the search for "magic remedies:" The various social responses to covid-19 in Peru. *História Ciências Saúde-Manguinhos, 30* (Suppl 1), 1–10. https://doi.org/10.1590/S0104-59702023000100031

Macquarie University. (n.d.). *Languages in Australia*. https://www.mq.edu.au/research/research-centres-groups-and-facilities/healthy-people/centres/centre-for-language-sciences-clas/australian-voices/languages-in-australia

Mallenbaum, C. (2020, April 2). Lockdown life imitates art: People post fun pics of themselves, pets as part of Getty challenge. *USA Today*. https://www.usatoday.com/story/life/2020/04/02/lockdown-challenge-people-share-fun-pics-life-imitating-getty-art/5116478002/

Māori Dictionary. (2025). *Whānau*. https://maoridictionary.co.nz/word/10062

Marr, B. (2023, May 19) Short history of ChatGPT: How we got to where we are today. *Forbes*. https://www.forbes.com/sites/bernardmarr/2023/05/19/a-short-history-of-chatgpt-how-we-got-to-where-we-are-today

Martinez, J. (2024, November 22). Bay Area muxe community celebrates gender diversity in indigenous cultures. *CBS News Bay Area*. https://www.cbsnews.com/sanfrancisco/news/bay-area-muxe-community-gender-diversity-indigenous-cultures/

Martyr, K. (2020, March 21). Mexican superhero to promote social distancing. *DW*. https://www.dw.com/en/mexican-superhero-susana-distancia-swoops-in-to-promote-social-distancing/a-52873960

McClaughlin, M., Vilar-Lluch, S., Parnell, T., Knight, D., Nichele, E., Adolphs, S., Clos, J., & Schiazza, G. (2023). The reception of public health messages during the COVID-19 pandemic. *Applied Corpus Linguistics*, *3*, 1–19. https://doi.org/10.1016/j.acorp.2022.100037

McMeeking, S., & Savage, C. (2020, August). Māori responses to covid-19. *Policy Quarterly*, *16*(3), 36–41. DOI: https://doi.org/10.26686/pq.v16i3.6553

Meta. (2025). *About ThruPlay*. https://www.facebook.com/business/help/205146 1368219124

Migus, A., et al. (2020). COVID-19 epidemic phases: Criteria, challenges and issues for the future. *Bulletin de l'Academie nationale de medicine*, *204* e145–e156. https://doi.org/10.1016/j.banm.2020.07.004

MILENIO. (2020a, March 20). *Susana Distancia, la heroína durante coronavirus en México*. [Video]. YouTube. https://www.youtube.com/watch?v=eO5cUw6vjMY

MILENIO. (2020b, July 7). *Susana Distancia vuelve al ataque contra el coronavirus con 'Escuadrón de la salud.'* [Video]. YouTube. https://www.youtube.com/watch?v=HfJHaxuwDUE&t=346s

Miller, Z. (2021, July 17). *Biden grappling with 'pandemic of the unvaccinated. Associated Press*. https://apnews.com/article/joe-biden-health-government-and-politics-pandemics-coronavirus-pandemic-8318e3f406278f3ebf09871128cc91de

Min Official. (2020a, April 9). *Ghen Co Vy - Official English Version | Corona virus Song | Together we #EndCoV."* [Video]. YouTube. https://www.youtube.com/watch?v=wGoodWEtV8c

Min Official. (2020b, February 23). Ghen Cô Vy| NIOEH x K.HƯNG x MIN x ERIK | WASHING HAND SONG | CORONA SONG. [Video]. YouTube. https://www.youtube.com/watch?v=BtulL3oArQw

Ministry of Health. (2024). *Tatau kahukura: Māori health chart book 2024* (4th ed.). Wellington: Ministry of Health. https://www.health.govt.nz/system/files/2024-12/tatau-kFFahukura-maori-health-chart-book-2024-v4.pdf

MND Staff. (2025, February 24). Only in Mexico: Who is Dr. Simi and why is he so popular? *Mexico News Daily*. https://mexiconewsdaily.com/lifestyle/who-is-dr-simi-doll-and-why-is-he-so-popular/

MPA. (September 15, 2021). Number of print consumer magazines in the United States from 2002 to 2020 [Graph]. *In Statista*. https://www.statista.com/statistics/238589/number-of-magazines-in-the-united-states/

Nalewicki, J. (2020, March 31). This museum is asking people to remake famous artworks with household items. *Smithsonian Magazine*. https://www.smithsonianmag.com/smart-news/museum-asking-people-remake-famous-artworks-with-household-items-180974546/

National Cancer Institute. (n.d.). *Making health communication programs work (Pink Book)*. https://www.cancer.gov/publications/health-communication/pink-book.pdf

New Zealand Immigration Concepts. (n.d.) *English and the official languages of New Zealand.* https://www.new-zealand-immigration.com/blogs/english-and-the-official-languages-of-new-zealand

New Zealand Royal Commission. (2024, November 28). *The experiences of iwi and Māori.* https://www.covid19lessons.royalcommission.nz/reports-lessons-learned/experiences-of-the-covid-19-pandemic/the-experiences-of-iwi-and-maori

New Zealand Tourism. (n.d.). *The arrival of Māori.* https://www.newzealand.com/us/feature/arrival-of-maori/

Nguyen, C. V. (2020, April 5). Music video breakdown: Vietnam raises coronavirus awareness on 'Ghen Cô Vy.' *The Harvard Crimson.* https://www.thecrimson.com/article/2020/4/5/ghen-co-vy-corona-psa/

Nguyen, N. P. T., Hoang, T. D., Tran, V. T., Vu, C. T., Fodjo, J. N. S., Colebunders, R., Dunne, M. P., & Vo, T. V. (2020). Preventive behavior of Vietnamese people in response to the COVID-19 pandemic. *PLoS ONE, 15*(9), e0238830. https://doi.org/10.1371/journal.pone.0238830

Nguyen, Q. V., Cao, D. A., & Nghiem, S. H. (2021). Spread of COVID-19 and policy responses in Vietnam: An overview. *International Journal of Infectious Diseases, 103*, 157–161. https://doi.org/10.1016/j.ijid.2020.11.154

O'Kane, C. (2020, March 4). Catchy PSA about coronavirus turns into viral TikTok challenge about washing your hands. *CBS News.* https://www.cbsnews.com/news/coronavirus-prevention-vietnam-song-ghen-co-vy-tik-tok-challenge-about-washing-hands-quang-dang-john-oliver/

Obre, G. G. C. (2018, February 26). The untimely death of sports journalist Daniel Peredo provokes outpouring of grief in Peru. *GlobalVoices.* https://globalvoices.org/2018/02/26/the-untimely-death-of-sports-journalist-daniel-paredo-provokes-outpouring-of-grief-in-peru/

Oh, S. (2020, May 14). South Korea's success against COVID-19. *The Regulatory Review.* [Opinion]. https://www.theregreview.org/2020/05/14/oh-south-korea-success-against-covid-19/

Okuhara, T., Terada, M., Okada, H. & Kiuchi, T. (2024). Experiences of governments and public health agencies regarding crisis communication during the COVID-19 pandemic in the digital age: Protocol for a systematic review of qualitative studies. *JMIR Research Protocols, 13*, e58040. https://doi.org/10.2196/58040

One Disease. (n.d.). *About One Disease.* https://www.onedisease.org/about-one-disease

Optidge Internet Marketing Agency. (n.d.). *Mexico promotes social distancing efforts with the help of a new super hero.* https://optidge.com/mexico-promotes-social-distancing-with-new-super-hero/

Park, C. (2019). MERS-CoV infection in South Korea and strategies for possible future outbreak: Narrative review. *Journal of Global Health Reports, 201*(3): e2019088. doi:10.29392/joghr.3.e2019088

Paudyal, P., & Ozkosar, S. (2022). Storytelling to communicate public health messages during the COVID-19 pandemic; A systematic review. *European Journal of Public Health, 32.* https://doi.org/10.1093/eurpub/ckac129.636

Pham, N. C., Li, Y., Schapsis, C., Hossain, T., Pham, H. H., Fisher, D., & Yang, J. (2020). Intrinsic cultural factors that helped Vietnam overcome the CoViD-19 pandemic compared with other countries. *Asia Pacific Journal of Health Management, 15*(3):i425. DOI: 10.24083/apjhm.v15i3.425

Poirier, B., Soares, G., Cachagee, M., Hedges, S., Jamieson, L., & Hedges, J. (2023). Stories of community strength: Reflecting on strong COVID-19 vaccination uptake among Aboriginal and Torres Strait Islander communities. *First Nations Health and Wellbeing - The Lowitja Journal, 1.* https://doi.org/10.1016/j.fnhli.2023.100008

Population Reference Bureau. (2023). *2023 World population data sheet booklet.* https://2023-wpds.prb.org/wp-content/uploads/2023/12/2023-World-Population-Data-Sheet-Booklet.pdf

Potter, R. (2020, December 22). Pandemic election push cable news channels to peak in 2020. *The Hollywood Reporter*. https://www.hollywoodreporter.com/tv/tv-news/pandemic-election-push-cable-news-channels-to-peak-in-2020-4108610/

Potts, T. (2020, May 12). The j. Paul Getty Museum during the coronavirus crisis. *Museum Management and Curatorship*, *35*(3), 217–220. https://doi.org/10.1080/09647775.2020.1762360

Poushter, J., Gubbala, S., & Austin, S. (2024, February 5). 8 charts on technology use around the world. *Pew Research Center.* https://www.pewresearch.org/short-reads/2024/02/05/8-charts-on-technology-use-around-the-world/

PRWeek. (2021, March 18). *PRWeek's USA Awards 2021: The winners*. https://www.qgdigitalpublishing.com/publication/?i=699529&p=30&view=issueViewer

Puttkamer, L. (2020, March 23). Susana Distancia: The Mexican superhero fighting the spread of Coronavirus. *parCitypatory*. https://parcitypatory.org/2020/03/23/coronavirus-susana-distancia/

Redacc̀ion El Universal. (2020, August 7). The Health Squad: Mexico turns to cartoon characters to promote COVID-19 health measures. *El Universal.* https://www.eluniversal.com.mx/english/health-squad-mexico-turns-cartoon-characters-promote-covid-19-health-measures/

Romero, L. (2020, October 27). The Getty Museum Challenge: A social media campaign inspiring re-creations of masterpieces. *Medium.* https://lisa-romero.medium.com/the-getty-museum-challenge-a-social-media-campaign-inspiring-re-creations-of-masterpieces-edc1e43d2bc1

Rose, A. (2020, April 29). Indigenous musicians go viral with COVID-19 awareness video, 'Wash Your Hands.' *NME Australia*. https://www.nme.com/news/music/indigenous-musicians-go-viral-with-covid-19-awareness-video-wash-your-hands-3606404

Sánchez, F. O. (2022, May 13). In memory of cultural figures the U.S. lost to COVID-19. *NPR*. https://www.npr.org/2022/05/13/1091258643/u-s-cultural-figures-lost-to-covid-19

Secretaría de Salud México. (2020a, March 21). *Susana Distancia*. [Video]. YouTube. https://www.youtube.com/watch?v=KL-4FTrWR2s

Secretaría de Salud México. (2020b, April 25). *Susana Distancia Niñas, Niños y Adolescentes*. [Video]. YouTube. https://www.youtube.com/watch?v=EG1rQT1DXDQ&list=PL_-nl6fTOV3lsP4SSYd12nhZXWKhb_X2i&index=8

Secretaría de Salud México. (2020c, April 13). *Susana Distancia ¡No estamos de vacaciones!* [Video]. YouTube. https://www.youtube.com/watch?v=F1R1mxpDLzo

Secretaría de Salud México. (2020d, December 16). *#SusanaDistancia para salir a comprar*. [Video]. YouTube. https://www.youtube.com/watch?v=KCHjezMwv8c

Secretaría de Salud México. (2020e, December 16). *#SusanaDistancia*. [Video]. YouTube. https://www.youtube.com/watch?v=SCV6I0_m4vs&list=PL_-nl6fTOV3lsP4SSYd12nhZXWKhb_X2i&index=2

Sellnow, T. L., & Seeger, M. W. (2021). *Theorizing crisis communication*. (2nd ed.). Wiley.

Shearer, E., & Mitchell, A. (2021, January 12). News use across social media platforms in 2020. *Pew Research Center.* https://www.pewresearch.org/journalism/2021/01/12/news-use-across-social-media-platforms-in-2020/

Shorty Awards. (2021) *From the 13th annual Shorty Awards: #GettyMuseumChallenge finalist in hashtag*. https://shortyawards.com/13th/gettymuseumchallenge

Stats NZ Tatauranga Aotearoa. (2025, May 16). *Māori population estimates: Mean year ended 31 December 2024 (2023-base)*. https://www.stats.govt.nz/information-releases/maori-population-estimates-mean-year-ended-31-december-2024-2023-base/

Stolberg, S. G., & Alba, D. (2021, July 15). Surgeon General assails tech companies over misinformation on Covid-19. *New York Times*. https://www.nytimes.com/2021/07/15/us/politics/surgeon-general-vaccine-misinformation.html?searchResultPosition=3

Suárez, V., Quezada, M. S., Ruiz, S. O., & De Jesús, E. R. (2020). Epidemiology of COVID-19 in Mexico: From the 27th of February to the 30th of April 2020. *Revista Clínica Española*, *220*(8), 463–471. https://doi.org/10.1016/j.rce.2020.05.007

Susana Distancia. (n.d.). *Semáforo COVID-19*. Facebook. https://www.facebook.com/SusanaDistancia/about

Susana Distancia. (2025). *Susanadistancia*. [Page]. Instagram. https://www.instagram.com/susanadistancia/?hl=en

SusanaDistancia. [@SusanaDistancia]. (2020, March). *Semáforo COVID-19*. X. https://x.com/susanadistancia?lang=en

Sutton, J., & Fischer, L. M. (2021, January). Understanding visual risk communication messages: An analysis of visual attention allocation and think-aloud responses to tornado graphics. *American Meteorological Society*. DOI: 10.1175/WCAS-D-20-0042.1

Te Ranga Tupua collective secures $2.8m to prepare for Covid-19 cases. (2021, November 17). *New Zealand Radio (NZR)*. https://www.rnz.co.nz/news/te-manu-korihi/455946/te-ranga-tupua-collective-secures-dollar2-8m-to-prepare-for-covid-19-cases

Ministry of Māori Development Te Puni, K., Ministry of Māori Development. (2022, June 17). *Te Tai Hauāuru/Te Ranga Tupua – Phase 1*. https://www.tpk.govt.nz/en/nga-putea-me-nga-ratonga/covid-19-information-for-maori/maori-communities-covid19-fund/the-work-of-kaitono/te-tai-hauauru

Tho, N. A. (2022, January). The role of occupational safety and health in the implementation of the socio-economic recovery program in the post-Covid-19 period. *Newsletter on Occupational Safety and Working Environment*. https://vnniosh.vn/wp-content/uploads/2023/12/Newsletter-No-1_2022_1_compressed.pdf

Timm, J. C. (2020, April 24). Trump says he was being sarcastic with comments about injecting disinfectants. *NBC News*. https://www.nbcnews.com/politics/donald-trump/trump-says-he-was-being-sarcastic-comments-about-injecting-disinfectants-n1191991

U.K. Parliament Committees. (2021, September 28). *Written evidence submitted by End the Virus of Racism (OSB0173)*. https://committees.parliament.uk/writtenevidence/39436/pdf/

UCSF Institute for Global Health and Sciences. (n.d.) *Mexico's response to COVID-19: A case study*. https://globalhealthsciences.ucsf.edu/wp-content/uploads/2024/02/mexico-covid-19-case-study-english.pdf.

UNESCO. (2020). *Museums around the world in the face of COVID-19*. [Report]. https://unesdoc.unesco.org/ark:/48223/pf0000373530

United Nations. (2020, May 8). *Secretary-General denounces 'tsunami' of xenophobia unleashed amid COVID-19, calling for all-out effort against hate speech*. [Press release]. https://press.un.org/en/2020/sgsm20076.doc.htm

United Nations Department of Economic and Social Affairs. (2020, May). *The impact of COVID-19 on Indigenous peoples*. [Policy Brief no. 70]. https://desapublications.un.org/policy-briefs/undesa-policy-brief-70-impact-covid-19-indigenous-peoples

United Nations Development Programme. (n.d.). *Viet Nam. COVID-19 Pandemic*. https://www.undp.org/vietnam/covid-19-pandemic

Vainauskienė, V., & Vaitkienė, R. (2022). Challenges to the learning organization in the context of COVID-19 pandemic uncertainty: Creativity based response. *Creativity Studies*, *15*(2), 332–347. https://doi.org/10.3846/cs.2022.15109
Vega, I. N. M., Castillo, M. E. M., Incio, F. A. R., & Moreno, A. E. P. (2022, May-August). Communication and COVID-19: Communication strategies implemented by the Peruvian government during the second wave. *TELOS: Revista De Estudios Interdisciplinarios En Ciencias Sociales*, *24*(2), 288–301. https://doi.org/10.36390/telos242.06
Vergonia, J. P. (2020, March 12). *[Stay strong, Korea] How the world can learn from Korea's response to COVID-19*. https://www.korea.net/NewsFocus/HonoraryReporters/view?articleId=183149&pageIndex=1
Verma, A., Jin, Y., & Lui, B. F. (2024). Visual design as a facilitator of risk observance: Optimizing message reception and memorability for increased public engagement. In B. F. Lui & A. M. Mehta, (eds.). *Routledge handbook of risk, crisis and disaster communication*. (pp. 113–129). Routledge. DOI: 10.4324/9781003363330-11
VNNIOSH. (2023, April 12). *History*. https://vnniosh.vn/en/history/
Villar, E., Francke, P., & Loewenson, R. (2024). Learning from Perú: Why a macroeconomic star failed tragically and unequally on covid-19 outcomes. *SSM-Health Systems*, *2*, 1–3. https://doi.org/10.1016/j.ssmhs.2023.100007
Wamsley, L. (2020, March 4). Coronavirus fears have led to a golden age of hand-washing PSAs. *NPR*. https://www.npr.org/2020/03/04/811609241/coronavirus-fears-have-led-to-a-golden-age-of-hand-washing-psas
Wang, K. (2020, March 26). How a coronavirus safety-themed dance took the world by storm, according to the TikTok star who created it. *Business Insider*. https://www.businessinsider.com/coronavirus-song-dance-wash-hands-quang-dang-2020-3
WHO. (n.d.). *COVID-19 global circulation*. https://data.who.int/dashboards/covid19/
WHO. (2017). *WHO Strategic Communications: Framework for effective communications*. https://www.who.int/docs/default-source/documents/communicating-for-health/communication-framework.pdf
WHO. (2022a, January 19). *Coronavirus disease (COVID-19) advice for the public: Mythbusters*. https://www.who.int/emergencies/diseases/novel-coronavirus-2019/advice-for-public/myth-busters
WHO. (2022b, March 2). *COVID-19 pandemic triggers 25% increase in prevalence of anxiety and depression worldwide*. https://www.who.int/news/item/02-03-2022-covid-19-pandemic-triggers-25-increase-in-prevalence-of-anxiety-and-depression-worldwide
WHO. (2023a, December 31). *COVID-19 vaccination, world data*. https://data.who.int/dashboards/covid19/vaccines?n=c
WHO. (2023b, May 5). *Statement on the fifteenth meeting of the IHR (2005) Emergency Committee on the COVID-19 pandemic*. https://www.who.int/news/item/05-05-2023-statement-on-the-fifteenth-meeting-of-the-international-health-regulations-(2005)-emergency-committee-regarding-the-coronavirus-disease-(covid-19)-pandemic
WHO. (2023c, August 9). *Corona disease (COVID-19): Key facts*. https://www.who.int/news-room/fact-sheets/detail/coronavirus-disease-(covid-19)
WHO. (2023d, May 5). *WHO Director-General's opening remarks at the media briefing – 5 May 2023*. https://www.who.int/news-room/speeches/item/who-director-general-s-opening-remarks-at-the-media-briefing---5-may-2023
WHO. (2024a). *Number of COVID-19 cases reported to WHO (cumulative total)*. https://data.who.int/dashboards/covid19/cases?n=c
WHO. (2024b). *Number of COVID-19 deaths reported to WHO (cumulative total)*.

Wilson, J. (2015, April). *Society – Where New Zealanders live*. Te Ara—the Encyclopedia of New Zealand. https://teara.govt.nz/en/society/page-2
World Bank Group. (2024). *Urban population (% of total population)*. https://data.worldbank.org/indicator/SP.URB.TOTL.IN.ZS
World Factbook. (2025a, July 3). Korea, South. *CIA*. https://www.cia.gov/the-world-factbook/countries/korea-south/factsheets/
World Factbook (2025b, July 3). Mexico. *CIA*. https://www.cia.gov/the-world-factbook/countries/mexico/
World Factbook (2025c, July 3). Peru. *CIA*. https://www.cia.gov/the-world-factbook/countries/peru/
World Factbook (2025d, July 3). Vietnam. *CIA*. https://www.cia.gov/the-world-factbook/countries/vietnam/
World Bank Group. (n.d.). *Data. Individuals using the Internet (% of population)*. https://data.worldbank.org/indicator/IT.NET.USER.ZS
You, J. (2020). Lessons from South Korea's covid-19 policy response. *American Review of Public Administration*, *50*(6-7), 801–808. https://doi.org/10.1177/0275074020943708
Zavalita Brand Building. (n.d.). *Zavalita bring Miguel Grau to life in the first spot of "Peru I Love You."* [English translation, internal document].
Zavalita Brand Building. (2023). *Peru, I love you. Don't just join us yet*. [English translation]. https://zavalita.pe/en/portfolio/peru-te-quiero-no-te-nos-unas-aun/

INDEX